Good Friends Great Tastes

A Celebration of Life, Food and Friendship

Debbie Meyer-Gore

PORTLAND, OREGON

Dedication

In remembrance of my parents, Louie and Brigitte Scherer,
who provided many wonderful food and travel experiences
that continue to inspire me.

Cover Design: Sarah Huerter, Kansas City, Missouri
Designer: Sara E. Blum
Photography: Joe Graber, Colleyville, Texas
Editors: Lindsay S. Brown, Lindsay L. Burt

Library of Congress Cataloging-in-Publication Data

Meyer-Gore, Debbie.
  Good friends, great tastes / by Debbie Meyer-Gore. -- 1st American ed.
    p. cm.
  Includes index.
  ISBN 1-933112-32-8 (hardcover : alk. paper)
  1. Entertaining. 2. Cookery. I. Title.
  TX731.M4255 2007
  642'.4--dc22

2006029766

Distributed by Publisher Group West

ISBN 10: 1-933112-32-8
ISBN 13: 978-1-933112-32-9

Printed in China
9 8 7 6 5 4 3 2 1

First four printings under ISBN 0-9676269-0-0

Collectors Press books are available at special discounts for bulk purchases, premiums, and promotions. Special editions, including personalized inserts or covers, and corporate logos, can be printed in quantity for special purposes. For further information contact: Special Sales, Collectors Press, Inc., P.O. Box 230986, Portland, OR 97281. Toll free: 1-800-423-1848.

For a free catalog write to:
Collectors Press, Inc., P.O. Box 230986, Portland, OR 97281
Toll free: 1-800-423-1848 or visit collectorspress.com.

Table of Contents

Dear Friends,

I'm very excited about the new edition of *Good Friends Great Tastes* and can't wait to share with you all the new delicious recipes I've included. My goal for the book is to provide you reliable, realistic recipes and timesaving tips that will stimulate your palate and simplify your cooking experience.

When *Good Friends Great Tastes* was released in 2000, the collection of recipes was culled from my youth and life experiences. Six years have passed and my knowledge and collection of favorite recipes continues to grow. A broadened culinary perspective, a busy family life and the experience I've gained managing two culinary schools inspired me to update *Good Friends Great Tastes*. Generous friends and new acquaintances have shared their favorite recipes to be included.

I have been passionate about "what's for dinner" since the age of ten. Many of my childhood memories are associated with food. Having grown up in a bicultural home (my mom was German and my father American), I was introduced to international travel at a young age. My love of travel expanded my palate and garnered a passion for unique and unusual food.

Although we entertain often, our busy schedules no longer allow us to spend a full day in preparation for company. In this stage of life we entertain more casually, hosting friends and family, serving elegant food made from realistic recipes. Cooking at home is more economical than dining out and we appreciate the slower pace of gatherings in our home. Creating a memorable meal and reducing the stress of preparation has become paramount to our gatherings.

We hope you enjoy this improved collection as much as we have enjoyed the journey. We also hope that you will be truly inspired in the kitchen, which is the heart of our home and yours.

Bon Appétit!

Debbie

Debbie
debbie@goodfriendsgreattastes.com
www.goodfriendsgreattastes.com

Planning the Event

What type of event do you want to have? Do you want to have a sit down dinner? Will children be involved? Would a buffet be easier? What is the weather forecast? Should you have the event outside? How many people would you like to have as guests for this gathering? A rule of thumb is to allow at least two days to prepare for the event. Of course there will be times that call for a spontaneous gathering—when you simply feel the need to be surrounded by friends or family. You may have little time to plan, but most people are thrilled to be treated to a home-cooked meal and don't mind eating off the everyday dishes.

Menu Tips

A well-planned meal should follow the basic food groups. Meat served with a vegetable and starch balances texture and nutrition, but color should also be a consideration. If your salad has a lot of yellow peppers in it, then yellow squash is not the best vegetable to serve. If you are making scalloped potatoes with cheese, then don't have a cheesy vegetable in the menu selection. Even the appetizer should avoid repetition of flavors. If the main dish has bacon crumbled on top then don't serve an appetizer with bacon. Consider the duplication of ingredients when planning your menu, balancing color and texture for presentation. Don't make all of your favorites for a get together; instead plan a menu where the prepared dishes complement the occasion, e.g. a cheese tray and other elegant appetizers for a wine tasting. Sometimes a little duplication is difficult to avoid and is acceptable. If your salad has nuts and so does the dessert, it is acceptable because they are served at different times and involve very different flavors. The table decorations and theme should coordinate with the menu and mood you are creating.

Outline your desired menu and consider the number of ovens you can access and the amount of time you have. Plan so that there are several things that can be made ahead of time. Consider using the shopping list (page 334) provided in the book and hang on to it until you are totally prepared for your event. The shopping list has a space for other errands to be added such as picking up a tablecloth from the cleaners, getting additional chairs or stopping to get liquor and mixers for the event. Think of the details all the way down to the ice, beverage napkins, flowers and candles. When you save trips to the store you save time. Think of the things that you can get done ahead of time or while the kids are in bed. Make your grocery list, set the table, pull out the dishes you will need, check your supplies in the bar, polish silver if necessary. The more organized you are the more fun you will have.

In order to save time in the kitchen, read through the entire recipe before you make your shopping list. The shopping list in the book is organized by aisle to avoid running all over the store. You may set this up on your own computer on a table and customize headings to suit your needs. Include non-food items on your list too, such as skewers, toothpicks or parchment paper. With an organized shopping list, you will not miss any items. If something in the recipe would taste better bought on the day of the event, then keep your list and circle that item or put a checkmark by it so you know you must go back to the store. There is also a space on the organized shopping list in the book that is designated for the ingredients you think you already have in stock. Check your cabinets before making a trip to the store. This helps you avoid duplication and saves money and unnecessary trips to the store that waste time.

Before food preparation begins, measure and chop ingredients so that you can relax and have a good time while entertaining. Find opportunities to get things done early. Wash lettuce or toast nuts ahead of time. Consider this your party too, and minimize stress with early preparation. Clean up as you go and you will not have such a chore at the end of your preparation. This is a lesson that has taken me years to learn.

With an excellent menu, bread is not a necessity. If bread is served, find a great local bakery and select something interesting that goes with what you are serving. A great example would be jalapeño cheese bread with the Green Chili Egg Strata (page 91) or walnut scallion bread with a beef dinner entrée. If you choose to serve sweet and savory bread (such as raisin bread and walnut scallion bread) at the same meal, do not mix them in the same basket or they will take on the flavor of the stronger one. Cut the bread in thick slices instead of sandwich slices. Serve the bread with good quality butter, slightly softened. It is not necessary to serve the bread warm, although it is a nice touch.

A good host/hostess will ask their guests if they have any food allergies before planning the menu. Shellfish and peanuts can be hazardous to some, so be sure to inquire. When serving a seafood appetizer, it is nice to serve a non-seafood appetizer as well. Avoid duplication of ingredients when serving two appetizers. One may have meat and the other may have cheese or seafood. The number of appetizers you serve may depend on the time guests arrive and when you are sitting down for dinner. If you are planning to wait on late arriving guests, or introductions need to be made, additional time for appetizers may be needed. If the group hasn't seen one another in a while, more than one appetizer may be needed to allow guests time to mingle.

Your invitation may prompt friends to ask, "What can I bring?" If you decide to share the responsibility, select a menu and assign them a dish or let them be creative and use their own recipes. Let them know what you are serving and allow them to decide what the best complement to the meal is. If you are assigning something, be sure to send the recipe to them in enough time and include clear instructions. Assigning them their specialty will benefit you both. If you are unsure of their cooking abilities, allow them to choose what dish to bring, e.g. appetizer, salad, dessert. Remember to ask the person bringing the appetizer to arrive earlier than the other guests.

Plan the event to reflect your personality and style. Your generosity of spirit when opening your home to friends is more important than having everything perfect. Written invitations are not necessary for every occasion, but are a nice touch when guests must plan ahead, or an accurate head count is needed. Request a reply whether the invitation is written or verbal. This helps to plan the seating arrangements and the amount of food needed.

Timing and Serving

Determine the approximate time you would like your meal to begin and outline (on paper) the time you need to prepare each item. Allow enough mingling time (at least an hour) and allow for late arrivals to have time to visit as well. Serve an appetizer and beverages while guests are visiting. You will need time to dress the salad and complete any other final preparations. With your outline you will stay on track and avoid frustration.

Wine and Beer

Ask a local merchant you can trust for advice when you are serving a group of people. Let the merchant know if your friends are knowledgeable of wine and indicate if cost is a consideration for you. There are wonderful white and red wines available that are not expensive but are considerably better than box wine. If wine comes in a magnum, it can be transferred to inexpensive carafes for easy serving. There are 5 glasses of wine per regular sized bottle; a magnum is equivalent to 2 bottles or 10 glasses. A wonderful recommendation for a magnum is La Vieille Ferme that comes in a red and white wine.

When serving beer, offer a variety of beers. Provide a selection that may be fun for experimenting and may stimulate conversation. I prefer glass bottles instead of cans. You might want to try Italian beer if the dinner is Italian or Mexican beer if you have a Southwest inspired menu. In most cases, both beer and wine should be offered since many guests may not drink wine.

When serving alcohol, always have bottled waters available or offer guests a glass of water with dinner. Sparkling waters (flavored/unflavored) are great to have on hand and are festive for those not drinking.

After the Meal

For after dinner coffee, it is best to purchase whole beans and grind them yourself. Ground coffee should be used shortly after grinding because it loses flavor after about four hours. Do not store beans or ground coffee in the freezer. The freezing of beans changes the flavor due to condensation. Instead, store beans and ground coffee in an airtight container away from light. The ground beans may be stored in the refrigerator. Those that drink regular coffee seem to prefer unflavored blends and those that drink decaffeinated seem to drink flavored blends. Refrigerated flavored creamers or half-and-half are good in coffee and are a nice alternative to flavored coffees. To please both the serious coffee drinkers and those that like theirs doctored up, serve a flavored creamer.

Once you have planned a few events in your home and are pleased with the results, start keeping a notebook. List a few menus that you know you like in the notebook with the page number of the recipe and the book or magazine from which it came. Include the month and year of the publication for easy reference. List who came to dinner, what you served, if you enjoyed the combination, and what you would change. The exact menu can be duplicated for another group of friends and the event will come together more easily the next time you entertain.

Keep a camera on hand as you never know when there will be a great photo opportunity. These pictures can later be used for birthdays and celebrations.

Creating the Mood & Setting the Table

Creative Containers

You can find unique ideas for your table by thumbing through magazines and looking through your cabinets. There are some wonderful ways to make creative arrangements. Use a silver champagne bucket, silver mint julep cups, teapots, mason jars or rose bowls. The possibilities found in your own cabinets are endless. A candy dish turned over can make a base for another bowl to sit on top, which creates height and interest. You can fill containers with flowers, ornaments, fruits or vegetables depending on the occasion.

Arrange roses in a rose bowl by cutting stems short and using a fair amount of roses tightly tied together to create an elegant rounded arrangement. White roses and white tapers together on a table are very elegant. A mirror under a rose bowl with or without votives can create a dramatic ambience.

Candlelight

Candles can be used day or evening and add warmth and atmosphere. A votive by each place setting creates additional light and is a special touch. Scented votives should be avoided when serving food as the flavor of the food can be impaired.

Always use new candles on the table when entertaining. Be sure and trim the wicks so they don't sputter when lit. It is worth buying quality candles because they burn less quickly and you don't run the risk of losing the color coating when peeling off the tight plastic on the outside.

Use different heights of candleholders and put the same color and size candle in each one. My favorite colors to use are white, ivory or gold. Odd numbers are best for floral arrangements and candle arrangements. You can also create a beautiful table arrangement by arranging an odd number of flower filled vases of varying heights and shapes.

Displaying food on a footed cake plate can help you to add height to a table. Place vases or candleholders on top of the plate and surround the base with additional candles or vases for a unique centerpiece.

A rose bowl or tumbler can be used with a candle (in a glass holder) placed in the middle and greenery or flowers inserted between the outside glass and the votive in the glass holder. Add color to your table by coordinating napkins to the centerpiece.

Arrange trays of the same size or same type candles in varied heights to make a beautiful display on a coffee table or mantel.

Florist blocks can be cut in semi-circles to fit around the base of a tall candleholder or footed bowl. You can then push holly, greenery or flowers into the form. Secure the foam with florist tape and push tapers gently into the foam. Put taller tapers to the inside and shorter to the outside. Fill in with holly, ivy, flowers or berries to hide the foam.

Natural Looks

Vegetables such as artichokes and small pumpkins can be hollowed out to hold a votive candle. Slide a tall taper inside a bundle of asparagus and tie with a ribbon. Look in your produce section at the grocery store for ideas to add seasonal color to your table.

Place a single rose on top of a napkin at each place setting for a personal touch.

Inexpensive flowers can be purchased at the grocery store. Arrange them yourself or provide your own vase or container and have them arranged while you shop.

Whole lemons, limes or cranberries add color to the bottom of a clear vase arranged with flowers. If you are ambitious, use a potato peeler or citrus zester to create designs in the skins of the lemons and limes.

Nature can be an inspiration for adding color to any table. Gourds and pumpkins in various shapes and sizes make a beautiful table setting. Arrange in odd numbers and add ambience by placing small, unscented votives in clear glass holders between the gourds to provide extra light. Gourds will spoil quickly so check your arrangement frequently, or use French leaves (decorative paper leaves found in gourmet or kitchen stores) to line beneath the gourds.

For a more dramatic presentation, lightly spray fruits or vegetables with a gold or silver metallic paint.

A large bowl of fresh artichokes or a mixture of artichokes, lemons and avocados creates a refreshing centerpiece. I saw this on a trip to Napa Valley, California, and it was on top of a natural wood table. A simple and elegant idea!

French leaves make an excellent base for a platter with cheese or place a single leaf on top of a dinner or salad plate and set a clear soup bowl on top. Rather than a doily, it adds a simple autumn or spring touch depending on the color you use.

Napkins, Napkin Rings and Place Cards

Fun napkin rings are an easy addition to any table setting. For a truly unique look make your own by wrapping small fresh flowers or greenery around a homemade ring made from a pliable stem, like a birch twig. Twist the birch twig into circles and tie off with florist wire. You can then wrap a flowers stem around the ring or group foliage into small bunches and bind the stems with wire to the ring. The same technique can be used to slip over tapers.

Make a place card out of small flowerpots for a spring party by gluing a place card to one side and tie with raffia or ribbon. Attach a pack of seeds to napkin rings made from raffia or wire for a garden meeting or a spring brunch.

At holiday time, ornaments are an inexpensive way to add color. Add a decorative ornament to each person's wineglass as a party favor. They also make easy place card holders by writing the person's name on a solid color ornament with a special metallic marker. Jody Huerter of Leawood, Kansas, fills the ornaments with salt and uses a paperclip where the hook would go to hold a place card. In order for the ornament to sit upright you may need a small circle of wire covered with metallic stars (as seen at holiday time in craft stores) to hold the ornament in place on top of the table.

Chili peppers tied together with raffia makes a festive Southwest style napkin holder.

Make place cards out of small pumpkins by writing names on them with a metallic pen.

A small stocking with names written in glitter and filled with candy is a great place card idea for kids or adults.

Cloth napkins are best. Simple white restaurant napkins can be purchased at specialty kitchen stores.

A napkin folded into the shape of a square and tied like a present, with a beautiful ribbon is a nice touch for a holiday or birthday table. Cut a piece of cardboard in a square to insert in the napkin to help maintain consistent size and shape while folding. Carefully slide the cardboard out once the ribbon is tied. For a dessert party, add a delicate dessert fork to the napkin and ribbon ensemble (see Desserts section photograph).

Buy an assortment of festive beverage napkins (paper and cloth) and keep them on hand for casual and elegant dining.

Festive Ideas

Assorted colors of small jelly beans or Runts (a brightly colored hard-coated candy) add color to the bottom of a glass vase. Add Gerber daisies (without water) for an easy centerpiece at a child's party.

A buffet set with a nice white tablecloth and a large bow (placed slightly off center) with extra streamers makes the table look like a large gift. This is a festive idea for birthday or holiday gatherings.

A large wicker basket (painted or not) can be lined with a garbage bag and filled with ice for a cute holder for chilled wines. Carafes or open wine can be immersed in the ice and guests can serve themselves.

For a picnic celebration, line a terra cotta pot with foil and the outside edges with romaine lettuce leaves. Fill the center of the pot with salad and tie raffia around the outside of the pot. It is a fun and unique presentation and if you forget to take it home, the cost is minimal. Square wire baskets (normally used for organization) make great containers for vegetables that have been cut uniformly for dipping. Be creative in your use of serving containers!

Music played softly on the stereo or radio helps fill the voids in conversation when not all guests have arrived and some of the guests do not know each other. Choose background music that does not interfere with talking until the guests get comfortable. Turning the television on when entertaining is inappropriate unless the theme of the party centers around the event, e.g. Super Bowl, Kentucky Derby, Oscars.

Make the food presentation on the dinner plates uniform in appearance. Setup is typically like reading a clock. Starch at 10, meat at 2 and vegetable at 6. Each plate should be placed on the table so when guests look around the table it is visually pleasing. Wipe off any dribbles of sauces with a napkin before serving.

Themed Parties

For an Oktoberfest theme (celebrated in Munich, Germany) a menu of Rouladen (page 164) can be prepared. A more casual evening would consist of sauerkraut, bratwurst, crusty dinner rolls, Warm German Potato Salad (page 136) and beer. In Bavaria, royal blue and white checked tablecloths are common table coverings. In German restaurants a colored square tablecloth is placed diagonally over a white tablecloth or a white square over a colored tablecloth. A variety of German beers can be found in most liquor stores. Taped accordion music of German songs can help create a festive atmosphere. (Refer to menu 15 in the *Menus and Wine Pairings* section, page 19.)

For Italian parties use red and white checkered tablecloths. When hosting a themed gathering, choose authentic menu items from the country or region including the beverages served. To add to the atmosphere, play background music that is consistent with the theme. Sending invitations to your guests may inspire their contributions to the "Evening in Italy" and encourage suggestions to carry out the theme. (Refer to menu 24 in the *Menu and Wine Pairings* section, page 22.)

The Spanish practice of serving tapas dates back to King Alfonso X in the thirteenth century. Due to an illness he was required to take small bites of food with wine between meals. Once recovered, he mandated that wine be served with small bites of food in the region of Castille where he governed. The tradition continues throughout Spain although some question the origin of the tradition. Tapas are often served in taverns "tabernas" and some restaurants accompanied by wine or sherry. Olives, nuts, cured serrano ham (Spanish Jamón serrano), regional sausages and manchego cheese are some of the common items that are available and may be found in gourmet specialty stores. A tapas party can be a fun gathering where dinner consists only of a variety of appetizers. Button mushrooms sautéed with olive oil and garlic, tuna salad on toast points, potato croquettes, calamari and fried or marinated sardines are some of the other delicious items found on a tapas menu.

For economical decorations at a wine tasting dinner, fill a champagne bucket to overflowing with red and green grapes. Tie each white cloth napkin with a floral pick of grapes. Try a wine with each course, pairing each wine to complement the food. Avoid preparing spicy foods for a wine tasting because they deaden the palate and certain wines will be less appealing than if paired with milder foods.

A festive Cajun party can be staged to resemble a dark intimate Cajun restaurant. Put black lace over white tablecloths and hang crystals on candelabras. Serve hurricanes and play authentic Cajun music. Hurricane mix is a powdered drink mix that can be found in many liquor stores. (Refer to menu 7 or 25 in the *Menu and Wine Pairings* section, page 17 and page 22.)

For a bistro atmosphere, string small white lights in the trees on a patio and use white tablecloths. A gazebo lined with lights also creates a beautiful setting.

Vicki Morgan, a friend since childhood, entertained her Bunco group in Little Rock, Arkansas, with a unique themed dinner. She planned a menu with a safari theme and renamed all the courses. The main course was "Wild and Cheesy Chicken Casserole" and "Safari Slaw" was the salad. She turned sturdy boxes upside down and arranged them in different heights on each guest table and for the buffet. She draped the boxes with burlap and different animal print fabrics, and lighter colored burlap was used as tablecloths over all the tables. She placed wooden animal figurines and painted flowerpots on top of the boxes and tables. The flowerpots were painted with animal print designs and animal print tissue was used inside (greenery could also be used) to make the centerpieces. Each table had a mix of animal prints and was slightly different. Naming the items on the menu for a buffet is a good idea as well as marking each dish with a place card. It is nice to know what is being served in a buffet whether or not it is a themed dinner.

For a humorous baby shower idea, use the smallest disposable infant diapers and put them around mason jars as vases or use them as cozies for canned beverages. Rattles and baby trinkets can also be tied to each napkin with ribbon and given to the mother-to-be at the end of the shower. To create a diaper holder for nuts or mints, cut 4-inch triangles from white paper, fold the bottom point up and bring the other two sides to the middle and fasten with a tiny safety pin.

For outdoor parties, galvanized buckets, wheelbarrows or wagons make great coolers for beverages. Create a beach party cooler out of a round galvanized bucket by tying a grass skirt around the outside.

Glassware and Silver

Serving magnums of wine is more economical, especially for large groups. Transferring the wines from the magnum to carafes is more appealing and also easier to handle.

Brandy snifters, martini glasses and open face champagne glasses can double as dessert dishes. For a decorative touch, tie a wire edge ribbon to the stem. Martini glasses or similar shaped margarita glasses are wonderful for individual portions of shrimp cocktail. Hang large peeled shrimp over the edge of the glass and put the sauce in the center.

China, silver and crystal does not have to be used only at the holidays. If you feel that just getting together is a special event, then by all means use them. Toasting is acceptable but clinking glasses is not recommended when using fine crystal or antique stemware. Both are delicate and chip easily.

Many antique China sets have wide mouth coffee cups and these are perfect for appetizer portions of soups.

Chargers are normally used as decoration under a dinner plate, but are big enough to make great serving pieces. Line them with kale or lettuce for cheese or appetizer platters. Place a pedestal cake plate under a charger to create height.

Use silver spreaders to serve dips for dressy or casual entertaining. These also make a great hostess gift.

For breakfast use a footed cake plate to serve bagels, muffins or Danishes. Taking time to add interest to everyday meals makes guests feel very special. It is a nice touch and no more difficult than serving breakfast pastries on a dinner plate. Topping a footed cake plate with a smaller footed cake plate makes a creative tiered serving piece for appetizers and assorted desserts. Garnish with fresh flowers.

I recommend putting salad dressings, mayonnaise, mustard, ketchup or any other condiments in glass bowls, divided dishes or glass banana split dishes. These inexpensive dishes are more sanitary than dipping knives in jars and much more visually appealing.

Glass banana split dishes are the perfect size for dips, crackers and olives for two.

Setting the Table

The difference in formal and informal table settings is the number of utensils used. The setting should always be traditional.

The pattern of the plate should face the guest.

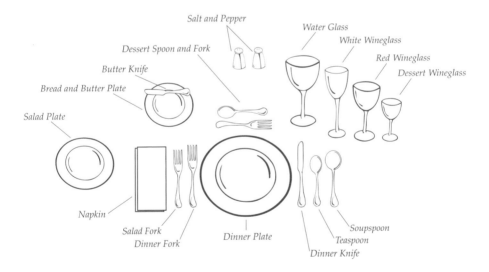

Wineglasses should be placed with the largest one closest to the plate, above the knife, working down to the smallest on the outside. Additional glasses are positioned in order of use and the course they are accompanying. If using a water glass, this should be the first glass above the knife. If serving champagne, the glass should be placed behind and between the water and white wineglass. Wines are generally not poured until everyone is seated, the host has checked the flavor and the appropriate course is presented.

Knives are on the right and forks on the left. Knife blades should always be turned toward the plate.

A rule of thumb for properly setting the table is that the utensils are placed in the order they will be used, working from the outside in. The salad fork is placed to the left of the dinner fork, which is next to the plate.

The butter knife should sit straight across the top of the bread and butter plate.

A teaspoon is placed to the right of the knife with the soupspoon to the right of the teaspoon.

Dessert forks and spoons may be placed horizontally above the plate with the fork tines facing right and the spoon facing left. An alternative is to serve the dessert with the dessert fork or spoon on the dessert plate and a spoon on the saucer with the coffee, handle parallel to the handle of the cup. Do not place the coffee cup and saucer on the table until dessert is served.

The host should announce dinner, tell guests where to sit or have place cards to avoid confusion. Once all the guests are seated, the host serves the guests from the left. If the host chooses to pass the serving pieces, passing begins with the person to the right of the host. All platters and bowls are passed to the right and the host is the last one served. To signify the start of the meal, the host puts their napkin in their lap and all guests should follow the host's lead. When the host begins to eat, guests should begin their meal.

Let the host or waitperson know you are finished with your meal by laying down your utensils properly. Place them side by side, your knife should be on the right with the blade turned in toward the fork on the left. On a clock, tines would be at 10:00 and handles at 10:20. Dishes should be removed from the right by your host or waitperson and the dishes should never be stacked when clearing the table.

Menus & Wine Pairings

◆ denotes may be prepared ahead

Chicken Menus

Menu 1
Crab Stuffed Mushrooms, p. 65 ◆
Bibb Lettuce with Feta, Sautéed Apples and Pears with Red Wine Vinaigrette, p. 130
Red Wine Vinaigrette, p. 130 ◆
Cornish Game Hens with Honey Glaze and Caramelized Onions, p. 198
Honey Glaze, p. 198 ◆
Sautéed Spinach, p. 198
Rice Medley, p. 198
Chocolate Sacks Filled with White Chocolate Mousse, p. 260 ◆
Wine recommendation for appetizer: Champagne
Wine recommendations for dinner: White Burgundy or Chardonnay

Menu 2
Spicy Shrimp Dip, p. 71 ◆
Salad with Balsamic Vinaigrette, p. 141
Balsamic Vinaigrette, p. 141 ◆
Baked Sour Cream Marinated Chicken, p. 175 ◆
Lemon Rice Pilaf, p. 228
Pineapple Carrot Cake with White Chocolate Cream Cheese Frosting, p. 269 ◆
Wine recommendations for appetizer: Gewürztraminer or Viognier
Wine recommendations for dinner: Pinot Noir or Chardonnay

Menu 3
Artichoke and Shrimp Cocktail, p. 79 ◆
Salad with Creamy Champagne Vinaigrette, p. 143
Creamy Champagne Vinaigrette, p. 143 ◆
Chicken in Puff Pastry with Basil Cream Sauce, p. 180
Wild Rice
Fruit Torte, p. 279 ◆
Wine recommendations for appetizers: Pinot Grigio or Orvieto
Wine recommendation for dinner: Chianti

Menu 4

Appetizer Brie Cheesecakes, p. 41 ◆
Crab Cakes with Rémoulade, p. 67 ◆ (Serve when guests are seated)
Mixed Field Greens with Stilton, Grapes and Honey Vinaigrette, p. 132
Honey Vinaigrette, p. 132 ◆
Cajun Creamed Chicken in Puff Pastry Shells, p. 186 ◆
Sour Cream Chocolate Cake with Cream Cheese Chocolate Frosting, p. 267 ◆
Wine recommendations for appetizer and first course: Chenin Blanc or Riesling
Wine recommendations for dinner: Pinot Noir or Fumé Blanc

Menu 5

Honey Pecan Brie Pastries, p. 44 ◆
Artichoke, Hearts of Palm and Feta Salad with Lemon Vinaigrette, p. 123
Lemon Vinaigrette, p. 123 ◆
Bacon and Arugula Stuffed Chicken Roulades, p. 178 ◆
Wild Rice
Puff Pastry Berry Napoleons with Mascarpone, p. 275 ◆
Wine recommendation for appetizer: Pinot Noir
Wine recommendations for dinner: Chardonnay or Côtes du Rhône

Seafood Menus

Menu 6

Bacon Tomato Tartlets, p. 59 ◆
Spinach Salad with Balsamic Maple Vinaigrette and Sugared Pecans, p. 126
Balsamic Maple Vinaigrette and Sugared Pecans, p. 126 ◆
Grilled Salmon with Spinach and Gorgonzola Cream, p. 206
Tomato Pie, p. 246
Fresh Fruit Tarts with Grand Marnier Cream, p. 277
Grand Marnier Cream, p. 277 ◆
Wine recommendations for appetizer: Sonoma Chardonnay or Conundrum
Wine recommendation for dinner: Fumé Blanc

"Nothing makes you more tolerant of a neighbor's noisy party then being there."

Menu 7
Crab Tartlets, p. 66 ✦
Green Olive Dip, p. 38 ✦
Mixed Field Greens with Stilton, Grapes and Honey Vinaigrette, p. 132
Honey Vinaigrette, p. 132 ✦
Cajun Spiced Shrimp with Mushrooms, p. 216
Raspberry Bread Pudding with Cajeta Sauce, p. 266 ✦
Wine recommendation for appetizers: Champagne
Wine recommendation for dinner: Chardonnay

Lamb Menus

Menu 8
Artichoke Dip, p. 37 ✦
Puff Pastry with Sherry Mushrooms (serve when guests are seated), p. 82
Fresh Tomato, Kalamata and Feta Salad with Shallot Herb Vinaigrette, p. 122
Shallot Herb Vinaigrette, p. 122 ✦
Rosemary Grilled Lamb, p. 203 ✦
Port Wine Sauce, p. 162 ✦
Potatoes Gruyère, p. 231
Baklava, p. 286
Homemade Vanilla Ice Cream, p. 284 ✦
Wine recommendations for appetizers: Fumé Blanc or Chardonnay
Wine recommendation for dinner: Rioja

Menu 9
Brie with Apples, Cranberries and Pecans, p. 42 ✦
Artichoke, Hearts of Palm and Blue Cheese Salad
with Lemon Vinaigrette (See variation), p. 123
Lemon Vinaigrette, p. 123 ✦
Lamb Chops with Juniper-Rosemary Marinade, p. 163
Feta Potatoes, p. 239 ✦
Fudge Truffle Cheesecake, p. 262 ✦
Wine recommendations for appetizer: Petit Syrah or Côtes du Rhône
Wine recommendations for dinner: Cabernet or Super Tuscan

Beef Menus

Menu 10

Pineapple Shrimp Skewers with Honey Marinade, p. 74 ✦
Orange and Romaine Salad with Lime Vinaigrette and Sugared Pecans, p. 131
Lime Vinaigrette and Sugared Pecans, p. 131 ✦
Tropical Fiesta Steak with Island Marinade and Caribbean Salsa, p. 159 ✦
Caribbean Salsa, p. 159 ✦
Black Beans with Cilantro Pesto Rice, p. 230
Cilantro Pesto, p. 230 ✦
Decadent Toffee Dessert Sauce, p. 288
Wine recommendation for appetizer: Dry Gewürztraminer
Wine recommendations for dinner: Beaujolais or Syrah

Menu 11

Blue Cheese-Parmesan Toasts, p. 43 ✦
Artichoke Red Pepper Tartlets (See variation), p. 59 ✦
Spinach Salad with Prosciutto, Capers and Cornichons, p. 127
Beef Tenderloin, p. 160 ✦
Mashed Potatoes with Caramelized Onions, p. 237 ✦
Green Bean Bundles, p. 242 ✦
Pecan Crust Ice Cream Pie with Caramel Sauce, p. 285 ✦
Wine recommendations for appetizers: Sauvignon Blanc,
White Bordeaux or Italian Vernaccia
Wine recommendations for dinner: Bordeaux or Cabernet-Merlot Blend

Menu 12

Pistachio Goat Cheese Strudel, p. 48 ✦
Sage Sausage Stuffed Mushrooms, p. 60 ✦
Hearts of Palm, Artichoke, Olive Salad with Red Wine Vinaigrette, p. 125 ✦
Beef Tenderloin, p. 160
Garlic Chive Mashed Potatoes, p. 236 ✦
Marinated Green Been Bundles, p. 247 ✦
Best Rolls Ever, p. 102 ✦
Coconut Cream Cake, p. 272 ✦
Wine recommendation for appetizers: Pinot Gris from Alsace
Wine recommendation for dinner: Australian Cabernet

Menu 13

Artichoke Dip, p. 37 ◆
Baked Goat Cheese Salad with Herb Vinaigrette, p. 129
Herb Vinaigrette, p. 129 ◆
Beef Tenderloin, p. 160
Red Zinfandel Sauce, p. 149 ◆
Potato, Mushroom and Spinach Tart, p. 232
Naturally Sweet Carrots, p. 252
Cappuccino Sundaes, p. 298
Wine recommendation for appetizers: Fumé Blanc
Wine recommendation for dinner: Red Zinfandel

Menu 14

Goat Cheese Torte with Sun-dried Tomatoes, Pesto and Pine Nuts, p. 47 ◆
Salad with Spicy Vinaigrette, p. 140
Spicy Vinaigrette, p. 140 ◆
Herb Crusted Prime Rib with Port Wine Sauce, p. 162 ◆
Julienne Vegetable Medley, p. 244
Portobello Mushrooms topped with Whipped Sweet Potatoes, p. 234
Chocolate Praline Squares with Coffee Whipped Cream, p. 263 ◆
Wine recommendation for appetizers: California Chardonnay
Wine recommendation for dinner: Australian Shiraz

Menu 15

Sausage En Croûte with Homemade Mustard, p. 58
Homemade Mustard, p. 58 ◆
Spiced Peaches
German Rouladen with Rich Brown Gravy, p. 164 ◆
Red Cabbage, p. 248 ◆
Potato Dumplings (found in grocery stores and German specialty food stores)
Amaretto Cheesecake, p. 255 ◆
Wine recommendation for appetizer: Riesling
Wine recommendation for dinner: Gewürztraminer

"Food is our common ground, a universal experience."

~James Beard

Menu 16

Marinated Feta with Pita Toasts, p. 45, 65 ♦
Salad with Balsamic Apricot Vinaigrette, p. 144
Balsamic Apricot Vinaigrette, p. 144 ♦
Osso Buco, p. 202 ♦
Wild Mushroom Risotto, p. 229 ♦
Chokahlúa Cheesecake, p. 256 ♦
Wine recommendations for appetizers: Viognier or Pinot Noir
Wine recommendation for dinner: Chianti Classico Riserva

Menu 17

Hearts of Palm and Artichoke Crostini, p. 35 ♦
Crab Tartlets, p. 66 ♦
Salad with Dates and Creamy Feta Dressing (See variation) p. 142 ♦
Beef Tenderloin, p. 160
Twice Baked Potatoes with White Cheddar and Rosemary, p. 238
Green Beans with Balsamic Brown Butter, p. 254
Bananas Foster, p. 283
Homemade Vanilla Ice Cream, p. 284
Wine recommendation for appetizers: White Burgundy
Wine recommendation for dinner: California Pinot Noir

Casual Menus

Menu 18

Shrimp with Garlic and Roasted Red Peppers, p. 78 ♦
Salad with Hoisin Vinaigrette, p. 145 ♦
Hoisin Marinated Pork Tenderloin, p. 169 ♦
Magic Meat Sauce, p. 154 ♦
Asparagus with Soy Sauce and Sesame Seeds, p. 242
Brown Rice
Vanilla Flan, p. 274 ♦
Wine recommendation for appetizer: Pinot Grigio
Wine recommendations for dinner: Pinot Noir, Red Zinfandel or Shiraz

"For me, each dish is like a song; it has to touch me in some way."

~Charles Dale, Aspen Restaurateur

Menu 19

Cheese Pecan Spread, p. 51 ✦
Salad with Spicy Vinaigrette, p. 140
Creole Mustard Marinated Pork Tenderloin with Red Wine Cherry Sauce, p. 168 ✦
Red Wine Cherry Sauce, p. 147 ✦
Chewy Chocolate Caramel Bars, p. 294 ✦
Wine recommendation for appetizers: Sauvignon Blanc
Wine recommendation for dinner: Shiraz

Menu 20

Southwest Layer Dip, p. 52 ✦
Southwest Caesar Salad with Homemade Croutons, p. 128
Dressing and Homemade Croutons, p. 128 ✦
Chicken Enchiladas with Green Chili Salsa, p. 196 ✦
Easy Fruit Pecan Crisp, p. 283 ✦
Beverage recommendations for appetizer and dinner:
Margarita Martinis (p. 109) and assorted beers

Menu 21

Spinach Dip with Crudités, p. 37
Horseradish Shrimp Dip, p. 75 ✦
Marvelous Meat Marinade, p. 158 ✦
Tomato Pie, p. 246
Corn Maque Choux, p. 253
Butterscotch Apple Crisp. p. 282
Homemade Vanilla Ice Cream, p. 284 ✦
Wine recommendation for appetizers: Côtes du Rhône
Wine recommendation for dinner: Chateauneuf-du-Pape

Menu 22

Tortilla Roll Ups, p. 54 ✦
Broccoli Salad with Nuts and Raisins, p. 138 ✦
Picnic Potato Salad, p. 137 ✦
Brisket with Honey Barbecue Sauce, p. 166 ✦
Blackberry Cobbler, p. 280 ✦
Beverage recommendations for appetizers: Beer and Margarita Martinis, p. 109
Wine recommendation for dinner: Grenache Shiraz

Menu 23
Tex-Mex Won Tons, p. 53
White Bean Chicken Chili, p. 120 ◆
Jalapeño Cornbread, p. 105 ◆
Buttermilk Brownies with Buttermilk Icing, p. 292 ◆
Beverage recommendation for appetizer and dinner: Assorted beers

Pasta Menus

Menu 24
Puff Pastry Pinwheels, p. 57 ◆
Tomato Basil Bruschetta, p. 40 ◆
Salad with Balsamic Vinaigrette, p. 141 ◆
Pasta with Mascarpone, Parmesan and Fresh Sautéed Vegetables, p. 222
Tiramisu, p. 290 ◆
Wine recommendation for appetizer: Vernaccia
Wine recommendations for dinner: Chianti or Valipolicella

Menu 25
Hot Crab Dip, p. 69 ◆
Salad with Mandarin Oranges, Capers and Red Onion and Spicy Vinaigrette, p. 140
Spicy Vinaigrette, p. 140 ◆
Pasta with Chicken, Cream and Creole Spice, p. 224
Creole Spice, p. 224 ◆
Rum Bundt Cake with Whipped Cream, p. 265 ◆
Wine recommendations for appetizer: Riesling or Viognier
Wine recommendation for dinner: Gewürztraminer

Brunch Menus

Menu 26
Hot Pepper Peach Dip, p. 51 ◆
Spinach Salad with Balsamic Maple Vinaigrette with Sugared Pecans, p. 126
Balsamic Maple Vinaigrette and Sugared Pecans, p. 126 ◆
Shrimp with Asparagus in Puff Pastry Shells, p. 88 ◆
Amaretto Cake, p. 270 ◆
Beverage recommendations for brunch: Champagne and coffee

Menu 27

Fruit Ambrosia, p. 83 ◆
Sausage and Spinach Quiche, p. 92
Rosemary Potatoes, p. 240
Baked Apple Donuts, p. 98
Beverage recommendations for brunch: Spicy Bloody Mary Pitchers (p. 106) and coffee

Menu 28

Fruit with Lime Cream, p. 89
Lime Cream, p. 89 ◆
Quick Eggs Benedict, p. 85
Rosemary Potatoes p. 240
Sour Cream Coffee Cake, p. 101 ◆
Beverage recommendations for brunch: Mimosas and coffee

Menu 29

Fruit Ambrosia, p. 83 ◆
Hash-brown Egg Pie, p. 95 ◆
Breakfast Pie, p. 94
Ciabatta Apple Cinnamon Toast, p. 100 ◆
Raspberry Streusel Muffins, p. 97
Beverage recommendations for brunch: Spicy Bloody Mary Pitchers (p. 106),
Mimosas and coffee

Menu 30

Fresh Fruit Mélange with Citrus Dressing, p. 83 ◆
Citrus Dressing, p. 83 ◆
Spinach and Egg Pinwheel with Shrimp Sauce, p. 86 ◆
Bacon Tomato Tartlets, p. 59 ◆
Rosemary Potatoes, p. 240
Easy Cream Cheese Danish, p. 96 ◆
Beverage recommendations for brunch: Champagne and coffee

"Tell me what you eat and I will tell you who you are."

~Jean Anthelme Brillat-Savarin

Secrets from the Kitchen

Throughout the years I have been cooking I have learned helpful tips and have some recommendations for ingredients. I would like to share these discoveries with you so you may also enjoy them. Some of these tips are repeated in recipes in this book where applicable, along with other useful information.

Taste Tips

Good quality butter such as Land O'Lakes is necessary. Inexpensive butters seem to have more water. Since butter is sold priced by the pound, it is not necessary to buy salted butter. Salt in butter is only used as a preservative. Using unsalted butter and adjusting seasoning is perfectly fine. I noted whether I used unsalted butter in testing. If not noted, lightly salted butter was used. My favorite butter comes from England (Somerdale salted butter) and Ireland (Kerrygold) and is sold in specialty grocers. I only use these imported butters when their wonderful flavor can be appreciated. I would serve these butters with bread or when tossing vegetables or topping a potato.

I use Hellmann's or Best Foods Real Mayonnaise only (they are the same product, just named differently in different parts of the country).

Pomi Tomatoes are shelf stable fresh tomatoes. They taste great in soups and sauces. They are found with the canned tomatoes but come in a shelf stable cardboard box.

Tomato paste and anchovy paste come in tubes that are great because recipes usually call for such small amounts. The tomato paste is generally found on the aisle with the canned tomatoes and the anchovy paste is with the canned tuna and other fish products. They will need to be refrigerated once opened.

Chopped or minced garlic in a jar is wonderful for marinades or meatballs. For sauces and other recipes, I chop fresh garlic.

Parmigiano-Reggiano would be my recommendation for any recipe that uses Parmesan, but sometimes it is difficult to find. Grate your own Parmesan even if it is not Parmigiano-Reggiano. United States renditions are aged 14 months and the Parmigiano-Reggiano is aged 2 years. The flavor of pre-grated Parmesan does not compare to freshly grated.

I cook with sea salt and keep both coarse and fine salt on hand. Sea salt has been used through the ages and is a result of the evaporation of seawater; the salt is a residue. Kosher salt is coarse grained and doesn't have any additives. Don't over salt. Put shakers on the table so guests may add additional salt to their taste. Taste test your sauces as you are cooking to determine if extra salt is needed. In most cooking, I use fine sea salt. For grilling steaks, I use kosher salt.

Have you ever felt like something is missing from a recipe? When this happens, I use a sprinkle of *Tony Chachere's*. *Tony Chachere's Creole Seasoning* (original flavor) is a combination of salt, red pepper and other spices. *Tony Chachere's* is in the spice section of most grocery stores or visit their web site at www.cajunspice.com or call 1-800-551-9066 to find a store that carries *Tony's* in your area.

A few drops of Tabasco red pepper sauce in chicken soup enhances the flavor.

Broth and bouillon are similar because they are the result of cooking meat or vegetables in water. Stock on the other hand is created the same way and then strained to remove any impurities. Stock is the result of cooking meat, fish or vegetables in water (like broth) but sometimes additional spices are added. I use stock and broth interchangeably. I prefer the ones that are a wet thick paste that must be refrigerated. My favorite is Better than Bouillon from Superior Touch Bases. The base must be mixed with water according to package directions before using.

Cooking rice in a broth enhances the flavor. My favorite brand is Better than Bouillon. Other components can add additional flavor as well. Sauté 1/4 cup (2 medium) finely chopped shallots or garlic (1 medium clove minced) prior to adding the rice and liquid. For Thai meals, coconut milk can be diluted (14 ounces coconut milk and 8 ounces water) for 2 cups white or brown rice, which adds additional flavor. One of my favorite combinations is to add 1/2 cup toasted slivered almonds to rice once cooked. When the almonds are used in the rice, I prefer long grain white rice, cooked in chicken broth with 1/4 cup sherry added to 1 3/4 cups broth. Serve with a mushroom cream sauce as in the recipe on page 184. Fresh corn, fresh herbs or a rinsed can of black beans and cilantro, all have their place depending on the ethnicity of the main dish you are serving.

Demi-glace is used in recipes when making a brown sauce. Most come as a concentrate and will need water added. In a store bought demi-glace, the complicated process has been done for you. A beef or veal reduction is made from boiling the bones for a 24-hour period to form a thick glaze. Vegetables, spices and a small addition of Madeira or sherry are added during the process to give the reduction a unique flavor.

Kitchen Bouquet Browning and Seasoning Sauce adds color to your sauce. You only need a few drops for Rich Brown Gravy (page 164) or a Balsamic Sauce (page 157).

For most recipes that have bacon as an ingredient, I buy the thick hickory-smoked bacon. If a brand of bacon like Pederson's or Applegate Farms is available, I prefer this bacon because it contains no nitrates. Nitrates are a preservative.

Chocolate chip cookies taste better when they are made with shortening rather than butter. A few drops of butter flavoring can be added or butter flavored shortening is also good. Cookies made with shortening store better and longer, staying moist without tasting stale.

All-purpose flour is used in all recipes in *Good Friends Great Tastes* unless otherwise noted.

When frying, we use peanut oil. It has a higher smoke point. If someone has peanut allergies, substitute a different type of oil such as non-hydrogenated lard or coconut oil.

If you cook vegetables such as asparagus or broccoli in boiling water, cook until tender-crisp with the lid on, approximately 9 minutes. Once the lid is removed and the vegetables are drained, do not cover them again. If you do, they turn a dull unappetizing shade of green.

Unsweetened coconut milk can be purchased in Asian grocery stores and might be found in the Asian section of your grocery store. The sweetened type on the beverage aisle cannot be substituted.

Whipped cream is such a wonderful treat especially in the summer over fresh strawberries. For two cups whipped cream, whip one cup (1/2 pint) heavy cream in a bowl that will hold at least 2 cups. (Heavy cream doubles in volume, when whipped.) Chill the heavy cream in the bowl you are whipping it in along with the beaters for 10 minutes in the freezer for best results. Whip with an electric mixer and as it starts to form soft peaks add 1 tablespoon of confectioners' sugar and 1 teaspoon vanilla. Taste and add more sugar if needed. Whip until it forms peaks. Do not over whip or it will turn to butter. To intensify the flavor of the berries toss them in a small amount of superfine sugar.

Light olive oils have been put through a filtration process but are no lighter in calories or fat. They will have a lighter, less classic olive oil flavor. Virgin olive oil and extra virgin olive oil have been cold pressed, which is a chemical-free process that involves only pressure and a lower level of acidity. The lower the acidity the higher the grade. Extra virgin olive oil is the finest and fruitiest of the olive oils and is less acidic. A deeper color of oil exemplifies a more intense flavor. Those olive oils that just state "olive oil" on the label are a combination of refined olive oil and virgin or extra virgin olive oil.

Use naturally occurring, non-hydrogenated oil such as cold pressed extra virgin olive oil, butter and other animal fats (lard, duck fat), expeller-expressed sesame and flax oil and the tropical oils—coconut and palm when possible. Peanut oil and non-hydrogenated lard have high smoke points and can be used to fry. Sesame oil is good for stir-fry and olive oil can be used for moderate temperatures but does not have a high smoke point. Avoid safflower, corn, sunflower, soybean, canola and cottonseed oil for recipes that require heating.

Balsamic vinegar is made from the Italian white Trebbiano grape and is aged in barrels to give it the dark color and pungent sweetness. Balsamic vinegar is great in salad dressings or drizzled over mozzarella and tomatoes and sprinkled with fresh chopped basil and olive oil. You can also boil balsamic vinegar to a syrup state and drizzle it over grilled steaks. It is delicious!

Salad is meant to be dressed lightly with a salad dressing. Do not drench. If you have any doubt that you put enough on, offer additional dressing in a small glass bowl with a spoon. Toss salad just before serving unless otherwise stated or greens will be limp. Some vinaigrette dressings will solidify due to the temperature in the refrigerator and the type of oil used. If this happens, run warm water over the jar to melt the build-up and re-whisk.

Ice-glazed frozen, boneless skinless chicken breasts bought in bulk are great for chicken dishes. One breast is equivalent to 1 cup when cubed or sliced. When grilling, grill extra chicken breasts and freeze them. You can defrost them later and add them to a casserole. The fresh grilled flavor tastes better than boiled chicken or chicken prepared in a microwave oven.

Ground white pepper is usually used instead of black in cream sauces. The flavor is slightly milder than black pepper, and it is more appealing than having dark flecks in your sauce.

Spices do have a shelf life. For best flavor replace ground spices after 3 years, whole spices after 4 years, leafy herbs and seasoning blends after 2 years, and seeds and extracts every 4 years.

White and yellow onions may be used interchangeably. I prefer white for Mexican food and yellow for most every other dish.

Preparation

One of my biggest secrets for everyday meals is to keep my favorite cookbook and a blank pad and pencil in the car. I find I am more likely to cook something good if I can run into the store directly after work or run errands without having to go home. I will sit in the car in the parking lot, make a shopping list, shop and be ready to cook when I get home. You can keep copies of my "organized shopping list" in the car or create one on your computer.

Cooking spray with flour added is the best to use on your bakeware. Other cooking sprays leave a yellow sticky residue.

Sifting passes ingredients through fine mesh to remove large pieces. It incorporates air and will change measurements. Measuring the ingredients after they have been sifted will give you the correct amount that should be added to the recipe, unless otherwise stated.

Devein shrimp by removing the gray-black vein from the back of the shrimp. You can do this with a sharp tip of a knife or the prong of a fork. This is optional on small and medium shrimp but recommended on large shrimp.

Linda Gore of Colleyville, Texas, taught me this great tip. It is sometimes hard to know how much of the asparagus stalk you should trim off. If you take the asparagus and bend it, it will break where the tender stalk meets the tough stalk.

Shrimp with Asparagus in Puff Pastry Shells (page 88) and Cajun Creamed Chicken in Puff Pastry Shells (page 186) are elegant enough for company because it is served in puff pastry shells. Frozen puff pastry dough also comes in sheets and can be cut into shapes such as stars and flowers. Use the shapes as a topping for fresh fruit. Cut into a shape and sprinkle with regular sugar before baking or sifted confectioners' sugar after baking, for a tasty addition to a fruit dessert.

Instead of relying on package labels, always use a measuring cup. It is best to measure liquids in glass measuring cups and solids in metal or plastic measuring cups. Solids can then be leveled off with a knife to ensure proper measurements.

If you accidentally oversalt a dish while it is still cooking, drop in a peeled potato to absorb the excess salt. It is a quick fix. Remove the potato before serving.

Although recipes state oven temperatures and cooking times, they are not always exactly accurate for your oven. Be sure to set your timer a few minutes earlier than the completed cooking time so that you can check the dish and avoid burning accidents. In turn, you may have to leave the dish in a little longer if your oven is not as hot as the oven in which the recipe was tested. I recommend having your oven calibrated to the correct temperature if it isn't new. A magnetic, mounted oven thermometer will also work and can be left in the oven to check the temperature to see how closely your controls are to the actual temperature.

When sautéing in butter, add a small amount of olive oil to the butter to keep it from burning.

When thickening sauces, there are several agents typically used. Arrowroot or arrowroot flour is probably the least called for but can be found in health food stores, Asian markets and some supermarkets. It should be mixed with a cold liquid and added to a hot mixture. Cornstarch is blended the same way with equal parts cold water blended with the dry powder. It should be blended to the consistency of heavy cream. When using flour and water as a thickener it is a thin paste called slurry. I prefer blending equal parts softened butter and flour to make a paste and whisking it into the hot liquid. This method is foolproof for sauces and gravies and is called a beurre manié (burr mahn-YAY) and is French for kneaded butter.

Kitchen Tools, Storage and Keeping Things Clean

It is highly suggested that a pepper mill or coffee grinder that is designated for grinding spices is used for recipes that call for ground or cracked pepper.

Kitchen shears are a great asset. They make cutting basil in strips or mincing parsley easier. You can use them to trim pie crusts too.

A portable egg timer allows you to time things that are in the oven when you need to go to another room in the house where the oven timer cannot be heard. The extra timer and the oven timer can both be used when you are timing more than one recipe.

Cheeses grate quickly and easily with the proper attachment on a food processor. For finely shredded, a microplane cheese grater works best.

Quiche dishes, pie plates and springform pans often have a size of 9 or 10 inches stated in a recipe. I have never experienced a problem using a 9-inch plate for a 10-inch or vice versa.

The color of your finished baked goods will be affected by the color of the bakeware you use. Light bakeware will result in lighter baked goods and darker bakeware will yield darker baked goods. Adjust cooking time accordingly.

Refrigerate fresh basil with a damp paper towel inside a plastic bag for up to 4 days. It will turn brown if you store it in the store container.

Ice that sits too long in the freezer takes on the flavor of what is being stored. When entertaining, be sure to have fresh ice, or buy a bag to use for the party.

When making potato dishes ahead, be sure and cook them and reheat before serving. Potatoes will turn brown over time if exposed to air when they are raw.

Brown sugar sometimes gets hard when stored in the box. It is best to store it in an airtight container. If it does become hard, peel half an apple and put it in the box for several hours or overnight. The sugar will soften and can be transferred to an airtight container.

Food storage is made easy and visible if you use sealable plastic bags. Several sizes are good to have on hand. Use one food item for each bag. Plastic sealable bags can be used to marinate meats too. Seal well before putting in the refrigerator. Get a step ahead in your recipes by storing pre-measured ingredients in plastic bags (grated cheese, chopped nuts, minced onions) so recipes can quickly be assembled the day of the event. Glass canning jars with lids are useful for storing your homemade vinaigrette. Use canning labels to identify each item.

Wrap celery in foil before placing it in the refrigerator. It will stay fresh longer.

Parchment paper is great for lining jelly roll pans and baking sheets. Things will not stick and cleanup is easier.

Spray plastic storage dishes with cooking oil before pouring tomato-based sauces in them. It will keep them from staining.

Meta West, a Family and Consumer Science teacher from Abilene, Kansas, passed on this tip for cleaning up after cooking. It is best to use cold water to soak dishes that held eggs, flour, starch, cream and milk. Hot water is best for those dishes that have contained oils, butter, sugar and syrup. Meta suggests using a paper towel to wipe away excess butter and oil prior to soaking. After dishes are soaked, all dishes should be washed with soap in hot water for sanitary purposes.

Meta also informed me the ideal temperature for your refrigerator thermostat is 37°F. This temperature will preserve foods better and keep foods from freezing.

My friend Irem Himam from Balikesir, Turkey, taught me how to best remove burnt foods from saucepans and skillets. Add a drop of dish soap and enough water to cover the bottom of the pan. Bring to a boil on the stove and the pan will be easier to clean.

To erase red wine stains off of counter tops, sprinkle with baking soda and leave for a few minutes. Wipe up the baking soda with a wet dishcloth and the stain should disappear. For red wine on carpets, sprinkle with iodized table salt and let sit. The salt will absorb the red wine. Scoop the excess off the carpet after several minutes and vacuum. If you get wine or coffee on table linens or clothing, don't pre-treat with bar soap; instead launder in detergent in warm or hot water. If the stain remains, soak article in all-fabric bleach before laundering again. Point out all stains to the dry cleaners if you are letting them care for your tablecloths and napkins.

Timesavers

Appetizers

Tomato-Mozzarella Crostini is a great appetizer! Cut a baguette into 1/4-inch slices. Slice 2 to 3 tomatoes in 1/4-inch slices. Place a tomato on top of the bread and top with a slice of fresh mozzarella. Bake at 350°F until cheese melts (approximately 10 minutes.) Sprinkle with thinly sliced fresh basil, drizzle with balsamic vinegar and serve warm.

Need a super quick appetizer? Pizzas of many varieties can be made from packaged refrigerated pizza dough. Buy some thinly sliced Cajun ham from the deli and thinly sliced mozzarella. Roll the meat and cheese up in the dough to the size of a fat cigar. Bake according to package directions and slice into 1-inch slices. Serve with a side of warmed spaghetti sauce.

Jane Plato of Southlake, Texas gave me this idea. In place of a sauce, spread 1 (13.8-ounce) package of Pillsbury refrigerated pizza dough with 1 (5.2-ounce) box of Boursin cheese (garlic and fine herb flavor) Top with 1/2 cup minced red onion and 1 each of thinly sliced yellow squash and zucchini. Bake according to package directions. Cut into 2 x 2-inch squares. Delicious!

Would you like a great tasting salsa? Combine 1 large bottle of picante sauce, 1 bunch fresh chopped green onions (white and pale green part only), 6 diced tomatoes (1/4-inch pieces), 1 large minced garlic clove and 3 chopped avocados (1/4-inch pieces). Mix up a few minutes before your event. It adds a homemade flavor.

Everyone loves chili con queso. Melt 1 (32-ounce) package of processed American cheese with 1 (8-ounce) package cream cheese and 1 (10-ounce) can of Ro*Tel Diced Tomatoes and Green Chilies over a double boiler or in a slow cooker. Serve warm with tortilla chips. If you want a variation or want to add some pizzazz, add fried spicy sausage, drained and crumbled to this combination. For another great combination, defrost and squeeze all the water out of 1 (10-ounce) box of spinach and add to the cheese/Ro*Tel tomato mixture or add 1 (15-ounce) can of chili without beans. Combinations of onion and jalapeño will add more spice and can be included in any of these combinations. For a special treat, put a cool scoop of guacamole in the bottom of a bowl. Pour warm chili con queso over the top. Serve with tortilla chips.

Richard Fennema of Coppell, Texas, gave me this tip for a quick and tasty marinade using Pickapeppa Sauce. Use 1 (6-ounce) bottle of undiluted Pickapeppa Sauce for 1 1/2 pounds of pork tenderloin. Let the meat marinate 1 hour at room temperature or up to 8 hours in the refrigerator. Grill to desired doneness and serve the meat with a chunky Caribbean Salsa (page 159). This meat marinade makes a colorful, hearty appetizer on a piece of lightly toasted baguette or a delicious main dish.

Cynthia Seymour, a friend from the Knots Landing Dinner Group (a group of us that watched the television series together for years), uses regular biscuits from the refrigerator section as a bun for appetizer ham sandwiches. Bake according to package directions and brush with melted butter and sprinkle with dried dill weed. Serve with sweet, hot mustard, thinly sliced ham and Swiss cheese. Delicious!

Cabécou goat cheese is a wonderful cheese that is delicious served with honey. To make four 1-ounce portions (the cheese comes in small round disks), pour 1/4 cup, slightly warmed or room temperature honey over the cheese and serve sprinkled with toasted walnuts or pecans (about 1/2 cup) for an extra treat. Serve with water crackers.

Thinly sliced bread can be cut into rounds with a cookie cutter and spread with a soft cheese such as Boursin (a triple cream cheese flavored with herbs). Top with a thinly sliced cucumber round and top with a sprig of dill. Elegant and light!

Marietta Kane of Colleyville, Texas, visits me at the cooking school and gave me this super quick appetizer. Take a round of Brie (8-ounce round or 16.9-ounce round) and place on a decorative platter or cake stand. Spoon olive tapenade (a bottled mixture of olives and spices) over the top and surround with bread rounds or crackers. Delicious and quick! Triple cream Brie is our favorite.

Joe Graber, my friend and the photographer for this book, created this easy and elegant appetizer. He uses fresh basil pesto as the bed for sea scallops that have been sautéed in butter approximately 2 minutes per side or until translucent. Allow 3 large sea scallops per guest.

Mary MacDowell of Colleyville, Texas, came up with a super easy and versatile appetizer. Butter a thawed sheet of phyllo dough using a pastry brush. Layer with another piece of phyllo and butter. Continue until you have 4 sheets stacked. Cut them lengthwise into 4 long rectangle strips (approximately 2 inches wide). Place a teaspoon of a soft cheese such as Boursin (garlic and fine herb flavor) on one corner. Top with a 1 x 1/2-inch (1/4 inch thick) piece of the raw meat of choice. Fold one corner over the filling, making a triangle, then fold the angle over again and again until the whole strip is folded. (They should be triangles or resemble Greek spanakopita.) Tuck the loose end neatly into the triangle shape. Brush with melted butter and bake at 400°F until golden, about 20 minutes. Beef filet, chicken breast, pork tenderloin or salmon may be used.

Jennifer Brightman-Moschel of Grapevine, Texas, is one of our instructors at the cooking school. For a quick appetizer she uses the frozen phyllo dough bite-size shells. She pre-bakes them and fills them with a dollop of apricot jam, small chunks of pear and tops with crumbled blue cheese. She bakes just a few additional minutes until the cheese melts. Top with toasted walnuts if desired.

Salads and Vegetables

Make a great summer salad by layering fresh sliced tomatoes with mozzarella slices (each 1/4 inch thick) so they slightly overlap, and sprinkle with fresh chopped basil, balsamic vinegar and lightly drizzle with olive oil. For an elegant and colorful presentation alternate tomato and mozzarella in a circle, drizzle with oil and vinegar and add a basil leaf in the middle.

For a quick egg salad, hard boil 4 eggs and grate into a bowl. Mix 1/4 cup Hellmann's or Best Foods Real Mayonnaise, 2 tablespoons sweet pickle relish, a pinch of sugar and salt and pepper to taste. Serve warm on fresh wheat bread. A pinch of sugar added to the water keeps the shells from cracking when the eggs are boiling.

David Gore makes a great squash side dish. Cut up unpeeled yellow squash and zucchini (approximately 6 whole vegetables). Finely chop one medium onion and finely dice 2 slices of bacon (1/4-inch pieces). Cook bacon and onion together until the onion is translucent. Add 1 (10-ounce) can Ro*Tel Diced Tomatoes and Green Chilies and the squash. Simmer, covered, until squash is tender. Taste and if salt is needed, sprinkle with *Tony Chachere's Creole Seasoning* to taste. If not using Ro*Tel, add 1/2 cup water so that the vegetables steam. Fred Hubbard of Trophy Club, Texas, mixes Dave's cooked squash with cooked pasta for a light lunch.

Brunch

For an added flavorful brunch idea, mix together 1/2 cup good jam with 1 stick soft butter. Form into cylinder on wax paper and refrigerate until firm. This can be cut in slices and served with muffins or toast. This is a wonderful tasty, colored butter.

My dad, Louie, made a wonderful pancake treat. He thinned his batter by adding more milk to make it more of a crêpe-like batter (approximately 2 cups milk to 1 cup dry pancake mix). Once they were cooked, he rolled canned or fresh peach slices up inside and placed them seam-side down on the plate. He rubbed butter across the top and sprinkled them with sugar. They are great!

For a breakfast treat, butter Jewish rye bread on one side and spread with cream cheese on the other side. Put the buttered side down in a pan as though you are making a grilled cheese sandwich. Top the side with cream cheese with thin sliced warmed pastrami. Simultaneously fry an egg and top pastrami with the fried egg. This combination is a delicious open-faced breakfast sandwich.

For a festive holiday brunch idea, arrange canned unbaked cinnamon rolls on a baking sheet (approximately 17 rolls) in the shape of a Christmas tree and bake according to directions. Drizzle with frosting to look like lights strung on a tree. Use red and green gumdrops or cherries between rolls as ornaments.

Champagne drinks are popular for brunch. Pour a glass of champagne and top off with a small amount of orange juice for a mimosa or cranberry juice for a poinsettia.

Dinner

Hamburgers don't have to be boring! My friend Jeanne Graber's mother, Claudette Patane, from Midlothian, Texas, mixes 1 (2.2-ounce) package dry beefy onion soup mix with 2 pounds ground beef or try mixing the hamburger meat with 1 (10-ounce) can Ro*Tel Diced Tomatoes and Green Chilies, drained. Both are great!

Defrost boneless, skinless chicken breasts and marinate overnight in Italian dressing and then roll in a stuffing mix. Drizzle 2 tablespoons butter mixed with one garlic clove chopped over the top of the marinated breasts and bake at 350°F for approximately 25 to 30 minutes. These can also be sliced and added to a salad.

Judy Hendrix of Sewickley, Pennsylvania gave me this recipe for a super topping to go over grilled meat. Mix a combination of savory ingredients such as blue cheese, shallots, garlic, herbs and Worcestershire sauce into soft butter. Pipe onto wax paper and freeze. When guests arrive, take them from the freezer to soften. You can use a knife to release them from the paper to top steaks or pork chops.

Dessert

Need a quick but elegant dessert? Mix 2 cups softened vanilla ice cream with 2 tablespoons Kahlúa and 1/4 cup Amaretto or Frangelico. Pour into a brandy snifter or open-face champagne glass that has been tied with a foil-edged ribbon at the base. Use the large side of your cheese grater to grate white chocolate on top. Serve this dessert with a spoon. This will make 2 servings.

Simple Garnishes

Purple or green kale is a leafy vegetable that makes a wonderful liner for a plate of appetizers, sandwiches or vegetables. Most grocery stores sell kale. To revive limp leaves, let them soak in cool water 30 minutes. Dry with paper towels before placing on the serving platter. Swiss chard also works well as a garnish.

During the holidays, add greenery from the Christmas tree to your appetizer and cake platters. Add colorful pinecone ornaments to dress up the greenery.

A small hollowed out pumpkin or red cabbage is a fun way to serve a dip. A small pumpkin can be used as a soup bowl in the fall months.

Miniature vegetables are unusual and appealing. You can find these at upscale grocery stores. They require less preparation since they are used whole. Squash, zucchini and carrots are usually available in this size.

Grapes cut into small bunches are quite decorative on a cheese tray. Fill in bare areas on the cheese tray, piling up the small clusters and hiding stems. The guests can put a small cluster on their appetizer plate, rather than struggling to pull single grapes off. For frosted grapes, dip the grapes in egg whites and then sprinkle them with superfine sugar. Let them harden and they will have the appearance of a first winter frost. To tell if grapes are fresh, shake them. If they cling to their stems, they're fresh; if they fall off, they're past their prime. Champagne grapes are tiny grapes that are beautiful on a cheese platter and can be found at upscale grocery stores that carry specialty produce.

If apples or pears are used, brush them lightly with lemon juice to keep them from discoloring. Dip tips of thinly sliced green apple in paprika and add to a cheese platter for color and interest. Add shredded purple cabbage beneath the fanned slices to create a colorful bed for the apples.

Star fruit (carambola) is a wonderful garnish when cut crosswise into 1/4 inch thick slices. It is yellow and resembles a star. Add as an edible decoration to cheese trays, desserts or salads.

Edible flowers have several decorative uses. You can mix an egg white with a few drops of water and brush the mixture onto all surfaces of the flower. Sprinkle with superfine sugar and let dry for a special look. They may be used in this way or directly from the package to decorate the top of white frosted miniature cupcakes. Edible flowers may also be used to dress up a salad, to garnish a plate of cookies or glued to a place card as decoration. Use a Bundt cake pan to make an ice ring for a punch bowl, add edible flowers to the water before freezing.

Flowers of any kind add color and style to appetizer and dessert platters. Pastel roses are especially good for showers, weddings and teas.

A Bundt cake looks festive when the center of the cake is filled with fresh flowers. Crumble foil and put in the center so you have a base for the stems and so fewer flowers will be needed.

Chop fresh parsley and sprinkle it around the outside edge of a plate for added color.

When using fresh herbs in a main dish, reserve sprigs to later garnish the plates. It is best to use herbs found in the recipe for garnish; parsley is the exception. If it is necessary for presentation to add color to the plate, choose flavors that are complementary, e.g. finely chopped green and red pepper for the Shrimp with Cilantro Pesto Cream Sauce (page 218). When serving a sauce, try pouring the sauce outside of the meat rather than on top. Fanning meat over a mound of potatoes with sauce drizzled around the outside makes a nice presentation. Pay attention to plate presentation in restaurants and collect new ideas.

Purchase empty condiment bottles (squeeze variety) to create edible plate designs. (The opening for squeezing must be fairly small.) Fill bottles with a thick enough sauce from your menu and draw designs on the outside edge of the plates you are using to serve the food. The sauce must be a consistency that won't run. Raspberry Sauce (page 260) or vanilla sauce (you may use melted vanilla ice cream) is often used as a decorative accent on a dessert plate. To paint heart shapes on a dessert plate, place a dollop of vanilla sauce in the center of the plate (creating a circle) and dot drops of Raspberry Sauce, an inch apart, at the edge of the circle. Stick a toothpick in the center of each dot and pull up or down to form a heart. The slice of dessert is then placed on top of the sauce. Practice on a separate plate before decorating the guests' plates.

> *"One of the delights is eating with my friends, second to that*
> *is talking about eating. And for an unsurpassed whammy,*
> *there is talking about eating while you are eating with friends.*
> *People who cook talk about food."*
>
> ~*Laurie Colwin*

Appetizers

Appetizers

 Kitchen tools needed

 May be prepared ahead

*Picture Features: Puff Pastry Pinwheels, page 57 • Appetizer Brie Cheesecakes, page 41
Horseradish Shrimp Dip, page 75 • Warm Spinach Artichoke Dip, page 36 • Assorted Cheeses*

Hearts of Palm and Artichoke Crostini

Makes: 36

- jelly roll pan
- cheese grater

2 (6-ounce) jars marinated artichokes, drained and chopped
3 stalks hearts of palm, coarsely chopped
3/4 cup Hellmann's or Best Foods Real Mayonnaise
1/4 cup sour cream
1 1/4 cups freshly grated Parmigiano-Reggiano cheese
2 medium garlic cloves, minced
1/8 teaspoon Tabasco red pepper sauce
1 baguette cut into 1/4-inch slices
Sweet paprika

Preheat broiler. In a medium bowl, mix the artichokes with the next six ingredients. If the bread seems too moist, toast slightly on a jelly roll pan without mixture under the broiler and turn over. Spread 1 tablespoon of the mixture on top of each baguette slice and sprinkle with paprika. Broil on the top rack of the oven about 2 inches from the heat until mixture is bubbly and starting to turn lightly golden. Watch carefully as not to burn. Temperatures of ovens vary! It would be best for you to know how long your broiler takes to toast, so toast one with topping before toasting them all. You want to be sure the mixture gets heated through and begins to turn lightly golden indicating that the cheese is melting. Continue to broil the remainder of the batch. Serve warm.

Tips: If baguette slices are large, cut them in half. Women tend to eat appetizers that are smaller in size. Make filling up to a day ahead of time and keep in the refrigerator, covered. Purchase the bread from the store bakery or specialty baker on the day of the gathering. This is also great with walnut scallion bread, if available in your area.

Warm Spinach Artichoke Dip

Serves: 6

 • cheese grater

2 (10-ounce) packages frozen chopped spinach
1 (14-ounce) can artichokes, drained and chopped
1 tablespoon jalapeño, seeded and minced
1 teaspoon minced garlic
1/4 cup minced onion
2 cups grated Monterey Jack cheese
1 (8-ounce) package cream cheese
1 cup freshly grated Parmigiano-Reggiano cheese
1 teaspoon Tabasco red pepper sauce
1/2 teaspoon *Tony Chachere's Creole Seasoning*
1 cup half-and-half
1/2 cup Hellmann's or Best Foods Real Mayonnaise
1 small tomato chopped or cherry tomato fanned, for garnish

Preheat the oven to 350°F. Defrost spinach and squeeze out all the water. Mix with all the other ingredients. Bake in a 10-inch deep pie pan or 2-quart casserole dish until bubbly, approximately 30 minutes. Sprinkle top lightly with additional *Tony Chachere's* and garnish with tomato for added color. Serve with tortilla chips and side of salsa for a casual gathering. Serve without salsa and offer guests crackers instead of chips if the meal is more elegant. You can make ahead and refrigerate, just heat before the guests arrive.

Variations: Goat cheese (1/2 cup) can be substituted for the Parmigiano-Reggiano. Cooked, crumbled bacon (about 4 slices) may also be added to either mixture. Bacon adds excellent flavor.

Carrie Hoffman: Overland Park, Kansas
Carrie took me under her wing during high school. Our friendship continued when we both attended Kansas State. This recipe's combination of ingredients grew from her original recipe after experimenting.

Spinach Dip with Crudités

Serves: 8

1 (10-ounce) package frozen
  chopped spinach
1 (16-ounce) container sour cream
1 cup Hellmann's or Best Foods
  Real Mayonnaise
3 green onions, finely chopped
  (white and pale green
  part only)
1 (8-ounce) can water
  chestnuts, drained and
chopped (optional)
1 (1.4-ounce) package Knorr
  Vegetable Recipe Mix

Defrost spinach and squeeze out all the water.
Blend all ingredients together, cover and
refrigerate. Make this a minimum of 2 hours
ahead. Stir before serving. Serve with crackers
or crudités (seasonal raw vegetables). Everyone
should have this in their collection of recipes if
they don't already!

Tip: If you own a potato ricer it is excellent for
squeezing the liquid out of frozen spinach.

Artichoke Dip

Serves: 6

 • cheese grater

2 (14-ounce) cans artichoke
  hearts, drained
1 cup Hellmann's or Best Foods
  Real Mayonnaise
1 cup freshly grated
  Parmigiano-Reggiano cheese
3 medium garlic cloves, minced
Dash of Tabasco red pepper
  sauce

Preheat the oven to 350°F. Chop the artichokes
and mix with remaining ingredients. Bake in a
quiche dish or an ovenproof dish until thoroughly
heated and bubbly, about 30 to 45 minutes. I
prefer to mix this together and let it sit overnight.
Bake before serving. Serve with water crackers.

*Variations: Lynne Borkowski, a friend from
working together at Caviar to Cabernet, cooks,
drains and crumbles 16 ounces of bacon and
sprinkles this on top before baking. It makes
a hearty appetizer and the bacon adds great
flavor. For a Southwest flair, I have also made
the basic recipe and added a 7-ounce can of
chopped green chiles. Cooked, chopped shrimp
(about 1 cup) added to the basic recipe adds a
seafood twist!*

Chilled Artichoke Vegetable Dip

Serves: 6

1 (14-ounce) can artichoke hearts, drained
1 (1-ounce) package Hidden Valley Original Ranch dry dressing mix
2 cups sour cream
1/8 teaspoon Worcestershire sauce
1/8 teaspoon freshly squeezed lemon juice

Chop the artichokes and combine with the remaining ingredients. Refrigerate at least one hour or overnight. Serve with fresh vegetables.

Special Note: Miniature vegetables are unusual and appealing on party platters. You can find these at upscale grocery stores. They require less preparation since they are used whole. Squash, zucchini and carrots are available in this size.

Green Olive Dip

Serves: 8

• Microplane cheese grater
• electric mixer

2 (8-ounce) packages cream cheese, softened
1/4 cup Hellmann's or Best Foods Real Mayonnaise
1/3 cup freshly grated Parmigiano-Reggiano cheese
1/4 cup finely chopped green onion (white and pale green part only)
6 slices bacon, cooked and crumbled
1 (5-ounce) jar pimento stuffed olives, drained and chopped
1/4 teaspoon Tabasco red pepper sauce

Using an electric mixer, combine the cream cheese with the other ingredients. Refrigerate until ready to serve. This dip keeps 5 to 7 days in the refrigerator. If desired, cook an additional strip of bacon or reserve 1 strip to crumble over the top.

Tips: Thick hickory smoked bacon tastes best for this recipe. Serve dip with water crackers. Water crackers are plain, unsalted crackers that allow the flavor of the dip to be appreciated!

Lynne Borkowski: Grapevine, Texas
This recipe is easy and delicious and is great with cocktails. Lynne and her husband Richard are friends that don't mind unannounced guests. We have had quite a few impromptu gatherings to taste new recipes.

Zucchini Bites

Serves: 4

- channel knife
- cheese grater

2 medium zucchini, washed and unpeeled
1/3 cup Hellmann's or Best Foods Real Mayonnaise
1/2 cup freshly grated Parmigiano-Reggiano cheese
1 tablespoon thinly sliced fresh basil
Sweet paprika, to serve

Preheat broiler. Score sides of zucchini with a channel knife starting at the top of the zucchini and scraping down in 3 straight lines around the zucchini each 1/3 of the way around, creating a design in the skin of the zucchini. Slice the zucchini in 1/4-inch slices. Mix together the mayonnaise, Parmigiano-Reggiano and basil. Arrange the zucchini slices on a foil-covered baking sheet. Spread 1/2 teaspoon of the mixture on each slice of zucchini. Temperatures of ovens vary! It would be best for you to know how long your broiler takes to toast, so toast one with topping before toasting them all. Broil on the top rack of the oven about 2 inches from the heat. You want to be sure the mixture gets heated through and begins to turn very lightly, golden indicating that the cheese is melting, about 30 seconds. Watch carefully as not to burn. Sprinkle with paprika and serve warm. The topping mixture may be made a day ahead and refrigerated until ready to use.

Variations: 1/4 cup chopped kalamata olives can be added to this mixture. Chopped red pepper can be used as a garnish for a more colorful combination once they are removed from the broiler. To add spice, omit the basil and use chopped jalapeño and 1/2 cup chopped onion. Melba toast rounds can be substituted for zucchini.

Special Note: A channel knife is a kitchen tool that has a small sharp "v" that peels the skin away, creating a design in the surface of the vegetables.

Tomato Basil Bruschetta

Serves: 6

4 ripe tomatoes, cored
1/2 cup finely chopped fresh
   basil leaves
1 tablespoon chopped fresh
   parsley
1/2 red onion, finely chopped
3 medium shallots, finely
   chopped (about 1/3 cup)
1/2 teaspoon salt
1/2 teaspoon ground black pepper
1 1/2 cups olive oil
1/2 cup water
1 teaspoon finely chopped fresh
   oregano or 1/3 teaspoon dried
1 tablespoon red wine vinegar
1 loaf Italian bread or a French
   baguette
3 large garlic cloves, peeled and
   sliced lengthwise

Dice the tomatoes (no need to remove skin or seeds) into 1/4-inch pieces and place in a large bowl. Add the basil, parsley, onion and shallots. Season the mixture with salt and pepper to taste. Pour in the olive oil, water, oregano and vinegar. Marinate for 3 hours at room temperature. Refrigerate prior to serving. May be made a day ahead, but refrigerate after it marinates. Cut bread into 1-inch slices. Toast slightly in oven and rub top and sides with sliced garlic cloves. When ready to serve, drain off excess liquid. Top the bread with a generous amount of the tomato mixture or serve bread and tomato mixture separately allowing guests to assemble.

Tip: Kitchen shears are a definite asset. They make cutting basil in strips or chopping parsley much easier.

"What I am most attracted to in my friends are their spirits: they are people who love life, who are passionate, who take risks to live fully, who are sensitive to feelings and idiosyncrasies, who share this goodness with me."

~Alexandra Stoddard

Appetizer Brie Cheesecakes

Makes: 24

- blender
- electric mixer
- mini muffin pans

4 crispy cracker breads, zwieback
  or Melba toasts
2 tablespoons melted butter
6 ounces cream cheese
4 1/2 ounces Brie cheese,
  with rind
1 large egg
1 tablespoon dry sherry
1/8 teaspoon salt
1/8 teaspoon garlic powder
1/8 teaspoon black pepper
24 small fresh basil leaves
6 cherry tomatoes, quartered
Small basil leaves for garnish

Preheat the oven to 350°F. Spray the 24 mini muffin pans with cooking spray. Crush crackers in a blender. Combine the crushed crackers and melted butter in a bowl. Press the cracker mixture into the bottom of the muffin cups. Beat together cream cheese, Brie, egg, sherry, garlic powder, salt and pepper with an electric mixer until combined. This may be made 1 day ahead, covered and refrigerated. The mixture will be lumpy. Place 1 teaspoon of the cheese mixture in each muffin tin. Place a basil leaf on top of each cup. Cover the basil leaf with more cheese mixture almost until flush with the top and bake 10 to 12 minutes. Cool slightly. Use a knife to loosen from tins and top each with a cherry tomato wedge and additional basil leaf. Serve slightly warm. Cracker bread can be found with the specialty crackers.

Tip: This idea of miniature cheesecakes can be used for a sweet dessert cheesecake as well. Substitute a recipe from the dessert section. I would not recommend the batter for Chokahlúa Cheesecake be used for this procedure. A firm cheesecake such as the Amaretto Cheesecake (page 255) works well as a miniature cheesecake. The decoration on top could be an edible flower or fruit. The cracker base can be made from graham crackers or gingersnaps mixed with butter for a dessert cheesecake. Bake miniature dessert cheesecakes 10 to 12 minutes or until edges are slightly golden.

Brie with Apples, Cranberries and Pecans

Serves: 16

- jelly roll pan
- 2-inch cookie cutter
- serrated knife
- parchment paper
- rolling pin

2 frozen puff pastry sheets (from a 17.3-ounce box)
2 tablespoons unsalted butter
1/4 cup brown sugar
1/4 cup dried cranberries
1 Granny Smith apple, peeled, cored and coarsely chopped (about 1 cup total)
1/4 cup chopped pecans
1 tablespoon brandy or cognac
2 (8-ounce) wheels of Brie cheese
1 egg yolk, beaten with 1 tablespoon cold water

Preheat the oven to 400°F. Defrost the pastry sheets according to package directions (approximately 20 minutes). With a rolling pin, roll dough just enough to remove the creases where the dough had been folded. Combine the next six ingredients in a small saucepan. Cook over medium-low heat until sugar is dissolved and apples are slightly softened. Cut Brie in half so there is a top and a bottom (the more chilled the Brie the better). Cover bottom half with apple mixture and top with remaining Brie. Using the Brie box or Brie as a guide, cut a circle slightly bigger than the Brie from the left side of the dough. Put the Brie in the center of the right uncut piece of dough. Reserve the extra dough for cutouts. Fold the two opposite sides toward each other and bring toward the center. You are wrapping to cover all of the cheese. Neatly top with the circle of cutout dough. Press the edges together to seal. Place seam-side down on a jelly roll pan lined with parchment paper. Brush with egg mixture. Decorate the top with cutouts from the leftover pastry and brush with egg mixture again. Repeat with the second Brie round and second sheet of pastry. The Brie may be refrigerated up to 1 day before baking. Bake 20 to 25 minutes or until golden. Let sit 20 to 30 minutes before moving to a serving platter with a spatula. Serve warm with a small knife or spreader and water crackers.

Tip: Judy Waitkus of Colleyville, Texas, suggests cutting the Brie into small wedges once baked and cooled, or at least cutting one wedge out. This encourages the guests to try the Brie since

(continued on next page)

42

most do not want to be the first to slice into the beautiful Brie. One (16.9-ounce) wheel of Brie cheese may be substituted for 2 (8-ounce) rounds of Brie cheese.

Judy prefers to make two small wrapped Brie rounds because it is more convenient for a buffet table. You may have one at each end or use the second one as a replacement for the other.

Variation: Apple brandy or Calvados may be used in place of brandy. Other nuts such as shelled pistachios can be substituted. Brie is a vehicle for both sweet and savory ingredients so use your imagination for this beautiful pastry wrapped version.

Blue Cheese-Parmesan Toasts

Serves: 6

- cheese grater
- jelly roll pan

1 cup Hellmann's or Best Foods Real Mayonnaise
2 medium garlic cloves, minced or pressed
1/8 teaspoon cayenne pepper
3/4 cup finely crumbled blue cheese
1 1/2 cups freshly grated Parmigiano-Reggiano cheese
3/4 cup finely chopped green onions (white and pale green part only)
24 slices (1/4-inch thick) baguette or sourdough bread

Preheat the oven to 400°F. Combine the mayonnaise with the next 5 ingredients. (Mayonnaise mixture may be made several days ahead and refrigerated.) When ready to serve, spread a generous tablespoon of the cheese mixture on each slice of bread. Arrange on a jelly roll pan and bake until the cheese topping starts to bubble and the toasts are golden around the edges. Transfer the toasts to a large platter and serve warm.

Variation: If you run out of time...blue cheese alone, melted on bread is delicious. Once warmed and slightly melted, drizzle with honey and sprinkle with chopped pecans.

Honey Pecan Brie Pastries

Serves: 6

- 1 (1/2-inch) round cookie cutter
- pastry brush
- parchment paper

1/2 cup finely chopped pecans, divided use
1 frozen puff pastry sheet (from a 17.3-ounce box)
1 egg yolk, beaten with 1 tablespoon cold water
1 (6-ounce) Brie cheese round, rind removed
1 tablespoon honey

Preheat the oven to 350°F. Toast the nuts for 3 to 4 minutes. Raise the temperature to 400°F. Thaw the pastry sheet for 20 minutes on the counter. With your fingers smooth the crease where the pastry was folded. With a 1 1/2-inch round cookie cutter, cut the pastry into approximately 28 rounds. Brush the tops of the pastries with the egg mixture and place on a parchment lined baking sheet. Bake for approximately 10 to 15 minutes until tops are golden. Remove from baking sheet and gently pull each one apart to make 2 layers. Mash together the cheese and 1/3 cup toasted nuts. (Make this a day ahead and bring to room temperature before using.) Drop 1/2 teaspoon of filling onto half of the pastry rounds and top with another round. Top each pastry with a drop of honey and gently spread (see tip). Sprinkle with the remaining nuts (honey should make the nuts adhere—press down if needed). Bake approximately 3 to 5 minutes so cheese begins to melt. Very easy and impressive!

Tips: Use the back of a spoon to spread the honey on top of pastries. Brushing the tops tends to tear the pastry. Also, when thawing the frozen puff pastry sheets, it is best to unwrap it completely and separate the two sheets. Because they are so compactly packaged, they will not defrost otherwise. They take approximately 20 minutes at room temperature. You may bake pastry ahead and assemble two hours before guests arrive.

Variation: Any dried fruit or nut variety can be mixed in the cheese. Complementary preserves such as fig, apricot or raspberry could be spread on the inside of the small pastries for additional flavor.

Marinated Feta with Roasted Garlic and Kalamata Olives

Serves: 4

• Microplane grater or zester

1 medium garlic bulb
1/4 cup olive oil
1 tablespoon minced fresh rosemary, or 1 teaspoon dried rosemary
1 tablespoon fresh thyme, or 1 teaspoon dried thyme
1 tablespoon minced fresh chives, or 1 teaspoon dried chives
1 teaspoon cracked black pepper
1/2 lemon, zest only
8 pitted kalamata olives, sliced
1 (8-ounce) block feta cheese
1 roasted red pepper or seeded Roma tomato, diced (1/4-inch pieces)

Preheat the oven to 400°F. Cut 1/4-inch off the pointed end of the bulb of garlic to expose the cloves. Place garlic in a baking dish, drizzle with olive oil and toss to coat. Place cut side up and cover tightly with foil. Roast the garlic until the skin is golden and garlic is tender, approximately 40 minutes or until cloves are tender. Cool slightly before removing 6 cloves. Smash cloves and set aside. Save the remainder for another use. In a small saucepan, heat the oil until warm (when you dip the rosemary in the oil, it will sizzle). Remove from heat, let stand 5 minutes and then add the herbs, pepper, zest, olives and garlic. (If you add the herbs when the oil is too hot, it will spatter.) Let the oil mixture sit until the mixture is cool. Add the cheese, pour the oil over the cheese and let the cheese marinate in the oil mixture a minimum of 2 hours un-refrigerated and up to 24 hours refrigerated. When you are ready to serve, put the cheese on a platter, leaving part of the herb mixture with the cheese. Top with chopped red pepper or tomatoes. While the cheese is marinating, make Pita Toasts (page 65) to serve along with the dish.

Tips: Zest of a lemon is the peel only and requires a tool like a Microplane grater for easiest zesting. You want only the yellow skin not the white pith. Leftover marinated cheese is good crumbled over salad.

Goat Cheese and Olive Finger Sandwiches

Serves: 6

- holiday or other 2-inch cookie cutter
- blender, food processor or electric mixer

1/3 cup good quality ripe black olives

1 cup (4 ounces) crumbled plain goat cheese

2 ounces cream cheese

1 green onion, minced

1 medium garlic clove, minced or pressed

1/8 teaspoon Tabasco red pepper sauce

1 loaf good quality sliced white bread (sour dough is firm and works well)

1/4 cup minced parsley

Remove pits from the olives if necessary and chop the olives. Put the olives, goat cheese, cream cheese, green onion, garlic and Tabasco sauce in a blender or food processor or use an electric mixer to blend. Use cookie cutter to cut out shapes in the bread. Do not use crusts. Cut out the bread shapes and spread the goat cheese, olive mixture on one side of bread. Top with another bread cutout. The filling should spill out the sides enough that chopped parsley will outline the shape when you dip them. Dip the edge of the sandwiches in the minced parsley. The olive mixture can be made ahead. Bring to room temperature before using. The bread can be cut out and stored overnight in an airtight container.

Tips: This is a great holiday tea or party item. It can be used for any occasion or served as a spread. If these ingredients don't appeal to you, use a chicken salad with finely chopped ingredients or some other filling (see page 133 for Artichoke Chicken Salad). Garnish the plate with fresh greenery and cranberries during the holidays. To easily remove pits from olives, place them on a work surface and roll over them with a rolling pin, then pick out the pits.

"Wrinkles only go where the smiles have been."

~Jimmy Buffett

Goat Cheese Torte with Sun-Dried Tomatoes, Pesto and Pine Nuts

Serves: 16

- plastic wrap
- springform pan (9- or 10-inch)
- mesh strainers

1 1/2 cups oil packed sun-dried tomatoes, finely chopped
1 cup prepared pesto
1 cup toasted pine nuts
3 (11-ounce) packages plain goat cheese
2 (8-ounce) packages cream cheese
2 tablespoons milk or half-and-half
Water crackers or thinly sliced baguette

Preheat the oven to 400°F. Before you begin, allow the sun-dried tomatoes and pesto to drain in strainers. Remove excess oil or liquid from both with paper towels. On a baking sheet, toast the pine nuts until just lightly golden and shiny, approximately 3 to 4 minutes. Set aside. Mix the goat cheese, cream cheese and milk or half-and-half together until smooth. Line a springform pan with plastic wrap, leaving a 4-inch overhang. Pat the sun-dried tomatoes evenly into the springform pan as the first layer. Press half of the goat cheese mixture onto the sun-dried tomatoes. Next, spread the pesto over the goat cheese. Spread the remaining goat cheese over the pesto evenly and carefully. Sprinkle the pine nuts evenly over the goat cheese. Cover the pine nuts with the plastic wrap and chill until ready to serve. (Chill a minimum of 3 hours up to two days before serving.) To serve unwrap the plastic wrap from the top of the goat cheese. Take the torte and turn it upside down onto a cake plate or serving platter. Unbuckle the springform and carefully remove the plastic wrap from the torte. A beautiful presentation!

Tips: You may cut this recipe in half and use a smaller springform pan, loaf pan and if absolutely necessary due to lack of equipment, you may layer these ingredients in the same manner in a bowl of approximately the same size. It will appear more rustic rather than uniform but will still have the same great flavor. Since the sun-dried tomatoes are most visible, choose tomatoes with a vibrant red color.

Rena Marson:
Denver, Colorado
Rena is the author of the cookbook,
Cooking with Rena, *and also owned*
Tastefully Yours Catering and The
Parlour Café in Grapevine, Texas.
Rena creates fabulous food with
presentation and flavor in mind and
this is one of my favorites with the
red and green layers!

Pistachio Goat Cheese Strudel

Serves: 8

- pastry brush
- jelly roll pan
- electric mixer

- serrated knife

1 (8-ounce) package plain goat cheese, softened
1 (3-ounce) package cream cheese
1/3 cup finely minced red onion
1 teaspoon minced garlic
1 large egg yolk
8 drops Tabasco red pepper sauce
1/4 teaspoon Worcestershire sauce
2 teaspoons freshly squeezed lemon juice
3/4 cup shelled, finely chopped salted pistachios, divided use
9 phyllo dough sheets, thawed (18 x 12-inch sheets, see tips)
1/2 cup (1 stick) unsalted butter, melted

Preheat the oven to 375°F. In a bowl, beat the goat cheese, cream cheese, onion, minced garlic, egg yolk, Tabasco, Worcestershire and lemon juice until smooth. Stir in 1/2 cup chopped pistachios. Unroll the phyllo and place one sheet on a jelly roll pan and brush with butter. Repeat this procedure twice with 3 additional sheets, brushing each with butter. Spoon 1/3 of the cream cheese mixture onto the long side of the phyllo dough and form into a long cigar shaped roll along the length of the dough. Finish by tightly rolling the dough up in a jelly roll style. Brush with additional butter and place on another lightly greased jelly roll pan. Repeat this procedure making two more rolls. With a serrated knife, cut rolls into 1-inch pieces and place filling side up 1 inch apart on the greased jelly roll pan. Sprinkle with remaining pistachios. Bake until dough is slightly golden, about 13 to 16 minutes. Serve warm.

Tips: For best results, thaw the phyllo by placing in the refrigerator overnight. Cover the phyllo with a slightly dampened dishtowel while working so phyllo does not dry out. Once baked, these can be frozen and reheated for use at another time. Thaw, cut and bake as directed. These are also a delicious accompaniment to salad. If only 9 x 14-inch phyllo sheets are available, make four rolls instead of two. Spraying olive oil cooking spray on the phyllo sheets is an alternative to brushing butter on the phyllo.

Lisa Flugstad: Bloomington, Minnesota
When I was at a culinary conference in Minneapolis, I stayed with my grade school friend, Paula Dyrhaug. She hosted a gathering for me to sample her friend's favorite recipe and this was Lisa's contribution. Because it is delicate, it pairs nicely with white wine or champagne.

Blue Cheese and Date Cheese Spread

Serves: 12

- cheese grater
- electric mixer

1 cup pecans
3 (8-ounce) packages cream cheese
1 cup (4 ounces) crumbled blue cheese
2 cups grated sharp Cheddar cheese
1 (8-ounce) package dates, chopped

Preheat oven to 350°F and toast pecans 3 to 4 minutes. Mix cream cheese, blue cheese, Cheddar cheese and chopped dates together. You may make this as a spread or make into one large or two small cheese balls. Coarsely chop the toasted pecans. If making into cheese balls, roll in pecans, otherwise sprinkle nuts on top of a spread. This can be made 2 days ahead. Do not roll or sprinkle nuts on top until the day you are serving. Serve dip with water crackers.

Tip: A small hollowed out pumpkin or red cabbage is a colorful way to serve a dip.

Jeanne Graber: Colleyville, Texas
Jeanne is a dear friend. We used to spend every Tuesday evening visiting over wine and appetizers when she worked near my house. She made this fabulous mixture as a cheese ball when my parents came to town to visit and she and Joe invited us for dinner. I love the blue cheese and date combination. The sweet and sharp flavors blend nicely.

Party Sandwiches

Servings: 8

- electric mixer
- serrated knife

1 unsliced 8- to 10-inch long loaf pumpernickel bread or other dense specialty bread
1 bunch green onions, finely chopped (white and pale green part only)
1/2 teaspoon *Tony Chachere's Creole Seasoning*
1 (8-ounce) package cream cheese, softened
Hellmann's or Best Foods Real Mayonnaise
Romaine lettuce leaves
2 tomatoes, thinly sliced (1/8-inch slices)
1 1/2 pounds thinly sliced rare roast beef, from the deli
1 pound bacon, cooked crisp and drained

Slice bread in half lengthwise and hollow out the top of the loaf about 1/2 inch deep. The bread loaf should be about 3 1/2 inches wide. In a medium bowl, mix the green onion and *Tony Chachere's* into the cream cheese. Fill the cavity of the bread with the cream cheese mixture. Spread the bottom half generously with mayonnaise. Cover to the edge of the bread. Layer the lettuce on the bottom half of the bread, followed by the tomatoes and roast beef. Top with the bacon slices. Top with the hollowed out bread filled with cream cheese. Wrap in plastic wrap until ready to serve.

May be made 8 hours ahead. Slice sandwich diagonally at 2-inch intervals with a serrated knife.

Tips: The bread that is dense and large enough should come from a specialty baker and may need to be special ordered. Serve with soup for a complete meal.

Variations: The Fresh Tomato, Kalamata and Feta Salad (p. 122) would be a great way to jazz up this sandwich by leaving the tomatoes in the sandwich and adding chopped feta and olives. Drizzle the tomatoes with the vinaigrette before putting in sandwich. Another yummy combination!

Jody Huerter: Leawood, Kansas
Jody and her family were our next-door neighbors while growing up in Kansas City. She is a wonderful cook. When either of us needs ideas for table settings or menus, we call each other. Jody suggested this sandwich for a couple's shower. It was perfect for the occasion. We served this sandwich along with a few interesting dips, crackers and a vegetable platter. There were no leftovers!

Cheese Pecan Spread

Serves: 8

• cheese grater

1/2 cup coarsely chopped pecans
2 cups grated Cheddar cheese
3/4 cup Hellmann's or Best Foods
  Real Mayonnaise
2 tablespoons finely chopped
  green onion (white and pale
  green part only)
4 strips cooked bacon, drained
  and crumbled

Combine all ingredients and chill 12 hours. Serve with bagel chips or water crackers.

Variations: My friend Becky Loboda from Mission Hills, Kansas, makes a simple dip similar to this by blending grated Monterey Jack cheese with mayonnaise (use the proportions above as a guide). She blends in a little dried minced onion, to taste, and serves it with water crackers. I do the same with Swiss cheese, ground white pepper and chives, to taste.

Beth Lemaster: Flower Mound, Texas
Beth gave me this recipe after taking it to a party where her friends called after the party to request the recipe.

Hot Pepper Peach Dip

Serves: 12

• cheese grater
• electric mixer

2 cups (8 ounces) grated
  mozzarella cheese
2 (8-ounce) packages cream
  cheese
1 (7.6-ounce) jar Rothchild Hot
  Pepper Peach Preserves
1 tablespoon jalapeño, seeded
  and chopped
1 teaspoon paprika
1 teaspoon chopped parsley
1 teaspoon dry minced onion

Set aside approximately 1 cup grated cheese to sprinkle over the dip. Mix the remaining cheese and ingredients together with an electric mixer. Put dip in one to two bowls depending on the size. Sprinkle the 1 cup grated cheese over the top and refrigerate. May be made up to two days ahead. This dip is spicy yet slightly sweet. It is delicious! Serve with water crackers.

Tip: The Hot Pepper Peach Jam can be found at gourmet retailers or call Rothchild Berry Farms for a store near you at 1-800-356-8933. Peach jam and red pepper flakes (to taste) would be a substitute if you cannot find the jam.

Southwest Layer Dip

Serves: 8

3 ripe avocados, peeled and
seeded
2 tablespoons freshly squeezed
lime juice (juice from 1
medium lime)
1 large garlic clove, minced or
pressed
1 (1.25-ounce) package taco
seasoning
1 (8-ounce) carton sour cream
2 (9-ounce) cans bean dip
2 cups (8 ounces) grated
Cheddar cheese
1 medium tomato, diced (1/4-
inch pieces)
1 (4.25-ounce) can ripe black
olives, chopped
1 bunch green onions, finely
chopped (white and
pale green part only)

Mash the avocados with the lime juice and
garlic. Set aside. Mix the taco seasoning with the
sour cream and set aside. In a decorative large
glass bowl or a 9 x 13-inch baking dish, spread
the bean dip on the bottom of the dish. Layer
the mashed avocados over the bean dip, then
the sour cream mixture. Sprinkle the cheese over
the layered mixtures and sprinkle the chopped
tomatoes, black olives and green onions evenly
over the surface. You may make this dip 24
hours ahead. Serve with tortilla chips.

Tip: The mashed avocados, lime juice and
garlic are the start of a great guacamole. Laurie
Martell Pino of Denver, Colorado, is a friend from
college. She increases the number of avocados to
4 or 5 and adds 1 to 3 tablespoons total garlic,
depending on your taste, 1/2 of a red onion
(finely chopped), 1/3 cup salsa, black pepper,
chili powder and salt, to taste. Sour cream may
be added to the guacamole if you like a creamier
consistency. Fresh seeded, minced jalapeño
peppers can be added if you want to add spice.

Easy Southwest Dip

Serves: 6

1 (16-ounce) container sour cream
1/2 cup Hellmann's or Best Foods
Real Mayonnaise
1 (1.4-ounce) package Knorr
Vegetable Recipe Mix
1 cup chunky salsa
2 teaspoons chili powder
1/4 cup chopped fresh cilantro
(stems removed)

In a medium bowl, combine the sour cream,
mayonnaise, dry soup mix, salsa, chili powder
and cilantro. Cover and refrigerate a minimum
of 2 hours. Serve with tortilla chips.

Tex-Mex Won Tons

Serves: 6

- mini muffin pans
- cheese grater

24 won ton wrappers or 6 egg roll wrappers
1 (9-ounce) can bean dip
1/4 cup finely chopped onion
1 1/2 teaspoons taco seasoning
1/8 teaspoon ground cumin
1/2 cup grated Cheddar cheese
Salsa
Sour cream

Preheat the oven to 350°F. Spray the mini muffin pans with a cooking spray. Press 1 won ton wrapper into each muffin cup and press so it stays open and adheres to the sides. Bake the wrappers for approximately 7 to 9 minutes so the edges start to get golden. Mix the beans, onions, and seasonings together. (This may be prepared ahead.) Fill the cups and top with cheese. Bake approximately 5 to 8 minutes until cups appear crisp and cheese melts. Top with a small dollop of salsa and sour cream. Serve warm.

Tips: Since oven temperatures vary, it is best to test one won ton wrapper to be sure suggested time to bake is the right amount of time for your oven. Egg roll wrappers may be cut to the same size of a won ton wrapper (approximately 2 x 2 inches) if necessary.

Variation: My gourmet version of this appetizer filling is made with 1/2 pound precooked shrimp mixed with 4 ounces cream cheese and 1 cup grated Cheddar cheese, 1 roasted red pepper (from a jar), minced and 1 canned chipotle chile in adobo, minced. Fill won ton cups and bake approximately 5 to 8 minutes until cheese melts. Top with a small dollop of homemade guacamole (page 52) or prepared guacamole from the grocery store produce area.

"This is the happiest conversation where there is no competition, no vanity, but a calm, quiet interchange of sentiments."

~*Samuel Johnson*

Tortilla Roll Ups

Serves: 8

• electric mixer

2 (8-ounce) packages cream
cheese
4 green onions, finely chopped
(white and pale green
part only)
1/4 cup grated Cheddar cheese
1 large garlic clove, minced or
pressed
1/4 cup salsa
1 package flour tortillas
Extra salsa for dipping

Mix together the cream cheese, onions, Cheddar cheese, garlic and salsa. Thinly spread on one side of a flour tortilla. Roll up to the size of a cigar. Be sure ends have enough filling. Wrap with plastic wrap and refrigerate overnight or until firm. Slice in 1/2-inch slices and serve with extra salsa.

Tip: Chopped black olives, minced jalapeños, drained green chiles or canned, drained black beans are also great additions to the basic mixture.

Special Note: When planning your appetizers balance the ingredients so there is a variety. Don't have them all be cream cheese based. Look at what ingredients are overlapping and choose things that complement one another and are not too similar in color, taste or texture.

Tamale Dip

Serves: 8

2 (15-ounce) cans or jars of
tamales, with juice
1 (16-ounce) can chili without
beans
1 (8-ounce) jar picante sauce
2 (5-ounce) jars old English
cheese
1 medium onion, finely
chopped

Chop tamales and reserve any juices from the cans. In a large bowl, mix together the tamales and reserved juice with the rest of ingredients. This may be made ahead and refrigerated. Bake in a quiche pan for 15 to 20 minutes or until bubbly. Serve warm with tortilla chips. As an alternative you may heat over double boiler and serve out of a fondue pot or slow cooker, but I think a quiche pan or pie pan is more appealing. A processed American cheese can be substituted for the old English cheese.

Cocktail Meatballs

Serves: 8

- chafing dish or slow cooker
- slotted spoon
- toothpicks

Meatballs
1 1/2 pounds ground chuck
(80/20 ground beef)
6 1/2 ounces evaporated milk
1 cup instant rice
1 egg
1/2 cup finely chopped onion
1/2 teaspoon salt
1 teaspoon minced garlic
1/4 teaspoon chili powder

Sauce
2 cups ketchup
1/2 cup brown sugar
2 tablespoons liquid smoke
1 teaspoon minced garlic
1/2 cup chopped onion

Preheat the oven to 350°F. Combine the ground chuck with the next 7 ingredients and shape into meatballs. For a cocktail party they should be walnut size. Combine sauce ingredients in a medium saucepan and heat slowly to dissolve the brown sugar. Put meatballs in a baking dish and pour the sauce over them. Bake meatballs about 1 hour. Remove meatballs with a slotted spoon into a serving dish that will keep them warm, such as a chafing dish or slow cooker. Stir sauce so that the juices of the meatballs blend with the sauce. Spoon the sauce over the meatballs. Serve with toothpicks. These may be made ahead and frozen. Defrost and reheat. Serve warm.

Tip: These meatballs are dual purpose. Substitute the meatballs made from ground beef in the recipe (page 223) for spaghetti with meatballs.

Special Note: Chopped or minced garlic in a jar is great for marinades or meatballs. For sauces and other recipes, I mince or press (with a garlic press) fresh garlic.

Melissa Weikel: Topeka, Kansas
Melissa and I have been friends since college. After graduation we both lived in Dallas and were able to get together fairly often. Now we live in separate cities. We only get together once a year, but we always manage to enjoy a new restaurant and good conversation. Everyone loves these bite-size meatballs with their slightly sweet flavor.

Danish Meatballs with Dill Sauce

Makes: 80 meatballs

- whisk
- chafing dish or slow cooker
- double boiler
- toothpicks

Meatballs
1 pound ground beef
1/2 pound ground veal
1/2 pound ground pork
2 teaspoons salt
1/4 teaspoon black pepper
2 large eggs
1/3 cup finely chopped onion
1/2 cup heavy cream
1 cup bread crumbs
Additional salt and pepper, to taste

Sauce
1 cup (2 sticks) butter
1/4 cup flour
2 cups chicken broth
1 (16-ounce) container sour cream
1/4 cup chopped fresh dill or 1 1/2 tablespoons dried dill weed
Salt and pepper, to taste

Preheat the oven to 375°F. Combine the ground meats, salt, pepper, eggs, onion and cream. Shape into meatballs and roll in bread crumbs. Bake the meatballs for about 35 minutes. Taste meatballs and add a sprinkle of salt and pepper if needed. To make the sauce, melt the butter in a large pan. Whisk in flour and gradually stir in broth. Cook over low heat stirring constantly until sauce bubbles and thickens. Stir in sour cream and dill. Add salt and pepper, to taste. Serve the meatballs warm in a chafing dish or slow cooker. Pour sauce over meatballs and serve with toothpicks. Meatballs can be made ahead and frozen (without sauce) or refrigerated with sauce. For frozen meatballs, thaw, then heat in the oven and make the sauce. For refrigerated meatballs with sauce, heat in a double boiler.

Joan Willhite: Yellow Springs, Ohio
When I was a retail buyer, Joan was my work counterpart in Ohio. When we all met for corporate gatherings it was like family getting together. Joan doubles this recipe because these meatballs get eaten so quickly.

Puff Pastry Pinwheels

Serves: 6

• serrated knife

**1 frozen puff pastry sheet
(from a 17.3-ounce box)
2 tablespoons honey mustard
1/4 pound thinly sliced prosciutto
(paper thin), finely chopped
1 cup freshly grated
Parmigiano-Reggiano cheese**

Preheat the oven to 400°F. Let the frozen pastry thaw 20 minutes on countertop, separate the dough so you defrost just one sheet and refreeze the other. You will know the dough is ready to work with when it unfolds easily. Lay the pastry out flat and where it has folded, press out creases as needed. Use a small amount of water if necessary. Spread mustard on top of pastry. Arrange the prosciutto evenly to cover all the pastry and sprinkle with cheese. Starting at the long end, roll the pastry up like a jelly roll but just to the middle of the dough. Roll the other side the same way. Where the two rolls meet in the middle, use a small amount of water to seal. (If there is time, allow the roll to be refrigerated 15 minutes as it is easier to cut. The pastry can even be made up to this point the night before, but remember to wrap it in plastic wrap before refrigerating.) Just before baking, cut the pastry into 1/2-inch slices with a serrated knife. Place the slices on a lightly greased baking sheet. Flatten slightly with a spatula. Bake 10 minutes until lightly golden and turn over with a spatula. Bake approximately 5 minutes more or until center is no longer doughy and shiny. These are best warm but may be served at room temperature. Once these appetizers have cooled slightly, they can be cut in half again to serve more people. I use my kitchen shears to chop the prosciutto.

Variation: A super variation of this recipe replaces the prosciutto with serrano ham (Spanish aged ham), the Parmesan with manchego cheese (a sheep's milk cheese) and the honey mustard with quince preserves, paste or jam. Spanish and spectacular! (The Spanish Jamón (ham) serrano has distinctly more flavor, and significantly less salt than country ham and less fat than prosciutto.) Either variation makes a super brunch bread or appetizer.

Sausage En Croûte with Homemade Mustard

Serves: 6

- 1-inch cookie cutters
- pastry brush

1 frozen puff pastry sheet (from a 17.3-ounce box)
2 pieces kielbasa sausage, each 6 inches long
1 egg yolk, beaten with 1 tablespoon cold water

Homemade Mustard
2 (2-ounce) containers dry mustard
1 cup white vinegar
2 large eggs, beaten
1 cup white sugar
Pinch of salt

Preheat the oven to 375°F. Let the frozen pastry thaw 20 minutes on countertop, separate the dough so you defrost just the one sheet and refreeze the other. You will know the dough is ready to work with when it unfolds easily. Lay the pastry out flat and where it has folded, press out creases as needed. Cut pastry crosswise in half. Wrap each piece of sausage in pastry, trimming pastry as necessary and sealing edges with the egg mixture. Use pastry trimmings and small cookie cutters to decorate the Sausage En Croûte. Brush with more egg and place on an ungreased baking sheet. (This may be made ahead to this step, loosely covered and refrigerated.) Bake for 35 to 40 minutes or until browned and puffed. Remove from the oven and cool slightly. To make the mustard, combine the dry mustard and white vinegar. Let the mixture sit overnight. The next day add eggs, sugar and salt and heat to the desired consistency. Refrigerate until ready to serve. Serve with the Sausage En Croûte.

"Be at peace with God. Whatever you conceive him to be, and whatever your labors and aspirations, in the noisy confusion of life, keep peace with your soul."

~Max Ehrmann, Desiderata

Bacon Tomato Tartlets

Makes: 24

- mini muffin pans
- cheese grater

1 (12-ounce) can flaky biscuits
6 slices bacon, cooked, drained and crumbled
1 medium tomato, seeded and diced (1/4-inch pieces)
3/4 cup grated mozzarella cheese
1/2 cup Hellmann's or Best Foods Real Mayonnaise
1 teaspoon dried basil
3/4 teaspoon garlic salt
1 teaspoon dried thyme
1/2 teaspoon dried oregano

Preheat the oven to 350°F. Split the biscuits into 3 pieces. (The flaky biscuits pull apart easily into their natural layers.) Spray muffin pans lightly with cooking spray. Press the split biscuits into the mini muffin cups. You will not use the entire can of biscuits. Mix the remaining ingredients together and fill each of the unbaked pastry cups with the mixture. Bake the tartlets for 10 to 14 minutes or until slightly golden around edges. These can be frozen and reheated for unexpected guests. Bake, remove from pan, completely cool and freeze. Reheat from frozen state by heating for 10 to 14 minutes at 350°F on a baking sheet.

Special Note: To seed a tomato, slice the tomato perpendicular to the stem. Squeeze the halves while scraping the seeds off with a knife or use a spoon to remove seeds.

Variations: Omit bacon if you would like to serve these as a vegetarian appetizer or breakfast bread where bacon is being served.

For blue cheese lovers, eliminate the tomato and spices, replace the mozzarella with 1 (4-ounce) package blue cheese crumbles and add 3 minced green onions (white and pale green part only). Walnuts (1/4 cup) may be added to this mixture if desired.

For an artichoke variation, mix the mayonnaise with 1/3 cup finely chopped roasted red pepper, instead of mozzarella cheese, use Swiss cheese or Gruyère cheese. Use 1/2 teaspoon dried thyme in place of spices and add a (14-ounce) can of drained and chopped artichokes and one medium clove of minced or pressed garlic. Prosciutto (1/2 cup, finely chopped) or 10 cooked shrimp are another delightful combination with the artichokes.

Frank and Darcel Kutcher: Frisco, Texas
While Frank and I worked together, we often discussed his family's culinary creativity. He and his wife, Darcel, have three children but still manage to cook great meals and entertain friends frequently. This is one of my favorite recipes in the book due to its versatility and great flavor!

Sage Sausage Stuffed Mushrooms

Makes: 30 to 50

30 large fresh white
mushrooms (or 50, if small)
1/4 cup (1/2 stick) butter, melted
1 (16-ounce) package sage
flavored pork sausage
1 tablespoon finely chopped
green onion (white and pale
green part only)
1/4 teaspoon black pepper
1 large garlic clove, minced or
pressed
1 tablespoon chopped fresh
parsley
1 (8-ounce) package cream
cheese

Preheat the oven to 350°F. Wipe the excess dirt from the mushrooms with a damp paper towel. Gently separate the mushroom stems from the caps. Set the stems aside (see tips). Place mushroom caps on a rack in a broiler pan. (This keeps mushrooms from getting soggy in their own juices.) Drizzle mushrooms with melted butter. You may use less butter if preferred. Brown the sausage and onion in a skillet (do not drain). Mix in the spices, parsley and cream cheese. Heat to blend all ingredients and melt cheese. Stuff mushrooms with about 1 tablespoon of filling. These may be made up to 1 day ahead and refrigerated until ready to bake. Bake 20 to 25 minutes just before serving.

Tips: Stems are discarded unless you would like to chop very fine and include in the sausage mixture. This will increase the yield. A melon baller is a great tool to use to scoop the filling into the mushrooms.

Variation: Use your imagination and experiment with hot sausage or andouille sausage as a substitute for the sage sausage. Recipes are only a guideline for cooking. By changing the type of cheese or meat in a recipe you can become the inventor! Look at your recipes in a new light. What can you change to expand your own collection? This filling is also delicious mixed into scrambled eggs.

Buffalo Chicken Wing Dip

Serves: 8

- electric mixer
- cheese grater

1 fully cooked deli chicken
(rotisserie chicken)

1/3 cup buffalo wing sauce, or
more to taste

2 (8-ounce) packages cream
cheese

1/2 cup blue cheese or Gorgonzola
cheese, crumbled

1 bunch green onions, minced
(white and pale green
part only)

1/2 cup bottled ranch dressing

2 cups grated Cheddar cheese

Preheat the oven to 350°F. Debone the chicken and discard bones and skin. Shred or chop the chicken into small pieces. In a medium bowl, mix the buffalo wing sauce with the chicken pieces. Set aside. With an electric mixer, blend the cream cheese with the blue cheese, onions, and ranch dressing. Spread the cream cheese on the bottom of a 9 x 13-inch baking dish. Sprinkle the chicken over the top and bake approximately 15 minutes or until heated through. Top with Cheddar cheese and bake until cheese is melted approximately 5 minutes. Serve with tortilla chips.

Tips: We prefer to grate our own Cheddar. It melts better than the pre-grated cheeses. My wing sauce had "inferno" as the heat index so the amount you use is dependent on the heat you want to add.

Shelly Castor: Phoenix, Arizona
Shelley contacted me when she was in town and I had not seen her in years. We had a memorable evening reminiscing and she sent me several of her favorite recipes when she left. She and her husband Joe and two sons are big football fans and find this to be perfect for a football party. The spiciness makes it a super "beer pairing".

Chicken Lettuce Wraps

Serves: 4

- whisk
- vegetable peeler (to peel ginger)

Marinade
1 teaspoon cornstarch
2 teaspoons dry sherry
2 teaspoons water
2 tablespoons oyster sauce (optional)
1 tablespoon less sodium soy sauce
2 teaspoons peanut sauce
2 teaspoons teriyaki sauce
1 teaspoon sugar
1 teaspoon sesame oil

Chicken
4 (8-ounce) boneless, skinless chicken breasts
3 tablespoons olive oil
8 shiitake mushrooms, cleaned, stems removed and minced
1 teaspoon minced fresh ginger
2 medium garlic cloves, minced or pressed
2 green onions, minced (white and pale green part only)
1 small dried red chili, minced
1 (8-ounce) can water chestnuts, minced
1 (8-ounce) can bamboo shoots, minced
Bibb, Boston or iceberg lettuce leaves

Sauce
1/4 cup sugar
1/2 cup water
2 tablespoons less sodium soy sauce

(ingredients continued on next page)

Mix all the marinade ingredients together with a whisk. Dice the chicken breast into 1/8- to 1/4-inch cubes. Add the chicken to the marinade and toss to coat. Allow the chicken to marinate 15 minutes at room temperature. To make the sauce, dissolve the sugar in the water and add the remaining ingredients. Refrigerate until ready to serve. Once the chicken has been marinated, heat 3 tablespoons olive oil in a large sauté pan or skillet. Add the mushrooms, ginger, garlic, onions, chili pepper, water chestnuts and bamboo shoots. Sauté until mushrooms soften. Add the chicken and marinade and continue to sauté, stirring constantly until chicken is cooked through and the mixture is thickened. Remove the chicken mixture from the pan with a slotted spoon onto a platter. (The filling for the lettuce may be made ahead, cooled, refrigerated and reheated if serving the next day.) Chicken mixture is to be served warm inside lettuce leaves. Pass sauce separately.

(continued on next page)

2 tablespoons rice vinegar
2 tablespoons ketchup
1 tablespoon freshly squeezed
lemon juice (juice from 1/2
medium lemon)
1 tablespoon Chinese hot mustard
1 teaspoon hot chili sauce
with garlic
Dash of sesame oil

Tips: This is a family favorite worth doubling for a main course for four! A single sauce recipe works for the doubled portion. Dicing is easier when the chicken is still slightly frozen.

Sandra Dunn: Southlake, Texas
Sandra volunteers with us at the cooking school. She passed this recipe onto me and it is delicious. It looks like a lot of work but once you get the hang of it, it moves quickly and is worth the effort!

Cajun Sour Cream Dip

Serves: 4

1 (16-ounce) carton sour cream
2 tablespoons Hellmann's or
Best Foods Real Mayonnaise
1 tablespoon sweet paprika
3/4 teaspoon dried thyme
3/4 teaspoon dried oregano
3/4 teaspoon onion powder
1/4 teaspoon cayenne pepper
1/2 teaspoon garlic powder
1/4 teaspoon black pepper
1/4 teaspoon sugar
1 teaspoon *Tony Chachere's
Creole Seasoning*
1/4 teaspoon Tabasco red pepper
sauce, or more to taste

Stir all ingredients together, chill and serve with your favorite potato chips. (Kettle Chips are yummy and sturdy enough for dipping!) Make ahead so the flavors have time to blend.

Variation: For blue cheese lovers add 1/3 cup of crumbled blue cheese. Either version is also good with crudités (fresh vegetables).

Special Note: Paprika comes in hot and sweet. Paprika is made from grinding sweet red pepper pods. Hungarian paprika is considered to be superior to paprika from Spain or South America. As with other dried spices and herbs, paprika should be stored in a dark place away from sunlight.

Shannon Curry-Rackers: Pembroke, Massachusetts
Shannon and I worked together at Viacom in Dallas. I stay in touch with her via email since she now lives in Connecticut. We enjoyed many laughs together and shopping for deals on antiques. This homemade dry seasoning and recipe was enclosed with a Christmas card!

Thai Chicken Strudel

Serves: 6

- pastry brush
- jelly roll pan
- cheese grater

10 phyllo dough sheets, thawed (18 x 12-inch sheets)

2 (8-ounce) boneless, skinless chicken breasts

Chicken stock or broth

3/4 cup bottled oriental peanut sauce

2 carrots, grated and finely chopped

2 green onions, finely chopped (white and pale green part only)

1 cup grated Monterey Jack cheese

2 tablespoons chopped cilantro (stems removed)

1/2 cup butter, melted

Thaw the frozen phyllo dough according to package directions. (I prefer the 8 hours in the refrigerator method.) Preheat oven to 375°F. Cover the chicken breasts in broth and boil for approximately 20 minutes. Cool chicken slightly and dice into 1/4-inch cubes or shred using two forks. Mix the chicken with the peanut sauce, carrots, onions, cheese and cilantro. Melt the butter in a small saucepan. Unwrap the phyllo dough and lay out on work surface. Cover with a very lightly dampened dishtowel so dough does not dry out. Brush a jelly roll pan with butter. Lay out one sheet of phyllo dough on the prepared sheet and brush with butter. Repeat with 9 additional sheets. Sprinkle the chicken mixture along the long side of the dough in a 3 inch wide area. Roll the dough up and brush the outside with more butter so it is completely covered. (This may be made to this step up to 2 days ahead, refrigerated uncovered (until butter hardens) and baked before serving.) Bake seam-side down on the jelly roll pan for 20 to 30 minutes or until golden. Serve sliced on appetizer plates with forks. If only 9 x 14-inch phyllo sheets are available, make two rolls instead of one.

Tips: You may bone and skin a precooked, 2-pound rotisserie chicken and use this meat instead of chicken breasts. Many produce departments have pre-grated carrots in small bags that work nicely. If serving this as a light dinner, pair it with the Asian Slaw with Peanut Dressing (page 134).

Crab Stuffed Mushrooms

Serves: 6

1 1/2 pounds medium fresh mushrooms (30 to 35)
5 tablespoons butter, divided use
1/2 cup finely chopped onion
1 large garlic clove, minced or pressed
1/2 cup bread crumbs
1/4 cup chopped fresh parsley
2 tablespoons dry sherry
1/2 teaspoon Worcestershire sauce
1/2 teaspoon salt
1/4 teaspoon cayenne pepper
1/4 cup Hellmann's or Best Foods Real Mayonnaise
3 tablespoons freshly grated Parmigiano-Reggiano cheese
8 ounces fresh lump crabmeat
Tony Chachere's Creole Seasoning

Preheat the oven to 350°F. Wipe excess dirt from mushrooms with a damp paper towel. Gently separate the mushroom stems from the caps. Set caps aside. Chop the mushroom stems into bits and set aside. Melt 3 tablespoons butter in a large skillet. Add chopped mushroom stems, onion and garlic. Sauté 3 to 5 minutes or until tender. Stir in the bread crumbs and next 7 ingredients until well blended; gently stir in crabmeat. Spoon crab mixture evenly into mushroom caps and place on a rack in a broiler pan. (This will eliminate mushrooms getting soggy in their own juices.) Drizzle with the remaining 2 tablespoons butter. Sprinkle lightly with *Tony Chachere's Creole Seasoning*. Bake the stuffed mushrooms for 20 to 25 minutes. You can make the crabmeat filling a day ahead. Fill caps and bake just before guests arrive. Serve warm.

Tips: This filling can also be used with portobello mushrooms and served as a side dish with a grilled steak.

Pita Toasts

Serves: 6

3 pita breads
6 tablespoons unsalted butter, softened
1 tablespoon fresh parsley, minced
1 teaspoon chives
1 1/2 teaspoons freshly squeezed lemon juice
1 large garlic clove, minced or pressed
Salt and ground black pepper, to taste

Preheat the oven to 450°F. Cut each piece of pita bread in half and then crosswise, to form quarters. Separate into 24 pieces. Blend softened butter with other ingredients and let mixture stand at room temperature for 1 hour. Spread the butter mixture on the inside of the bread. Bake for approximately 5 minutes or until crisp (watch carefully). The butter mixture can be made ahead and brought to room temperature.

Tips: These are a great accompaniment to a salad or with hummus. The herb butter can be used with any bread for a special touch.

Crab Tartlets

Serves: 6

• mini muffin pans
• cheese grater

1 (12-ounce) can flaky biscuits
6 ounces canned crab or fresh
  lump crabmeat
2 green onions, finely chopped
  (white and pale green
  part only)
1/4 cup grated Monterey Jack
  cheese
1/4 cup grated Cheddar cheese
1/4 cup Hellmann's or Best Foods
  Real Mayonnaise
1/2 teaspoon freshly squeezed
  lemon juice
1/8 teaspoon curry powder
1/3 cup (1/2 of an 8-ounce can)
  water chestnuts, drained and
  chopped
Sweet paprika
Fresh chopped parsley

Preheat oven to 350°F. Split the biscuits into 3 pieces. (The flaky biscuits pull apart easily into their natural layers.) Spray muffin pans lightly with a cooking spray. Press split biscuits into the mini muffin cups. If using fresh lump crabmeat, squeeze moisture out. If using canned crabmeat, rinse and squeeze moisture out. In a medium bowl, mix crab with the next 7 ingredients. Fill each of the unbaked pastry cups with mixture. Sprinkle with paprika and fresh parsley. Bake for 10 to 14 minutes until lightly golden.

Tip: These freeze well. Bake them, remove them from the pan and cool. Freeze in a sealable bag. To reheat, preheat oven to 350°F. Bake on a baking sheet approximately 10 to 12 minutes. Try one before serving or cut one in half to be sure center is warm.

> *"Live Life to the Fullest. You have to color outside the lines if you want to make your life a masterpiece. Laugh some everyday. Keep growing, keep dreaming, follow your heart. The important thing is not to stop questioning."*
>
> ~Albert Einstein

Crab Cakes with Rémoulade

Makes 8

- whisk
- cheese grater

5 tablespoons butter, divided use
1 celery stalk, minced
1/2 small red pepper, minced
1/2 small onion, grated
1 tablespoon flour
1 teaspoon dry mustard
1/2 teaspoon *Tony Chachere's Creole Seasoning*
1/2 cup whole milk
8 ounces fresh lump crabmeat
3/4 cup dry bread crumbs, divided use (not all may be needed)
1 tablespoon fresh, chopped parsley
1 tablespoon freshly squeezed lemon juice (juice from 1/2 medium lemon)

Rémoulade
3 tablespoons Creole mustard
1 cup Hellmann's or Best Foods Real Mayonnaise
2 tablespoons drained chopped capers
1 tablespoon chopped fresh parsley
1 tablespoon fresh lemon juice
1/2 teaspoon cayenne pepper, plus more to taste
1/4 teaspoon *Tony Chachere's Creole Seasoning*

Biscuits for Mini Crab Cakes
Makes: 48
1 cup biscuit mix
1/2 cup (1 stick) butter, melted
1/2 cup sour cream

Heat 2 tablespoons butter and cook the celery, red pepper and onion until tender. Stir in flour, mustard and *Tony Chachere's.* Cook 1 minute. Gradually whisk in the milk and stir until mixture thickens. Remove from heat and mix in crabmeat gently. Add 1/2 cup bread crumbs, parsley and lemon juice. If the dough does not seem firm enough, add remaining 1/4 cup crumbs. Form into 2- to 3-inch round patties if you are serving as a sit down appetizer, or into bite-size patties if you are serving them on the mini biscuits. Cook in the remaining 3 tablespoons butter until brown. To make the Rémoulade, combine all ingredients and chill. Serve as a sauce for the crab cakes or any other seafood. Both the crab cakes and the Rémoulade can be made ahead. The Rémoulade can be stored in the refrigerator for 4 days and crab cakes can be made a day ahead, refrigerated and reheated in the oven. If you would like mini crab cakes on a flaky biscuit, double the crab cake recipe and form into 48 by using a tablespoon as a guide. Combine the biscuit ingredients and turn the dough onto a floured surface. Knead five or six times. Roll into 1/2 inch thickness and cut with a 1-inch round cookie cutter. Place on lightly greased baking sheet. Bake the biscuits at 450°F for 8 to 10 minutes or until lightly browned. Cool. Split biscuits and put a small amount of Rémoulade on the inside of each biscuit and a mini crab cake on each. The mini biscuits can be made ahead and frozen.

Tip: A 1/3 cup solid measuring cup is a great guide for forming the crabcakes.

Nut Crusted Shrimp with Pineapple Aïoli

Serves: 8

- whisk
- cooling rack
- thermometer (to test oil temperature)

Nut Crusted Shrimp
3 cups corn flake crumbs
2 teaspoons salt
2 (2.25-ounce) packages macadamia nuts, ground (about 1/2 cup)
1/4 cup sugar
1/2 teaspoon cayenne pepper
1 cup flour
2 large eggs
1 cup milk
2 pounds (about 40 medium) shrimp, peeled, tail on
Peanut oil for frying

Pineapple Sauce
Makes 1 cup
1/4 pound fresh pineapple, cored and finely diced (1/4-inch pieces)
1/3 cup sugar
2 teaspoons pear or raspberry vinegar
1 large garlic clove, minced or pressed
1 tablespoon finely diced red onion (1/4-inch pieces)
Pinch of salt
1 jalapeño pepper, seeded and minced

(ingredients continued on next page)

You can crush your own corn flakes in a food processor or you can purchase them already ground. Mix the corn flakes with the next 4 ingredients. Put the flour in a separate bowl large enough to batter shrimp. With a whisk, beat the eggs and milk together in another bowl. Roll the shrimp in egg then flour then again in egg and then the cornflake mixture. Heat the oil in a skillet to 360°F. Fry shrimp just until golden, about 2 to 3 minutes. Drain on a cooling rack so shrimp do not get soggy. You may place a paper towel under the rack to catch the grease. To make the pineapple sauce, mix the fresh pineapple with the next 6 ingredients in a medium saucepan. Bring to a boil. Reduce the heat and simmer 10 minutes. Cool. Once cool, mix 1/2 cup of the pineapple sauce (freeze remainder to make additional batches) with mayonnaise, garlic, cilantro and lime juice. Stir together with a whisk and chill. The shrimp and aïoli can be made ahead. Reheat the shrimp in a 170°F oven. Serve the shrimp warm with the aïoli as a dipping sauce.

Tip: It is best to take the pineapple sauce recipe and just adapt it (times 4) to 1 pound of pineapple. Freeze the other 3 portions of sauce in individual bags for later use.

(continued on next page)

Pineapple Aïoli

1/2 cup prepared Pineapple
Sauce (previous page)

1 cup Hellmann's or Best Foods
Real Mayonnaise

2 large garlic cloves, minced or
pressed

1 bunch cilantro, coarsely
chopped

2 tablespoons freshly squeezed
lime juice (juice from 1
medium lime)

*Variations: This is the perfect coating to add
coconut to (1 cup) for a crunchy coconut shrimp.
Other nuts (e.g. honey roasted peanuts, almonds)
may be substituted for macadamia nuts.*

Special Note: Aïoli is a fancy term for a
flavored mayonnaise. It started as a garlic
mayonnaise and has taken on many new
flavors since the original homemade version.

Hot Crab Dip

Serves: 12

 • chafing dish
• cheese grater

6 tablespoons butter

1/2 cup finely chopped green
onion

2 tablespoons flour

1 (8-ounce) bottle clam juice

1 cup half-and-half

1 (8-ounce) package cream
cheese

1 1/2 cups grated Swiss cheese

1 tablespoon prepared
horseradish

2 teaspoons Worcestershire
sauce

1 teaspoon cayenne pepper

1 pound fresh lump crabmeat

1/4 cup fresh chopped parsley

Melt butter in a skillet. Add the green onions
and sauté for about 2 minutes. Add the flour
and whisk 1 minute. Gradually whisk in clam
juice. Bring to a boil stirring often until mixture
thickens, approximately 3 minutes. Whisk in
the half-and-half and bring to a boil. Boil 1
minute, stirring constantly. Reduce to low.
Add cheeses, horseradish, Worcestershire
sauce and cayenne. Stir until cheese melts.
Add the crabmeat and parsley into the mixture
and stir to combine. Put in a chafing dish
to serve. Serve warm with crackers. This
can be made a day ahead, refrigerated and
slowly heated on the stove (stir occasionally)
before transferring into a chafing dish.

Tip: If canned crabmeat is substituted, rinse
and squeeze all moisture out.

Shrimp Tartlets

Serves: 6

• mini muffin pans
• cheese grater

1/3 pound shrimp (you may use precooked shrimp)
1 (3-ounce) package crab boil
3/4 cup Hellmann's or Best Foods Real Mayonnaise
1/3 cup grated Swiss cheese
1/3 cup freshly grated Parmigiano-Reggiano cheese
1/2 teaspoon Worcestershire sauce
1/4 teaspoon Tabasco red pepper sauce
1 (12-ounce) can flaky biscuits
Sweet paprika

Preheat oven to 350°F. Cook shrimp as directed on crab boil package with the crab boil spice package. Peel, devein and chop. Mix the shrimp, mayonnaise, cheeses, Worcestershire and Tabasco together. (Shrimp mixture may be made up to 2 days ahead and refrigerated until you are ready to use.) When you are ready to bake, split each biscuit into 3 pieces. The flaky biscuits pull apart easily into their natural layers. Spray muffin pans lightly with cooking spray. Press the split biscuits into the mini muffin pans. Fill each of unbaked pastry cups with the shrimp mixture. Sprinkle with paprika. Bake the tartlets for 10 to 14 minutes or until slightly golden around the edges. Serve warm.

Special Note: Cooking spray with flour added is the best to use on your bakeware (especially non-stick bakeware). Other cooking sprays leave a yellow sticky residue.

> *"Cooking is knowing who you are and then doing something practical—and delicious—with that knowledge."*
>
> *~Perri Klass*

Spicy Shrimp Dip

Serves: 12

• electric mixer
• cheese grater

2 pounds uncooked shrimp
1 (3-ounce) package crab boil
1 (8-ounce) package cream
cheese, softened
1/2 cup Hellmann's or Best Foods
Real Mayonnaise
1 cup Thousand Island dressing
1/4 cup minced green onion
(white and pale green
part only)
1 small onion, grated
4 teaspoons Tabasco red pepper
sauce
1 tablespoon seasoned salt (such
as Lawry's Seasoned Salt)
1 tablespoon prepared
horseradish, drained
Fresh parsley, chopped (for
garnish)

Boil shrimp in water according to crab boil directions. (Crab boil is found in the spice section of the grocery store.) Peel, devein and chop the cooked shrimp. Use a mixer to blend the cream cheese, mayonnaise and Thousand Island dressing. Fold in the shrimp, green onion, grated onion, Tabasco sauce, seasoned salt and horseradish. Make at least 8 hours ahead of serving time so flavors blend. Refrigerate until ready to serve. Garnish with a sprinkling of parsley before serving with crackers or vegetables.

Special Note: Devein shrimp by removing the gray-black vein from the back of the shrimp. You can do this with a sharp tip of a knife or the prong of a fork. This is optional on small and medium shrimp, but recommended on large shrimp.

Mary King: Coppell, Texas
Mary and I sat across from each other when we were buyers together. When there was a birthday celebration, everyone would bring an appetizer or dessert. This was an office favorite and I have held onto her recipe for years!

Spiced Shrimp with Red-Eye Gravy and Grits

Serves: 8

- whisk
- 6-inch bamboo skewers, soaked in water
- food processor or coffee bean grinder

Marinade
1 3/4 teaspoons red pepper flakes
2 teaspoons fennel seeds
2 teaspoons ground black pepper
Zest of 2 lemons
2 tablespoons finely chopped shallots (one medium shallot peeled and finely chopped)
1 cup olive oil
16 large shrimp, peeled, tail on (see note on next page)

Grits
1 garlic bulb
1 cup instant or stone ground grits
4 cups chicken stock or broth, divided use
2 tablespoons unsalted butter
1/4 cup heavy cream
1/2 cup grated Cheddar cheese
1/4 cup freshly grated Parmigiano-Reggiano cheese
Salt and pepper, to taste

Red-eye Gravy
8 ounces bacon, diced (1/4-inch pieces)
1/3 cup brewed black coffee
1 cup balsamic vinegar
2 cups chicken broth or stock
2 tablespoons minced garlic
1 cup diced tomatoes with onions (from a 14.5-ounce can)
1 teaspoon red pepper flakes
1 tablespoon fresh thyme

Heat the oven to 400°F and cut the pointed end off the bulb of garlic just so the cloves are exposed. Cut a piece of foil large enough to wrap the garlic in and drizzle the garlic with olive oil and wrap in foil. Place in a small baking dish and bake approximately 50 minutes or until the cloves are tender. The roasted garlic will be used in the grits recipe. To make the marinade put the dry spices in a coffee bean grinder or food processor to grind and blend. In a large glass bowl, add the zest, ground spices and shallots to the olive oil and blend with a whisk. Add the shrimp to the marinade. Let marinate for 30 minutes at room temperature. Skewer the shrimp by inserting one skewer in the head end of the shrimp and a skewer in the tail end of the shrimp. (You may put several shrimp on a skewer this way and it will prevent them from curling when grilled.) While the shrimp are marinating, make the sauce and grits. Read the package directions for the amount of water needed for boiling grits and use the chicken broth as a replacement. (You may not need all four cups.) Follow the package directions for cooking the grits and whisk to get lumps out. Once grits are smooth, add the butter, cream and cheeses. Stir until smooth. Once garlic is tender and slightly cooled, squeeze the cloves out, discarding the peel. Chop if necessary and stir into the grits. Add salt and pepper to taste. If making ahead, before serving, you may need to thin with extra broth. Grits should be pourable. To make the gravy, fry the bacon until crisp and remove with a slotted spoon onto a paper towel. If grease is over 3 tablespoons, remove excess. Add the coffee and the balsamic

(continued on next page)

vinegar to the pan. Bring to a boil and cook until reduced by half. Add the chicken stock and continue to cook until reduced by half. Add the garlic, 1 cup tomatoes with juice (refrigerate remaining for another use), red pepper, thyme and crispy bacon. Simmer until heated through. (The gravy and grits can be made ahead and reheated.) Grill the marinated, skewered shrimp until pink and slightly coiled. To serve, place a large scoop of warm grits on a small plate, leaving the edge around the grits to spoon the gravy. Take the grilled shrimp off the skewers and put them on top of the grits. Spoon the gravy around the outside of the grits. Serve with forks, encouraging guests to try all three elements together!

Tips: It is easiest just to throw whole pepper-corns in the food processor before mixing spices and grind them. Measure correct amount and reserve the extra. The instant grits just need less time to cook. You do not want to overcook the shrimp so you may undercook them slightly and finish them in the oven at 350°F so you may monitor them.

Special Note: Shrimp by the pound are sold by the number of shrimp per pound. When the sign says U/10 it means 10 to a pound. The higher the number the smaller the shrimp.

Pineapple Shrimp Skewers with Honey Marinade

Serves: 4

- 8 (6-inch) bamboo skewers, soaked in water
- vegetable peeler (to peel ginger)

24 large shrimp, tails on

Marinade
1/4 cup finely chopped green onions (white and pale green part only)
1 teaspoon minced garlic
1 tablespoon fresh ginger, minced
1/4 cup rum
1/3 cup honey
1 tablespoon whole black peppercorns
1 teaspoon crushed red pepper
2 tablespoons sesame oil
1 tablespoon Chinese plum sauce
1 fresh pineapple for garnish

Rinse, peel and devein shrimp, keeping tail intact. Mix marinade ingredients, excluding the pineapple. Add the shrimp and toss to coat. Let them sit overnight in the refrigerator to marinate. Prepare grill. Core pineapple and cut pineapple into chunks to use on skewers. Alternate the marinated shrimp and pineapple on skewers using 3 shrimp and 4 chunks of pineapple per skewer. Grill until shrimp turns pink, 2 to 5 minutes on each side.

Tip: Use the leftover hollowed out pineapple shell as a decorative bowl for Black Beans with Cilantro Pesto Rice (page 230).

"The celebration of great taste comes from the complexity of premium, quality ingredients; popular intensive flavors, and aromas; consistency in quality and flavor delivery and the delicious linger on the palate."

~Bhawana Sinha, Sensory scientist

Horseradish Shrimp Dip

Makes: 3 cups

1 pound shrimp, uncooked
(reserve 5 for garnish)
1 (3-ounce) package crab boil
3/4 teaspoon *Tony Chachere's
Creole Seasoning*, divided use
4 green onions, minced (white
and pale green part only)
3 tablespoons prepared
horseradish, drained
3 tablespoons Hellmann's or
Best Foods Real Mayonnaise
1 (8-ounce) package cream
cheese, softened
1/4 cup chopped celery
1/2 yellow bell pepper, chopped
1 tablespoon freshly squeezed
lemon juice (juice from 1/2
medium lemon)
1/4 teaspoon dried dill
1/4 teaspoon cayenne pepper
1 tablespoon chopped fresh
parsley
Fresh parsley for garnish

Cook shrimp according to crab boil directions and drain. Peel, devein (reserve 3 to 5 whole shrimp for garnish) and chop shrimp into pieces. Mix together shrimp with 1/2 teaspoon of *Tony Chachere's* seasoning and all remaining ingredients. Chill for at least 3 hours. Taste and if more salt is needed, add *Tony Chachere's* for salt and spice. If only spice is needed, add a bit more cayenne. Serve in a dish or hollowed out cabbage and garnish edge by alternating shrimp and parsley leaves. Sprinkle dip with remaining 1/4 teaspoon *Tony Chachere's* for color. Serve with vegetables and crackers.

Shrimp Egg Rolls

Serves: 6

- wire cooling rack
- tongs or shallow basket for frying
- thermometer (to test oil temperature)
- pastry brush
- vegetable peeler (to peel ginger)

Apricot Dipping Sauce
1 (18-ounce) jar apricot jam
2 tablespoons less sodium soy sauce
3 tablespoons minced green onion (white and pale green part only)
2 teaspoons minced fresh ginger
1 teaspoon minced garlic
1 tablespoon freshly squeezed lime juice (juice from 1/2 medium lime)
1 teaspoon Asian hot chili sauce or 1 dash Tabasco red pepper sauce

Egg Rolls
1 1/2 pound peeled and deveined shrimp, tails removed
3/4 teaspoon salt
1/2 cup fresh cilantro
1 tablespoon cornstarch mixed with 1 tablespoon cold water
1 (16-ounce) package egg roll wrappers
Oil for frying (peanut oil)

Mix all of the apricot dipping sauce ingredients together in a saucepan over low heat. Once thoroughly combined, set the dipping sauce aside until ready to serve. The sauce may be made ahead, refrigerated and reheated. Mix the shrimp, salt and cilantro together. Follow the back of the egg roll package directions for stuffing and seal the egg roll edges by brushing them with the cornstarch mixture. To fry, heat the oil in a skillet to 360°F. Add 3 rolls at a time. Fry approximately 2 to 3 minutes on each side until nicely golden. (Keep oil to 360°F or the rolls will absorb grease.) Remove onto a cooling rack (place over jelly roll pan lined with paper towels to catch grease). To serve, cut at a diagonal and serve with the apricot dipping sauce.

Tips: Any remaining egg roll wrappers may be frozen in a sealable bag and used at another date. A thermometer with a cord and a beeper is perfect for checking the temperature of your oil.

Variation: Peanut sauce is another wonderful accompaniment. These are delicious for brunch if you fry 1 (16-ounce) package of pork breakfast sausage and mix with 1 (8-ounce) bag of coleslaw. Roll mixture in egg roll wrappers, seal with the cornstarch mixture and fry. Serve with the apricot dipping sauce.

Special Note: When you mix cornstarch with cold water, do this just before using. The cornstarch mixture will harden if it sits too long.

Spring Rolls with Hoisin Sauce   Serves: 6

• vegetable peeler (to peel ginger)

Spring Rolls

12 (12-inch) rice paper rounds
12 Bibb lettuce leaves, washed
and dried
1 (4-ounce) package of Thai rice
noodles, cooked according to
package directions
1 cup grated carrot
1/3 cup fresh mint, coarsely
chopped
1/3 cup fresh cilantro, stems
removed and coarsely
chopped
1/3 cup fresh basil, coarsely
chopped
24 large shrimp, cooked,
peeled and deveined (tails
removed) and sliced,
lengthwise

Hoisin Sauce

1/2 cup hoisin sauce
1/4 cup rice vinegar
1 tablespoon minced fresh
ginger
1 teaspoon hot chili oil

Fill a large bowl with very warm water and line
2 baking sheets or jelly roll pans with plastic
wrap. Dip 1 sheet of rice paper into the warm
water and leave it in the water several seconds
until it is soft and pliable. Remove to work
surface (lined jelly roll pan) and cover with a
damp paper towel. Repeat until all rice papers
are softened. On a piece of plastic wrap or wax
paper arrange a lettuce leaf in the middle of the
rice paper, leaving a 1-inch border around the
outside edge. Top with a heaping tablespoon
of rice noodles, spreading down the center of
the lettuce. Cover the noodles with about 1
tablespoon of grated carrot and sprinkle equal
amounts of the three fresh herbs over this and
2 slices of the cooked shrimp. Fold in the 2
opposite sides of the rice paper and tightly roll
up. Transfer to the second plastic lined jelly roll
pan and cover with plastic. Continue until all 12
are finished. These may be prepared 4 hours
ahead of serving. (Covering and refrigerating
the finished rolls keeps them from drying out.
They will also slice more easily if they have
time to chill.) In a small bowl, whisk together
all ingredients to make the hoisin sauce. Chill if
making a day ahead. When ready to serve, cut
each spring roll in half diagonally and arrange
on a platter, cut side up. Serve with the room
temperature dipping sauce or your favorite spicy
peanut sauce. (I like to have both available.)

Tip: If you have problems with the papers tearing,
the lettuce will help to strengthen the spring roll.

Special Note: Hoisin is also called Peking
Sauce and is a reddish brown sauce made
with soybeans and is often used in Chinese
food. It is slightly sweet and spicy.

Shrimp with Garlic and Roasted Red Peppers

Serves: 4

1 pound shrimp, peeled and deveined
Coarse sea salt
1/3 cup olive oil
3 large garlic cloves, coarsely minced
1 dried Thai red chili, stem and seeds removed, cut into two pieces
1/2 teaspoon sweet paprika
Chopped parsley for garnish
Roasted red peppers, for garnish

Dry the shrimp with paper towels and sprinkle lightly with coarse sea salt. Let rest at room temperature for 10 minutes. Heat the olive oil in a skillet until hot and add the minced garlic and Thai pepper. When the garlic starts to turn golden, add the shrimp. Cook over medium-high heat until the shrimp are pink and slightly coiled. Remove from heat and stir the paprika in with the shrimp. Outline your serving platter with slices of roasted red peppers, creating a star pattern with the slices, then pile the shrimp in the center and sprinkle with chopped parsley. Serve with baguette slices and toothpicks for skewering. Leftover shrimp are delicious mixed with warm pasta.

Smoked Salmon with Caper Relish

Serves: 8

Caper Relish
3/4 cup finely diced red onion
3 tablespoons capers, drained and rinsed
3 tablespoons chopped, fresh dill (stems removed)
4 teaspoons Dijon mustard
1 tablespoon freshly squeezed lemon juice (juice from 1/2 medium lemon)

Smoked Salmon Rounds
16 slices (1/2 inch thick) fresh baguette
4 ounces cream cheese
4 ounces thinly sliced fresh smoked salmon, cut in 16 pieces

Preheat the oven to 350°F. To make the relish, mix the first 5 ingredients together. (Make ahead if desired and refrigerate until ready to use.) Toast the baguette rounds in the oven for approximately 5 minutes until edges are crispy but bread is still soft. Spread a layer of cream cheese on the top of each toast round and top each with a piece of smoked salmon. Put a small spoonful of relish on top of the salmon.

Fresh smoked salmon that is available is typically already thinly sliced. Sometimes called gravlax, the fresh raw salmon is cured in a salt-sugar-dill mixture. Any leftovers can be stored tightly wrapped in the refrigerator for 1 week.

Artichoke and Shrimp Cocktail

Serves: 6

1 cup Hellmann's or Best Foods
Real Mayonnaise
2 1/2 ounces horseradish
1 1/2 teaspoons dry mustard
1 tablespoon freshly squeezed
lemon juice (juice from 1/2
medium lemon)
1 (6.5-ounce) jar marinated
artichokes (with marinade),
chopped
1 teaspoon *Tony Chachere's
Creole Seasoning*
1 1/2 pounds shrimp, peeled,
deveined, cooked and chilled

Mix the mayonnaise with the next 5 ingredients. Refrigerate for at least 8 hours. Add the shrimp just before serving. Serve either in martini glasses with small forks or as a dip with water crackers.

Tip: Shrimp takes just minutes to cook. Once water is boiling, add shrimp and remove pan from heat. You want the shrimp to turn pink and be slightly coiled. Drain the water and chill the shrimp until ready to serve.

Special Note: *Tony Chachere's Creole Seasoning* can be located on the spice aisle of most grocery stores. Horseradish typically comes in a 5-ounce jar so use half of the jar.

Julie Lancaster: Grapevine, Texas
Julie made this unforgettable appetizer for my 40th birthday, which I celebrated on September 22nd, 2001, eleven days after 9-11. In the aftermath of this national tragedy, Julie made my birthday very special with a poolside gathering decorated in a patriotic red, white and blue theme.

Calamari with Apricot Dipping Sauce Serves: 4

- whisk
- thermometer (to test oil temperature)
- vegetable peeler (to peel ginger)

Apricot Dipping Sauce
1 (18-ounce) jar apricot jam
2 tablespoons less sodium soy sauce
3 tablespoons minced green onion (white and pale green part only)
2 teaspoons minced fresh ginger
2 large garlic cloves, minced or pressed
1 tablespoon freshly squeezed lime juice (juice from 1/2 medium lime)
1 tablespoon Asian hot chili sauce or a dash of Tabasco red pepper sauce

Marinade
2 egg whites (from large eggs)
1 egg
3 sliced jalapeño peppers with seeds
1 pound cleaned calamari (without tentacles)
1/4 cup fish sauce (nam pla)

Breading
3 1/2 cups flour
2 cups cornstarch
1 teaspoon baking powder
1/4 cup chili powder
3 tablespoons coarse sea salt or kosher salt
Peanut oil for frying

Mix all of the apricot dipping sauce ingredients together in a saucepan over low heat. Set the sauce aside until ready to serve. It may be made ahead, refrigerated and reheated. Slice the calamari into 1/2-inch wide strips if necessary. In a mixing bowl, whisk egg whites and egg until foamy. Add the jalapeño pepper slices, calamari slices and nam pla to the mixture and let sit at least an hour or overnight in the refrigerator. Mix the breading ingredients together. Coat the calamari and the jalapeño peppers in the breading. Heat the oil to 360°F (test with a thermometer). Fry approximately 30 to 40 seconds or until crispy. Drain on paper towels. Move to a serving platter and serve with the warm apricot dipping sauce.

Julie Esstman: Irving, Texas
Julie and her husband, Mike, are active philanthropists and help with many community projects. They hosted a martini party for charity. I prepared the food for the event and Vince my hair stylist sang Sinatra. Julie shared this recipe with me while planning the event.

Escargot with Shallot Cream in New Potatoes

Makes: 12 escargot

- jelly roll pan
- whisk

1 (7-ounce) can large snails
6 small new potatoes
1 tablespoon olive oil

Shallot Cream
1/2 cup dry white wine
1/2 cup chicken broth
2 medium shallots, finely chopped (about 1/4 cup)
1/2 teaspoon dried thyme
1 small bay leaf
1 cup heavy cream
2 garlic cloves, minced or pressed
2 teaspoons cornstarch mixed with 2 teaspoons cold water
1 tablespoon butter
1/2 teaspoon black pepper
1/4 teaspoon salt
2 tablespoons minced parsley, divided use
Tony Chachere's Creole Seasoning

Preheat oven to 400°F. Rinse snails and let dry on a paper towel. Wash the potatoes and cut in half. Put potatoes raw side down on a jelly roll pan that has been coated with 1 tablespoon oil. Bake the potatoes on the middle oven rack for 30 to 35 minutes or until potatoes are tender. Make sauce while potatoes are baking. Combine the wine, broth, shallots, thyme and bay leaf in a skillet and bring to a boil over high heat. Reduce to 3 tablespoons liquid. Add the cream and garlic and boil until reduced to 2/3 cup. Reduce heat and whisk the cornstarch mixture into the hot liquid (whisk out any lumps) and heat until liquid boils and thickens (about 2 minutes). (Make the sauce a day ahead and reheat, if desired.) Stir in the snails, butter, pepper, salt and 1 1/2 tablespoons parsley. Remove the bay leaf. Cool the potatoes enough so that you may handle them. Scoop out the meat of the cooked potato so you can put the escargot in the center. If necessary cut off rounded side of potato so they may sit evenly on a plate. Spoon a snail with the sauce into the center of the scooped out potato and sprinkle lightly with *Tony Chachere's* and the remaining minced parsley.

Tips: This sauce is divine! Try it on fish, chicken or pasta. The escargot may be served as a seated first course on a piece of toasted baguette with the sauce spooned over the toast and snails.

Jerie Wylie: Keller, Texas
Jerie is a friend from my first job out of college. She explained her recipe for escargot on a drive out to Napa Valley with the Knots Landing Dinner Group for her 40th birthday celebration. I came home and experimented with her recipe and this recipe is the result.

Puff Pastry with Sherry Mushrooms

Makes: 10

- 2-inch cookie cutter (for fall, a leaf shape is perfect!)
- parchment paper

1 frozen puff pastry sheet
(from a 17.3-ounce box)
1/3 cup plus 1 tablespoon
unsalted butter, divided use
3 cups (6 ounces) assorted
fresh mushrooms (shiitake,
oyster, white), cleaned,
shiitake stems removed
2 medium shallots, finely
chopped (about 1/4 cup)
1/4 cup dry sherry
1 cup low sodium chicken
stock or broth
1/4 cup heavy cream
Pinch of white pepper
1 tablespoon flour

Preheat the oven to 400°F. Defrost the puff pastry for approximately 20 minutes while making the mushroom mixture. Heat the 1/3 cup butter in a skillet and add the mushrooms. Cook until tender, approximately 5 minutes. Remove the mushrooms from the pan with a slotted spoon. In the same pan, sauté the shallots until softened and translucent. Add the sherry to the pan and deglaze the pan, scraping any bits off the pan. Add the broth and cream and cook until slightly thickened. Add the mushrooms back to the pan. Add the white pepper. Blend the remaining tablespoon of butter with the flour to make a paste. Add to the hot liquid stirring to blend until the desired thickness is reached. (This may be made a day ahead, refrigerated and reheated.) With the defrosted pastry, cut out shapes (such as leaves or hearts) and place on a baking sheet that has been lined with parchment paper. Bake 14 to 18 minutes (depending on the size of the dough shapes) or until they are lightly golden. Serve the sherry mushroom mixture warm over the warm puff pastry.

Tips: This is a delightful first course but must be served with a fork. Champagne or white wine is a perfect accompaniment. Baby bellas, chanterelles, oyster and shiitake all add to the interesting flavor.

Special Note: Mushrooms should be wiped off with a damp paper towel or if necessary, rinse lightly with cold water.

Brunch, Breads & Beverages

Kitchen tools needed

 May be prepared ahead

Picture Features: Cranberry Juice and Champagne • Bacon Tomato Tartlets, page 59
Fresh Fruit Mélange, page 83 • Rosemary Potatoes, page 240 • Spinach and Egg Pinwheel with
Shrimp Sauce, page 86 • Amaretto Cake, page 270

Fresh Fruit Mélange with Citrus Dressing

Serves: 8

 • melon baller (optional)

Salad
1 pint strawberries, sliced
1 pint blueberries
3 kiwis, peeled and sliced
1 medium cantaloupe, cut into
  uniform chunks or balls
1 medium honeydew melon, cut
  into uniform chunks or balls
Mint leaves as garnish

Gently toss strawberries, blueberries, kiwis, cantaloupe and honeydew together. Combine dressing ingredients and pour over fruit mixture. Serve chilled and garnish with mint leaves.

Tip: Any fruit combination is good in this salad. Oranges, pineapple or blackberries can be added or substituted. Varying the color is the most important thing for presentation.

Citrus Dressing
1/2 cup orange juice
1/4 cup freshly squeezed lemon
  juice (juice from 2 medium
  lemons)
3 tablespoons sugar

Fruit Ambrosia

Serves: 4

3 medium oranges, peeled and
  divided
2 bananas, sliced
1/2 cup orange juice
3 tablespoons honey
1 tablespoon freshly squeezed
  lemon juice (juice from 1/2
  medium lemon)
1/4 cup sweetened coconut flakes
Maraschino cherries (optional)

Combine oranges and bananas and toss gently. Combine orange juice, honey and lemon juice in small bowl; stir well and pour over fruit. Toss gently. Sprinkle with coconut and top with halved cherries. Chill before serving, if desired.

Overnight French Toast

Serves: 6

- whisk
- jelly roll pan
- sifter

4 large eggs
1/4 cup sugar
1/4 teaspoon ground nutmeg
2/3 cup orange juice
1/3 cup milk
1/2 teaspoon vanilla
1/2 teaspoon ground cinnamon
9 slices French bread, cut in
   1-inch slices (from a
   16-ounce loaf)
2/3 cup butter, melted
1/2 cup chopped macadamia
   nuts (optional)
Confectioners' sugar for garnish
Syrup of your choice

Whisk the eggs thoroughly. Add the next six ingredients to the eggs and whisk until well combined. Spray a 9 x 13-inch baking dish with cooking spray. In a single layer, place the bread slices in the baking dish and pour the egg mixture over the bread. Turn the slices to coat thoroughly. Cover and refrigerate overnight. When ready to bake, preheat the oven to 400°F. Spread melted butter over the surface of a jelly roll pan, place bread slices on top of the butter in a single layer. Bake the slices for 15 to 20 minutes until golden. Garnish with the chopped nuts and sifted confectioners' sugar. Serve with butter and warm syrup.

Tips: This is a great basic recipe if you want to take it a step further and either serve with fresh berries, make a raspberry sauce or sauté apples for alongside the French toast. Various fruits or nuts can be used so the opportunities are endless. Liqueurs such as Amaretto, Grand Marnier, Frangelico or Chambord can be substituted for the 1/4 cup of orange juice. Nuts can be chosen for pairing. An example would be chopped hazelnuts with Frangelico or almonds with Amaretto.

Marla Payne: Coppell, Texas
Since this wonderful French toast is made ahead of time, it alleviates morning confusion when you have visitors. A few of us got together and cooked an extravagant New Year's Eve dinner and then we all stayed all night. Marla made this for New Year's Eve Day. It's wonderful!

Quick Eggs Benedict

Servings: 6

2 (10-ounce) packages frozen puff pastry shells (12 shells total)
12 medium eggs
12 slices Canadian bacon, warmed slightly in microwave, skillet or oven
12 tomato slices (1/2 inch thick)
1 (0.9-ounce) packet Knorr Hollandaise sauce, prepared according to directions
Pimento strips
Sliced black olives
Fresh parsley

Preheat the oven to 400°F. Bake pastry shells, according to directions on a baking sheet, but undercook slightly so shells are starting to puff and still very light colored. Allow the shells to cool before removing the perforated tops with a sharp knife and scooping out the middle dough, being careful not to make holes in the shell. Place shells on a large baking sheet. Carefully crack 1 raw egg into each shell. Reduce the oven to 325°F and bake until egg is set, approximately 20 to 25 minutes, watching carefully. Heat Canadian bacon while eggs are cooking. To serve, place a tomato slice on top of the slice of heated Canadian bacon. Set the cooked pastry top on the bacon and set on top of the egg. Spoon Hollandaise sauce over the egg baskets and garnish with crossed strips of pimentos, black olive slices and sprigs of parsley.

Tip: Parchment paper is great for lining jelly roll pans and baking sheets. Things will not stick and cleanup is easier.

Variation: A Crab Cake (page 67) would accompany this meal nicely. Serve the Crab Cake (without the Rémoulade) alongside Quick Eggs Benedict instead of Canadian bacon.

"Cooking is an uncertain art, hostage to the quality of ingredients you are able to obtain, the temperature of your oven, the weather, even your mood."

~Ruth Reichl

Spinach and Egg Pinwheel with Shrimp Sauce

Serves: 8

- whisk
- jelly roll pan (11 1/2 x 17)
- cheese grater
- electric mixer
- rubber spatula
- wax paper

Egg Pinwheel
7 large eggs, separated
Butter or shortening to grease pan
3/4 teaspoon salt, divided use
1/4 teaspoon cream of tartar
1/3 cup butter
6 tablespoons unsifted flour
Dash of cayenne pepper
1 1/4 cups milk
1/2 cup grated Cheddar cheese
1/2 cup freshly grated
  Parmigiano-Reggiano cheese

Filling
2 (10-ounce) packages frozen,
  chopped spinach
1/4 cup finely chopped onion
2 tablespoons butter
1/4 teaspoon *Tony Chachere's
  Creole Seasoning*
1/4 cup grated Cheddar cheese
1/2 cup sour cream
2 tablespoons freshly grated
  Parmigiano-Reggiano cheese

(ingredients continued on next page)

If you are planning to serve the pinwheel immediately after baking, make the sauce ahead of time. The pinwheel only takes 15 minutes to bake. Place egg whites and egg yolks in separate bowls. Let the egg whites warm for one hour. Grease the bottom of a jelly roll pan, line the pan with wax paper then grease the wax paper. Preheat oven to 350°F. With a mixer at high speed beat the egg whites with 1/4 teaspoon salt and cream of tartar until stiff peaks form. Melt 1/3 cup butter in a large saucepan and remove from heat. With a wire whisk, stir in the flour, cayenne and the remaining 1/2 teaspoon salt until smooth. Return to heat and start to gradually whisk in the milk. Bring to a boil stirring constantly. Reduce heat, simmer, stirring until the mixture is thick and starts to come together, leaving the bottom of the pan. With a mixer, beat in cheeses so that they are incorporated. With whisk, beat the egg yolks in their separate bowl and mix them into the cheese mixture. With a spatula (using an under and over motion) fold in 1/3 egg whites into cheese mixture. Carefully fold in the remaining whites and thoroughly combine. Turn the mixture onto prepared jelly roll pan. Bake 15 minutes or until the surface is puffed and firm to fingers. While the soufflé is baking, make the filling by cooking the spinach according to the package directions. Drain excess water. In a medium skillet, sauté the onion until golden in 2 tablespoons butter.

(continued on next page)

Shrimp Sauce
1 tablespoon butter
1 tablespoon flour
2 1/2 ounces half-and-half
1 (10.5-ounce) can condensed
  cream of shrimp soup
3/4 cup grated Cheddar cheese
2 tablespoons Sautérnes
  (sweet wine)
1/2 pound cooked fresh shrimp,
  peeled, deveined, tails off
  (reserve 8 shrimp with tails on
  for garnish)

Add the cooked spinach, *Tony Chachere's,*
Cheddar cheese and sour cream, mixing well
and remove from the heat. With a spatula
loosen the edge of the baked soufflé and invert
onto a piece of waxed paper sprinkled with
freshly grated Parmigiano-Reggiano. While it is
still warm peel off the waxed paper. Spread the
warm soufflé evenly with the prepared filling.
From the longer side, roll up the soufflé. Place
the roll seam-side down on a cutting board and
slice into 1-inch slices. This pastry does freeze
well, but before reheating it remember to spray
the foil heavily with cooking spray and sprinkle
with additional Parmigiano-Reggiano to keep foil
from sticking. Take the sliced pastry from the
freezer and place in the refrigerator for 24 hours
to dethaw. Reheat in the prepared foil on a jelly
roll pan for 30 minutes at 350°F. To make the
sauce, make a roux of butter and flour. Mix in
the half-and-half and whisk to thicken. Add the
condensed soup, cheese and wine. Whisk until
the sauce thickens and continue to cook over
low heat. Add the cooked shrimp and bring to
a boil. Spoon the shrimp sauce over the sliced
egg pinwheels. Garnish with a whole shrimp.

Tip: A 0.9-ounce packet of Hollandaise sauce
is a quick alternative to the shrimp sauce.

Shrimp with Asparagus in Puff Pastry Shells

Serves: 4

• whisk

18 pears fresh asparagus, trimmed, cut in 1-inch pieces
3 tablespoons butter, divided use
2 cups (4 ounces) fresh sliced mushrooms
2 tablespoons flour
3/4 cup chicken stock or broth
1/4 cup white wine
1/2 cup heavy cream
4 dashes Tabasco red pepper sauce
1 tablespoon chopped fresh dill weed, or 1 teaspoon dried dill
Pinch of white pepper
Sprinkle of *Tony Chachere's Creole Seasoning,* or more to taste
8 ounces frozen shrimp, defrosted, peeled, deveined, tails removed
4 frozen puff pastry shells (from a 10-ounce package)

Blanch the asparagus pieces (see Special Note on next page) and set aside. Preheat the oven to 400°F. In a medium skillet, melt the butter and add the mushrooms. Cook just until softened. Add the flour to coat the mushrooms. Slowly add the broth, wine and heavy cream to the flour-coated mushrooms, stirring with a whisk to remove any lumps. Add the Tabasco and continue whisking over low heat until thickened. Stir in the dill weed, white pepper and *Tony Chachere's.* Stirring occasionally, keep the mushroom mixture covered and on a very low temperature to keep warm while baking the puff pastry shells. (The mixture may be made ahead, refrigerated and reheated.) Bake the shells on a baking sheet for approximately 18 to 20 minutes until puffed and golden, just before serving. Near the end of the pastry shells bake time, add the shrimp to the mixture. Cook the shrimp approximately 3 to 5 minutes until just slightly coiled and pink. Add the blanched asparagus to the sauce and heat through. (Keep the pan uncovered or the asparagus will turn an unappetizing green color.) Taste and adjust the seasoning if needed. Remove the baked pastry shells from the oven and with a sharp knife, remove the perforated tops. Spoon about 1/3 cup of the shrimp mixture into the opening of each baked puff pastry shell and top with the cut out piece. This can be served as a light main dish with a salad.

(continued on next page)

Tips: Puff pastry shells are in with other packaged doughs in the freezer section of the grocery store. There is no need to defrost them before you bake them. You just place them on a baking sheet and bake 18 to 20 minutes at 400°F. They add some elegance to main dishes. You may make this filling with a combination of shrimp and sea scallops, crabmeat or any combination of seafood (even chicken would work).

Special Note: To blanch is to plunge food (asparagus, in this case) into boiling water for 2 to 3 minutes then into cold or ice water to stop the cooking process. It helps to heighten and set the color.

Lime Cream

 Makes: 1 cup

 • Microplane grater or zester

2 teaspoons lime zest
1 (8-ounce) container sour cream
2 tablespoons sugar
2 tablespoons freshly squeezed lime juice (juice from 1 medium lime)
Assorted fruit (see tips)

Mix all of the ingredients together in a bowl and refrigerate. This recipe can be made 24 hours ahead. This may be used as a dip for mixed fruits such as strawberries, bananas, cantaloupe, honeydew, kiwi or any other fruit. If serving fresh sliced apples, bananas and pears, you will need to brush them with a small amount of lemon or lime juice to keep them from discoloring.

Tips: Another special way to serve the lime cream is to drizzle it over cantaloupe slivers that have been topped with mixed berries and kiwi. Fruit can also be put on skewers for a buffet and lime cream served alongside.

Creole Pork with Garlic Grits

Serves: 4

• cheese grater

2 teaspoons salt
1 teaspoon black pepper
1/4 teaspoon cayenne pepper
2 pounds pork tenderloin,
  thinly sliced (1/8 inch thick)
1 cup flour
2 tablespoons butter
1 tablespoon olive oil
5 medium garlic cloves,
  minced or pressed
1 1/2 cups finely chopped onion
3/4 cup finely chopped celery
1/2 cup finely chopped green
  pepper
1 pound fresh tomatoes, finely
  chopped (1 1/2 large tomatoes)
1 1/2 cups chicken stock or broth

Garlic Grits
2 cups white (quick cooking)
  or yellow grits
6 cups water
1 1/2 teaspoons salt
1/2 cup grated Cheddar cheese
1/4 cup grated Parmigiano-
  Reggiano cheese
2 medium garlic cloves,
  minced or pressed
4 tablespoons unsalted butter
1 cup milk

To make the creole pork, mix together the salt, black pepper and cayenne pepper and rub into the meat with your fingers. Then coat (dredge) the pork with the 1 cup flour. (You may do this in a sealable plastic bag.) Melt the 2 tablespoons butter and the olive oil together in a large skillet. Turn heat up to medium. Thoroughly brown the coated pork in the hot butter and oil mixture. Remove the meat from the skillet and set aside. In the pan drippings, sauté the garlic, onions, celery and green pepper until they are soft. Add the browned pork back to the skillet and add the tomatoes and chicken stock. Cover, reduce heat and simmer on low for approximately one hour or until the meat is tender, stirring occasionally. Ten minutes before serving, heat the liquid to boiling while stirring. (Sauce should thicken due to the flour coating on the pork.) To make the garlic grits, check the grits package for the proportion of liquid required. Adjust as needed. Cook grits in the suggested amount of water seasoned with the salt until they are tender yet pourable. Remove from the heat and add the grated cheeses, garlic, butter and milk, stirring to thoroughly combine. Place the lid on grits and keep warm either on the stovetop or in the oven until ready to serve. Be careful not to burn the bottom of the grits. Add a bit more milk, water or broth if they get too thick. Serve by spooning the seasoned pork and sauce over the garlic grits.

(continued on next page)

Tips: A slow cooker (or a Dutch oven placed in a warm oven) works well for simmering if you cannot tend to a pot on the stove. This dish would be tasty prepared with chicken as well. Grits may be cooked in chicken broth, if desired.

Julie and Joe Lancaster: Grapevine, Texas
This delicious dish was served at a party hosted on a Sunday afternoon. The flavor of the slow cooked pork with the garlic and tomatoes is fabulous! Joe and Julie have plenty of space to entertain so they served this buffet style for over 30 people, along with several other brunch dishes. This is always a huge hit!

Green Chili Egg Strata

Serves: 12

6 slices French bread (1/2 inch thick)
3 tablespoons butter, softened
2 cups grated Cheddar cheese
2 cups grated Monterey Jack cheese
2 (4.5-ounce) cans green chiles
6 large eggs
2 cups milk
1 1/2 teaspoons *Tony Chachere's Creole Seasoning*
1 1/2 teaspoons sweet paprika
1 teaspoon dried oregano
1/4 teaspoon black pepper
1/2 teaspoon garlic powder
4 tablespoons finely chopped yellow onion
1/4 teaspoon dry mustard
1 Jalapeño, seeded and minced (optional)

Trim crusts off the French bread slices. Spread the softened butter on one side of the bread. Arrange the bread, buttered side down in 9 x 13-inch baking dish or two 10-inch quiche dishes. Sprinkle the grated cheeses evenly over bread. Distribute the chiles over the cheese. In a bowl whisk together the eggs and milk, adding all of the seasonings, onion and dry mustard. Pour the egg mixture over the cheese and chiles. Cover with plastic wrap and chill overnight or at least 4 hours. Preheat oven to 325°F. If you prefer a spicier version, remove the seeds from a fresh jalapeño and finely mince. Sprinkle on top of the strata before baking. Bake strata uncovered for 50 minutes or until the top is lightly browned. Let the dish stand for 10 minutes before serving.

Tips: Serve with warm flour tortillas, butter and salsa on the side. The idea for this dish came from a stay at the Briar Patch Inn in Sedona, Arizona. They served a homemade breakfast that was similar. We were seated for breakfast next to a babbling brook in beautiful surroundings.

Variation: For a different flavor, add 8 ounces fried, drained chorizo sausage.

Sausage and Spinach Quiche

Serves: 8

- cheese grater
- whisk
- glass pie pan or quiche pan

8 ounces pork sausage
2 tablespoons butter
3 tablespoons finely chopped green onion (white and pale green part only)
1/2 cup grated Cheddar cheese
3/4 cup grated Swiss cheese
1 teaspoon dried Italian seasoning
1 1/2 cups (2.5 ounces) fresh spinach, chopped
1 large garlic clove, minced or pressed
8 large eggs, beaten
1/2 cup half-and-half
1 (3-ounce) package cream cheese, softened

Preheat oven to 350°F. Spray a 10-inch quiche dish with cooking spray and set aside. In a skillet, fry the sausage until no pink remains and drain well. Remove the sausage from the skillet and set aside. In the same pan, melt the butter and sauté the chopped green onion until translucent. Mix the onion, sausage, grated cheeses and Italian seasonings together in the skillet. Spread the sausage mixture over the bottom of the prepared quiche dish. Using the same pan you cooked the sausage in, sauté the chopped spinach with the garlic until spinach is wilted. Spread the cooked spinach over the top of the sausage mixture. Beat the eggs and half-and-half together with a whisk. Soften the cream cheese in the microwave 15 to 20 seconds. Add the softened cream cheese to the egg mixture and whisk to thoroughly incorporate. Pour the mixture over the spinach. Bake the quiche until the egg mixture has set, approximately 45 minutes. Slice and serve warm. This quiche also reheats nicely if made ahead.

Tips: Choose any sausage you prefer—spicy, regular, sage or turkey. You may use 1/2 teaspoon dried oregano and 1/2 teaspoon dried basil in place of Italian seasoning.

"We cannot tell the precise moment when friendship is formed. As in filling a vessel drop by drop. There is at last a drop which makes it run over; so in a series of kindnesses there is at least one which makes the heart run over."

~James Boswell

Chorizo, Tortilla, Fresh Tomato Quiche

Serves: 8

- cheese grater
- quiche pan or pie pan

5 ounces frozen, chopped
  spinach
8 ounces chorizo sausage
3/4 teaspoon vegetable oil
2 corn tortillas cut into 1-inch
  strips
1/4 cup flour
3/4 teaspoon chili powder
1/2 teaspoon salt
1 medium tomato, diced (1/4-
  inch pieces)
1/3 cup salsa
3 green onions, finely chopped
  (white and pale green
  part only)
1 jalapeño, seeded and minced
5 large eggs, beaten
3/4 cup milk
1 cup grated Monterey Jack
  cheese

Preheat oven to 350°F. Thaw the spinach and squeeze out any moisture. Remove the casing from the sausage and crumble. Fry the chorizo in a skillet and drain. Lightly brush the bottom of a 9-inch pie pan with oil. Place the tortilla strips in the bottom of the dish, slightly overlapping. Combine the flour, chili powder and salt in a bowl. Sprinkle 1/2 of flour mixture over the tortillas. Combine the tomatoes, salsa, green onions and jalapeño. Layer the tomato mixture over the flour mixture. Sprinkle the tomato layer with the remaining flour mixture. Sprinkle the cooked chorizo sausage on top of the flour mixture. In a medium bowl combine the eggs, milk, spinach and a 1/2 cup of the grated cheese. Pour the egg mixture evenly over the chorizo. Bake uncovered for 30 minutes. Sprinkle with the remaining cheese and bake 5 minutes longer. Slice and serve warm. This quiche freezes and reheats easily.

Special Note: Chorizo is a coarsely ground pork sausage flavored with garlic, chili powder and other spices.

Breakfast Pie

Serves: 8

- whisk
- cheese grater
- glass pie pan
- wire cooling rack

1 (16-ounce) package pork sausage
1 (9-inch) refrigerated pie crust
1 1/2 cups grated Swiss cheese
4 large eggs
1/4 cup finely chopped green bell pepper
1/4 cup finely chopped red bell pepper
2 tablespoons finely chopped onion
1 cup half-and-half

Preheat oven to 375°F. Cook the sausage thoroughly, drain and crumble. Prepare the crust according to package directions in a 9-inch pie pan, but do not bake. Mix together the grated cheese and cooked sausage and sprinkle in pie shell. Beat the eggs in a medium bowl. Combine the remaining ingredients and add to the beaten eggs. Pour the eggs over the sausage mixture and bake for 40 to 45 minutes, until the eggs have set. Cool the pie on a rack for 10 minutes before serving. You may make this dish ahead of time and reheat.

Tip: Any flavor sausage may be used but spicy is our favorite!

Julie McAllister: North Richland Hills, Texas
Julie is one of the original Knots Landing Dinner Club members. Our group met at our first job out of college. We started as a Knots Landing watch party and blossomed from there. We still enjoy our eating adventures and take pride in the recipes. I requested this from Julie after she made it for a baby shower and I had a second helping. It is delicious!

Hash-Brown Egg Pie

Serves: 8

- electric mixer
- glass pie pan or quiche pan
- cheese grater
- whisk

2 1/2 cups frozen hash-brown potatoes (shredded or cubed)
7 slices bacon
5 large eggs
1 1/2 cups grated Pepper Jack cheese
1/3 cup milk
2 green onions, finely chopped (white and pale green part only)
1 medium tomato, seeded, diced (1/4-inch pieces)
1/2 teaspoon *Tony Chachere's Creole Seasoning*

Prepare a quiche pan or pie pan with cooking spray. Pat the 2 1/2 cups uncooked hash-browns into the bottom of the pan. Cook the bacon until crisp, drain and crumble. Set aside. In a bowl, beat eggs with an electric mixer or whisk until fluffy. Stir in all the remaining ingredients including the cooked bacon. Pour the egg mixture over the hash-browns, cover with plastic wrap and refrigerate overnight. Preheat oven to 325°F. Bake the pie for 40 to 50 minute. The pie is done when a knife inserted comes out clean and the top of the pie is slightly golden.

Variation: This wonderful quiche is a variation of one introduced to me by Donna Gray of Kansas City, Kansas. Donna used ham instead of bacon and no tomatoes.

Special Note: Pepper Jack is a mild cheese; it is a Monterey Jack that is enhanced with flecks and shavings of pepper.

> *"One cannot think well, love well, or sleep well, if one has not dined well."*
>
> ~*Virginia Woolf*

Easy Cream Cheese Danish

Serves: 12

- electric mixer
- whisk

Cream Cheese Danish
2 (8-ounce) cans refrigerated crescent rolls
2 (8-ounce) packages cream cheese
1 cup sugar
1 large egg
1 teaspoon vanilla
Fresh berries (optional)

Glaze
1/2 cup confectioners' sugar
1/2 teaspoon vanilla
3 tablespoons milk

Preheat the oven to 350°F. Spray the bottom of a 9 x 13-inch baking dish with cooking spray. Unroll the first can of uncooked crescent dough and spread it along the bottom of the prepared pan. Seal the perforations in the dough by pressing the seams together with your fingers. Mix the cream cheese, sugar, egg and vanilla together with an electric mixer until smooth. Spread this mixture evenly on top of the crescent dough. Spread the second can of dough out flat on a work surface and seal the perforations with your fingers to make a solid rectangle. Place this rectangle over the top of the cream cheese mixture. Bake for 30 minutes. For the glaze, whisk the confectioners' sugar, vanilla and milk together. While the danish is warm, spread the glaze over the top. Once completely cooled, place in the refrigerator. Cut in squares and serve. Garnish with fresh berries if desired.

Laurie Tittle: Arlington, Texas
Laurie and I met when I spoke to a women's group in Arlington, Texas. We struck up a conversation as I was packing to leave, and she offered to email me several of her favorite recipes. I love making this dish for weekend guests.

Raspberry Streusel Muffins

Makes: 1 dozen

- wooden spoon
- sifter
- muffin pans

- Microplane grater or zester

Muffins

1 1/2 cups flour
1/4 cup sugar
1/4 cup packed brown sugar
2 teaspoons baking powder
1/4 teaspoon salt
1 teaspoon ground cinnamon
1 large egg, beaten
1/4 cup unsalted butter, melted
1/2 cup milk
1 1/4 cups fresh raspberries
1 teaspoon grated lemon zest

Streusel Topping

1/2 cup chopped pecans
1/2 cup packed brown sugar
1/4 cup flour
1 teaspoon ground cinnamon
1 teaspoon lemon zest
2 tablespoons unsalted butter, melted

Glaze

1 tablespoon freshly squeezed lemon juice (juice from 1/2 medium lemon)
1/2 cup confectioners' sugar

Preheat oven to 350°F. Prepare muffin pans with cooking spray. Sift all the dry ingredients, then measure. Mix the flour, sugars, baking powder, salt and cinnamon together in a medium bowl. Make a well in the center and place the egg, melted butter and milk in the well. Stir with a wooden spoon just until ingredients are combined. Gently stir in the fresh raspberries and lemon zest. (If desired, you can make the batter the night before and refrigerate.) Fill each muffin cup 3/4 full with batter. Combine all of the dry streusel ingredients and stir in the melted butter. Sprinkle this mixture over each muffin. Bake for 20 to 25 minutes. While muffins are baking, make the glaze by mixing lemon juice with the confectioners' sugar. Right after removing the baked muffins from the oven, drizzle the glaze over the warm muffins with a spoon. Serve them warm.

Tip: Mini muffin pans may be used instead of regular sized muffin pans.

Special Note: Sifting passes ingredients through fine mesh to remove large pieces. It incorporates air and will change measurements. Measure ingredients after they are sifted and that is the correct amount that should be added to the recipe, unless otherwise stated.

Twila Baker: Dallas, Texas
Twila and I met at Kansas State University and we both ended up in Dallas. Our "Dinner Club" was started by Joan Lewis, Twila's sorority sister. Twila hosted a girl's get together and made these for one of our brunches. They are mouth watering when served warm.

Baked Apple Doughnuts

Makes: 1 dozen

- muffin pan or mini muffin pan
- cheese grater

Doughnuts
1 1/2 cups flour
1 3/4 teaspoons baking powder
1/2 teaspoon salt
1/2 teaspoon ground nutmeg
1/2 cup sugar
1/2 cup shortening
1 egg, beaten
1/4 cup milk
1/2 cup peeled, grated apple

Topping
1/3 cup sugar
1 teaspoon ground cinnamon
1/2 cup (1 stick) butter, melted

Preheat the oven to 350°F. Prepare the muffin pan with cooking spray. Sift all the dry ingredients, then measure. Mix together the flour, baking powder, salt, nutmeg, and sugar. Cut in shortening until mixture is fine. Mix together the egg, milk and grated apple and add all at once to the dry ingredients, mixing quickly but thoroughly. Fill greased muffin cups 2/3 full. Bake for 20 to 25 minutes or until they are golden brown on top. Remove the doughnuts from the pans. For the topping mix the sugar and cinnamon together. Immediately roll the tops of doughnuts in the melted butter then in the cinnamon sugar mixture. Serve warm.

Cream Cheese Brown Sugar Bites

Makes: 24

- mini muffin pan
- electric mixer

1 (8-ounce) package cream
  cheese, softened
1 egg yolk (from a small or
  medium egg)
1/4 cup sugar
3/4 cup brown sugar
1 teaspoon ground cinnamon
1 (12-ounce) can refrigerated
  flaky biscuits
6 tablespoons butter, melted

Preheat the oven to 350°F. Make the filling by mixing together the softened cream cheese, egg yolk and sugar with an electric mixer. In another bowl, mix together the brown sugar and cinnamon. Set aside. Prepare mini muffin pans with cooking spray. Split each flaky biscuit into thirds by tearing into their natural layers. Spoon a small amount of the filling onto the split muffin. Fold over and pinch together forming a half moon. Roll in the melted butter, then in brown sugar and cinnamon mixture. Put one in each muffin cup with the rounded side up. Bake the pastries for 10 to 14 minutes or until lightly golden. Serve warm.

Sausage Crescents

Makes: 4 dozen

• pastry brush

1 (16-ounce) package pork
  sausage
1 (8-ounce) package cream
  cheese, softened
2 (8-ounce) packages
  refrigerated crescent rolls
1 egg white, beaten
Poppy seeds

Preheat oven to 350°F. Lightly brown the sausage and drain. While the sausage is warm, add the cream cheese and stir until it is melted and the mixture has a creamy texture. Remove from the heat and cool completely. Separate the crescent rolls into 2 rectangles. Form a line of sausage mixture lengthwise down the center of each rectangle. Fold over the long sides of the pastry to cover the sausage. Place the pastries on an ungreased baking sheet, seam-side down. Brush with the egg white and lightly sprinkle the tops with poppy seeds. Bake 20 minutes until crust is golden. When cooled slightly, slice into 1 1/2-inch slices and serve warm. These can be made ahead, frozen and reheated.

Variations: Any flavor sausage may be used. Crescents make delicious rolls that can become a great accompaniment to many types of meals or snacks. Consider the possibilities with cooked chicken, cream cheese, cooked mushrooms and green onions or ham, cream cheese and dill. We've used honey and prosciutto or even pesto and Parmesan. The opportunities are endless. The crescents can be made as rolls with a thin layer of mixtures spread on each individual roll or rolled with fillings as stated and used as a breakfast bread or appetizer.

Melissa Ripley: Southlake, Texas
Melissa and I met through mutual friends and we hosted a spring brunch together.
These were a hit and the kids and adults loved them. Make plenty; they go fast!

Ciabatta Apple Cinnamon Toast

• jelly roll pan

1 loaf ciabatta bread,
   sourdough or baguette, sliced
   (approximately 20 slices)
1 (8-ounce) container of
   mascarpone cheese
5 McIntosh apples, peeled and
   thinly sliced
1/4 cup sugar
1 teaspoon ground cinnamon
Pure maple syrup (optional)

Preheat the broiler. Place the bread slices on a jelly roll pan or baking sheet and spread a thin layer of mascarpone cheese over each slice of bread. Cover entire slice of bread with overlapping slices of apple. Mix the sugar and cinnamon together and sprinkle over the apples. Broil 6 inches from the broiler until the apples are tender and the edges of the bread are golden. Watch carefully so the edges do not burn. Serve hot with maple syrup as a topping, if desired.

Special Note: Mascarpone is a buttery rich double cream to triple cream cheese made from cow's milk. It is delicious when paired with gingersnaps, raisin bread and fruits. McIntosh apples cook quickly so they are ideal for this recipe.

Cindy Cannon: Phoenix, Arizona
Cindy and I worked together and she has the most incredible infectious laugh. She would bring cookbooks from home and share her favorite recipes with me.

Sour Cream Coffee Cake

Serves: 8

- electric mixer
- springform pan (9-inch or 10-inch)
- sifter

Coffee Cake
1 cup (2 sticks) unsalted butter
2 cups sugar
2 large eggs
1 cup sour cream
1 teaspoon vanilla
2 cups flour
1 teaspoon baking powder
1/4 teaspoon salt

Topping
1 cup chopped pecans
1 1/2 tablespoons sugar
1 teaspoon cinnamon

Preheat oven to 350°F. Spray the bottom and sides of a springform pan with cooking spray. Dust lightly with flour. In a large bowl, cream together the butter and sugar until the mixture is light and fluffy. Beat in the eggs and fold in the sour cream. Add the vanilla, stirring to incorporate thoroughly. Sift remaining dry ingredients, then measure. Add them to the creamed mixture. In a separate bowl, mix together the topping ingredients and set aside. Pour half of the batter into the prepared pan and sprinkle with half of the topping. Repeat with remaining batter. Bake approximately 1 hour, until a toothpick comes out clean. Serve warm or at room temperature. This freezes well. Defrost, warm (if desired) and serve.

Tips: To add color to your table, garnish top with fresh raspberries (approximately 1 cup). This coffee cake may be made in a Bundt cake pan as well. Layer small amount of topping, then half of the batter, another layer of topping (as a filling) and remaining batter. Bake approximately 50 minutes or until a toothpick comes out clean.

Lee Martell: Murrysville, Pennsylvania
Laurie, Beth and Julie Martell are three of Lee's daughters that have recipes in the book. Lee gave Julie and I this recipe when we lived together in college. This is a delicious coffee cake recipe!

Best Rolls Ever

Makes: 40 rolls

- rolling pin
- pastry brush

- 1 (2 1/2- to 3-inch) round biscuit cutter
- thermometer, to test temperature of water

3/4 cup (1 1/2 sticks) butter, divided use
2 large eggs
1/2 cup sugar
1/2 cup lukewarm water
2 packages dry active yeast (rapid or regular)
1 3/4 cups lukewarm milk (Jane uses dried skim mixed with water)
5 1/2 cups flour
1 tablespoon salt

Tips: If making and baking for a dinner party the next day or later in the day, let the rolls rise two times, get them cut, rolled in butter and folded and put in the cake pan. Cover them with plastic wrap and put them in the refrigerator. They will rise a little in the refrigerator; however allow approximately 2 hours while sitting out at room temperature (uncovered) for them to completely rise before baking. This allows you to be with your guests instead of in the kitchen cutting and preparing rolls.

If you plan to make the bread and bake immediately, melt 1/2 cup (1 stick) butter, but check the temperature to be sure it is not over 115°F. (I like to stay at 113°F to be safe.) Beat the eggs in a small bowl and set aside. Measure out the sugar into a large bowl. In a separate bowl measure out the warm water (lukewarm water to activate yeast is between 105°F-115°F) and add the room temperature yeast and a pinch of sugar from the large bowl. Stir the yeast, water and the pinch of sugar together and set aside in a warm place (70°F-85°F) for 5 to 10 minutes. If it begins to swell and foam, the yeast is alive, active and capable of leavening bread. Add yeast mixture to the remaining sugar in the large bowl and stir in the lukewarm milk (105°F-115°F). Measure out the flour in a separate bowl and stir in the salt. Add 3 cups flour to the yeast mixture and stir to blend. Stir in the eggs and melted butter and add the remaining flour in two additions. Cover and place in a warm place (not in the oven but perhaps near an oven that has been on) and let rise until double in size, punch down and let rise again. Punch down again. Melt the additional 1/4 cup (1/2 stick) butter in a 9 x 13-inch baking dish. Let the butter cool. On a floured surface, knead the dough and roll the dough out to a 3/8 inch thickness with a rolling pin. Use the 2 1/2-inch to 3-inch round biscuit cutter to cut out rolls. With the melted butter in the baking dish, brush the insides of the cut out dough with the butter and fold in half. Brush the outside as well. Cover lightly with a slightly dampened cloth and let rise in the baking dish until double in size. Preheat the oven to 350°F before baking. Bake until lightly golden approximately 20 to 25 minutes. (You do not want centers to be doughy.)

Sweet Rolls

Makes: 40 rolls

1/2 cup (1 stick) butter, melted
1 1/4 cups brown sugar
3 tablespoons honey
2 tablespoons heavy cream or
  half-and-half
1 1/2 cups pecans, chopped
Extra melted butter for
brushing over dough
Cinnamon and sugar mixed
  together for sprinkling

To make sweet rolls made with the same dough, melt the butter and add the brown sugar, honey, cream and nuts. Pour the brown sugar mixture into the bottom of a 9 x 13-inch baking dish. On a floured surface, knead the dough and roll out to a rectangle with a rolling pin (approximately 3/4 inch thick). Brush the top of the dough with the extra melted butter and sprinkle with the cinnamon and sugar. Roll up the dough into a log and cut into 20 rolls (if using only half of the dough). Place rolls in the baking dish on top of the brown sugar mixture. Let rise to double in size. Preheat the oven to 350°F while dough is doubling. Bake the rolls for approximately 20 to 25 minutes or until lightly golden. Turn the baking dish over onto a serving platter so that the nuts and brown sugar mixture spills over the rolls. Serve warm from the oven.

Tips: Jane, the recipe contributor, prefers to use Parkay margarine. She also usually uses one half of the dough for these dinner rolls and the other half of the dough for her cinnamon rolls.

Variation: The recipe above makes gooey caramel nut rolls. If you prefer to make regular cinnamon rolls, do not melt the butter with the 4 extra ingredients, instead spread the kneaded dough with butter and sprinkle with the cinnamon and sugar mixture. Follow the directions for cutting the rolls and place in a greased pan. While these are baking make a glaze from confectioners' sugar (page 96) and drizzle over the warm buns straight out of the oven.

Jane Langlais: Southlake, Texas
Jane is one of the original members of "Dinner Club" along with her husband Don. Jane and her husband have moved out of the country several times due to work assignments. While she is away I attempt to make her rolls and always use butter and regular milk. They are never quite as airy and light as hers so this must be her "secret."

Sausage-Apple Bread

Serves 6

• whisk

1 (16-ounce) package pork
sausage
1/2 cup finely chopped onion
1/4 cup diced green pepper
(1/4-inch pieces)
1 medium garlic clove, minced
or pressed
4 ounces cream cheese
1 large apple, peeled, cored
and diced
2 (8-ounce) packages
refrigerated crescent rolls
1 egg yolk, beaten with one
tablespoon of cold water

Preheat the oven to 375°F. Fry the sausage with
the onion, pepper and garlic. Drain if needed.
While the sausage is warm, add the cream
cheese and stir until it is melted and mixture has
a creamy texture. Add the diced apple and mix
together. Cool the mixture completely. Separate
the crescent rolls into 2 rectangles. Form a line
of sausage mixture lengthwise down the center
of each rectangle. Fold over the long sides of the
pastry to cover the sausage. Place the pastries
on an ungreased baking sheet, seam-side down.
Brush the tops with the egg yolk and bake 18
to 20 minutes until golden. Slice in 2-inch
slices while warm and serve with a fork and an
accompaniment such as fresh fruit.

Tips: Use your imagination and create
combinations of sautéed mushrooms, chopped
tomatoes or cooked sausage and bacon. This is
an easy recipe to make for a group and to get
your eggs and bread in one dish!

*Variation: For an alternative you can encase
scrambled eggs as well. Whisk 3 eggs together
with 1/4 cup milk or cream and fold in 1/2 cup
grated cheese and a tablespoon of onions and
green or red pepper if desired. Scramble eggs.
Sprinkle with salt and pepper. Proceed with
filling the crescent rolls with the egg mixture.
Slice and serve warm from the oven.*

Sherryn Harris: Dallas, Texas
*I met Sherryn (B.J. to her friends) through her neighborhood women's organization. I held
a cooking demo for them and they were certainly an enthusiastic and memorable group.
Sherryn shared this recipe with me after the event.*

Jalapeño Cornbread

Serves: 12

1 red onion, finely diced (1/4-inch pieces)

1/2 cup (1 stick) butter, plus 2 tablespoons for sautéing

2 (15.25-ounce) cans corn

2 jalapeños, seeded and chopped

2 (14.75-ounce) cans creamed corn

1 (8-ounce) package cream cheese

1 (4-ounce) jar pimento, drained

6 large eggs

3 (8.5-ounce) boxes "Jiffy" Corn Muffin Mix

Preheat the oven to 400°F. Sauté the diced red onion in the 2 tablespoons butter. Drain the regular corn. Remove seeds from the jalapeños and finely chop. Soften the cream cheese in the microwave for 10 seconds. In a large bowl, mix all of the ingredients together. Pour the batter evenly into a greased 9 x 13-inch baking dish. Bake for 20 to 30 minutes.

Variation: Roasted red peppers from a jar (drained) can be used in place of the pimento.

Vince Martinez: Dallas, Texas
Vince Martinez, my friend and hair stylist gave me this recipe. He is a great cook and knows all his recipes by memory. Vince has fun and lives life to the fullest. He cooks the same way. He experiments by mixing unusual flavors and spices together.

Orange-Pineapple Spice Tea

Serves: 4

4 cups hot brewed tea

1/3 cup sugar

3 cups orange juice

1 cup unsweetened pineapple juice

3 (3-inch) cinnamon sticks, broken into pieces

3/4 teaspoon whole cloves

1/2 teaspoon whole allspice berries

Combine the hot tea and sugar in a large pan. Stir in the fruit juices. Add spices and bring to a boil. Cover and reduce heat, simmering 30 minutes; strain tea to remove spices. This is wonderful served cold or hot!

Sparkling Cranberry Tea

Serves: 4

8 cups apple-cranberry drink
(other cranberry combinations
can be used)
2 cups double strength tea
1 (10-ounce) bottle or can of
lemon/lime carbonated drink
Ice

In a pitcher mix first 3 ingredients together.
Pour over ice. This is a nice alternative to iced
tea. A flavored tea with orange and cinnamon
spice can also be used.

Spicy Bloody Mary Pitcher

Serves: 8

1 (46-ounce) bottle chilled
spicy hot vegetable juice
2 cups vodka
2 tablespoons freshly squeezed
lime juice (juice from 1
medium lime)
1/8 teaspoon celery salt
1/8 teaspoon cayenne pepper
1 1/2 teaspoons Worcestershire
sauce
1 teaspoon bottled horseradish,
drained
Ground black pepper, to taste
Ice
Celery stalks
Small wedges of fresh lime for
garnish (optional)
Spicy pickled green beans
(optional)
Tabasco red pepper sauce
(optional)

In a 2-quart pitcher mix together the first 7
ingredients. Add enough cracked black pepper
so you can see the flecks floating in the pitcher
when stirred (about 1 teaspoon). Pour the drink
over ice in individual glasses and garnish with a
celery stalk and lime wedge or a spicy pickled
green bean. Pass around the Tabasco sauce
for those who want to add more heat to their
bloody mary.

Special Note: Spicy pickled green beans can
be found in gourmet stores.

Beach Buzzes

Makes: 8

• blender

3/4 cup 80 proof white rum
1/2 cup vodka
4 medium, ripe peaches, pitted, with peal
6 ounces frozen pink lemonade concentrate
12 ice cubes

Put first 4 ingredients in blender and blend to chop peaches. Keep a pitcher close by in case blender gets too full. Pour half of the blended mixture into a pitcher. Add ice to the blender and blend to create a slushy frozen drink. More ice may be needed. Serve immediately or repeat with the second half. These are not overly sweet and make a refreshing pool side drink! Store in the freezer and blend again before serving.

Tip: Ice that sits too long in the freezer takes on the flavor of what is being stored. When entertaining, be sure you have fresh ice or buy a bag to use for the party.

Pineapple-Banana Punch

Serves: 40

• blender or food processor

1 (12-ounce) can frozen concentrate lemonade
1 (12-ounce) can frozen concentrate orange juice
6 bananas, puréed
1 (46-ounce) can pineapple juice
1/2 cup sugar
1 (2-liter) bottle of lemon-lime carbonated drink

Prepare the lemonade and orange juice according to package directions and combine. Purée the bananas in a blender or food processor. Mix the pineapple juice, puréed bananas and sugar into the lemonade/orange juice mixture. Freeze in a gallon container overnight. Defrost two hours before serving and add the lemon/lime drink.

Mojitos

Serves: 2

• cocktail shaker with strainer

8 teaspoons superfine sugar
1/4 cup freshly squeezed lime
   juice (juice from 2 medium
   limes)
1/2 cup white rum
Crushed ice
24 fresh mint leaves
1 cup club soda
Additional limes wedges for
   garnish

In a cocktail shaker, shake the sugar, lime juice and rum together until the sugar dissolves. Fill two highball glasses 1/3 full of crushed ice. Put 12 fresh mint leaves on top of the ice in each glass. Layer with another 1/3 of ice. Pour the lime mixture equally over the ice in both glasses. Pour enough club soda to the top of the glass. (You may not use the entire cup.) Add a fresh lime wedge for garnish.

Tip: If this is increased to pitcher size, add 1 or 2 (3-ounce) boxes of fresh mint leaves per pitcher rather than counting the leaves.

Susan and Russ Bee: Rockwall, Texas
My former boss, Susan, and her husband Russ, gave us this wonderful cocktail recipe.
They have become our fun and festive dinner companions over the years. The combination
of lime and mint is very refreshing!

Margarita Martini

Serves: 2

• cocktail shaker with strainer

Simple Syrup
2 cups sugar
1 cup water

Margarita Martini
1/2 cup freshly squeezed lime juice (juice from 4 medium limes)
2 tablespoons simple syrup (recipe above)
1/2 cup tequila
1/4 cup orange liqueur
Ice

To make the simple syrup, mix together the sugar and water in a small pan, heat until sugar dissolves. Combine all of the remaining ingredients in a cocktail shaker with ice and shake 30 times. Strain into the chilled martini glasses. Taste and squeeze a bit more lime into mixture if it's too sweet. Store leftover syrup in a sealed jar and refrigerate for later use.

Tip: Grand Marnier, Cointreau and Gran Gala are both orange liqueurs. Choose your price point.

Orange Vodka Cosmopolitan

Serves: 2

• cocktail shaker with strainer

1/4 cup orange vodka or regular vodka
2 tablespoons orange liqueur
1/4 cup cranberry juice
1 tablespoon freshly squeezed lime juice (juice from 1/2 medium lime)
3/4 cup crushed ice

Mix together all ingredients in a martini shaker with ice and shake 30 times. Strain into chilled martini glasses and serve.

Tips: While making the drinks we either chill the glasses in the freezer or fill them with ice. We store our vodka in the freezer.

Variation: You can use pomegranate juice in place of cranberry if desired and rum as an alternative to vodka.

Frozen Coconut Lime Cooler

Makes: 2

• blender

1/2 cup canned cream of coconut (Coco Lopez)
1/4 cup tequila
Zest of one lime
3 tablespoons freshly squeezed lime juice (juice from 1 1/2 medium limes)

Stir the coconut milk well before measuring. In a blender blend all of the ingredients until smooth. Add 2 cups ice cubes, blend again and serve in chilled martini glasses. The cooler is not too sweet and is refreshing!

Peach–Amaretto Eggnog

Serves: 16

• electric mixer
• whisk
• 6 quart punch bowl

1/2 cup peach brandy
1/2 cup amaretto
1 quart half-and-half
1 quart heavy cream
12 large eggs
1 (16-ounce) box confectioners' sugar
2 cups dark rum
1 teaspoon nutmeg (optional)

Chill a 6-quart punch bowl. Chill the brandy, amaretto, half-and-half and cream before starting. Separate the eggs. Set whites aside and refrigerate. In a medium bowl, beat egg yolks with the confectioners' sugar until sticky. As mixture turns sticky, gradually add the rum. Chill this mixture 2 to 3 hours in the refrigerator. Once chilled for the allotted time, take the egg whites out and whip them until they are stiff but not dry. In the cold punch bowl, mix together the cream, half-and-half, brandy and amaretto. Add the sugar, egg yolk and rum mixture to the cream and liquor mixture. Whisk together. Once the two are mixed, carefully fold in the egg whites. Sprinkle with nutmeg.

Tip: If this is for a small gathering the recipe may be cut in half. Cover and refrigerate for up to 3 days. Be sure to stir before serving because the alcohol settles to the bottom.

Soups & Salads

Soups & Salads

 Kitchen tools needed

 May be prepared ahead

Picture Features: Fresh Tomato, Kalamata and Feta Salad with Shallot Herb Vinaigrette, page 122
Ham and Bean Chowder, page 113, Party Sandwiches, page 50

Wild Rice Soup with Sherry and Cream   Serves: 6

• whisk

6 cups chicken stock or broth, divided use
1 cup wild rice blend
6 tablespoons unsalted butter, divided use
1 cup yellow onion, finely chopped
2 cups (4 ounces) coarsely chopped fresh mushrooms
1 stalk celery, finely chopped
1/4 cup flour, divided use
2 carrots, peeled and thinly sliced
1/2 teaspoon *Tony Chachere's Creole Seasoning*
1/4 teaspoon dry mustard
1/4 teaspoon Herbes de Provence
1/4 teaspoon ground white pepper
1 bay leaf
1 cup heavy cream
1/4 cup dry sherry

Bring 2 cups of the chicken stock or broth to a boil in a large saucepan and add rice. Bring back to a boil, then reduce the heat and simmer until all the water is absorbed, according to package directions. In a large soup pot or saucepan, melt 4 tablespoons of the butter and add onions. Cook until onions are translucent, about 5 minutes; add the mushrooms and celery. Sauté approximately 3 more minutes until celery and mushrooms are softened. Sprinkle 2 tablespoons of the flour over the vegetables and blend. Slowly add the remaining 4 cups chicken stock while stirring with a whisk. (This will thicken the soup.) Stir in 1/2 teaspoon *Tony Chachere's,* the mustard, Herbs de Provence, white pepper and bay leaf. In a separate bowl, mix the remaining 2 tablespoons flour with 2 tablespoons soft butter to make a paste. Bring the soup to a boil and stir in the paste with a whisk. Continue to stir until soup reaches desired consistency. Thin with additional stock if desired. Lower the heat, add the rice and sherry and serve warm.

Variations: Boil and debone a 4-pound chicken and reserve the broth. Use the broth for the recipe and the chicken to make the soup heartier.

Add 3 ears fresh corn (frozen may be substituted) and 8 ounces cooked smoked sausage (andouille or kielbasa), cut into slices. This makes a hearty chowder.

Follow the recipe exactly but you may choose in any of the versions to use a combination of more unusual mushrooms versus button mushrooms. For this seafood version, split the stock between lobster and chicken stock (3 cups each) and add 1 pound of lump crabmeat for a delicious seafood-rice soup. Just before serving add 1/4 teaspoon Tabasco red pepper sauce.

Sally Graber:
Lawrence, Kansas
Sally Graber was my inspiration for this recipe. Sally is a vivacious lady and dear friend. She is the mother of my cookbook photographer, Joe Graber.

Roasted Corn Chowder

Serves: 6

- whisk
- blender or food processor

3 ears fresh corn, shucked and roasted
1 medium red pepper, roasted
1 poblano pepper, roasted
1 small canned chipotle chile in adobo (optional)
2 (14.75-ounce) cans creamed corn, divided use
3 slices bacon, diced (1/4-inch pieces)
1 medium yellow onion, finely chopped
1/3 cup green onion, minced (white and pale green part only)
1/4 cup flour
3 cups chicken stock or broth
1 bay leaf
1/4 teaspoon *Tony Chachere's Creole Seasoning*
1/2 cup heavy cream
Dash of Tabasco red pepper sauce (optional)

Preheat the broiler or grill. Place the corn and peppers on a baking sheet and roast in the broiler (or place on grill), turning occasionally, until all sides are blackened. Place the blackened peppers in a paper bag to steam. When cool enough to handle, remove the outside charred skin and discard the inside seeds and stems. Coarsely chop the peppers and remove the corn from the cob. Set the corn aside. Place the poblano pepper, red peppers and 1 can of corn in the blender. If you prefer a spicier soup with a slight kick, add the chipotle at this time. Pulse several times to coarsely chop the vegetables, leaving some red and green pieces for texture. In a large soup pot or saucepan, sauté the bacon until slightly crispy. Add the onions and continue to cook until translucent, about 5 minutes. Sprinkle the flour over the sautéed bacon and onions and stir to coat ingredients. Cook just until flour is lightly golden. Whisk in the stock and add the bay leaf. Bring to a boil while whisking. Reduce heat to a simmer and add the puréed vegetables, remaining can of creamed corn, roasted corn and *Tony Chachere's*. Simmer for 10 minutes on very low heat. Add the cream and season to taste. Thin with more stock, if desired. Serve warm.

Special Note: You can also roast the peppers over direct flame on your stovetop if you have a gas stove. Using tongs, hold the peppers over the flame, turning occasionally, until all sides are blackened. Complete the recipe as directed.

Variation: Shrimp, crab or kielbasa sausage may be added. If you would like this to be vegetarian, sauté the onions in butter or oil and complete the recipe as directed. This recipe can be made without roasting the vegetables and even potatoes cooked and diced may be added. We just like the depth of flavor that the roasting adds.

Ham and Bean Chowder

Serves: 6

 • cheese grater

1 (16-ounce) bag dried Great Northern white beans or navy beans
2 quarts water
4 smoked ham hocks
2 cups diced yellow onion (1/4-inch pieces)
1/2 cup finely chopped celery
2 teaspoons freshly minced garlic
1 bay leaf
2 whole cloves
1/4 teaspoon pepper
3 (14.5-ounce) cans chicken stock or broth
1 (14.5-ounce) can chopped tomatoes
2 cups grated Cheddar cheese

Rinse the beans. Cover the beans with water in a 6-quart soup pot or saucepan and bring to a boil. Cover and boil for two minutes. Remove from the heat and let beans soak for one hour. Drain the beans, reserving the liquid. Return beans to the soup pot; add 4 cups reserved liquid, ham hocks, onion, celery, garlic, bay leaf, cloves, pepper and chicken stock combined with enough water to measure 6 cups. Bring to a boil, lower the heat and simmer 2 to 2 1/2 hours or until the meat is tender. Remove the meat and set aside. Remove the bay leaf and cloves and discard. Add the tomatoes with their juice to the soup. Cut the meat off the ham hocks and return the meat to the soup (discard the hocks). Skim off the fat, if desired. Add the cheese, stirring until melted. Cheese that you grate yourself will melt better. Serve chowder warm.

Tip: Wrap celery in foil before placing it in the refrigerator. It will stay fresh longer. Fat is easier to remove once the soup is cooled and chilled. Skim off fat and reheat for serving.

Variation: On our Spain excursion we tasted a similar soup but thinly sliced chorizo sausage was added. It was delicious. In either version, 1 tablespoon smoked Spanish paprika is a nice addition to the soup.

Brigitte Scherer: Kansas City, Kansas
This is a wonderful soup and everyone has teased me that they would never get the recipe if it weren't for the publishing of Good Friends Great Tastes. *It is one of the most flavorful soups I have ever eaten. My mother was the queen of good soups.*

Lentil Soup

Serves: 8

1 (16-ounce) package dried
lentils
2 slices bacon, diced (1/4-inch
pieces)
1 carrot, thinly sliced
2 stalks celery including tops,
chopped
1 medium garlic clove,
minced or pressed
1 medium onion, finely chopped
3 Knorr Extra Large Beef Bouillon
Cubes
6 cups water
1/4 teaspoon pepper
1/2 teaspoon dried oregano
1 (14.5-ounce) can chopped
tomatoes
1 link good quality kielbasa
sausage, thinly sliced
2 teaspoons red wine vinegar

Rinse lentils and set aside. In a large stockpot or Dutch oven, sauté the bacon with the carrots, celery, garlic, and onion over medium heat until the onion is translucent, about 5 minutes. Add the lentils, bouillon cubes, water, pepper, and oregano. Bring to a boil; reduce heat to simmer. Simmer covered for 1 hour. Add the tomatoes with their juice and simmer another 15 minutes. Add the kielbasa and the red wine vinegar. Continue to simmer to warm the sausage, about 15 minutes. If the soup is too thick for your liking, add a cup more water. Stir to let flavors blend. Further thinning can be done if desired, but add more beef cubes as you dilute with water to keep flavors balanced. This soup freezes well.

Tip: Crusty French bread from the refrigerator section of the grocery store goes well with this soup. Serve the bread with softened butter.

Special Note: A lentil is a tiny, lens-shaped dried seed that has long been used as a meat substitute. The French or European lentil, sold with the seed coat on, has a grayish-brown exterior and a creamy yellow interior. When cooking with beans (legumes) or onions, tomatoes are typically added late in the recipe, once the beans are cooked or onions are translucent, because the acid from the tomato stops the cooking process of these items.

"Don't undermine your worth by comparing yourself with others. It is because we are different that each of us is special."

~Nancye Sims

Restaurant Style Baked Potato Soup   Serves: 10

- cheese grater
- whisk

4 cups diced onions (1/4-inch pieces)
8 tablespoons (1 stick) butter
1/2 cup flour
1/4 cup chicken base powder mixed with 8 cups water
1 1/4 cups instant potato buds
4 cups half-and-half
1/2 teaspoon seasoned salt
1 teaspoon dried basil
Dash of Tabasco red pepper sauce
2 cups diced, baked potatoes or more if you prefer
Grated Cheddar cheese (grate your own)
4 slices bacon, cooked, drained and crumbled
Chopped green onion tops (dark green) for garnish

In a medium skillet over low heat, sauté the onions in butter, 10 to 15 minutes. Do not brown. Add flour to the onions and butter, and cook 4 to 5 minutes to make a roux. Do not brown. In a separate bowl, mix chicken base mixture with the potato buds. Use a whisk to blend until smooth. Add base mixture to roux, mixing slowly with a whisk. Cook 15 to 20 minutes. Whisk in the half-and-half and cook for 10 more minutes. Do not boil. Add salt, basil and red pepper sauce. Before serving, add the 2 cups diced, baked potatoes. Garnish with Cheddar, bacon and green onions.

Tip: A good quality chicken stock or broth may be used in place of the chicken base mixture. Do not dilute with water.

Mary Pat Johnston: Overland Park, Kansas
Mary Pat, my college "running buddy" gave me this recipe years ago when she lived in Cincinnati. It closely resembles the thick restaurant style potato soup. Mary Pat likes to bake her potatoes with the skin on before adding the chunks to the soup.

Creamy Tomato Basil Soup

Serves: 8

• blender or food processor

1 (28-ounce) can chopped, drained tomatoes or
12 Roma tomatoes, peeled and chopped
3 cups tomato juice
2 cups chicken stock or broth
3/4 cup fresh basil
1 1/2 cups heavy cream
3/4 cup (1 1/2 sticks) unsalted butter, cut in chunks
1/2 teaspoon salt
1/2 teaspoon black pepper
Freshly grated Parmigiano-Reggiano cheese (optional)

Combine tomatoes, tomato juice and chicken stock in a large saucepan. Simmer for 30 minutes. Add basil. Slightly cool and transfer in batches to a food processor or blender and process until smooth. Do not get the batch too large or the pressure will cause the processed soup to leak out the lid. Return to the saucepan over low heat. Whisk in cream, butter, salt and pepper. Whisk until the butter is melted and the soup is thoroughly heated. Garnish with freshly grated Parmigiano-Reggiano cheese. This can be made 1 to 2 days ahead.

Tip: To peel tomatoes, drop them in water that has come to a boil. Remove from water after 2 to 3 minutes and they should peel easily. If using canned, the drained liquid can be the base for the juice you need. You will need to add additional tomato juice from a can or jar to get 3 cups.

Special Note: Pomi Tomatoes are shelf-stable fresh tomatoes. They taste great in soups and sauces and one (26.55-ounce) box works well for this soup. They are found with the canned tomatoes but come in a shelf-stable cardboard box.

Cynthia Granados: San Antonio, Texas
Cynthia was part of the original Single Girl's Dallas Dinner Club before she moved away. We love this soup because it is similar to a soup we enjoy from a well-known Dallas Bakery.

Appetizer Brie Soup with Homemade Croutons

Serves: 4

• mesh strainer

2 cups (4 ounces) fresh shiitake mushrooms
4 cups chicken stock or broth
1 (1.1-pound) wheel Brie cheese, rind removed
2 tablespoons unsalted butter
1 large garlic clove, minced or pressed
3 medium carrots, peeled and thinly sliced
2 medium shallots, finely chopped (about 1/4 cup)
2 cups half-and-half
1/2 teaspoon pepper, or more to taste
2 tablespoons dry sherry (optional)

Homemade Croutons
3 tablespoons unsalted butter
3 tablespoons olive oil
3 medium garlic cloves, minced or pressed
1 baguette, crust removed and cut in 1-inch cubes

Preheat the oven to 350°F. Wipe the mushrooms with a damp paper towel to remove excess dirt. Remove the tough part of the mushroom stem and slice. Set mushrooms aside. In a large stockpot or Dutch oven, bring the stock to a boil. (This is an important step.) Stir in the Brie and continue to stir until the Brie is melted. Strain mixture into a bowl and discard the solids. In the same pan, melt the butter. Add the garlic, mushrooms, carrots and shallots. Sauté until shallots are translucent and vegetables are tender, about 5 minutes. Stir in the reserved stock mixture, half-and-half, pepper and sherry. Bring to a boil. Simmer, covered for 10 minutes. Make the croutons by heating butter and oil together in a large sauté pan. Add the garlic and cook until garlic is fragrant. Add the bread cubes and cook over medium heat, tossing to coat. Place croutons on a baking sheet and bake for approximately 5 to 10 minutes until lightly golden and crispy. (If made ahead, store in an airtight container.) The outside should be crisp and golden. Ladle the soup into bowls and top with homemade croutons.

Variation: Fresh baby spinach (approximately 1 cup chopped) may be added to this for a nutritious twist on a decadent soup. For a heartier soup you may add cooked rice.

Special Note: The larger wheels of Brie vary in measurement; a few ounces up or down will not affect the success of the soup. Instead of a chowder consistency, the soup is a thin consistency. Don't skip the croutons; they add wonderful flavor.

Clam Chowder

Serves: 6

• whisk

2 slices bacon, diced (1/4-inch pieces)
1 medium yellow onion, finely chopped
3 tablespoons flour
1 quart half-and-half
1 (10.5-ounce) can cream of celery soup
1 (10.5-ounce) can cream of potato soup
4 medium potatoes, peeled, cubed and cooked
10 ounces chicken or vegetable stock or broth
1 (10-ounce) can whole baby clams, drained
1 teaspoon pepper
1 1/2 teaspoons dried thyme
1 teaspoon dried tarragon (optional)
1 teaspoon *Tony Chachere's Creole Seasoning* or salt, to taste
1 tablespoon dry sherry

In a large stockpot or Dutch oven, cook the bacon and when starting to crisp add the onion. Continue to cook until the onion is translucent, about 5 minutes. Sprinkle the flour over the sautéed onion and bacon, stirring to coat the ingredients. Cook just until the flour is lightly golden. Whisk in the half-and-half slowly, allowing the flour to thicken the mixture. Add all remaining ingredients, except for the sherry, and simmer. Just before serving add the sherry. Serve warm. This recipe is easy and delicious!

Tip: If you would like a slightly thinner chowder, add more chicken broth. For a thicker soup you may increase the flour slightly. You may use fresh tarragon (1 tablespoon) in place of dried.

Gloria Long: Lenexa, Kansas
The Long family lived down the street from us while we were growing up.
When mom passed away, they brought us this delicious soup. It was comforting
and delicious so when I saw Gloria again, I asked for the recipe. There were many
wonderful cooks in our neighborhood.

Steak Soup

Serves: 6

• whisk

2 1/2 pounds round steak, cut into bite-size pieces
1 pound ground beef
9 cups water, divided use
2 tablespoons McCormick Beef Base
1 tablespoon coarsely ground black pepper
4 carrots, peeled and sliced
4 stalks celery, thinly sliced
1 onion, finely chopped
1 1/2 cups frozen mixed vegetables
1 (28-ounce) can chopped tomatoes
1/2 cup (1 stick) butter
1 cup flour
2 teaspoons Kitchen Bouquet Browning and Seasoning Sauce

In a medium skillet over medium heat, brown the round steak. In a separate pan, cook the ground beef and drain off the grease. Combine the meats, 8 cups water, beef base and pepper in a large stockpot or Dutch oven. Add the carrots, celery and onion. Bring to a boil and simmer until steak is done, about 30 minutes. In the last 15 minutes before you are ready to serve, stir in the frozen mixed vegetables and the tomatoes with their juice. (Vegetables should be cooked enough and warmed through to be tender before serving.) Make the soup thickener by melting the butter in a saucepan and slowly whisking in 1 cup flour. Add 1 cup cold water and some hot soup liquid until smooth. When smooth, add to the hot soup. Continue to whisk the soup over the heat to be sure there are no clumps of thickener. The heat will allow the thickening process to occur. Add Kitchen Bouquet to enhance color and flavor.

Special Note: Beef flavor base is usually found in the spice section of the grocery store. This is a great soup to freeze. Allow it to cool completely before freezing.

Brigitte Scherer: Kansas City, Kansas
My mother made this Kansas City restaurant favorite for years and served it with crusty rolls or French bread. This is a hearty soup for a cold winter day.

White Bean Chicken Chili

Serves: 6

4 (8-ounce) boneless, skinless
  chicken breasts
1 tablespoon olive oil
2 medium onions, finely
  chopped
4 medium garlic cloves,
  minced or pressed
2 (4-ounce) cans chopped
  green chiles
2 teaspoons ground cumin
1 1/2 teaspoons dried oregano
1/4 teaspoon cayenne pepper
3 (16-ounce) cans Great Northern
  white beans, undrained
6 cups chicken stock or broth
3 cups grated Monterey Jack
  cheese, divided use
Salt and pepper, to taste
Sour cream (optional)

Cover the chicken with water in a large stockpot or Dutch oven and simmer until tender and no pink remains. Drain and set the chicken aside to cool. Heat the oil in the same pot over medium heat and add the onions, garlic, chiles, cumin, oregano and cayenne pepper. Add the undrained beans and chicken stock and bring to a boil. Cube the chicken and add to the pot. Reduce the heat and add 2 cups of the cheese, and salt and pepper, to taste. Remove from the heat and garnish with the remaining cheese and a dollop of sour cream.

Tip: You may use a small chicken or a precooked deli chicken (rotisserie chicken). When using either chicken, clean the chicken by discarding the skin and bones, reserving the meat. Canellini beans (white kidney beans) could be used in place of Great Northern white beans.

Special Note: Broth and bouillon are similar because they are the result of cooking meat or vegetables in water. Stock is the result of cooking meat, fish or vegetables in water (like broth) but sometimes, additional spices are added. The stock is then strained to remove any impurities. I use stock and broth interchangeably.

Kathryn Farr: Pensacola, Florida
Kathryn has been my friend since Kindergarten and was my college roommate.
She acquired this delicious recipe when she lived in Pensacola, Florida. She passed
this on to me when four of us from high school had a reunion at her place.
This recipe is such a winner!

Chicken Gumbo

Serves: 6

- large cast iron pot
- whisk
- wooden spoon

2 medium onions
7 stalks celery
1/2 green pepper
1 cup olive or peanut oil
1 1/4 cups flour
2 large ripe tomatoes, diced
(1/4-inch pieces)
5 cups chicken stock or broth
2 teaspoons cayenne pepper,
or more, to taste
1 bay leaf
1 tablespoon *Tony Chachere's Creole Seasoning*
1 (10-ounce) can Ro*Tel Diced Tomatoes and Green Chilies
1 teaspoon ground black pepper
1 small garlic bulb, peeled and cloves minced
1 whole chicken for frying (approximately 3 1/2 pounds)
Cooked long grain white or popcorn rice

Finely chop the onions, celery and green pepper. Set aside. Heat the oil on high in a large cast iron pot until it starts to smoke. Shake in the flour while constantly stirring with a wire whisk to create a roux. Continue whisking until this combination becomes the color of a brown paper bag or peanut butter (may be as dark as milk chocolate), but be careful not to burn. Keep the stove fan on as you work. Add the onions, celery and pepper immediately when the roux is the right color. The mixture will cool down and may splatter. Continue stirring using a wooden spoon. Stir until onions are translucent, about 5 minutes. You should still be cooking on high heat. Add the chopped tomatoes and 5 cups of chicken stock. Keep stirring to blend. Add the cayenne pepper, bay leaf, *Tony Chachere's,* Ro*Tel tomatoes, black pepper, garlic, and 1 whole chicken. Continue to cook over medium-high heat or the roux will separate. Cook 1 hour until chicken falls off the bone. Skim off excess fat with a large spoon. Remove the carcass and pull off the meat (discarding skin); return the meat to the pot. Cook rice according to package directions. Serve gumbo spooned over rice in individual bowls.

Variation: *Thinly sliced kielbasa sausage (16 ounces) may be added to gumbo and is highly recommended. This is a family favorite.*

David Gore: Grapevine, Texas
Dave is my "soul" and "food" mate. We spend a couple nights a week in the kitchen cooking together. This is spicy and addicting! Serve with crusty French bread. Dave prefers to use a long grain rice from Texas or Louisiana. Popcorn rice is delicious and smells like popcorn when cooking.

Fresh Tomato, Kalamata and Feta Salad with Shallot Herb Vinaigrette

Serves: 8

- whisk
- vegetable peeler (to peel ginger)

Shallot Herb Vinaigrette
1/3 cup red wine vinegar
2 teaspoons dried oregano
1 tablespoon Dijon mustard
1 medium shallot, finely chopped
  (about 2 tablespoons)
1 large garlic clove, minced
1 teaspoon minced fresh ginger
2/3 cup extra virgin olive oil
Salt and pepper, to taste

Salad
4 medium tomatoes, sliced
  (1/2 inch thick)
1/3 cup pitted kalamata olives
1/3 cup crumbled feta cheese

To make the vinaigrette, combine the first 6 ingredients in a bowl and whisk. While continuing to whisk, gradually add oil in a thin stream. It should be slightly thick. Season the vinaigrette to taste with salt and pepper. The vinaigrette may be made ahead and refrigerated. Arrange tomatoes on either a large platter to pass or on individual salad plates. Sprinkle with olives and feta cheese. Drizzle with desired amount of dressing. Cover and refrigerate remaining vinaigrette. The vinaigrette may be stored for up to a month and used on a variety of salads.

Variation: Substitute cooked and crumbled bacon in place of olives for a different flavor.

Special Note: Virgin olive oil and extra virgin olive oil have been cold pressed, which is a chemical free process that involves only pressure and a lower level of acidity. The lower the acidity the higher the grade of oil. Extra virgin olive oil is the finest and fruitiest of the olive oils and is less acidic. A darker color of the oil means the oil flavor is more intense. Those olive oils that just state "olive oil" on the label are a combination of refined olive oil and virgin or extra virgin olive oil.

Artichoke, Hearts of Palm and Feta Salad with Lemon Vinaigrette

Serves: 8

1 (14-ounce) can artichoke hearts, drained and coarsely chopped
1 (8.8-ounce) jar hearts of palm (about 7 to 8 stalks), sliced
1/4 cup minced green or red onion
2 medium garlic cloves, minced or pressed
2 tablespoons freshly squeezed lemon juice (juice from 1 medium lemon)
1/3 cup extra virgin olive oil
4 ounces (1 cup) crumbled feta cheese
Pepper, to taste
1 1/2 heads romaine lettuce, torn into bite-size pieces
2 fresh tomatoes, cut into wedges for garnish
Kalamata olives, for garnish (optional)

Toss the artichoke hearts with the next 7 ingredients. Chill until ready to serve. When ready to serve, toss the romaine with the artichoke mixture. Garnish each plate with tomato wedges and olives, if desired. This salad has a unique Mediterranean flavor and is one of our favorites.

Variation: Blue cheese may be used instead of feta cheese and if you want dried, crumbled bacon added...go for it!

Special Note: Hearts of palm are the inner edible portion of the stem of the cabbage palm tree and the flavor is reminiscent of an artichoke.

"Happiness in the ancient, noble verse, means self-fulfillment and is given to those who use the fullest whatever talents God or luck or fate bestowed upon them."

~Arthur H. Prince

Chilled Asparagus Salad

Serves: 4

24 asparagus spears, trimmed

Vinaigrette
1 teaspoon salt, plus more to taste
1/2 teaspoon black pepper
1/2 teaspoon minced garlic
1/4 teaspoon sugar
1/2 teaspoon dry mustard
1 teaspoon Creole mustard
1/8 teaspoon cayenne pepper
Dash of Worcestershire sauce
Dash of Tabasco red pepper
  sauce
3 tablespoons red wine vinegar
5 tablespoons extra virgin
  olive oil
5 tablespoons Spectrum
  Grapeseed Oil
2 tablespoons heavy cream
2 teaspoons chopped parsley

Break asparagus where the tough stalk and the tender asparagus meet by bending gently. Blanch asparagus by plunging into boiling water for 3 minutes then into cold or ice water to stop the cooking process. Set aside. To make the vinaigrette, mix all the ingredients together in a jar with a lid. (Canning jars work nicely.) Shake the jar to blend ingredients. Arrange the asparagus on plates and drizzle desired amount of vinaigrette over asparagus (refrigerate remainder). If making several days ahead of time, do not add cream. Add cream to the vinaigrette just before serving.

Tip: A dash is considered to be somewhere between 1/16 and 1/8 teaspoon and is accomplished by adding the ingredient (usually a liquid) to food with a quick, downward stroke of the hand.

Special Note: Like many herbs and botanicals, there is a very small amount of oil in grapeseed and it is difficult, expensive and impractical to extract using typical expeller extraction systems. That is why virtually all grapeseed oil is chemically extracted. Spectrum's Grapeseed Oil is produced using the most benign method available—alcohol extraction—and then it is ultra-refined to assure that no alcohol residue is left behind. It is healthier to digest grapeseed oil than canola, corn or vegetable oil.

Hearts of Palm, Artichoke and Olive Salad

Serves: 6

• whisk

Vinaigrette
3 tablespoons red wine vinegar
1/2 teaspoon Dijon mustard
1/2 teaspoon salt
1/2 teaspoon pepper
1/3 cup extra virgin olive oil

Salad
1 (14-ounce) can hearts of
  palm, drained and sliced
1 (14-ounce) can artichoke
  hearts, drained and sliced
1/2 cup chopped green pepper
1/2 cup chopped red pepper
10 pimento-stuffed green
  olives, halved
10 black pitted kalamata olives,
  halved
6 leafs from a head of Boston or
  Bibb lettuce
Quartered hard-boiled eggs
  (optional)
Halved cherry tomatoes (optional)

To make the vinaigrette, whisk the first 4 ingredients together. While continuing to whisk, add oil in a thin stream. Vinaigrette will thicken slightly. Toss the first 6 salad ingredients with desired amount of the vinaigrette. Chill 1 hour before serving. To serve, place salad on a leaf of Boston or Bibb lettuce and top with hard-boiled egg and tomatoes, if using. The vinaigrette may be made ahead and refrigerated.

Variation: Crumbled blue cheese or feta is good sprinkled on top of this salad. For a unique presentation for a picnic, serve the salad in hollowed out red, green or yellow peppers. The vinaigrette is delicious for marinating vegetables such as yellow squash, zucchini, carrots, broccoli and cauliflower. Create your own combination. Boston, Bibb and Butterhead are the same lettuce.

Donna Edwards: Dallas, Texas
Donna made this salad at one of the very first Dinner Club gatherings, and it has been a favorite ever since. It is elegant, colorful and simple. What more could a busy gourmet ask for?

Spinach Salad with Balsamic Maple Vinaigrette and Sugared Pecans

Servings: 8

• wax paper, foil or parchment paper

Balsamic Maple Vinaigrette
3 tablespoons balsamic vinegar
2 tablespoons pure maple syrup
1 medium shallot, finely chopped
  (about 2 tablespoons)
2/3 cup extra virgin olive oil
1/8 teaspoon salt
1/4 teaspoon pepper

Sugared Pecans
3 tablespoons sugar
1 1/2 tablespoons water
1/4 teaspoon salt
1/8 teaspoon pepper
1 cup pecan halves

Salad
8 cups fresh baby spinach
6 slices bacon, cooked, drained
  and crumbled (optional)
1/3 cup diced (1/4-inch pieces)
  or thinly sliced red onion
1/3 cup dried cranberries or
  cherries
1/3 cup blue cheese or feta
  cheese
Freshly ground pepper, to taste

To make the vinaigrette, mix all the ingredients in a jar with a tight fitting lid and shake vigorously. For the sugared pecans, heat the sugar, water, salt and pepper together in a small saucepan until bubbly. Add the pecans and toss to coat. Cook over medium-low heat until coated and caramelized. (They will become shiny and the outside and coating will begin to harden.) Once they start cooking, they need to be constantly stirred or they will burn. Once the pan begins to smoke and pecans are fragrant, place the pecans on wax paper to cool. (If making ahead, store in a sealable plastic bags or airtight container.) Toss the desired amount of the vinaigrette with the spinach, bacon, red onion, cranberries and blue cheese. Top with pecans and grind fresh pepper over the top, if desired. Refrigerate remaining vinaigrette.

Tip: We cook a whole week's worth of bacon by using the "hands free" method. Preheat the oven to 350°F. Line a jelly roll pan with foil. Place as many slices of bacon as will fit on the pan. Bake 25 to 35 minutes depending on the thickness of the bacon and desired doneness.

Special Note: Glass canning jars with lids are useful for storing your homemade vinaigrette. Identify the vinaigrette or dressing by labeling the outside with a canning label.

Variation: *Red leaf lettuce or any combination of lettuces may be used in place of spinach. Almonds and walnuts are also delicious sugared. For color and texture, add mandarin oranges, unpeeled slices of Red Delicious apples, or diced pear, if desired. Pear, champagne or raspberry vinegar may be substituted for the balsamic vinegar. This dressing made with balsamic also pairs well with greens mixed with tomatoes, toasted pine nuts, diced red onion and feta or blue cheese.*

Spinach Salad with Prosciutto, Capers and Cornichons

Serves: 4

• cheese grater

Spinach Salad
1 (9-ounce) bag baby spinach or arugula
4 thin slices prosciutto, finely chopped
2 hard-boiled eggs
2 tablespoons capers, drained and rinsed
2 tablespoons minced cornichons
2 tablespoons chopped fresh chives
6 cherry tomatoes, quartered

Lemon Dressing
1 1/2 tablespoons freshly squeezed lemon juice (juice from 1/2 medium lemon)
1/2 teaspoon salt
1/4 teaspoon black pepper
3 tablespoons extra virgin olive oil

Place the spinach (or arugula) in a large bowl. Add the prosciutto. Use the cheese grater to grate the hard-boiled eggs. Set aside. In a separate bowl, make the dressing by mixing all the ingredients together. Add the capers, cornichons, chives and tomatoes to the greens. Toss with desired amount of dressing. Dressing may be made ahead and refrigerated.

Special Note: Cornichon is French for "gherkin." Cornichons are crisp, tart pickles made from tiny gherkin cucumbers. If it is easier to chop the prosciutto with kitchen shears, then do so.

"Know Your Passion, Show Your Passion"
"Your interests, wishes, and happiness determine what you actually do well, more than intelligence, aptitudes or skills do."

~*Richard Bolles*

Southwest Caesar Salad with Homemade Croutons

Serves: 4

- cheese grater
- whisk, blender or food processor

Dressing

1/2 cup Hellmann's or Best Foods Real Mayonnaise
1 1/2 tablespoons chicken broth
1 tablespoon less sodium soy sauce
1 tablespoon freshly squeezed lemon or lime juice (juice from 1/2 medium lemon or lime)
1 1/2 teaspoons minced canned chipotle chiles in adobo sauce
1 teaspoon brown sugar
Salt and pepper, to taste

Homemade Croutons

3 tablespoons olive oil
3 tablespoons unsalted butter
3 medium garlic cloves, minced or pressed
1/4 teaspoon *Tony Chachere's Creole Seasoning*
1/4 teaspoon dried basil
1 baguette, crust removed and cut in 1-inch cubes

Salad

1 large head romaine lettuce, torn into bite-size pieces
2 medium tomatoes, seeded and diced (1/4-inch pieces)
1/2 cup frozen corn kernels, thawed and drained
4 tablespoons freshly grated Parmigiano-Reggiano cheese

Preheat the oven to 350°F. To make the dressing, whisk mayonnaise, chicken broth, soy sauce, lemon juice, minced chiles and brown sugar in a medium bowl to blend (or use a blender or food processor). Season to taste with salt and pepper. Dressing may be prepared a day ahead. Cover and refrigerate. To make croutons, heat oil and butter together in a large skillet. Add garlic and spices. Add bread cubes and cook over medium heat, tossing to coat. Put croutons on a baking sheet and bake for 5 to 10 minutes until lightly golden and crispy. Check after 5 minutes since oven temperatures vary slightly. Store cooled croutons in airtight container if making ahead. To make the salad, mix lettuce, tomatoes and corn in a large bowl. Add 2 tablespoons Parmigiano-Reggiano cheese and desired amount of croutons. Toss salad with desired amount of dressing. Sprinkle with remaining 2 tablespoons cheese and serve.

Special Notes: Adobo is a paste that is made from ground chiles, herbs and vinegar. Canned chipotle chiles are smoked jalapeños in adobo sauce. They are inexpensive and usually found on the aisle with other Hispanic foods. Freeze leftover adobos individually in sealable plastic snack bags.

Baked Goat Cheese Salad with Herb Vinaigrette

Servings: 4

• strainer
• whisk

Herb Vinaigrette
3 sprigs (2 tablespoons of leaves)
  fresh rosemary
3 sprigs (1 tablespoon of leaves)
  fresh thyme
3 sprigs (1/3 cup of leaves)
  fresh oregano
1/2 cup extra virgin olive oil
1/2 teaspoon Creole mustard
3 tablespoons balsamic vinegar
1/4 teaspoon salt
1/4 teaspoon freshly ground
  pepper

Salad
1 (11-ounce) log plain goat
  cheese
Bread crumbs
4 cups (7 ounces) mixed greens
  (such as gourmet salad mix and
  romaine)

Preheat the oven to 350°F. To make the herb vinaigrette, combine the rosemary, thyme, oregano and olive oil in a saucepan over medium-high heat. Bring to a boil, remove from the heat and let cool. Strain the oil and discard the herbs. This may be made ahead. Add the mustard, vinegar, salt and pepper to the seasoned oil, whisking with a wire whisk. Cut cheese log into 8 rounds on a plate and chill 15 minutes until firm. Gently roll the goat cheese in the bread crumbs to coat them. Place them on a baking sheet. Bake 10 minutes and set aside. To make the salad, drizzle lettuce with the desired amount of the vinaigrette and toss to coat. Evenly divide the salad on 4 salad plates. Serve each with 2 goat cheese rounds, delicately placed on plates.

Tip: The goat cheese rounds are great in other salads with vinegar, oil and spice combinations. Olive oil may be used instead of seasoned oil and the goat cheese rounds can be rolled in pecans or walnuts before baking.

Julie Lancaster: Grapevine, Texas
Julie and I met through our good friend Lynne. She invited us for a great dinner by her pool and made this salad from fresh herbs in her garden. Julie changed the mustard from Dijon to Creole and changed the greens from a mix of radicchio, Bibb, and watercress to romaine and mesclun. Julie's recipe came from Paula Lambert. Paula is the founder of the Mozzarella Company in Dallas.

Bibb Lettuce with Feta, Sautéed Apples and Pears with Red Wine Vinaigrette

Serves: 6

• whisk

Red Wine Vinaigrette
1/2 cup sugar
1/2 cup red wine vinegar
1 teaspoon Dijon mustard
1/2 teaspoon salt
1 teaspoon celery seed (optional)
2 small garlic cloves, minced
   or pressed
1 cup extra virgin olive oil

Salad
1/4 cup coarsely chopped
   pecans
1 red-skinned apple
1 mildly soft red pear with
   skin on
1 tablespoon butter
1 head Bibb or Boston lettuce
1 cup (4 ounces) crumbled
   feta cheese

Preheat the oven to 350°F. To make the red wine vinaigrette, heat sugar and vinegar in a saucepan until the sugar is dissolved. Remove from heat and whisk in the next 4 ingredients. While continuing to whisk, slowly add oil in a thin stream. Continue to whisk to thicken slightly. Serve immediately or refrigerate until ready to serve. To make the salad, toast the pecans on a baking sheet for 3 to 4 minutes. Cut apples and pears in 1/4-inch slices. Do not peel. Sauté the pears and apples in melted butter, until they start to soften slightly. Wash lettuce and tear into bite-size pieces. Toss the lettuce with feta, fruits, nuts, and as much vinaigrette as desired. You will have leftover dressing that will keep nicely in any sealed jar in the refrigerator. The dressing can be used on any green salad and can be refrigerated in an airtight container for up to 1 month. Bring to room temperature and whisk before using.

Variation: Blue cheese can be substituted for feta. Raspberry vinegar may be substituted for red wine vinegar. Strawberries or mandarin oranges can replace the apple and pear. Thinly sliced red or green onions are also a nice addition.

Special Note: Use ingredients like sunflower seeds, raisins, dried cranberries, and nuts, like cashews or toasted pine nuts in salad. Nuts are toasted to bring the oils to the surface and make them more flavorful. Avoid acidic things like tomatoes when using dried fruits in salad.

Orange and Romaine Salad with Lime Vinaigrette and Sugared Pecans

Serves: 6

- wax paper, foil or parchment paper
- whisk

Salad
1 head romaine lettuce
1 large red onion, thinly sliced
2 kiwis, peeled and sliced
1 (11-ounce) can mandarin
   orange sections
1 star fruit (carambola (optional))
3/4 cup (3 ounces) crumbled
   blue cheese

Lime Vinaigrette
1/4 cup freshly squeezed lime
   juice (juice from 2 medium
   limes)
1 tablespoon honey
3 tablespoons red wine vinegar
3 tablespoons orange marmalade
1/2 cup olive oil
Salt and pepper, to taste

Sugared Pecans
3 tablespoons sugar
1 1/2 tablespoons water
1/4 teaspoon salt
1/8 teaspoon pepper
1 cup pecan halves

To make the salad, tear the lettuce into bite-size pieces and place in a salad bowl with the onion. To make the lime vinaigrette, combine the lime, honey, vinegar and marmalade with a whisk. Slowly add oil in a thin stream as you continue to whisk ingredients. Salt and pepper to taste. To make the sugared pecans, heat the sugar water, salt and pepper together in a skillet over medium heat until it begins to bubble. Add the pecans and toss to coat. Continue to cook over medium-low heat, stirring the nuts until they are shiny and begin to caramelize. You will feel the mixture begin to thicken and become sticky. Once this begins to occur, turn the nuts onto wax paper, foil or parchment paper. (The total cook time is approximately 5 minutes.) These may be made ahead and stored in an airtight container once cooled. Toss the lettuce and onions the with desired amount of vinaigrette and gently mix in the kiwi and oranges. Arrange the star fruit on the plate or on top of the salad and sprinkle with blue cheese and sugared pecans. Store leftover vinaigrette in a glass jar in the refrigerator for up to 1 month.

Special Note: Carambola do not need to be peeled and once ripe can be stored in the refrigerator for up to a week. Carambola (often called star fruit) is a wonderful garnish when cut crosswise 1/4 inch thick. It is yellow and resembles a star. It tastes good and looks festive on cheese trays, desserts and in salads.

Mixed Field Greens with Stilton, Grapes and Honey Vinaigrette

Serves: 6

• blender or food processor

Salad
1/4 cup sliced or slivered almonds, toasted
6 cups red leaf lettuce or other variety lettuce
1 1/2 cups (2.5 ounces) mixed gourmet salad mix
20 seedless red grapes
1 apple
1/3 cup crumbled Stilton or blue cheese

Honey Vinaigrette
1/4 cup coarsely chopped yellow onion
1/4 cup honey
1/4 cup white wine vinegar
2 teaspoons Tabasco red pepper sauce
1/2 cup Spectrum Grapeseed Oil

Preheat the oven to 350°F. For the salad, toast the almonds on a baking sheet for 3 to 4 minutes in the oven. Wash the lettuce and tear into bite-size pieces. If preparing ahead, wrap the washed lettuce in paper towels and store in the refrigerator until ready to use. To make the honey vinaigrette, put the first 4 ingredients in a blender or food processor. Process the vinaigrette until smooth. Slowly add oil in a thin stream through the top hole while the blender or processor is running. Continue processing. The mixture will thicken slightly. Shortly before you are ready to serve, halve the grapes and core the apple. Cut unpeeled apple into wedges and dice (1/4-inch pieces). Toss desired amount of dressing with salad greens, grapes, apples, cheese and almonds. Dressing may be made ahead and stored in refrigerator.

Tip: We sometimes prefer to compose salads, which means you toss the lettuce with the dressing and then you top the salad with all the other delicious components. This way the flavor components do not get lost in the bottom of the bowl and the salad is visually more appealing.

Special Note: Allow approximately 1 1/4 to 1 1/2 cups (approximately 2 ounces) of slightly packed lettuce per person, per serving as a side dish. Tart apples such as Granny Smith or Fuji are best in this salad. Mixed gourmet salad mix is typically a combination of young salad greens that add color and texture when mixed with other greens.

Artichoke Chicken Salad

Serves: 8

2/3 cup pecans
2 cups cooked, finely diced
chicken (1/4-inch pieces)
1 (14-ounce) can artichoke hearts,
drained and finely chopped
3 tablespoons Hellmann's or
Best Foods Real Mayonnaise
3 tablespoons sour cream
1/4 cup minced green onion
(white and pale green
part only)
1 garlic clove, minced or pressed
1/2 teaspoon salt
1/2 teaspoon pepper
Fresh parsley, minced (optional)

Preheat the oven to 350°F to toast the pecans, or toast them in a medium skillet turning frequently to prevent burning. Toast until nuts are fragrant, approximately 4 minutes. Mix the chicken with the toasted nuts and remaining ingredients. Chill a minimum of 5 hours. Serve on your favorite sliced bread for a delicious sandwich.

Tip: This filling is wonderful for an appetizer. Purchase prepared phyllo tart shells (found in freezer section) or small tart shells from the cracker section and bake if needed, according to package directions. Fill the shells with chicken salad and sprinkle with fresh parsley.

Rena Marson: Denver, Colorado
Rena and I met at a home improvement store where I was doing a demo.
Our paths continued to cross and we started the Remarkable Women group together.
This is a group of interesting women we have met over the past few years. We invite
them to come cook with us once a month, and each month the group is a different
group of women. Rena is a former Colleyville, Texas resident who now resides with
her partner, Stone, in Denver.

Asian Slaw with Peanut Dressing

Serves: 4

• whisk

Dressing
1/4 cup bottled Thai peanut sauce
(such as House of Tsang)
1/4 cup Hellmann's or Best
 Foods Real Mayonnaise

Slaw
1 (16-ounce) bag coleslaw
1/2 cup diced red pepper
 (1/4-inch pieces)
3 large green onions, minced
 (white and pale green
 part only)

To make the dressing, whisk the peanut sauce and mayonnaise together in a small bowl. Combine the salad ingredients in a large bowl and toss with the dressing. You can chill this a couple hours or serve immediately. See the variations to add color and texture.

Variations: For a tasty main course, add 4 grilled chicken breasts (2 pounds), or 1 pound sautéed shrimp.

Cilantro (1/2 cup) stems removed, cucumber (1/2 cup) unpeeled, diced and chopped, and shelled peanuts or cashews (1/2 cup) add great texture and taste to the salad. (Nuts should be added just before serving.)

If all ingredients are not in supply, the slaw with just the dressing is still a wonderful side dish especially for a casual meal like pork chops or hamburgers.

In our family, slaw is a base for many salads. Start with the bag of coleslaw, add 2 hard-boiled eggs, an avocado, cooked shrimp (1 pound) and mayonnaise to moisten the salad. Season with Tony Chachere's Creole Seasoning. This is a delicious recipe from my dear friend Melissa Weikel from Topeka, Kansas.

Oriental Cabbage Slaw

Serves: 10

Slaw
1/4 cup slivered almonds
1/4 cup chopped, shelled
  cocktail peanuts
1/4 cup shelled sunflower seeds
2 tablespoons sesame seeds
3 tablespoons butter
2 (3-ounce) packages oriental
  ramen noodles, uncooked
  (spice packs will be used)
1 head Napa cabbage, cored
  and shredded
8 green onions, finely chopped
  (white and pale green
  part only)

Vinaigrette
1/2 cup sesame oil
1/4 cup white wine vinegar
1/3 cup sugar
3 tablespoons less sodium soy
  sauce
1 teaspoon crushed red pepper
4 medium garlic cloves, minced or
  pressed

To make the slaw, sauté the nuts and sesame seeds in the butter in a small skillet until lightly toasted. Crush the ramen noodles and add to the skillet along with the spice packets. Toss to coat. Let the mixture cool. The ramen and nut mixture may be made earlier in the day and stored in an airtight container. To make the vinaigrette, mix all the ingredients together in a glass jar. Shake vigorously and refrigerate. Mix together shredded cabbage, green onions and sautéed ramen and nut mixture in a large bowl. Cabbage may be shredded and mixed with onions and refrigerated until ready to serve. Shake the vinaigrette to remix and toss the desired amount with the cabbage, nuts, seeds and noodles. Serve immediately.

Variation: This vinaigrette can be used on a green salad as well. Cashews may be substituted for cocktail peanuts. For those that like cilantro, 1/2 cup may be added. Add shredded chicken for a complete meal.

Special Note: Napa cabbage is cream colored with celadon tipped leaves. It is an elongated, not round head. A head will weigh approximately 2 pounds. Bagged coleslaw may be substituted.

Vicki Morgan: Little Rock, Arkansas
When Vicki, a friend since junior high school, gave me this recipe, it sent me on a quest for the best. I had variations of this recipe from Betty Krenger of Abilene, Kansas, and Kathy Anderson of Kansas City, Missouri, so I took the best ingredients from them and created my own version. It is different and a tasty side dish with Asian-spiced fish, chicken or grilled meats.

Thai Cucumber Salad

Serves: 4

Rice Wine Vinaigrette
3 tablespoons rice wine vinegar
1/4 cup sugar
1/2 teaspoon salt
1/3 cup hot water

Salad
3 cucumbers, sliced in thick slices and quartered (unpeeled)
1 cup finely chopped or thinly sliced red or green onion

In a saucepan, mix together the vinaigrette ingredients and heat until sugar dissolves. Allow to cool. Toss the cucumber and onion together. Stir and pour the vinaigrette over the cucumber and onion mixture. Serve on individual plates. This salad is crunchy and refreshing!

Tip: Flavors penetrate the cucumbers if you can toss the salad and let it stand at room temperature for 2 hours before serving.

Variation: Four tablespoons chopped jalapeño peppers with their seeds can be added to the salad if you love the heat of Thai! We like the sweetness of the dressing to accompany our hot dishes, such as Thai Chicken Curry, page 193, and Asian Peanut Chicken, page 194.

Warm German Potato Salad

Serves: 6

4 slices bacon
3/4 cup finely chopped onion
1 (10.75-ounce) can cream of celery soup
1/4 cup water
2 tablespoons white vinegar
1/2 teaspoon sugar
1/8 teaspoon pepper
2 (14.5-ounce) cans whole potatoes, drained and sliced
1/4 cup chopped fresh parsley

Cook the bacon in a small skillet until crispy, about 8 minutes. Remove from the skillet, reserving the drippings. Set the bacon aside until cool and then crumble. Cook the onion in bacon drippings until translucent, about 5 minutes. Blend in the soup, water, vinegar, sugar and pepper. Heat, stirring occasionally. Add potatoes, parsley and crumbled bacon. Simmer for 5 minutes. Serve warm. This recipe can be made ahead, refrigerated and reheated.

Brigitte Scherer: Kansas City, Kansas
This is another Scherer family favorite. My mother served this delicious potato salad with bratwurst or Reuben sandwiches. Reuben's are best made with thin-sliced deli pastrami, Swiss cheese, sauerkraut (rinse the sauerkraut before heating), with Thousand Island dressing as the spread. Butter the outside of your rye, pile the ingredients on, and toast in a skillet on both sides! Yum!

Picnic Potato Salad

Serves: 12

Potato Salad
3 large hard-boiled eggs, peeled and diced (1/4-inch pieces)
5 pounds red-skinned potatoes, peeled and diced (1/4- to 1/2-inch pieces)
6 tablespoons sweet pickle relish
1/2 large red onion, diced (1/4-inch pieces)
3 green onions, finely chopped (white and pale green part only)
7 slices bacon cooked, drained and crumbled
1 (8-ounce) can water chestnuts, drained and chopped
4 tablespoons McCormick Salad Supreme (found in spice section)
4 teaspoons *Tony Chachere's Creole Seasoning* (or more to taste)

Dressing
1 cup Hellmann's or Best Foods Real Mayonnaise
3 tablespoons Creole mustard
2 teaspoons red wine vinegar
1 tablespoon sugar

To hard boil eggs, put eggs in a saucepan and completely cover with cold water (2 inches above eggs). Cover the pan and bring water to boil (takes about 7 minutes over high heat). Turn off heat immediately and remove pan from heat. Let eggs stand, covered, 18 to 20 minutes. Plunge eggs into cold water. Crack the shells while rinsing under water and peel. For the potato salad, cover the potatoes with cold water in a large stockpot or Dutch oven. Boil until tender when pierced with a fork, approximately 15 to 20 minutes, depending on the size. Drain and cool slightly. To make the dressing, mix together the mayonnaise, mustard, vinegar and sugar. Set aside. For the salad, add all the other ingredients to the potatoes and then stir in the dressing mixture. Mix gently. Refrigerate.

Tip: This is best if it sits in the refrigerator for 24 hours so flavors blend.

> *"Cooking is like love. It should be entered into with abandon or not at all."*
>
> ~*Harriet Van Horne*

Broccoli Salad with Nuts and Raisins

Serves: 6

Salad
1 head broccoli or 2 broccoli
  crowns
1 cup raisins or dried cranberries
1/2 cup finely chopped red onion
3/4 cup shelled sunflower seeds
8 slices bacon, cooked, drained
  and crumbled

Dressing
2 tablespoons red wine vinegar
1 cup Hellmann's or Best Foods
  Real Mayonnaise
1/2 cup sugar

To make the salad, chop the broccoli into small pieces and mix with the next 4 ingredients. To make the dressing, mix all the ingredients together in a separate bowl. Toss the desired amount of dressing with the salad ingredients. The dressing may be made ahead and refrigerated until ready to use. Leftover dressing may be refrigerated for 2 weeks.

Variation: I have had this with salted peanuts instead of sunflower seeds and it was good! Broccoli slaw in the bag is a good substitute for heads of broccoli.

Chopped Greek Salad

Serves: 12

Salad
2 (10-ounce) bags hearts of
  romaine, chopped (or two heads
  romaine)
1 cucumber, peeled and diced in
  1/4-inch cubes
1/3 cup diced (1/8-inch) red onion
1/2 cup finely chopped black olives
6 cherry tomatoes, quartered
1/3 cup crumbled feta cheese

Dressing
2 tablespoons freshly squeezed
  lemon juice (juice from one
  medium lemon)
2 tablespoons white wine vinegar
2 tablespoons Cavender's Greek
  Seasoning
1/2 cup extra virgin olive oil

Toss all the salad ingredients together. Whisk the dressing ingredients together. When ready to serve, toss the desired amount of dressing with the salad and serve. Refrigerate any remaining dressing.

Amy Haney: Bedford, Texas
Our dear friends, Joe (the books photographer) and Jeanne Graber, introduced Amy and her husband, Chad, to us. The six of us travel to the Graber's lake house together and each couple is responsible for planning a meal or a course. Quality is the key requirement. This is definitely a group of good friends with great tastes!

Black-Eyed Pea Salad

Serves: 8

2 (15.5-ounce) cans black-eyed peas, drained and rinsed
1 (15.25-ounce) can corn, drained
1 1/2 cup zesty Italian dressing
1 medium bell pepper, chopped (any color)
1/2 cup minced fresh parsley
2 medium garlic cloves, minced or pressed
1 (14-ounce) can diced tomatoes
1 fresh tomato, diced (1/4-inch pieces)
Fresh cilantro, to taste

Mix all the ingredients together and marinate for 24 hours.

Variations: Tomatoes now have many seasonings. The jalapeño pepper/tomato combination may be used or Ro*Tel tomatoes with green chiles may be substituted. Black beans may be substituted, and the salad could be garnished with diced avocado. This salad may be used as a dip for tortilla chips as well.

Donna Edwards: Plano, Texas
Donna and her husband Gaylon entertain our Dinner Club quite often. Donna made this when we got together in the summer for Mexican food. Ashton Hampel, Donna's niece, re-created this combination with the two of them combining their own tastes for a Dinner Club poolside party with grilled meats.

Spicy Vinaigrette

Serves: 6

• blender or food processor

1 garlic clove
1 tablespoon orange juice
3 tablespoons red wine vinegar
1/2 teaspoon salt
1/2 teaspoon chili powder
1 tablespoon Dijon mustard
1/2 cup Spectrum Grapeseed
   Oil

Blend the first 6 ingredients in a blender or food processor. Blend on stir setting, and slowly add oil through the top hole in blender or through the feed tube on the processor until vinaigrette thickens slightly. Make ahead and serve with your favorite combination of lettuce and exotic ingredients!

Variations: Delicate ingredients should be used as a garnish on top of the tossed salad. mandarin oranges, avocado, and thin-sliced red onion rings dress up the top of this salad. Other combinations include lettuce tossed with diced water chestnuts, a tablespoon drained and rinsed capers and mandarin oranges; or a favorite, blue cheese, Sugared Pecans (page 126) and red onion.

Special Note: Oil is the last thing added to a salad dressing that you are trying to emulsify or thicken. Oil is added slowly in a thin stream at the same time as mixing rapidly either with a blender, processor, or whisk. It is usually done with ingredients such as vinegar and oil that cannot normally combine smoothly. This process disperses and suspends minute droplets of one liquid throughout the other to create a thick and satiny texture.

Mary Hutchinson: Topeka, Kansas
Mary was one of the original members of the "Single Girl's Dinner Club."
We had this salad dressing at one of our first Dinner Club gatherings in Dallas.
Mary cooked for us in her highrise apartment. Life has changed. She lives in Topeka with her husband, Steve, and has three children. Despite a busy schedule, Mary still enjoys cooking and was recognized as "Cook of the Week" in the Topeka Capital-Journal Food Section *several years ago.*

Balsamic Vinaigrette Dressing

Makes: 1 cup

• whisk

1/3 cup balsamic vinegar
1 teaspoon Dijon mustard
1 tablespoon sugar
1/2 teaspoon cracked black pepper, or more to taste
1/4 teaspoon salt
1 large garlic clove, minced or pressed
2/3 cup extra virgin olive oil

Whisk together the first 6 ingredients. While continuing to whisk, add the oil in a thin stream to thicken. Adjust the seasonings as needed. Make ahead and refrigerate.

Tips: Spices such as oregano and dried basil may be used to create variations of this dressing. When working to emulate a vinaigrette recipe you have tasted, the proportions typically are one part vinegar to two parts oil. Adjust to your palate as needed.

Special Note: Balsamic vinegar is made from the Italian white Trebbiano grape and is aged in barrels to give it a dark color and pungent sweetness. For a delicious and colorful salad, balsamic vinegar can be used drizzled over mozzarella and tomatoes and sprinkled with fresh chopped basil and olive oil.

Linda Gore: Colleyville, Texas
Linda, my mother-in-law, passed this recipe on to me and we make it frequently. Linda and her husband David spend the hot summer months at a resort they own in Almont, Colorado. They frequently entertain their daughters, Susan and Peri and their families, as well as many visitors.

Creamy Blue Cheese Dressing

Serves: 8

• whisk

1 cup Hellmann's or Best Foods
Real Mayonnaise
1 cup buttermilk
1 1/2 tablespoons freshly
squeezed lemon juice (juice
from 1/2 medium lemon)
1 teaspoon Worcestershire
sauce
2 medium garlic cloves,
minced or pressed
1 medium shallot, finely
chopped (about 2
tablespoons)
1/2 teaspoon black pepper
1 1/2 cups blue cheese
1/4 teaspoon *Tony Chachere's
Creole Seasoning*, or more
to taste
3/4 teaspoon Herbes de Provence
(optional)

In a bowl, whisk together the mayonnaise with
the next 6 ingredients. Stir the cheese into the
mixture. Add *Tony Chachere's* and the Herbes
de Provence. Refrigerate until ready to use. It
thickens nicely as it chills.

Tip: If you do not have buttermilk, you can take
1 cup milk and combine with 1 tablespoon
fresh lemon juice or vinegar. Give it about 5
minutes to thicken.

*Variations: Serve with a combination of romaine,
thinly sliced red onion, beets and toasted walnuts.*

*For a luncheon salad, combine romaine with
grilled chicken, toasted pine nuts, tomatoes,
avocados and diced red onion (1/4-inch pieces).*

*Other combinations for salad toppings include
hearts of palm, artichokes or pistachios.*

*For a quick and tasty salad, simply toss dressing
with a package of coleslaw. Add red onion or red
peppers or both for some color.*

*Replace the blue cheese with feta cheese. The
feta version is super with dried, chopped dates,
baby spinach and finely diced red onion (1/4-
inch pieces).*

*Serve the feta or blue cheese version as a dip
for crudités or chips!*

*Make the creamy dressing and leave out the
cheese. The creamy dressing appeals to children
and you can just sprinkle the cheese over the
salad for the adults.*

Creamy Chili Spiced Dressing

Serves: 8

1 cup buttermilk
1 cup Hellmann's or Best Foods Real Mayonnaise
1 tablespoon freshly squeezed lime juice (juice from 1/2 medium lime)
3/4 teaspoon chili powder
1/2 teaspoon dry mustard
1 jalapeño, seeded and minced
1 teaspoon *Tony Chachere's Creole Seasoning*

Combine all the ingredients in a medium bowl and use as a dressing for lettuce or coleslaw. Make ahead and refrigerate until ready to use. Match ingredients like black beans (rinsed and drained), diced avocado, fresh chopped cilantro, green onion and corn (or red pepper) for a colorful salad.

Variations: This dressing makes a great spread for sandwiches and burgers or as a dip for chips. Add 1 pound of cooked, chopped shrimp and you have a spicy shrimp dip. Yum!

Special Note: Organic black beans have far less sodium than other black beans. Check the label before buying. Jalapeños vary in heat intensity so you may use just half of one to start.

Creamy Champagne Vinaigrette

Makes: 2 cups

 • blender or food processor

1/3 cup sugar
1/3 cup champagne vinegar
1/4 teaspoon celery seed
1/2 teaspoon black pepper
1 tablespoon Dijon mustard
1/2 teaspoon *Tony Chachere's Creole Seasoning*
3/4 cup coarsely chopped white or yellow onion
3/4 cup extra virgin olive oil

In a blender or food processor, combine the first 7 ingredients. In a slow stream with the motor running (on the lowest setting), slowly drizzle in olive oil and blend until combined. The dressing will be slightly thick. If desired, make ahead and refrigerate until ready to use.

Tip: This is delicious over a chilled shrimp, lettuce, tomato, diced red onion and avocado salad or about any combination you can dream up! Lettuce with a fruit like strawberries or mandarin oranges and a pungent cheese like blue or feta pair nicely as well.

Balsamic Apricot Vinaigrette

Makes: 1 cup

• blender or food processor

1/2 cup canned apricots, drained
1/3 cup balsamic vinegar
1/4 cup honey
2 teaspoons Dijon mustard
1 garlic clove
1 teaspoon dried Italian seasoning
1/4 teaspoon salt
1/4 teaspoon pepper
1 tablespoon extra virgin olive oil

In a blender or food processor, combine apricots, vinegar, honey, mustard, garlic and seasonings; blend until smooth. With motor running, slowly drizzle in olive oil until combined. If desired, make ahead and refrigerate until ready to use.

Tip: Combine this dressing with lettuce, Sugared Pecans (page 126), diced apple or pears, cranberries, diced red onion, blue cheese and crumbled cooked bacon, if desired.

Special Note: Salad is meant to be dressed lightly with a salad dressing. Do not drench. If you have any doubt that you put enough on, offer additional dressing in a small glass bowl with a spoon. Toss salad just before serving unless otherwise stated or greens will be limp. Some vinaigrette dressings will solidify due to the temperature in the refrigerator and the type of oil used. If this happens, run warm water over the jar to melt the buildup and whisk.

Hoisin Vinaigrette

Serves: 4

- whisk
- vegetable peeler (to peel ginger)

2 tablespoons hoisin sauce
1 tablespoon rice wine vinegar
1 teaspoon minced fresh ginger
3 tablespoons plus 1 teaspoon
  extra virgin olive oil
2 teaspoons sesame oil

In a bowl, whisk together the first 3 ingredients. In a thin stream, drizzle the oils slowly into the mixture. Serve with any combination of lettuce or spinach. If desired, make vinaigrette ahead and refrigerate until ready to use.

Tips: This is delicious and works best with Asian-inspired menus such as the Asian Peanut Chicken (page 194) and Hoisin Marinated Pork (page 169). Dried ground ginger can be used in place of fresh (1/8 teaspoon).

Variations: Various lettuce, romaine or even cabbage slaw, can be the base of the salad, and additional ingredients like dried cranberries, toasted almonds or sugared nuts (page 126), minced green or finely diced red onions and red peppers add additional color and texture. Salted cashews and shelled sunflower seeds may be added, if desired. We even smoked a duck breast and sliced it over the top of a salad tossed with this dressing. We smoked the breast in a stovetop smoker with Earl Grey tea as our faux wood chips!

> *"If one advances confidently in the direction of his dreams to live the life he imagined, he will meet with a success unexpected in common hours."*
>
> *~Henry David Thoreau*

Cha Cha Chicken Salad

Serving: 12

4 (8-ounce) boneless, skinless chicken breasts
Tony Chachere's Creole Seasoning
1 (16-ounce) bag coleslaw
1 1/2 cups halved red seedless grapes
1 1/2 cups finely chopped celery
1 cup coarsely chopped walnuts
1 Asian pear, unpeeled and chopped
1 (12-ounce) bottle Briannas' Home Style Rich Poppy Seed Dressing

Lightly sprinkle chicken breasts with *Tony Chachere's Creole Seasoning*. Grill chicken 6 to 7 minutes per side, 15 minutes total, over moderate heat. Slice or cube the chicken breasts once cooked. Toss the chicken breasts with the next 5 ingredients. Toss with the entire bottle of dressing. This salad is best served immediately but will keep several days.

Tips: This is a fabulous salad for a light dinner or luncheon. Serve it on a leaf of red cabbage or leaf lettuce with a slice of fresh bakery bread on the side. If you leave the chicken out of this salad, it makes a great side salad for barbecue.

Special Notes: Asian pears are round and green to yellow in color with the consistency of an apple. If you can't find an Asian pear, then another variety can be substituted. The Asian pears are usually with specialty fruits in the grocery store and not with the other pears. Briannas' Dressing is sold at most grocery stores.

Vince Martinez: Dallas, Texas
Vince is my hair stylist and colorist and is very colorful himself. He sings great cocktail music internationally. I enjoy my hair styling sessions with him because he's got his finger on the pulse of the trendiest places to go in Dallas and usually has a wild story to go with it!

Meat & Seafood

Meat & Seafood

 Kitchen tools needed

 May be prepared ahead

*Picture Features: Beach Buzzes, page 107 • Orange and Romaine Salad with Lime Vinaigrette
and Sugared Pecans, page 132 • Pineapple Shrimp Skewers with Honey Marinade, page 74
Black Beans with Cilantro Pesto Rice, page 230 • Tropical Fiesta Steak with Island Marinade and
Caribbean Salsa, page 159*

Red Wine Cherry Sauce

Serves: 4

- whisk

2 tablespoons unsalted butter
2 medium shallots, finely chopped
(about 1/4 cup)
2 medium garlic cloves,
minced or pressed
1 cup beef stock or broth
1 cup chicken stock or broth
1 cup red wine (Cabernet)
1/3 cup currant jelly or cherry
preserves
1/2 teaspoon fresh thyme or
rosemary (or both)
1/4 cup dried tart Bing
cherries or dried cranberries
1 tablespoon cornstarch mixed
with 1 tablespoon cold water
Salt and pepper, to taste

To make the sauce, melt the butter in a medium saucepan over medium heat and sauté the shallots and garlic until the shallots are translucent, about 3 minutes. Add both broths, red wine, jelly, thyme and cherries. Boil until reduced to 1 cup, about 40 minutes. Reduce the heat and add half of the cornstarch mixture to the hot liquid while whisking. Bring back to a boil and cook until thickened, about 2 minutes. Add more of the cornstarch mixture if a thicker sauce is desired. Sauces thicken quickly with cornstarch. It should be thick enough to coat the back of a spoon. Do not over whisk.

Tip: Cornstarch is always mixed with a cool liquid, so you can use wine or broth instead of water without diluting the flavor. When doubling the recipe, allow plenty of time to reduce the broth mixture. A good quality broth or bouillon may be purchased. I prefer a good quality bouillon paste that must be refrigerated after opening or a cube such as Knorr. Both must be mixed with water.

Special Note: If you are serving steak with this sauce and you like blue cheese, crumble gorgonzola over the top of the steak and top with the sauce. This sauce is versatile and pairs with pork, lamb or beef. For cooking guidelines see the chart on page 324.

Perfect Red Wine Sauce

Serves: 4

• fine mesh strainer

1/4 cup (1/2 stick) unsalted
butter
2 medium shallots, finely chopped
(about 1/4 cup)
2 medium garlic cloves,
minced or pressed
2 slices onion
2 carrots, sliced
10 whole peppercorns
2 whole cloves (optional)
2 bay leaves
3 tablespoons flour
1 1/2 cups beef broth or stock
1 cup red wine (Merlot or
Cabernet)
1/8 teaspoon black pepper
1/4 teaspoon salt

Melt the butter in a medium skillet over medium-high heat and sauté the shallots, garlic, onion, carrots, peppercorns, cloves and bay leaves until the onion and shallots are caramelized. Lower the heat and add the flour. Stir to coat and cook until the flour is lightly browned. Add the beef broth and wine and bring to a boil, stirring constantly. Reduce heat and simmer uncovered for 10 minutes. Strain the sauce by reserving the liquid and discarding all the solids. Add pepper and salt to the reserved liquid. Once cooled, this may be refrigerated and reheated when ready to serve. For cooking Beef Tenderloin see page 160.

Tip: This sauce is easily doubled for serving a larger crowd, but you may need to thicken it by using beurre manié (equal parts of softened butter mixed with flour) mixed into the hot liquid. If a heartier beef flavor is desired, adjust by adding undiluted beef base or a small portion of a beef bouillon cube (Knorr) to desired taste.

Variations: *Dried or fresh herbs can be added to enhance the flavor of the sauce depending on what you are serving. Two sprigs fresh thyme or rosemary is ideal. Add when you are sautéing the onion and carrot.*

Mushrooms (shiitake and oyster are recommended) may be added at the point of sautéing for an earthy flavor.

Using port (tawny or rub) as a substitute for red wine creates an overall richness that is also delicious with red meats.

(continued on next page)

A piece of grilled beef can be enhanced with crumbled blue cheese or a tablespoon of Boursin cheese (garlic and fine herb or black pepper). Crumble the cheese over the meat with this sauce ladled over the top.

Jody Huerter: Leawood, Kansas
Jody, Jerry and their five children lived next door to us when I was growing up. Jody continues to be a great inspiration to me in my entertaining and has always encouraged high standards. This is one of her favorite recipes for guests. She makes this sauce for tenderloin, and I am honored to have her special recipe.

Red Zinfandel Sauce

- meat thermometer
- fine mesh strainer
- whisk

1 1/2 cups red **Zinfandel wine**
1 (14.5-ounce) can **beef stock or broth**
1 1/2 teaspoons **tomato paste**
2 tablespoons **unsalted butter, softened**
2 tablespoons **flour**
1/4 teaspoon **salt**
1/4 teaspoon **black pepper**

To make the sauce, heat the wine to boiling. Boil until reduced to 1/2 cup. Pour into a small saucepan. Add stock and tomato paste; boil 10 minutes or until reduced to 1 1/2 cups. In a small bowl, blend the butter and flour into a paste; whisk into the wine mixture. Heat to boiling while continuing to whisk until thickened. Strain the sauce through a fine mesh sieve into another pan and season with salt and pepper. If you are serving this sauce with a meat dish, add any drippings from meat to the pan. Keep warm until ready to serve. To serve, drizzle sauce over the main dish and serve extra sauce on the side. Sauce may be made ahead. If pairing Beef Tenderloin with this sauce, see page 160.

Perfect Cream Sauce

Serves: 6

 • whisk

4 tablespoons unsalted butter,
softened, divided use
2 tablespoons flour
1 medium shallot, finely chopped
(about 2 tablespoons)
1 medium garlic clove,
minced or pressed
1 cup chicken stock or broth
1 cup heavy cream
1/4 teaspoon Tabasco red
pepper sauce
Salt, to taste

Make a paste by blending 2 tablespoons of the soft butter with 2 tablespoons flour in a small bowl. Set aside. Melt the remaining butter in a medium skillet and sauté the shallot and garlic until the shallots are translucent, about 3 minutes. Add the chicken stock and heavy cream and bring to a boil. Add a tablespoon of the flour paste and whisk to thicken. If desired consistency is not reached, stir in more of the flour mixture. Lower the heat, stir in the red pepper sauce and taste. Add salt if desired.

Tip: In order to test a sauce to see if the sauce is thick enough, coat the back of a spoon with the sauce. Draw your finger through the sauce. If the sauce does not seep back into the line you drew or drip off the spoon, then it is thick enough. Keep sauce warm until ready to serve. If the sauce gets too thick, add a little more stock or cream.

Variations: Remove the sauce from the stove and stir in fresh herbs just before serving. Basil and thyme are two of our favorite choices. If you add the herbs too early, they turn black.

If using the sauce for fish, use seafood or vegetable stock or broth; for beef, use a beef stock or broth; and for pork, use a combination of equal parts chicken and beef stock or broth.

Additional ingredients like red bell pepper, mushrooms, leeks or sun-dried oil-packed tomatoes can change this sauce into several different types of sauce.

(continued on next page)

The mushrooms, peppers or leeks would need to be added with the shallots and garlic to soften them. (Basil Cream Sauce on page 180 is a rendition that is delicious.)

White wine, sherry, Cognac, vermouth and brandy (apple) can all change the flavor of this sauce. If using, the broth should be reduced by the amount used. White wine can be 1/2 cup, but the others should be no more than 2 tablespoons. Sherry added to a cream sauce pairs beautifully when mushrooms are used.

Bourbon (or whiskey) can turn this into an amazing sauce for anything (meat, fish, chicken or vegetables). Increase the quantity of shallots to 4 and garlic to 2 cloves. While sautéing the garlic and shallot in 2 tablespoons unsalted butter, add 2 coarsely chopped carrots. Add 2/3 cup bourbon and reduce by half before adding beef stock (3 cups). Boil again until beef stock is reduced to 1 cup (takes 30 to 45 minutes). Strain into another saucepan, add 1 tablespoon tomato paste, 1 teaspoon dried thyme and 2 teaspoons freshly cracked black pepper. Add one cup of cream and bring to a boil. Make the paste of flour and soft butter (4 tablespoons each) and whisk into the boiling liquid to thicken the sauce. Fabulous and flavorful!

1/2 cup grated Parmigiano-Reggiano cheese can be stirred into the basic sauce. It melts and makes this a super Alfredo.

1/2 cup crumbled Blue cheese and beef stock instead of chicken stock, makes a rich white sauce for beef. Garnish with fresh, chopped parsley.

For a spicy version, add 1 tablespoon of the Creole Spice (page 224) to the basic recipe. Use for pasta or meats.

Blue Cheese Mushroom Sauce

Serves: 4

1 cup Roquefort or blue cheese
1/2 cup unsalted butter
4 medium garlic cloves,
   minced or pressed
1 tablespoon Worcestershire sauce
1/2 cup finely chopped green
   onions (white and pale green
   part only)
5 cups (10 ounces) sliced, fresh
   mushrooms

Melt the cheese and butter together in a saucepan over low heat. Add garlic, Worcestershire, green onions and mushrooms. Stir ingredients together until well blended. Cook over low heat 3 to 5 minutes until mushrooms have softened. Pass the sauce separately for topping a main dish.

Variations: Toast or grill slices of sourdough (1/2 slice per person). Layer the blue cheese mixture on top, add a steak filet and top with some greens that have been tossed in a light vinegar and oil. Beautiful and delicious! If you would like to leave out the mushrooms, another great combination with just a few simple ingredients is to julienne 2 medium yellow onions and caramelize with a small amount of oil to prevent sticking. Cook the onions over low heat 30 minutes until golden. Add 1/2 cup cooked, crumbled bacon, 1 cup heavy cream and 1 cup Roquefort. Cook over low to reduce the cream to 1/2 cup. Serve as mentioned above, with the toast and steak on top! Yum!

Special Note: Roquefort is a blue cheese made from sheep's milk. It has a creamy, rich texture and a pungent, salty flavor.

Barb Boerner: Southlake, Texas
Barb and I met at a local gourmet store and continue to see each other at various local functions. We always manage to discuss food and recipes when we see one another. This is one of my favorites to make for friends.

Horseradish Sauce for Steaks

Serves: 8

 • electric mixer

1 cup heavy cream
1/2 cup prepared horseradish,
   drained
1/3 cup Hellmann's or Best
   Foods Real Mayonnaise
1 teaspoon dry mustard
Generous dash of cayenne pepper
Tony Chachere's Creole Seasoning
   and lemon pepper for steaks,
   if desired

Whip the cream with an electric mixer in a large bowl until it forms peaks. Gently fold in the remaining ingredients.

Bourbon Beef Marinade

Serves: 4

1 cup less sodium soy sauce
1/2 cup bourbon
1/4 cup Worcestershire sauce
2 tablespoons brown sugar
1/2 teaspoon ground ginger
4 large garlic cloves,
   minced or pressed
2 teaspoons black pepper
1 teaspoon ground white pepper
1/4 cup olive oil
1/4 cup water

Mix the marinade ingredients together in a large bowl. Marinate beef in the marinade for a minimum of 2 hours up to 2 days. Grill the meat to desired doneness. See the temperature chart (page 324) for guidelines. This marinade is enough for 3 to 6 pounds of meat.

Tip: For larger amounts of beef, double the marinade and marinate for up to 2 days before cooking. This is a delicious marinade for beef tenderloin to be used on an appetizer buffet for mini sandwiches. Slice thinly and have small rolls and condiments available.

Magic Meat Sauce

Serves: 4

• whisk

1 tablespoon sesame seeds
1/4 cup (1/2 stick) unsalted
  butter
3 tablespoons less sodium soy
  sauce
1/2 cup honey
1 teaspoon chili powder
1 teaspoon cornstarch mixed
  with 1 teaspoon cold water
1 bunch (1/2 cup) thinly sliced
  green onion (white and pale
  green part only)

In a small saucepan toast the sesame seeds over medium heat until lightly golden. Remove from the pan and set aside. In the same pan, melt the butter over low heat. Add the soy sauce, honey and chili powder. Stir to blend. Whisk the cornstarch mixture into the hot honey mixture and bring to a boil. Whisk until thickened, about 2 minutes. Remove from the heat and reheat just before serving. Drizzle the sauce over grilled meat and sprinkle with green onions and sesame seeds.

Tip: This little concoction is perfect when serving lamb or pork. The combination of the sweet glaze with the crisp green onion and sesame seeds turns a simple grilled piece of meat into the perfect dinner! Typically, we marinate pork tenderloin in a store-bought teriyaki marinade or the Hoisin Marinade (page 169) before grilling the tenderloin. Use the sauce, sesame seeds and green onions as the accompaniment. The textures complement the flavors and enhance the presentation!

Special Note: Chili powder spelled with an "i" is a blend of chiles. Chile powder with an "e" is a particular type of chile.

Mushroom–Red Onion Steak Topping   Serves: 4

1 cup ruby port
2 cups beef stock or broth
1/4 cup butter
4 medium garlic cloves,
  minced or pressed
6 cups (12 ounces) sliced fresh
  mushrooms
1 red onion sliced into thin rings
2 teaspoons fresh thyme
2 teaspoons finely chopped
  fresh oregano
2 teaspoons finely chopped
  fresh rosemary
1/2 teaspoon salt
4 teaspoons cornstarch mixed
  with 4 teaspoons cold water
8 tablespoons plain goat cheese

In a medium saucepan, mix together the port and beef stock over medium heat. Boil and reduce to 1 1/2 cups, approximately 20 minutes. Turn heat to low to keep warm. In a large skillet, melt the butter over medium heat. Sauté the garlic until fragrant; add the mushrooms and onion and sauté until onions are translucent, about 5 minutes. Add the herbs and salt. Add the reduced port and broth to the mushroom mixture. Whisk half of the cornstarch mixture into the mushroom mixture. Bring to a boil and allow the sauce to thicken, about 2 minutes. If you prefer a thicker topping, use additional cornstarch mixture. Pour over grilled steaks that have been seasoned with cracked pepper and lemon pepper. Crumble the goat cheese over the sauce.

Tip: Keep goat cheese refrigerated until ready to crumble. This topping is also good served as an appetizer with warmed pita bread triangles.

Special Note: If using dried herbs, use one-third the amount of fresh because they are more pungent. Adjust as needed to desired taste.

Shallot Cream Steak Sauce

Serves: 4

2 tablespoons butter
2 tablespoons minced garlic
2 medium shallots, finely
chopped (about 1/4 cup)
1/2 cup dry white wine such as
Sauvignon Blanc
2 tablespoons Dijon mustard
1 cup heavy cream
2/3 cup beef stock or broth
1 tablespoon cornstarch mixed
with 1 tablespoon cold water

Melt butter in a heavy skillet over medium heat. Add garlic and shallots and sauté until shallots are translucent, about 3 minutes. Add wine. Increase heat to high and boil until the liquid is reduced to half, about 4 minutes. Whisk in mustard, cream and stock. Boil until reduced to 1 1/4 cups, about 7 minutes. Reduce heat and whisk the cornstarch mixture into the hot liquid. Bring back to a boil and cook about 2 minutes until sauce coats the back of the spoon without dripping. You may mix in extra juices from steaks when they are taken off the grill. Roll steaks in cracked black pepper to add extra flavor. If you are serving a sliced tenderloin or filet mignon, you may fan slices out and slightly overlap them. Drizzle the sauce over the steak. Pass extra sauce at the table. This sauce can be made ahead and reheated slowly.

Tip: To crack peppercorns, put them inside a sturdy self-sealing plastic bag and crush with a meat mallet or rolling pin. You can also grind them in a coffee bean grinder that has been designated for spices only.

"To love and to be loved is to feel the sun from both sides."

~David Viscott

Balsamic Sauce for Steaks

Serves: 4

1/4 cup dry red wine
1/4 cup dry sherry
3 tablespoons balsamic vinegar
2 medium shallots, finely chopped
(about 1/4 cup)
2 garlic cloves, minced or pressed
1/3 cup butter
2 large egg yolks
Kitchen Bouquet Browning and
Seasoning Sauce (optional)

Bring the first 6 ingredients to a boil in a medium saucepan. Once boiling, reduce the heat to low and allow to cool down. Once the temperature has cooled down add the egg yolks to the saucepan and over low heat, continue to whisk until thickened. A few drops of Kitchen Bouquet may be added to create a slightly brown sauce, otherwise, the sauce is slightly pink. Pass the sauce separately at the table.

Variation: For a very delightful sauce for steaks or lamb, boil 1 cup balsamic vinegar and 1 chopped shallots until reduced to half and the consistency of syrup. Delicious!

Special Note: Kitchen Bouquet Browning and Seasoning Sauce adds color to your sauce. You only need a few drops for brown gravy or a balsamic sauce.

Julie Lancaster: Grapevine, Texas
Julie, my accountant, made this for grilled steaks. It is very flavorful.
She and her husband Joe, recommend rubbing steaks with olive oil and
sprinkling with coarse ground black peppercorns and coarse sea salt before
grilling. Pass sauce separately.

Marvelous Meat Marinade

Serves: 4

1/2 cup less sodium soy sauce
1/4 cup Pickapeppa Sauce
1/4 cup Worcestershire sauce
3 tablespoons olive oil
3 tablespoons balsamic vinegar
2 tablespoons brown sugar
2 large garlic cloves, minced
1 1/2 pounds pork tenderloin

In a large bowl or gallon-sized sealable plastic bag, mix the marinade ingredients together. Add the meat to the marinade. Marinate 24 hours. Grill the meat to desired doneness. We cook our pork tenderloin to 150°F and let it rest for 10 minutes before slicing. If you desire to choose a cut of beef, see the chart on page 324 for cooking temperatures.

Tip: If desired you may divide the marinade in half and use half to marinade meat and the other half to heat up and serve alongside the grilled meat.

Variation: Mary Hutchinson of Topeka, Kansas, simplifies things and just uses 1/3 cup less sodium soy sauce, 3 large cloves of garlic and 1/3 cup olive oil to marinate 1 1/2 pounds of pork tenderloin. This simple marinade recipe can be doctored up with molasses, mustard, brown sugar and even minced adobo chiles.

Special Note: Pickapeppa Sauce was created in Jamaica in the 1920s. The sauce is prepared with cane vinegar and aged in oak barrels. Pickapeppa Sauce has a sweet but mellow flavor that gives it an unmatched versatility and has been touted as Jamaican ketchup due to the many uses.

Cindy Kimbell: North Richland Hills, Texas
Cindy and her husband, Chip, own Elegant Lifestyle Magazine and Classic Lifestyle Magazine that are distributed locally. My husband, Dave, and I write monthly food and wine related articles for them. She loves to cook and shared her favorite marinade with me. It works well for flank steak, rib-eye, sirloin or filet mignon.

Tropical Fiesta Steak with Island Marinade and Caribbean Salsa

Serves: 4

 • zester

Marinade
Juice from 1 medium lemon
4 medium garlic cloves, minced or pressed
1/4 cup orange juice or juice from 1 orange
3 tablespoons olive oil
1 tablespoon Creole mustard
3 green onions, finely chopped (white and pale green part only)
1/4 teaspoon Tabasco red pepper sauce
1/2 teaspoon ground cumin
1 teaspoon chili powder
1 tablespoon dried oregano leaves
4 filet mignons, approximately 1/2 pound each

Caribbean Salsa
4 Roma tomatoes, seeded and diced (1/4-inch pieces)
1 papaya, peeled, seeded and diced (1/4-inch pieces)
1 cup red onion, diced (1/4-inch pieces)
2 limes
1 tablespoon mint, finely chopped
2 tablespoons brown sugar
1/2 teaspoon cumin
1 teaspoon chili powder
1 teaspoon crushed red pepper flakes
1/2 teaspoon salt
1 teaspoon Worcestershire sauce
1 avocado, chopped, for garnish

Mix marinade ingredients together in a large bowl. Add the meat and toss to coat. Marinate meat 8 hours in the refrigerator, turning meat occasionally. Make salsa at least 1 hour ahead. If made a day ahead, refrigerate and bring to room temperature before serving. To make salsa, combine tomatoes, papayas and onion in a large bowl. Zest and juice the limes, adding this to the tomato mixture. Add remaining ingredients, excluding avocado and stir to blend. For steaks, the approximate grilling time is 8 to 12 minutes for medium-rare and 11 to 15 minutes for medium. Grill to desired doneness and serve with salsa spooned over the top of the steaks. You could also brown the steaks in a small amount of olive oil in a pan on the stovetop and finish them to the desired doneness in the oven. For finishing in the oven, preheat the oven 350°F. Continue to cook the meat in the oven after browning it on the stovetop until the internal temperature reaches 130°F to 135°F for medium-rare and 135°F to 140°F for medium. Garnish with chopped avocado. This salsa can also be made for other occasions and served as an appetizer with tortilla chips.

Variation: Mango may be substituted for papaya.

Beef Tenderloin

Serves: 8

• probe thermometer

1 (4-pound) beef tenderloin
Olive oil
Salt and pepper

Preheat the oven broiler or prepare the grill as needed to sear the meat. Trim fat off the tenderloin (the butcher will typically do this). If searing on the grill, trimming the fat keeps the flame from flaring up while cooking. Let your tenderloin come to room temperature 45 minutes to an hour before cooking. About 10 minutes before searing the meat, rub the outside with olive oil and season with a little salt (coarse sea salt or kosher), pepper (fresh cracked) and garlic or your favorite spices. (If the ends of the tenderloin are very small, tuck them under for more even thickness.) Sear the outside of your beef tenderloin on the grill or under the oven broiler for 15 minutes, turning after 7 minutes. You can also sear the tenderloin on the stovetop in a large skillet in olive oil over medium-high heat. (This will seal in the juices before roasting the tenderloin.) Once the meat is seared, adjust the oven temperature to 350°F. Place the tenderloin in a roasting pan and finish cooking in the oven. Insert a meat thermometer in the thickest part of the tenderloin and be sure the thermometer is not hitting an oven coil. Remove the meat when the temperature is 8°F to 10°F less than the temperature desired, as it will continue to cook once removed. It will take approximately 1 hour to sear and bake a 4-pound beef tenderloin in the oven. We tend to cook our tenderloin to approximately 140°F for medium, and 135°F for medium-rare see chart on page 324. Remove the meat from the oven or grill and let rest uncovered for 10 minutes. The meat will continue to cook, the temperature will rise and the juices from the meat will redistribute. Slice in 1/4-inch slices and pass the sauce of your choice separately.

(continued on next page)

Tip: The thinner ends of the meat will be more done for those that prefer their meat more medium to medium-well. It is better to have the meat slightly underdone and put a few pieces back in for those not wanting any pink or red in their meat than to overcook the whole thing. Allow about 1/2 pound of tenderloin per person for dinner.

Special Note: The best meat thermometer I have found has a timer attached to it and a wire that attaches the alarm to the probe thermometer that goes in the thickest part of the meat. You set the temperature you would like to reach and the alarm sounds when the meat reaches this temperature. This type of thermometer is best because you can check the temperature on the outside thermometer without opening the door of the oven or grill.

Joan Lewis: McKinney, Texas
Joan started our Dinner Club in 1989. She blends this delicious combination before roasting her tenderloin in the oven. Mix equal parts of prepared yellow mustard with brown sugar to make a paste. Spread this over the tenderloin before roasting.

Herb Crusted Rib Roast with Port Wine Sauce

Serves: 8

- roasting pan with rack
- meat thermometer
- foil

Herb Crusted Rib Roast
1 (4-pound) standing rib roast
  or rib-eye roast
1 tablespoon black pepper
1 tablespoon chopped fresh
  parsley
2 teaspoons coarsely chopped
  fresh rosemary
1 teaspoon fresh thyme
2 teaspoons minced garlic
1 teaspoon salt

Port Wine Sauce
1 (14.5-ounce) can beef stock
  or broth
3/4 cup port wine
1 medium shallot, finely chopped
  (about 2 tablespoons)
1 bay leaf
2 tablespoons butter, softened
2 tablespoons flour

Remove rib roast from the refrigerator 1 hour before roasting. Preheat the oven to 350°F. Thirty minutes before putting the roast in the oven, combine the pepper, parsley, rosemary, thyme, garlic and salt in a small bowl and rub the mixture over entire surface of meat. Place the meat on a rack, in a roasting pan, fat side up. Insert a meat thermometer into the thickest part of the meat. (If the roast has bones, the thermometer should not touch the bones or any part of the oven.) Cook roast in the oven until internal temperature reaches 120°F to 125°F for rare to medium-rare (2 to 2 1/4 hours) or 130°F to 135°F for medium to medium-well (2 1/4 to 2 3/4 hours). Let meat rest 10 to 15 minutes before carving. While meat is cooking, prepare the sauce by combining the stock, port, shallots and bay leaf in a medium saucepan. Bring to a boil. Reduce heat and simmer uncovered 15 to 20 minutes. Remove the bay leaf. Make a thickener for the sauce by thoroughly blending the softened butter with the flour, to make a paste. Whisk the flour mixture into the hot liquid and bring to a boil while continuing to whisk until desired consistency is reached. This sauce should not be a thick gravy. Add more port if the sauce or broth gets too thick. Sauce may be made ahead, refrigerated and reheated.

Tip: This tip came from my mother-in-law, Linda Gore, Colleyville, Texas. When roasting meat in a roasting pan with a rack, crumple foil and place in the pan under the rack. This will keep the fat from splattering and smoking in the oven.

Variations: Au jus from the dry packaged sauce section of the grocery store would be an alternative to making this sauce. Au jus is a natural juice from beef that complements the meat. Dried rosemary may be used; use approximately 1/3 the amount.

Standing Rib Roast with Juniper-Rosemary Marinade

Serves: 8

- roasting pan
- meat thermometer
- foil

15 medium garlic cloves,
minced or pressed
30 juniper berries, crushed
1 tablespoon chopped rosemary
1/4 cup olive oil
1 (4-pound) standing rib roast,
beef tenderloin, lamb chops or
rack of leg of lamb

Combine the garlic, juniper berries, rosemary, and oil in a large bowl and rub over the meat. Store the meat in a sealable plastic bag in the refrigerator until ready to cook. Marinate a minimum of 2 hours up to 2 days. (If you marinate longer, more flavor is imparted.) Allow the meat to sit at room temperature for 1 hour before roasting. Insert your meat thermometer in the thickest part of the meat. (If the roast has bones, the thermometer should not touch the bones or any part of the oven.) Preheat the oven to 450°F. Roast the meat in a roasting pan in the lower part of the oven for 30 minutes. Reduce the oven temperature to 350°F. Roast approximately 1 hour and 45 minutes until the internal temperature is approximately 125°F. (See the chart for desired doneness of other meats on page 324) The thinner parts of the beef will be more done. Let the meat rest 10 minutes, uncovered, before carving.

Tip: Crush the juniper berries either in a coffee grinder that is used just for spices or in a sealable plastic bag with a rolling pin. Even though the meat has incredible flavor after marinating, I find the Perfect Red Wine Sauce (page 148) is a nice addition.

Special Note: A standing rib roast usually includes 3 ribs. A rib roast cannot be labeled prime unless it comes from USDA Prime beef.

Darren McGrady:

Plano, Texas

I met Darren by sending an email to him after his name appeared in our local paper. After meeting Darren, I asked him to teach some cooking classes at two cooking schools I manage. He was the former chef to Princess Diana and the Queen of England. He is gracious, kind and funny and has an incredible repertoire of stories to go with each recipe. This is a favorite he prepared that works fabulously with lamb, tenderloin or prime rib.

German Rouladen with Rich Brown Gravy

Serves: 6

- whisk
- cooking string or unwaxed dental floss
- tongs
- meat mallet

Rouladen
6 pieces top round steak (13 x 4 inches) cut 1/8 to 1/4 inch thick
Salt and pepper
Prepared yellow mustard
5 slices bacon, uncooked, diced (1/4-inch pieces)
1 medium onion, diced (1/4-inch pieces)
6 dill pickle spears, halved lengthwise
Flour
3 tablespoons butter
1 tablespoon olive oil
4 cups beef broth or stock

Potato Dumplings
1 (6.88-ounce) package potato dumpling mix

Rich Brown Gravy
1 (1 ounce) package dry onion soup mix
1/2 cup cold water
4 tablespoons flour mixed with 4 tablespoons cold water
2 teaspoons Kitchen Bouquet Browning and Seasoning Sauce

Preheat the oven to 150°F. With the backside (smooth side) of a mallet, tenderize the meat. Season the round steak very lightly with salt and pepper. Cut each piece of meat crosswise to make two 6 1/2 x 4 inch pieces. Spread one side of each piece of top round steak lightly with mustard and sprinkle with diced bacon and onion. Place a dill pickle on one end of the meat (if the pickle is too long, cut off excess). Roll the meat and tie with thread (or use a toothpick), tucking in the sides. Lightly roll the rouladen in flour and shake off the excess. In a large stockpot or Dutch oven, melt the butter and add the oil. Brown the rouladen lightly on all sides. To avoid crowding, you will have to brown a few at a time. Once all are browned, place them back into the Dutch oven and pour the broth over them. Simmer 45 minutes (do not boil), covered. Make the dumplings while the meat is cooking, according to package directions. Once rouladen has cooked 45 minutes, leaving the strings or toothpicks intact, remove the rouladen from the stock, reserving the liquid. Keep the rouladen warm on an ovenproof platter in the oven while making the gravy. To make the gravy, add the dry onion mix and water to the reserved juices. Heat the juices to blend the flavors. Add the flour mixture into the hot liquid while continuing to whisk. The flour mixture should be thin without lumps. Continue to whisk until there are no lumps of flour. Add the Kitchen Bouquet and whisk until the color is uniform. Add the rouladen and any extra drippings back to the gravy mixture and bring to a boil. Once the mixture boils, immediately lower heat to the lowest setting.

(continued on next page)

With tongs, gently place 2 rouladen per person on each plate. Remove toothpicks or string. Serve warm smothered in gravy. Tear open the dumpling and generously cover the dumpling with gravy. Pass extra gravy separately. You may refrigerate or freeze the rouladen just after cooking in the stock, after the meat has cooled. If freezing, defrost in the refrigerator and follow the recipe as directed.

Tip: Potato dumplings are found in some grocery stores or German specialty food stores. Red Cabbage page 248 and canned spiced peaches are delicious with this entrée. The round steak should not be so thin it is translucent.

Brigitte Scherer: Kansas City, Kansas
My mother and father got married in Germany after World War II. My mother came over on a ship to America with the other war brides. My mother taught me the art of keeping in touch with friends even when you are separated by distance. This is an authentic German dinner she cooked on special occasions. Serve Red Cabbage as a side dish (page 248).

Brisket with Honey Barbecue Sauce

Serves: 8

Brisket
1 (6-pound) brisket
2 tablespoons liquid smoke
Tony Chachere's Creole Seasoning
Garlic salt
1 tablespoon flour
1 oven cooking bag
1 1/2 cups water

Barbecue Sauce
1 tablespoon olive oil
1/2 cup finely chopped onion
1 1/2 cups ketchup
1/2 cup packed brown sugar
1/4 cup Creole mustard
1/4 cup apple cider vinegar
1 1/2 teaspoons chili powder
1 1/2 teaspoons black pepper
1 teaspoon garlic powder
1 1/2 teaspoons
    Worcestershire sauce
1/2 teaspoon celery salt
1 teaspoon Tabasco red
    pepper sauce
1/2 cup honey

Preheat the oven to 350°F. Season the brisket on the meaty side with the liquid smoke and sprinkle generously with *Tony Chachere's* and garlic salt. Shake 1 tablespoon flour (as directed on cooking bag directions) in the bag before adding beef. Put brisket fat side down in the oven bag and add the water to the bag. Make 6 slits in the top of the bag and close with the nylon tie provided. Lay in a baking dish fat side down. Do not let bag hang over side of the baking dish. Bake for 3 hours until fork tender. Remove meat from the bag and cool in the refrigerator in a clean baking dish. Meat may be cooled overnight and reheated and served the next day. To make the sauce, heat the oil over medium heat in a medium saucepan and add the onion. Sauté until translucent, about 5 minutes. Add remaining ingredients to the saucepan, stirring to blend. Heat to boiling. Reduce heat. Simmer covered for 30 minutes. Slice beef against the grain in 1/2 inch thick slices. To serve, spread barbecue sauce on top of the sliced beef and heat, covered, in the oven for 30 minutes at 350°F.

Garlic and Thyme Roasted Pork Loin with a Brandy Cream Sauce

Serves: 8

- meat thermometer
- roasting pan
- blender or food processor
- whisk

Roasted Pork Loin Roast
1 (4-pound) boneless pork loin roast
6 large garlic cloves
1 teaspoon salt
2 teaspoons black pepper
1/4 cup brandy
1/4 cup fresh thyme or 1 1/2 tablespoons dried thyme
1/4 cup olive oil
1 cup dry white wine

Brandy Cream Sauce
1/4 cup (1/2 stick) butter
1/2 cup finely chopped yellow onion
1 cup dry white wine
2 cups heavy cream
1/2 cup brandy
1 teaspoon salt
1 teaspoon black pepper
1 tablespoon cornstarch mixed with 1 tablespoon cold water

Remove roast from refrigerator 30 minutes before preparing the rub for the meat. Preheat the oven to 350°F. In a blender or food processor, combine garlic cloves with salt, pepper, brandy and thyme. Add olive oil slowly in a thin stream through the hole in top of the blender or feeding tube of food processor. Process to thicken slightly. Place the pork roast in a roasting pan. Coat the roast with the garlic and thyme mixture. Bake in the oven, uncovered, with a meat thermometer inserted into the center. Baste with 1/4 cup of white wine every 15 minutes for 1 hour. Roast approximately 1 1/2 hours or until internal temperature reaches 155°F. Make the sauce while pork is roasting. Melt butter in a medium skillet, add onion and sauté 3 to 5 minutes. Reduce the heat and add white wine. Simmer 15 minutes. Stir in cream, brandy, salt and pepper. Cook over medium-high heat, stirring to reduce liquid by 1/3, about 5 to 7 minutes. Whisk half of the cornstarch mixture into the hot liquid. Bring sauce to a boil to thicken, about 2 minutes. Only whisk in the remainder of cornstarch mixture if the desired consistency is not reached. The sauce should coat the back of a spoon without dripping. Once the meat is removed from the oven, let rest 10 minutes. Slice in 1/4- to 1/2-inch slices and serve. Pass sauce separately.

Variation: In place of the Brandy Cream Sauce, use the Red Wine Cherry Sauce (page 147). The herbs used in this recipe can be a combination of sage, rosemary and thyme, which is equally delicious.

Creole Mustard Marinated Pork Tenderloin

Serves: 6

2 pork tenderloins (2 1/2
   pounds total), trimmed

Marinade
1/2 cup olive oil
2 tablespoons brown sugar
2 tablespoons Creole or
   coarse-grained mustard
1/4 cup pure maple syrup
2 tablespoons less sodium soy
   sauce
1/3 cup hoisin sauce
4 large garlic cloves, minced or
   pressed
1/2 cup orange juice
1/2 cup cola

Place the tenderloins in a large sealable plastic bag. To make the marinade, whisk together all of the ingredients in a large bowl and pour over the tenderloins in the plastic bag. Marinate 4 to 8 hours in the refrigerator. For the meat, grill the pork approximately 15 to 25 minutes or until the temperature reaches 150°F in the center with a meat thermometer. Let the meat rest, uncovered, 10 minutes before slicing. The cola and orange juice help break down the fibers in the meat and make it very tender. Serve this with the Red Wine Cherry Sauce (page 147) if you would like a sauce to accompany the meat.

Tip: Creole mustard is made from vinegar-marinated brown mustard seeds with a hint of horseradish. It is available at most grocery stores. If you cannot find Creole mustard, substitute coarse-grained mustard.

Variation: A 4-pound pork roast may be substituted (marinade is plenty) and cooked in the oven at 350°F with a thermometer inserted. The internal temperature should be approximately 155°F. Let it rest 10 minutes so the juices disperse. Pork chops or grilled steaks taste wonderful after marinating in this mixture as well.

Special Note: Silver skin is the thin pearlescent membrane found on certain cuts of meat such as beef and pork tenderloin. It is a common practice to remove this part from the meat because it does not add any benefit to the cooking or eating of the meat.

Hoisin Marinated Pork Tenderloin   Serves: 6

2 pork tenderloins (2 1/2
    pounds total), trimmed
1 1/2 cups chicken stock or broth
1/2 cup brown sugar
1/2 cup less sodium soy sauce
1/3 cup hoisin sauce
3 large garlic cloves, minced or
    pressed
2 tablespoons apple cider vinegar
2 tablespoons olive oil

Place the tenderloins in a large sealable plastic bag. Mix chicken stock with the remaining ingredients in a large bowl and pour over the tenderloins in the plastic bag. Marinate for 8 hours if possible or until ready to cook. This is best cooked on the grill (approximately 10 to 15 minutes total) and tested with a meat thermometer. We like to cook the tenderloin to about 150°F and let it rest, uncovered, for 10 minutes so it continues to cook and reaches close to 160°F.

Tip: Tenderloins can be cooked in the oven as well. Brown the meat in a skillet on all sides in olive oil once it has been removed from the marinade. Preheat the oven to 350°F and if the skillet is ovenproof just transfer it to the oven. Again using a meat thermometer, test the temperature.

Special Note: Our favorite sauce to serve with this is the Magic Meat Sauce (page 154), brown rice and the Asian Slaw with Peanut Dressing (page 134) or a green salad with Hoisin Vinaigrette (page 145). Drizzle the meat and the rice with the sauce and serve a colorful vegetable like Naturally Sweet Carrots (page 252) or Sesame Asparagus (page 242) and be sure to use the wonderful garnish mentioned with the Magic Meat Sauce on page 154 (green onion and sesame seeds).

"Dance like no one's watching, love like you'll never be hurt, sing like no one is listening, and live like it's heaven on earth."

~William Purkey

Marinated Pork Tenderloin with Cumberland Sauce

Serves: 8

- jelly roll pan
- meat thermometer
- vegetable peeler (to peel ginger)
- whisk

3 pork tenderloins (3 3/4 pounds total), trimmed

Marinade
1/2 cup dry sherry
1/2 cup less sodium soy sauce
2 large garlic cloves, minced or pressed
1 tablespoon dry mustard
1 teaspoon dry, crushed thyme

Cumberland Sauce
2 1/2 cups tawny port, divided use
1 (10.5-ounce) jar currant jelly
2/3 cup fresh orange juice
3 tablespoons brown sugar
1 1/2 tablespoons minced fresh ginger
2 teaspoons dry mustard
1/4 teaspoon salt
1/4 teaspoon cayenne pepper
2 tablespoons cornstarch

Place the tenderloins in a large sealable plastic bag. Combine the marinade ingredients in a large bowl and pour over the tenderloins in the plastic bag. Marinate up to 24 hours in the refrigerator. Cook on the grill over hot coals for 15 to 25 minutes, approximately 10 minutes per side. The internal temperature should be 150°F. If you are unable to cook outdoors, preheat the oven to 375°F. Brown the pork tenderloin in a skillet over medium-high heat for 5 minutes until browned on all sides. Place the pork on a jelly roll pan and bake with a meat thermometer inserted, 15 minutes or until the meat thermometer reaches an internal temperature of 150°F. Make the sauce while the meat is cooking or up to 2 days ahead and reheat slowly. Bring 1 1/2 cups port and the next 7 ingredients to boil in a large saucepan. Reduce heat and simmer 20 minutes, stirring often. Stir together remaining 1 cup port and cornstarch in a separate small bowl until smooth. Stir into saucepan. Bring to a boil over medium heat while whisking constantly, approximately 2 minutes. Slice meat in 1/2 to 1 inch thick slices and drizzle sauce over the meat. Serve additional sauce on the side. Sauce may be reheated if made ahead.

Special Note: Cumberland sauce is popular with the English and is excellent with venison, duck or other game. Tawny port is a blend of grapes made from several different years and can be aged in wood as long as 40 years. Ruby ports are a lower grade, blended from several vintages and not aged as long.

Pork Tenderloin with Caramelized Onion Sage Sauce

Serves: 6

Pork

2 pork tenderloins (2 1/2 pounds total), trimmed
Salt and pepper
1 cup flour for dredging
2 1/2 teaspoons dried sage
Olive oil

Caramelized Onion Sage Sauce

2 medium shallots, finely chopped (about 1/4 cup)
2 medium yellow onions, thinly sliced
3 large garlic cloves, minced
14 fresh sage leaves, finely chopped, or 1 tablespoon dried sage
1 cup dry white wine
3 cups beef stock or broth
2 tablespoons unsalted butter, softened
2 tablespoons flour

Preheat the oven to 150°F. Slice the tenderloins in 1/4-inch slices. Lightly sprinkle pork with salt and pepper. Place the flour and sage in a shallow dish. Dredge the pork in the flour mixture, shaking off the excess. Heat 3 tablespoons oil, over medium-high heat in a large skillet. Working in batches, cook pork until brown, about 4 minutes per side. Add additional oil if necessary. Remove the pork to an ovenproof platter and place in a warm oven. Turn off oven. (You do not want meat to get tough.) To make the sauce, sauté the shallots, onions and garlic in the pan previously used, on medium-high heat about 15 minutes, adding more oil if needed. Reduce heat to medium and sauté until the onions are dark brown, about 35 minutes longer. Add the sage and wine. Bring to a boil. Add the pork to the skillet arranging in a single layer then add beef stock to cover. Simmer until heated through. Make a paste with the butter and flour in a separate small bowl and add to the pan, whisking to blend. Bring the sauce to a boil continuing to whisk until thickened.

Tip: For easy dredging place the flour and sage in a large plastic sealable bag. Add the meat and shake vigorously. Remove meat and proceed with recipe. If using canned broth, be aware that many contain a lot of salt. This is a comforting meal when served with mashed potatoes. Wild rice makes this a more elegant entrée.

Variation: Veal scaloppini (often spelled scallopini) also works well for this dish. Scallopini is a term for Italian cookery describing a thin scallop of meat (usually veal) dredged in flour before sautéing. If making with chicken, substitute chicken broth for beef broth.

Apple and Cornbread Stuffed Pork Roast with Bacon Thyme Gravy

Serves: 4

- whisk
- meat thermometer

1 cup cornbread stuffing
1/2 cup diced apple, unpeeled
  (1/4-inch pieces)
3 tablespoons minced onion
1/2 teaspoon *Tony Chachere's
  Creole Seasoning,* plus more
  to taste
1/2 teaspoon dried sage
2 cups chicken stock or broth,
  divided use
1 (4-pound) pork roast

Bacon Thyme Gravy
3 slices bacon, diced
  (1/4-inch pieces)
4 green onions, minced (white
  and pale green part only)
1/2 cup dry white wine
2 tablespoons flour
2 cups whole milk, half-and-half
  or heavy cream
1 teaspoon dried thyme

Preheat the oven to 350°F. Mix the cornbread stuffing with the apple, onion, *Tony Chachere's,* sage and 1/4 cup stock. Make deep slits in the pork to portion out how big of a slice you would like to serve. In the middle of each slice, make a deep slice to create a pocket to spoon the stuffing in. (You may make ahead to this point and refrigerate.) When ready to cook, place the pork roast in an ovenproof baking dish and add 3/4 cup stock in the bottom of the pan. Bake in the oven, uncovered, with a meat thermometer inserted into the center. Bake until the internal temperature is 155°F, approximately 1 1/2 hours. Allow the meat to rest 10 minutes, uncovered, before slicing. Temperature will rise to approximately 160°F and juices will redistribute during this time. While the meat is roasting, cook the bacon in a heavy skillet until crisp and drain on paper towels, reserving the bacon grease. Add onions to the skillet and sauté the onions in the reserved grease for about 3 minutes. Add the white wine to the skillet and boil until the liquid has reduced by half. Whisk the flour into the wine and oil mixture until all lumps disappear and slowly add remaining 1 1/4 cups broth while continuing to whisk. Slowly add the milk (you may not need all two cups). In order for a gravy or sauce to thicken it must start to boil while whisking. Allow the sauce to simmer on a mild boil while continuing to whisk until desired consistency is reached. Adjust consistency with additional milk if needed. Turn heat to low, add the cooked bacon and thyme to the sauce. Season to taste with additional *Tony Chachere's,* if desired. Serve over slices of stuffed pork.

(continued on next page)

Variation: *Fry the bacon and reserve the grease. Make a batter for dipping by combining 1 egg with 1 cup milk in a medium bowl. Dip 4 large, boneless, skinless chicken breasts in the egg then in seasoned flour (flour seasoned with Tony Chachere's). Sauté the chicken in the remaining bacon grease and olive oil if needed over medium-high heat for 4 minutes per side. Continue cooking the chicken in a 9 x 13-inch baking dish for 25 minutes at 350°F in the oven. Proceed by deglazing the dish with wine and continuing to make a sauce with reserved bacon grease to go on the chicken.*

Allison Brock: Rogers, Arkansas
Allison and Rusty are dear friends of Lynne and Richard Borkowski. Allison makes this with thick pork chops but I find a pork roast is easier to cook to the perfect temperature and tenderness.

Chicken Breasts Stuffed with Lobster in a Garlic Cream Sauce

Serves: 4

- meat mallet
- toothpicks or short bamboo skewers (soaked in water for 30 minutes)

Stuffed Chicken Breasts
2 tablespoons butter
1/4 cup minced yellow onion
1/4 cup chopped celery
1 cup crushed buttery crackers
2 tablespoons sherry
1/2 teaspoon garlic powder
1/2 teaspoon Worcestershire sauce
1 tablespoon chopped fresh
parsley
1 tablespoon finely chopped
green onion (white and pale
green part only)
Salt and pepper, to taste
4 (8-ounce) boneless, skinless
chicken breasts
8 ounces lobster meat steamed,
divided use
1/2 cup dry white wine

Garlic Cream Sauce
1 medium shallot, finely chopped
(about 2 tablespoons)
1 tablespoon butter
1 cup heavy cream
1 (5.2-ounce) box of Boursin
cheese (garlic and fine herb
flavor)

Melt the butter in a large skillet over medium heat. Add the onions and celery and sauté until the celery is soft and onions are translucent, about 5 minutes. Remove from the heat and add crackers, sherry, garlic powder, Worcestershire, parsley, green onion and salt and pepper. Stir to combine. Preheat the oven to 350°F. Place a piece of plastic wrap over the chicken breasts (this will keep them from splattering). Pound the chicken breasts to an even thickness by beating with the flat side of the meat mallet. Divide the lobster and cracker mixture over the top of the 4 breasts. Roll chicken up, tucking ends in and fastening with a toothpick or short bamboo skewers. Place breasts in a baking dish and pour the white wine over the chicken. Bake for 25 to 35 minutes or until juices run clear when pierced with a fork. Remove from the oven and set aside, keeping warm. Filling for the chicken breasts may be made a day ahead and refrigerated until ready to serve. To make the sauce, sauté the shallots in butter in a medium skillet until soft, about 3 minutes. Add heavy cream and cook over medium heat until liquid is reduced and slightly thickened. Cut cheese into cubes and add to the skillet. When mixture is thickened and cheese is melted, remove from heat. Serve chicken breasts with sauce.

Special Note: Lobster tail can be steamed at your local grocer and is not too expensive. One tail should be enough lobster meat. Boursin cheese typically comes in a small box and is displayed with specialty cheeses in the grocery store. The sauce from this dish is delicious tossed with pasta.

Baked Sour Cream Marinated Chicken

Serves: 6

6 (8-ounce) boneless, skinless
  chicken breasts
2 cups sour cream
1/4 cup lemon juice
4 teaspoons Worcestershire sauce
4 teaspoons celery salt
2 teaspoons sweet paprika
4 medium garlic cloves,
  minced or pressed
2 teaspoons salt
1/2 teaspoon black pepper
1 3/4 cups bread crumbs
1/2 cup butter
1/2 cup shortening

Defrost chicken breasts if they are frozen. Combine sour cream, lemon juice, Worcestershire, celery salt, paprika, garlic, salt and pepper in a large bowl. Add the chicken to the mixture and coat well. Refrigerate overnight. Preheat oven to 350°F. Remove chicken from sour cream mixture and roll in bread crumbs, coating evenly. Arrange in a single layer in a large shallow baking dish. Melt the butter and shortening in a small saucepan and spoon half over the chicken. Bake the chicken, uncovered, for 45 minutes. Spoon the remaining butter mixture over the chicken. Bake 10 to 15 minutes longer until chicken is tender and browned. Keep warm until ready to serve.

Special Note: A portable egg timer allows you to time things that are in the oven when you need to go to another room in the house where the timer cannot be heard. The extra timer and the oven timer can both be used when you are timing more than one recipe.

> *"Wine makes daily living easier, less hurried, with fewer tension and more tolerance."*
>
> *~Benjamin Franklin*

Chicken Breasts Stuffed with Prosciutto and Gruyère

Serves: 6

- jelly roll pan
- meat mallet
- whisk
- toothpicks or short bamboo skewers (soaked in water for 30 minutes)

Chicken

6 (8-ounce) boneless, skinless chicken breasts
Salt and pepper, to taste
6 paper thin slices prosciutto
1 (4-ounce) block Gruyère cheese, cut into 6 (2 x 1/2-inch slices)
1/3 cup flour
2 tablespoons butter
1 tablespoon olive oil

Sauce

3 tablespoons butter
3 medium garlic cloves, minced or pressed
2 medium shallots, finely chopped (about 1/4 cup)
1 1/2 cups (3 ounces) sliced fresh mushrooms
1 cup chicken stock or broth
1/2 cup white wine
1/2 cup sherry
1/2 teaspoon dried thyme, not ground
1/2 teaspoon dried oregano
1/2 cup heavy cream
1 tablespoon cornstarch mixed with 1 tablespoon cold water
Salt and pepper, to taste
Cooked wild rice blend, white or brown rice

Preheat the oven to 350°F. Place a piece of plastic wrap over the chicken breasts (this will keep them from splattering). Pound the chicken breasts to an even thickness by beating with the flat side of the meat mallet. Sprinkle lightly with salt and pepper. Top with one slice of prosciutto and cheese. Tuck in ends and roll jelly roll style. To hold each chicken roll, fasten with a wooden toothpick or short bamboo stick. In a large dish, add the flour and lightly coat each chicken breast. Combine the butter and oil in a large skillet over medium-high heat. Add each of the rolled chicken breasts, browning on all sides. Remove the chicken breasts to a baking dish and wipe out the skillet. At this point, you may refrigerate the browned chicken and continue the next day. To make the sauce, melt the butter in a large skillet and sauté the garlic and shallots until soft, about 3 minutes. Add the mushrooms, broth, wine, sherry, thyme and oregano. Simmer until mushrooms are tender, 10 minutes. Add the heavy cream and stir to blend ingredients. Pour sauce over the chicken and bake, covered, 25 to 30 minutes. Remove chicken breasts and arrange on a serving platter. Keep warm. Pour the remaining sauce that has mixed with the juices from the chicken while baking into a saucepan and simmer over medium heat. Add half of the cornstarch mixture to the hot liquid. Bring sauce to a boil to allow it to thicken. (This takes about 2 minutes.)

(continued on next page)

Only add remaining cornstarch mixture if desired consistency is not reached. Salt and pepper, to taste. (Remember, prosciutto will be slightly salty.) To serve, remove skewers and slice the stuffed breasts on an angle and place on top of cooked rice. Drizzle sauce over the chicken. Pass additional sauce separately.

Carrie Hoffman: Overland Park, Kansas
Carrie and I became friends in high school and later shared an apartment off campus at Kansas State University. Carrie got this wonderful recipe from a former business partner. The combination of shallots, sherry, thyme and heavy cream is delicious!

Bacon and Arugula Stuffed Chicken Roulades

Serves: 6

- toothpicks
- meat mallet
- whisk

Marinade

3 slices pepper or hickory smoked bacon, cut in half

6 (8-ounce) boneless, skinless chicken breasts

3/4 cup fresh arugula, watercress or baby spinach

1/2 cup teriyaki sauce (Kikkoman brand works best)

Lemon pepper

Olive oil

Parmesan Cream Sauce

4 tablespoons unsalted butter, softened

1/4 cup flour

2 medium shallots, finely chopped (about 1/4 cup)

2 medium garlic cloves, minced or pressed

2/3 cup dry white wine

3 cups chicken stock or broth

3/4 cup heavy cream

2/3 cup freshly grated Parmigiano-Reggiano cheese

Salt and pepper, to taste

Cooked wild rice blend or brown rice

Preheat the oven to 350°F. In a large skillet, cook bacon over medium heat until golden but still pliable. Drain on paper towels, reserving about 1/4 cup grease from the skillet. Place a piece of plastic wrap over the chicken breasts and pound to an even thickness by beating with the flat side of the meat mallet. Arrange half of the bacon slices on each breast and top with 2 tablespoons of the arugula. Roll chicken up, tucking in the ends to close, and use a toothpick to secure. Place the rolled chicken in a large dish and pour the teriyaki over the chicken and sprinkle with lemon pepper. Marinate approximately 3 hours in the refrigerator or 30 minutes at room temperature, turning occasionally. Add approximately 1 tablespoon of oil (if needed) to the reserved bacon grease and heat over medium heat. Add the rolled breasts (roulades) to the oil and brown on all sides, about 5 minutes total. Transfer the roulades to a 9 x 13-inch baking dish, reserving the grease in the skillet, and bake 30 to 40 minutes or until the juices run clear when chicken is pierced with a fork. While the chicken is cooking, make the sauce by mixing the butter and flour together in a small bowl to make a paste; set aside. Add the shallots and garlic to the skillet with the reserved bacon grease and sauté on low heat until shallots are translucent, about 3 minutes. Add the white wine to the skillet and increase the heat to medium. The wine will boil, loosening the browned bits that contribute to the sauce's flavor. Boil until the wine reduces by half. Add the stock and bring back to a boil. Boil 10 minutes until mixture reduces slightly. Add the cream and Parmigiano-Reggiano cheese and continue to whisk. Add the flour-butter paste to

(continued on next page)

178

the sauce and whisk. Continue whisking until sauce is thick enough to coat the back of a spoon without dripping. Season with salt and pepper and keep warm until ready to serve. When roulades are cooked through, remove toothpicks and slice diagonally. To serve, make a timbale of rice (drum-shaped uniform mound) using a 1/3 cup solid measuring cup as a scoop. Scoop rice onto a plate, smash down slightly and serve chicken over the bed of rice. Drizzle the chicken with sauce, passing additional sauce separately.

Tip: This may be made ahead and baked later. After refrigeration, bring the roulades to room temperature before baking. Depending on the size of the chicken breasts you may not need an entire breast slice per person so this is a recipe you can stretch if additional unexpected guests arrive. If you increase the recipe and brown quite a few breasts in the same oil, the bottom of the pan may blacken too much to make a sauce. Do not discard any of the bacon grease until you have completed the recipe in case you need to make your sauce starting with bacon grease due to the pan being unsuitable for sauce. In case the pan is too dark, wash it out. Use the reserved grease and start the sauce.

Special Note: Arugula is a semi-bitter, aromatic salad herb with a peppery mustard flavor.

Variations: Stuff the inside of the chicken with anything! (E.g. Boursin cheese, herbed or with black pepper, or any cheese, prosciutto or other vegetables like watercress or spinach). If you do not have teriyaki, mix 1/4 cup less sodium soy sauce with 2 tablespoons brown sugar. If desired, mushrooms may be sautéed with the shallots and garlic and the dish may be garnished with fresh, chopped chives. Since cream and sherry pair nicely, stir in 1/4 cup dry sherry into the original version above and simmer 5 minutes before serving...delicious.

Chicken in Puff Pastry with Basil Cream Sauce

Serves: 4

 • whisk

Puff Pastry Wrapped Chicken
2 (8-ounce) boneless, skinless chicken breasts
1 (17.3-ounce) box frozen Puff Pastry Sheets, thawed
2 teaspoons prepared pesto
1 egg yolk, beaten, mixed with 1 tablespoon cold water

Basil Cream Sauce
4 tablespoons unsalted butter, softened, divided use
2 medium shallots, finely chopped (about 1/4 cup)
1 medium garlic clove, minced or pressed
1 small red bell pepper, diced (1/4-inch pieces)
1 cup chicken stock or broth
1 cup heavy cream
2 tablespoons flour
2 tablespoons minced oil packed sun-dried tomatoes
1/4 teaspoon Tabasco red pepper sauce
Salt, to taste
1/4 cup thinly sliced fresh basil

Preheat the oven to 400°F. Wrap the chicken breasts in plastic wrap and pound the chicken with a meat mallet to get consistent thickness throughout. (Do this step only if necessary.) Remove excess moisture with a paper towel. Cut the breasts crosswise into 2 even-sized halves. Lay out the 2 sheets of pastry dough and cut in half diagonally. (You will be creating an envelope or be packaging the chicken breast in the dough.) Place the chicken breast in the center of each pastry triangle. Spread pesto evenly on top of each breast (approximately 1/2 teaspoon). Fold the short ends of pastry over the chicken; fold long side the of pastry over the chicken to create an envelope. Pinch the edges to seal. (Chicken should be entirely encased but without too much dough overlapping. Cut off excess dough.) Place pastry packages seam-side down on a baking sheet and brush with egg yolk. You may refrigerate until ready to bake (no more than a few hours). Bake until the pastry is golden and the bottom is done, about 20 to 25 minutes. (The chicken is perfectly cooked due to the heat that causes the breasts to steam.) For the sauce, melt 2 tablespoons butter and sauté the shallot, garlic and pepper. Add the chicken broth and heavy cream. Bring to a boil. Make a paste of the remaining 2 tablespoons butter and the flour. Add a tablespoon of the flour mixture to the hot liquid and whisk to thicken. Add the remaining if needed for desired consistency. Once thickened, lower heat and whisk in the tomatoes and Tabasco. Keep sauce warm while the chicken is cooking.

(continued on next page)

Taste and add salt, if desired. Remove the sauce from heat, stir in the basil and serve. If sauce gets too thick, add additional broth. Transfer chicken to plate and drizzle each packet with sauce before serving. Pass extra sauce.

Variations: This can easily be done with a skinned salmon fillet or pork (1 inch thick pieces are the key.) Use clam juice, seafood or vegetable stock or broth when making a sauce for fish.

With pork or beef, you may use half beef stock or broth, and half chicken stock or broth. You may encase the meat with something other than pesto. Sautéed mushrooms (drain off liquid) or cheese (such as Boursin pepper or herb cheese) are other options and spices can be varied according to taste.

You may replace part of the stock with white wine if desired or add 2 tablespoons sherry just before serving.

This sauce is a favorite. I will often make the sauce and add uncooked salmon or shrimp in the last 5 minutes of cooking. Serve over rice or pasta.

Special Note: If you have extra dough, make small cutouts of hearts or leaves and adhere to top for an extra special touch! This is tasty, quick and impressive enough for guests! Prepared pesto is typically near the pasta sauces.

Pollo Maria

Serves: 4

Chicken
2 tablespoons olive oil
4 (8-ounce) boneless, skinless
  chicken breasts
1/3 cup flour
1/2 ounce tequila

Sauce
1/2 cup (1 ounce) thinly sliced
  fresh mushrooms
1 cup half-and-half
1 teaspoon chicken base,
  undiluted
5 dashes of Maggi Seasoning
Salt and white or black pepper,
  to taste

Heat the oil in a large skillet. Coat the chicken breasts in flour and cook in the skillet until lightly browned on all sides. Drain the excess oil and continue to sauté breasts on low heat, approximately 4 minutes per side. While cooking, add the tequila to the pan and light or flambé. The alcohol will burn fast and the flame should die down quickly. Once the flame has died down, add the mushrooms to the skillet and gradually stir in the half-and-half and chicken base. Simmer until sauce starts to thicken. Add the Maggi Seasoning and salt and pepper, to taste.

Tip: When purchasing button mushrooms, look for firm, evenly colored mushrooms with tightly closed caps. If the gills are showing, the mushrooms are past their prime.

Special Note: Maggi is a seasoning sauce and can be found in your grocery store usually where liquid smoke is found. Chicken soup base is the consistency of a paste. It is a chicken stock that when mixed with water makes a great rich stock and can be used in recipes in place of broth. Flambé safety: To extinguish the flame after you flambé, keep the skillet lid in close proximity to the stove. Immediately place lid over the skillet if necessary. Without oxygen, the flame cannot burn. Alcohol ignites easily, so keep your face and clothing at a distance.

La Margarita: Irving, Texas
This is our getaway for our favorite Mexican food. We are warmly greeted by Gabriel and Adrian and are promptly served our margaritas by our friendly waiter, Joel. I was thrilled they shared their delicious Pollo Maria recipe with me. They serve it with sautéed, julienned carrots, squash and rice.

Chicken with Sour Cream and Smoked Paprika

Serves: 6

4 (8-ounce) boneless, skinless chicken breasts
2 tablespoons smoked sweet paprika
2 tablespoons unsalted butter
1 cup diced onion (1/4-inch pieces)
2 tomatoes, seeded and chopped (1/4-inch pieces)
2 cups chicken stock or broth
1 cup heavy cream
1 tablespoon cornstarch, or more if needed
1 cup sour cream
Salt, to taste
Cooked brown or white rice

Cut the chicken breasts into bite-sized chunks (1 x 1-inch) or strips (1 1/2 x 1 1/2-inch) and rub with the paprika. In a large skillet with a lid, melt the butter and sauté the onion until translucent, about 5 minutes. Add the chicken, tomatoes, stock and cream. Simmer until chicken is cooked through, approximately 20 minutes. Stir the cornstarch into the sour cream in a separate small bowl and add to the skillet. Cover and simmer approximately 8 minutes or until sauce reaches desired consistency. Taste and add salt if desired. Serve hot over rice. Easy and delicious!

Tip: Sour cream added to the pan can sometimes cause the sauce to separate. The cornstarch will help bring the sauce back together. Use an additional tablespoon of cornstarch dissolved in cold water if desired consistency is not reached.

Variation: Hungarian (sweet) paprika can also be used for a completely different flavor.

Special Note: Pimenton (smoked paprika from Spain) comes in three varieties—sweet and mild (dulce), bittersweet medium hot (agridulce) and hot (picante)—and normally keeps for two years.

Chicken with Mushroom Cream Sauce

Serves: 4

1 1/2 pounds boneless, skinless chicken breasts, cut in cubes or sliced in thin slices
1 cup flour
3 tablespoons unsalted butter
2 medium shallots, finely chopped (about 1/4 cup)
1 (8-ounce) package mushrooms, chopped
2 medium garlic cloves, minced or pressed
2 tablespoons white wine (sweet or dry), apple brandy or dry sherry
1 cup chicken stock or broth
1 teaspoon dried thyme
1 cup heavy cream
1 tablespoon coarse-grained mustard
2 tablespoons unsalted butter, softened, mixed with 2 tablespoons flour
Salt and ground white pepper, to taste
Cooked white, wild or brown rice

In a large plastic bag, add the chicken in with the flour and toss to coat. In a large skillet or Dutch oven over medium heat, melt the butter and add the shallots, mushrooms and garlic. Once the shallots are translucent, about 3 minutes, add the wine or apple brandy and cook until reduced by half. Add the chicken and sauté. Turn heat to medium-low and add the stock and thyme. Bring to a boil. Reduce the heat and add cream and mustard. Cover and simmer 30 to 40 minutes until meat is very tender. Whisk in the butter-flour mixture and continue whisking until desired consistency is reached. Season with salt and pepper and serve with rice.

Variations: You may use boneless beef chuck or thinly sliced pork tenderloin to change this recipe. Herbs, spices and onions (red or green onion) can be interchanged to create variations of this meal. Beef broth can replace chicken broth and for pork I like to do half chicken and half beef broth. If the sauce is too creamy for your taste, add a teaspoon of Worcestershire sauce to enhance the beef flavor.

3 slices of bacon, diced and cooked may be added. Use the grease from the bacon to cook the onions and mushrooms. Top the dish with minced fresh chives.

1/4 teaspoon Marjoram and 1 tablespoon of sweet Hungarian paprika can be substituted for other spices in the recipe.

Cajun spices work well for spicing this up (see Creole Spice page 224). One tablespoon per 4 breasts is plenty of spice. The spice works equally well with pork or beef. Leave the mustard out.

(continued on next page)

A favorite combination of ours came from our good friend Joe Graber. Joe does a version of this and adds 2 teaspoons ground green peppercorns or rinsed, drained and brined green peppercorns to the sauce.

The mushrooms in this recipe are optional. When we just need a quick family meal, we make this without mushrooms and everyone loves it!

Special Note: Shallots are a cross between onion and garlic. Peel them like an onion or clove of garlic. If unavailable, just use a combination of 3/4 onion and 2 garlic cloves, minced. The cream tenderizes the meat, making this recipe and its variations a perfect meal. We prefer a nice concentrated stock or broth that requires refrigeration once opened. For a change, serve any of these combinations in a baked puff pastry shell.

> *"I've learned the importance of chasing life's rainbows and that the pot of gold may sometimes be a heart of gold found around the least expected corner."*
>
> *~Author unknown*

Cajun Creamed Chicken in Puff Pastry Shells

Serves: 8

Seasoning Mix
1 tablespoon salt
1 1/2 teaspoons dried basil
1 teaspoon garlic powder
1 teaspoon onion powder
1 teaspoon ground white pepper
1 teaspoon sweet paprika
1 teaspoon dry mustard
1/2 teaspoon dried Herbes
   de Provence
1/4 teaspoon nutmeg

Chicken
6 (8-ounce) boneless, skinless
   chicken breasts
1/2 cup (1 stick) unsalted
   butter, softened, divided use
1/4 cup flour
1/4 cup white wine
1 cup diced onion
   (1/4-inch pieces)
2 cups (4 ounces) thinly sliced
   fresh mushrooms
1 cup diced red bell pepper
   (1/4-inch pieces)
1 cup diced green bell pepper
   (1/4-inch pieces)
1 1/2 cups heavy cream
1 cup whole milk
2 tablespoons dry sherry
2 (10-ounce) packages frozen
   puff pastry shells

Preheat the oven to 400°F. To make the seasoning mix, combine all the ingredients in a small bowl. Sprinkle 2 tablespoons seasoning over the chicken breasts and rub in with your hands. Cut the chicken breasts into bite-size cubes and set aside. Combine 1/2 stick (1/4 cup) butter with the flour in a small bowl to make a paste. Heat a large skillet or Dutch oven over high heat. When the skillet is hot, add the seasoned chicken and the remaining 1/2 stick of butter. Cover and do not stir for approximately 4 minutes. Uncover and stir, re-cover and cook an additional 4 minutes. (Be sure your oven vent is on the entire time because you are cooking at such a high heat.) Add the white wine (reserving the sherry), onions, mushrooms, bell peppers and remaining seasoning. Stir well, cover and cook 5 minutes. Reduce heat to medium. Uncover and add the butter-flour mixture a spoonful at a time. Stir as you add, until the mixture dissolves and the sauce thickens. Stir in the cream and heat until small bubbles come to the surface and erupt. Do not let boil. Let the bubbles erupt 3 times and stir after each eruption. Add the milk and heat again until another group of small bubbles erupt and the mixture is at a desired thickness. Turn the heat to low and stir in the sherry. Keep on low heat until ready to serve, stirring occasionally so it doesn't stick to the bottom of the skillet. Bake the pastry shells according to package directions just before serving. Remove the tops of the puff pastry shells after they are baked. Spoon a generous amount of the chicken mixture inside the baked puff pastry shells. Top each with the baked pastry shell top and serve.

(continued on next page)

Variation: Peeled and deveined shrimp make a super replacement for chicken. Shrimp would be the last thing added and takes only about 5 minutes to cook. A (14-ounce) can of artichoke hearts, drained and coarsely chopped, is a nice addition with the shrimp.

Special Note: I prefer to use a granulated garlic powder (small granules of dehydrated garlic) versus the garlic powder that resembles powder.

Creamy Lemon Chicken with Capers

Serves: 4

• whisk

4 (8-ounce) boneless, skinless chicken breasts
1 tablespoon olive oil
1/4 cup fresh lemon juice (juice from 1 1/2 large lemons)
1 tablespoon Creole Spice (page 224)
1/2 teaspoon chicken bouillon paste, undiluted
1 1/2 cups heavy cream
2 tablespoons capers, rinsed and drained
1 cup freshly grated Parmigiano-Reggiano cheese
2 tablespoons cornstarch mixed with two tablespoons cold water
1/2 cup frozen peas (optional)
9 ounces cooked pasta, 3 cups hot cooked rice or baked puff pastry shells

Cut the chicken into bite-size chunks (1 x 1-inch) or strips (1 1/2 x 1 1/2-inch). In a large skillet, heat a tablespoon of olive oil and add the chicken. Pour lemon juice over the chicken and sprinkle with Creole Spice. Sauté the chicken until browned on the outside. Add the bouillon paste to the skillet. Pour the cream over the breasts and bring to a boil. Reduce heat to a simmer and cover pan for 30 minutes. Add the capers and cheese; stir to blend. Add the cornstarch mixture to the hot liquid while whisking. Heat liquid to boiling allowing about 2 minutes for sauce to thicken. Sauce should coat the back of a spoon without dripping. Serve over hot cooked pasta, rice or in a baked pastry shell.

Tip: For most recipes calling for broth or bouillon, I use a base that is a paste called Better than Bouillon. If you have an extra large (2 cups) Knorr bouillon cube, 1/4 of the cube may replace the paste. A canned broth or stock will not work in this recipe because it is not concentrated enough.

Variation: To lighten this up we eliminate the Parmigiano-Reggiano and heavy cream. Dredge the chicken pieces in rice flour. In a large skillet, heat 2 tablespoons olive oil and sauté the chicken, 2 garlic cloves, minced or pressed, lemon juice and Creole Spice. Cook chicken until no longer pink and cooked through (use extra olive oil if needed); remove chicken from the skillet and set aside in a 150°F oven. Add 1/2 cup white wine to the skillet and boil until reduced by half, scraping the browned bits off the bottom of the pan. Mix 1 1/2 teaspoons of the chicken bouillon paste with 1 1/2 cups water in a separate medium bowl and add to the skillet.

(continued on next page)

188

Thoroughly heat the liquid and whisk the cornstarch mixture into the hot liquid; bring to a boil for about 2 minutes. Whisk to avoid lumps. Add capers and chicken. Once thickened, serve over cooked rice.

Special Note: Regular rice flour is a fine, powdery flour made from regular white rice. It can be used in recipes as a replacement for wheat flour when dredging meats or fish before sautéing. Cooking rice in a broth enhances the flavor. My favorite brand is Better Than Bouillon. Other components can add additional flavor as well. Sauté 1/4 cup finely chopped shallots or garlic (1 medium clove, minced) prior to adding the rice and liquid. For Thai meals, coconut milk can be diluted (14 ounces coconut milk and 8 ounces water) for 2 cups white or brown favorite combinations is to add 1/2 cup toasted slivered almonds to rice once cooked. When the almonds are used in the rice, I prefer long grain white rice, cooked in chicken broth with 1/4 cup sherry added to 1 3/4 cups broth. Serve with a mushroom cream sauce as in the recipe on page 184. Fresh corn, fresh herbs or a rinsed can of black beans and cilantro, all have their place depending on the ethnicity of the main dish you are serving.

Ryan Gore: Grapevine, Texas
My stepson, Ryan, helped me create this recipe. He has a sophisticated palate and recognizes the nuances that make a dish memorable.

Chicken Stroganoff

• whisk

4 tablespoons butter
1 medium yellow onion, diced
  (1/4-inch pieces)
1 garlic clove, minced
1 (8-ounce) package fresh
  sliced mushrooms
1 Knorr Extra Large Beef
  Bouillon cube
1 1/2 cups hot water
4 (8-ounce) boneless, skinless
  chicken breasts, cut in strips
1/4 teaspoon black pepper
1/8 cayenne pepper
1/8 teaspoon ground white pepper
1/4 teaspoon onion powder
1/8 teaspoon garlic powder
1/4 teaspoon dry mustard
1 teaspoon *Tony Chachere's
  Creole Seasoning*
1 tablespoon A.1. Steak Sauce
1/2 cup heavy cream
1 tablespoon cornstarch mixed
  with one tablespoon cold water
3/4 cup sour cream
Salt and pepper, to taste
1 tablespoon minced fresh parsley
Cooked white or brown rice or
  egg noodles

Melt the butter in a large skillet over medium heat and sauté the onions, garlic and mushrooms until the mushrooms are tender. Dissolve the bouillon cube in the hot water in a separate small bowl. Add the beef broth and the chicken strips to the skillet. Mix together the black pepper, cayenne pepper, white pepper, onion powder, garlic powder and dry mustard in a small bowl. Stir the spices into the skillet and add the *Tony Chachere's*, A.1 and cream. Cover and cook over low heat until the chicken is tender and no longer pink, about 20 minutes. Add half of the cornstarch mixture and bring to boil for about 2 minutes while whisking. Sauce should begin to thicken. Add more of the mixture if needed to achieve desired thickness. Remove from heat and whisk in sour cream. Season with salt and pepper. Sprinkle with parsley and serve over rice or noodles.

Tip: If a sauce breaks (separates) it is often due to sour cream being added. Cornstarch mixed with equal parts cold water in a separate small bowl and then added to the pan will bring it back together. Heat the sauce over medium heat whisking continually and sauce will pull together for desirable texture.

Variation: A whole chicken may be boiled with a piece of celery and a carrot for flavor if preferred. Debone the chicken, reserve broth and complete the recipe as directed. For a shortcut, debone a precooked rotisserie chicken from your local grocer. Stroganoff typically has mushrooms but this dish is also delicious without them.

(continued on next page)

Special Note: Sauces can be thickened by sprinkling sautéed vegetables with flour and then adding liquid or by adding a butter and flour mixture called a beurre manié after the sauce is made. Beurre manié (burr mahn-YAY) is French for kneaded butter and is a paste of equal parts softened butter and flour (2 tablespoons of each per 4 cups of liquid). Getting sauces to thicken requires raising the temperature to allow bubbles to break on the surface. Whisk the beurre manié into the hot boiling liquid and reduce heat to simmer. Allow a minimum of 10 minutes to cook so the flour loses its raw taste. Cornstarch can be used as well in place of the flour. (Mix 1 tablespoon cornstarch with 1 tablespoon cold liquid such as water, broth or wine to make a thin paste just before adding to the sauce.) The liquid must get hot enough for the cornstarch to activate and must be cooked for 2 minutes. Do not overheat or over stir for best results. The color consistencies of the sauces will differ slightly.

> *"With years richer life begins*
> *The spirit mellows,*
> *Ripe age gives tone to violins,*
> *Wine and good fellows."*
>
> ~*John Trowbridge*

Empress Stir-Fry Chicken

Serves: 4

1/4 cup soy sauce
2 tablespoons honey
2 tablespoons ketchup
2 tablespoons cider vinegar
1 medium garlic clove, minced
   or pressed
1/2 teaspoon ground ginger
1 tablespoon cornstarch
2 (8-ounce) boneless, skinless
   chicken breasts
1 tablespoon peanut oil, if
   necessary add a little more
   when sautéing
2 cups chopped onions (1-inch
   chunks)
2 cups sliced celery
1 (8.5-ounce) can water
   chestnuts, drained and sliced
Cooked brown or white rice

Combine soy sauce, honey, ketchup, vinegar, garlic and ginger in a medium bowl. Dissolve cornstarch into mixture and set aside. Cut chicken into chunks and set aside. Heat oil over high heat in a skillet or wok. Add onions, celery and water chestnuts. Stir-fry about 4 minutes or until vegetables are tender crisp (soft but not overcooked). Remove vegetables from skillet and set aside. Stir-fry the chicken in the same skillet until lightly brown. Add the soy sauce mixture to the chicken and continue to cook until mixture thickens, about 2 minutes. Add the cooked vegetables and heat thoroughly. Serve hot over rice. You may add cashews or peanuts and substitute your favorite vegetables if others are preferred.

Tip: A boxed Chinese rice from the grocery store adds additional oriental flavor.

Robin Murphy: North Richland Hills, Texas
Robin made this recipe years ago when we were getting together with the "group" to watch Knots Landing. We still get together often, but wonder how we ever made a commitment to a weekly gathering. This can be a complete family meal since the starch, vegetables and meat are all part of the dish.

Thai Chicken Curry

Serves: 4

4 (8-ounce) boneless, skinless chicken breasts

1 tablespoon olive oil, plus more if needed

4 teaspoons Thai green or red curry paste

2 fresh serrano chiles, minced (or 1 medium jalapeño, seeded and minced)

1 (14-ounce) can Thai coconut milk

3 tablespoons fish sauce (nam pla)

1 (8-ounce) can bamboo shoots, drained

4 teaspoons sugar

1 teaspoon undiluted chicken base or 1 (1 cup) chicken bouillon cube

2 teaspoons cornstarch mixed with 2 teaspoons cold water (optional)

1 cup (3-ounce package) fresh basil, chopped

Cooked brown or white rice

Cut the chicken breasts in bite-size chunks (1 x 1-inch) or strips (1 1/2 x 1 1/2-inch) and set aside. In a large skillet with a lid, heat the oil, curry paste and chiles and cook 3 minutes until fragrant. Add the chicken and stir to coat with the curry. Add the coconut milk, fish sauce, bamboo shoots, sugar and chicken base. Cover and cook over low heat, approximately 20 minutes, or until chicken is cooked through. If the sauce is too thin, whisk the cornstarch mixture into the hot liquid. Bring to a boil to thicken, about 2 minutes. Remove from the heat and stir in the basil. Serve hot over rice. (Rice is more flavorful when cooked in the chicken broth instead of water.)

Special Note: We recommend a Thai Kitchen curry paste that is sold in many grocery stores. The coconut milk used for drinks (Coco Lopez) is not the same as that used for Thai cooking. Thai recipes use unsweetened coconut milk. Less sodium soy sauce can be used in place of fish sauce and it still tastes great. I remove the seeds if I use a jalapeño but do not remove the seeds when using serranos.

Variations: This sauce is delicious made with any meat or seafood. Even grilled or baked salmon pairs nicely. Consider using leftover pork, beef or shrimp in the last stage of cooking. Shrimp takes just minutes to cook. If you would like some color added, dice a red pepper in 1/2-inch pieces and add just when you bring mixture to boil.

Additional broth could also be added to make a marvelous soup. There are Asian noodles that may replace rice if you wish.

Serrano chiles are slightly milder than jalapeño peppers and may be used interchangeably depending on your heat preference.

For a delicious variation, use the red curry paste and add 1/2 cup Thai peanut sauce to this dish. Start with 1 tablespoon minced serrano chile and adjust the spice to taste.

Asian Peanut Chicken

Serves: 4

• vegetable peeler (to peel ginger)

4 (8-ounce) boneless, skinless chicken breasts
1/2 cup Thai peanut sauce
1/4 cup less sodium soy sauce
1 (14-ounce) can Thai coconut milk
2 teaspoons sugar
2 tablespoons sesame oil
2 medium garlic cloves, minced or pressed
2 tablespoons minced fresh ginger
6 green onions, thinly sliced on the diagonal (white and pale green part only)
4 teaspoons Thai green curry paste
1 teaspoon undiluted chicken base or 1 (1 cup) chicken bouillon cube
1 tablespoon cornstarch mixed with 1 tablespoon cold water
2 red bell peppers, cut in 1-inch pieces
1 green bell pepper, cut in 1-inch pieces
1 serrano chile, minced
1/3 cup thinly sliced fresh basil
Cooked brown or white rice

Cut the chicken breasts in bite-size chunks (1 x 1-inch) or strips (1 1/2 x 1 1/2-inch) and set aside. In a small bowl, mix together the peanut sauce, soy sauce, coconut milk and sugar. In a medium saucepan, heat the sesame oil and sauté the garlic, ginger, green onions and green curry paste until garlic is fragrant. Add the chicken and chicken base; sauté until no pink remains. Add the peanut sauce mixture and stir to coat. Add the cornstarch mixture, whisking to avoid lumps. Heat to boiling and allow sauce to thicken, about 2 minutes. Add the red and green pepper chunks and the serrano chile. Remove from the heat and add the basil. Serve hot over rice. A family dinner winner! Serve with the Asian Slaw with Peanut Dressing on page 134 or salad with Hoisin Vinaigrette page 145.

Variation: Pork tenderloin (1 1/2 pounds) thinly sliced may be substituted for the chicken.

Special Note: Thai peanut sauce is usually in the Asian section of the grocery store.

Chicken Chalupas

Serves: 20

3 cups (12 ounces) grated
Monterey Jack cheese
3 cups (12 ounces) grated
Cheddar cheese
2 bunches green onion tops (dark
green part), thinly sliced
1 (10.75-ounce) can cream of
mushroom soup
1 (10.75-ounce) can cream of
chicken soup
1 (4.5-ounce) can chopped
green chiles
1 (16-ounce) container sour cream
1 (4.25-ounce) can sliced black
ripe olives
4 (8-ounce) boneless, skinless
chicken breasts, cooked and
cut in 1-inch pieces
20 (6-inch) flour tortillas
Bottled salsa or hot sauce

Preheat the oven to 350°F. Combine cheeses in a medium bowl and set aside. Combine half of the cheese mixture, half of the green onions, the mushroom and chicken soups, chiles, sour cream and olives in a large bowl. Set aside 1 1/2 cups of this mixture for the topping. Add the cooked chicken to the cheese mixture for the filling and mix well. Put 3 heaping tablespoons of filling on each tortilla and roll. Place tortilla seam-side down in a lightly oiled shallow 9 x 13-inch baking dish. Arrange tortillas in a single layer using 2 pans if necessary. Spread reserved topping mixture over tortillas and cover with the remaining cheese and onion tops. Refrigerate overnight or freeze. Bake uncovered 45 minutes. Let stand a few minutes before serving. Serve with salsa or hot sauce on the side.

Tip: One chicken breast equals approximately 1 cup.

Special Note: Green onions are often called scallions. The difference is scallions do not have the bulb developed and are milder than those onions where a bulb has started to mature. Often you will find both of these shapes within one bunch of onions. Chives are completely different. They are vivid green and have slender, hollow stems and have a very mild onion flavor.

Kathryn Farr: Pensacola, Florida
Kathryn contributed this recipe because when she entertains it is usually a large group and children are included. She prefers to prepare meals a day ahead because her four children keep her and Wes very busy. My memories of Kathryn include sharing chili dogs, ice cream sandwiches, corn nuts and Swannie's Yum Yums rather than gourmet meals, as we have known each other since Kindergarten and roomed together our first year of college.

Chicken Enchiladas with Green Chili Salsa

Serves: 6

• cheese grater

3 (8-ounce) boneless, skinless chicken breasts, finely chopped
1/2 teaspoon *Tony Chachere's Creole Seasoning*
1/2 teaspoon lemon pepper
1 tablespoon butter
1 small yellow onion, finely chopped
1 garlic clove, minced or pressed
1 (7-ounce) jar green chile/tomatillo salsa
1 (4.5-ounce) can chopped green chiles
2 cups grated Monterey Jack cheese, divided use
2 cups heavy cream
1/2 teaspoon salt
Olive oil for softening tortillas
12 corn tortillas
1 tomato, diced (1/4-inch pieces)
1 bunch green onion tops (dark green portion), for garnish

Preheat the oven to 350°F. Sprinkle chicken breasts with *Tony Chachere's* and lemon pepper. Grill 6 to 7 minutes per side over moderate heat. In a medium skillet, melt the butter and sauté the onion until translucent, about 5 minutes. Add the garlic just before the onion is fully sautéed. Combine the chicken, onion, garlic, green salsa, chiles and 1 cup cheese in a large bowl. Mix heavy cream and salt together in a separate small bowl and set aside. Coat the bottom of a large skillet with the olive oil. Dip each tortilla in the skillet about 5 seconds to soften then dip into the bowl containing cream and salt, coating each side. Fill each tortilla with the chicken mixture. Roll seam-side down and place in an ungreased 9 x 13-inch baking dish. Pour remaining cream over the rolled tortillas and sprinkle with remaining cheese. Bake enchiladas for 20 to 25 minutes. Garnish before serving with tomato and green onion tops.

Tip: If you choose not to grill the chicken, then use a pre-cooked 2-pound rotisserie chicken. Skin, debone and shred the meat. Frozen corn can be added to the mixture for a variation.

Special Note: When grilling, grill extra chicken breasts and freeze them. You can defrost them later and add them to a casserole. The fresh grilled flavor tastes better than boiled or microwaved chicken.

Mexican Chicken Delight

Serves: 6

• cheese grater

1 small package corn tortillas
(12 to 15 tortillas)
3 cups cooked chicken
3 tablespoons butter
1 medium onion, finely chopped
1 (10.75-ounce) can cream of
mushroom soup
1 (10.75-ounce) can cream of
chicken soup
1 cup chicken stock or broth
1 (10-ounce) can Ro*Tel Diced
Tomatoes and Green Chilies
1 (7-ounce) can chopped green
chiles, drained
2 cups grated Cheddar cheese

Preheat oven to 325°F. Cut tortillas into 1-inch wide strips. Boil the chicken and clean meat from the bone or use boneless chicken breasts that have been grilled, boiled or prepared in the microwave. (Approximately 3 breasts equal 3 cups meat.) Melt the butter in a skillet and sauté the onion until translucent. In a large bowl combine the soups, broth, tomatoes, cooked onions and green chiles with the chicken and mix well. In a 9 x 13-inch baking dish, layer the tortillas, chicken mixture and cheese. Bake for 40 minutes covered and an additional 15 minutes uncovered. Let the dish cool slightly and serve this with a salad, chips and hot sauce on the side.

Tips: This casserole is a great thing to make ahead and refrigerate until ready to bake. The refrigeration helps it to set up better. You may need to heat slightly longer (if it has been refrigerated) to warm through the center. White and yellow onions may be used interchangeably.

Debbie Smith: Lawrence, Kansas
Debbie lived with my family for a year while she finished high school because her parents moved out of the district. We enjoyed some of my mother's terrific meals together.

Cornish Game Hens with Honey Glaze and Caramelized Onions

Serves: 2

 • jelly roll pan or roasting pan

Honey Glaze
1/4 cup plus 2 tablespoons honey
1 1/2 cups Muscat wine or other
  sweet wine
1 cup chicken broth
2 tablespoons less sodium soy
  sauce
1/2 cup (1 stick) unsalted
  butter, cut into chunks

Onions
1 (10-ounce) basket of pearl
  onions
2 tablespoons unsalted butter
1/4 cup water
1 tablespoon honey

Rice
1 box wild rice medley, cooked
  according to directions

Cornish Hens
2 Rock Cornish game hens
  (2.5 pounds total), defrosted
Salt and pepper

Spinach
1 tablespoon unsalted butter
1 bunch (10 ounces) fresh
  spinach, washed and tough
  stems removed
Salt and pepper, to taste

Preheat oven to 425°F. To make the glaze, heat the honey in small heavy skillet over medium heat until the honey darkens and becomes fragrant, swirling the pan occasionally for about 3 minutes. Slowly add the wine and chicken broth and bring to a boil. Continue to boil the mixture until it has reduced to 1 cup, about 20 minutes. Add soy sauce and boil 3 minutes longer. When you are ready to serve the hens, bring the glaze to a boil and add the 1/2 cup butter. This can be made a day ahead, refrigerated and butter can be whisked in when reheating. For the onions, bring a medium saucepan of water to boil. Add the onions and blanch 2 minutes. Drain and rinse the onions under cool water. Cut off the end of each onion and peel. Melt the butter in a heavy skillet over medium heat. Add the onions to the skillet and sauté until golden brown and tender, almost 10 minutes. Add the 1/4 cup water and honey. Cover and simmer until onions are tender, about 5 minutes. Uncover and continue cooking until onions are caramelized, about 2 to 5 minutes. Keep warm. These can be made 8 hours ahead of serving, just let them rest covered at room temperature. Reheat the onions over medium heat, stirring constantly. Cook rice according to package directions. Season the hens with salt and pepper and arrange breast side up on a jelly roll pan. Bake until juices run clear when thighs are pierced with a fork, about 30 to 45 minutes. Keep warm.

(continued on next page)

198

Melt the tablespoon of butter over medium high heat and add the fresh spinach. Cover and cook until spinach is wilted, about 2 minutes. Drain and salt and pepper to taste. Divide the spinach among plates and place 1 hen on top of the spinach layer. Line the cooked rice underneath the hen on both sides. Drizzle lightly with the warm honey glaze. Place warm caramelized onions down the wing area or along the outside edge of the plate and drizzle hen generously with the remaining glaze.

Tip: For extra color add 1/2 cup fresh corn kernels to the rice.

Special Note: The Muscat grape has a sweet, musky flavor. It is a white or black grape and is typically grown in Italy, France, Greece, Spain and California.

"Through points of both commonality and divergence in culinary traditions, food can help unite, rather than divide, us in an increasingly fractious and fragmented world."

~Editor Darra Goldstein, Gastronomica magazine

Spice Cured Turkey

Serves: 12

- blender or food processor
- large roasting pan with rack
- large kettle
- meat thermometer

Brine Soaked Turkey
1 cup coarse sea salt
1/2 cup plus 2 tablespoons sugar
2 bay leaves
1 tablespoon dried thyme or 3
   tablespoons fresh thyme
7 whole cloves
1/2 tablespoon whole allspice
   berries
1/2 teaspoon whole juniper berries
1 teaspoon cracked black pepper
8 quarts (32 cups) water
1 (14-pound) turkey, defrosted

Spice Rub
1 1/2 tablespoons whole fennel
   seeds
1 large dried red chile
1/2 tablespoon whole allspice
   berries
1/2 tablespoon whole black
   peppercorns

Sage Butter
1 cup (2 sticks) unsalted butter
20 fresh sage leaves

Vegetable Stuffing
3 medium onions, coarsely
   chopped
1 large celery rib, chopped
1/2 cup celery leaves, chopped
24 garlic cloves, mashed
2 cups chicken broth or stock

In a very large stockpot, combine the coarse salt, sugar, bay leaves, thyme, cloves, allspice, juniper berries, black pepper and water. Bring to a boil over high heat. Remove from heat and cool to room temperature. Add the turkey to the cooled brine, breast side down. Cover and let rest overnight in the refrigerator. Prepare the spice rub by placing the measured spices in a small pan over medium heat and toast until fragrant, about 3 minutes. Remove from the heat and once cooled, transfer to a blender and grind. Set the rub aside. Make the sage butter by melting the butter in a saucepan and simmering until butter turns brown. Stir occasionally so solids do not stick to the pan and do not let the butter burn. Remove from heat and add the sage leaves. Let the leaves steep in the butter for 5 minutes. Remove the sage leaves with a fork and pour the butter in a glass or ceramic dish. Refrigerate overnight. Preheat the oven to 500°F. In a large bowl, toss the chopped vegetables with the mashed garlic and 1/2 tablespoon of the spice rub. Remove the turkey from the brine and place on a work surface. Spoon all but 2 cups of the vegetable stuffing into the chest and neck cavities. Using your fingers loosen the skin from the breast without tearing it. Evenly spread the sage butter under the skin and close the neck with toothpicks. Set the turkey breast side up in a roasting pan on top of a rack. Sprinkle the remaining spice over the bird and tie the legs together with kitchen string. Scatter the remaining 2 cups stuffing around the turkey and pour the chicken broth over the stuffing. Roast the turkey in the preheated oven for 20 minutes. Remove and cover the turkey loosely with foil and adjust the oven temperature to 350°F. Continue roasting for about 4 hours, basting frequently.

(continued on next page)

The turkey can be removed from the oven when the internal temperature of the thigh is 165°F to 170°F. Add water to the pan during cooking if the juices evaporate. Transfer the turkey to a carving board and let rest 15 to 20 minutes before slicing. Remove the stuffing from the turkey and serve alongside the sliced turkey. Serve with Turkey Gravy (following recipe).

Louella Hundt: Long Beach, California
I was a sportswear buyer for Louella several years ago. When we traveled to New York and Los Angeles as a group, she selected the restaurants where we would have dinner. She chose some of the best and most interesting places I have dined. She loves great atmosphere as much as the food. Her recipe for turkey requires soaking the turkey in brine, which makes the turkey extremely tender. This process and the unusual spice combination create a gourmet meal.

Turkey Gravy

Serves: 8

4 1/4 cups water, divided use
1 large Knorr chicken bouillon cube or 2 teaspoons chicken base
3 medium onions, coarsely chopped
1 1/2 carrots, washed and coarsely chopped
1 1/2 celery stalks, coarsely chopped
Rinsed neck, gizzard and liver from inside turkey
Pinch of dried thyme
1 1/2 tablespoons cornstarch
1 teaspoon Kitchen Bouquet Browning and Seasoning Sauce
Salt and pepper, to taste

Bring the water and chicken bouillon or base to a boil. Once dissolved, reserve 1/4 cup stock and set aside. Add the next 5 ingredients to the remaining broth. Simmer over low heat approximately 20 minutes until the neck is cooked. Strain all ingredients out, reserve neck and return broth to the pan. Cut off as much neck meat as possible and add to the broth. Mix together the cornstarch with the 1/4 cup reserved and cooled chicken broth until smooth. Add half of the cornstarch mixture to the hot liquid. Bring gravy to a boil for approximately 2 minutes until gravy is thickened. If mixture is not the desired consistency, add the remaining cornstarch mixture. Add 1 teaspoon Kitchen Bouquet or enough to get the desired caramel colored gravy. Salt and pepper to taste. Serve with turkey and dressing.

Special Note: I included this recipe because when I was in the retail world, I never went home for Thanksgiving. Over the years, I spent a lot of time on the phone with my mother walking me through the steps of this gravy making process.

Osso Buco

Serves: 6

1/3 cup flour plus 3
  tablespoons, divided use
2 teaspoons salt, divided use
1/2 teaspoon ground black pepper
6 veal shanks (about 4 pounds)
1/4 cup olive oil
1/3 cup unsalted butter, softened,
  divided use
1/2 teaspoon dried sage
1 teaspoon finely chopped
  rosemary
1 medium onion, finely chopped
3 large garlic cloves, minced or
  pressed, divided use
2 small carrots, finely chopped
1 rib celery, finely chopped
1 1/2 cups dry white wine
1 1/4 cups chicken broth or stock
2 tablespoons tomato paste

Gremolata
1 1/2 tablespoons fresh parsley,
  chopped
1 1/2 teaspoons lemon zest

Season the 1/3 cup flour with 1 teaspoon salt and the pepper. Put this mixture in a large sealable plastic bag or on a large platter and coat (dredge) the veal shanks in the flour mixture. Heat the oil and 2 tablespoons butter in a large Dutch oven and cook the meat over medium heat until golden on all sides. Arrange the meat in a single layer and sprinkle with the sage, rosemary, onion, 1 minced garlic clove, carrots and celery. Sprinkle the vegetables with the remaining salt and cook 10 minutes covered. (Onion must be translucent before continuing.) Add the wine, broth and tomato paste and turn heat down to low. Simmer 2 to 2 1/2 hours until the meat is fork tender. (You can place the Dutch oven in the oven at 300°F for the same amount of time.) Mix the remaining garlic, fresh parsley and lemon zest together to make the Gremolata and set aside. Remove the veal to a platter. Heat the remaining sauce to a boil on the stovetop. In a separate small bowl, mix together the remaining 3 tablespoons softened butter and 3 tablespoons flour. Add to the boiling sauce and continue to boil for 5 minutes, stirring constantly until the flour mixture thickens the sauce. When ready to serve, put a veal shank on each plate, spoon sauce over and sprinkle with the Gremolata mixture. Pass extra sauce separately. Serve with Risotto (page 229).

Variations: *This is an Italian version of pot roast. Use chuck roast or beef short ribs instead of veal chops for a less expensive version. Prepare the same way but use red wine and beef broth due to the different flavor of those cuts of meat. You will find the fatty meats will need additional salt before serving. Pass a small bowl of kosher salt or coarse sea salt or sprinkle meat before serving and top with sauce. If you are serving the next day, refrigerate; the fats will harden on the top and may be removed if desired. We enjoy soft polenta served with the short rib version. Follow package directions for preparing.*

Rosemary Grilled Lamb

Serves: 6

• meat thermometer

1/3 cup oil
2 teaspoons finely chopped
  fresh rosemary
3 garlic cloves, minced or
  pressed
1/4 cup coarse-grained Dijon
  mustard
2 racks of lamb (1 1/2 pounds
  each)

Make the marinade by combining the oil, rosemary, garlic and mustard. Pour into a large sealable plastic bag or marinade dish. Add the lamb and turn to coat. Refrigerate for 24 hours in the marinade. To cook the lamb outdoors, cook over moderate coals. Grill about 4 inches from heat for approximately 9 to 11 minutes. Desired doneness is 135°F for rare, 145°F for medium and 155°F for well done. If using a meat thermometer, the tip of thermometer should be in the center of meat not touching any bone, fat or grill. To cook the lamb in the oven, place the rack meaty side up and roast at 375°F using a meat thermometer and temperatures listed above for desired doneness.

Tips: We always prefer to pair a sauce with this marinated lamb. The Perfect Red Wine Sauce (page 148), Port Wine Sauce (page 162), and Red Wine Cherry Sauce (page 147) are sauces that complement the lamb. If using dried rosemary, use approximately 3/4 teaspoon.

> *"I feel a recipe is only a theme, which an intelligent cook can play each time with a vibration."*
>
> ~Madame Benoit

Sautéed Salmon with a Champagne Macadamia Cream Sauce

Serves: 4

- nut chopper
- whisk

4 (8-ounce) skinless salmon fillets
Salt, to taste
1 cup lightly salted macadamia
  nuts, coarsely chopped
5 tablespoons butter, divided use
1/2 cup pink sparkling wine or
  champagne
2 tablespoons flour
1 cup whole milk
1/2 cup fish or lobster stock
1/4 cup cream

Special Note: Béchamel sauce is made by stirring milk into a butter and flour mixture. This butter and flour mixture is called a roux. The thickness depends on the portion of butter and flour to the milk. If a few teaspoons of heavy cream are added with the milk, it tastes as though the whole sauce was made from cream.

Sprinkle the fillets with salt. In a skillet, sauté the macadamia nuts over medium heat in 1 tablespoon butter until lightly golden. Remove the pan from the heat and set aside 1/4 cup nuts for garnish. Add the champagne to the remaining 3/4 cup macadamia nuts and return to the stove. Cook the mixture until it boils, about 5 minutes. Turn down heat and keep warm. In another skillet, melt 2 tablespoons butter and add 2 tablespoons flour, whisking to blend. Cook until bubbles begin to form and stir in the milk. Continue to whisk as sauce thickens. Add the fish or lobster stock and simmer for an additional 5 minutes. Add the cream and simmer the roux until thickened to desired consistency. Add the roux to the nuts, butter and champagne mixture. Stir to blend and keep warm. Add salt to taste if needed. In a clean skillet, sauté salmon in 2 tablespoons butter until opaque in center, about 4 minutes per side. Place the salmon fillets on plates. Serve the sauce over salmon and sprinkle with the reserved salted macadamia nuts.

Tip: Mumm makes a pink sparkling wine called Mumm Cuvée Napa Blanc de Noirs. This sparkling wine is made from 85% Pinot Noir grape and 15% Chardonnay grape. It is a great accompaniment to this entrée.

Jane Langlais: Southlake, Texas
Jane and her husband Don moved to Australia with their son Reid for Don's work assignment. They have been part of the Dinner Club that started in 1989 and we missed them while they were away. They returned with this wonderful recipe, a knowledge and supply of great Australian wines and a new son, Luke!

Salmon with Honey–Soy Sauce

Serves: 4

• whisk

2 tablespoons honey
2 tablespoons less sodium soy
sauce
2 teaspoons Dijon mustard
4 tablespoons (1/2 stick)
unsalted butter
1 teaspoon olive oil
4 (6-ounce) salmon fillets
2 tablespoons dry white wine
2 green onions, sliced diagonally
into 1/4-inch pieces (white and
pale green part only)

Preheat the oven to 350°F. In a small bowl, whisk together the honey, soy sauce and mustard and set aside. Heat the butter and oil in a large skillet over medium heat and add the salmon fillets, skin side down. Cook the salmon 3 minutes per side. Remove the skin. (It should remove easily.) Transfer the cooked salmon to an ovenproof platter or baking dish and place in a 350°F oven while you make the sauce. (Salmon should be pink all the way through and flaky once removed from oven. This takes about 10 minutes.) Add the wine to the hot skillet and deglaze the pan scraping all the bits with a spatula. Add the honey mixture to the skillet and boil for 1 minute. Keep the sauce warm while baking the salmon. Stir the green onions into the sauce just before serving and pour over the cooked salmon.

Variation: We love to add 2 cups sliced fresh mushrooms (shiitake or button) and 1 garlic clove (minced or pressed) to this dish. Add these to the hot pan once fish is removed and sauté until mushrooms soften. Continue the recipe. Serve over brown rice with the Oriental Cabbage Slaw (page 135).

Grilled Salmon with Spinach and Gorgonzola Cream

Serves: 4

- pastry brush
- slotted spoon
- whisk

Spinach
1 package frozen whole leaf spinach
2 cups oil (preferably peanut)
Chopped fresh parsley, for garnish

Salmon
4 (8-ounce) skinless salmon fillets
2 tablespoons olive oil

Gorgonzola Cream Sauce
2 tablespoons butter
1 tablespoon chopped fresh dill
1/2 cup dry white wine
1 cup low salt chicken broth
1/4 teaspoon ground white pepper
1/2 cup heavy cream
1/4 cup Gorgonzola cheese
1 teaspoon cornstarch mixed with 1 teaspoon cold water

Red Pepper Garnish
1 red bell pepper
2 tablespoons olive oil
Black pepper

Thaw the spinach and squeeze out all excess water. Set aside. Prepare fillets by removing any remaining bones and brushing with 2 tablespoons olive oil. Measure out all cream sauce ingredients and put in small bowls. Cut up red peppers, discarding stem and seeds. Toss the peppers with the olive oil and sprinkle with black pepper. Set aside. Prepare and light the grill if using charcoal. Prepare the cream sauce by melting the butter over medium heat and adding the dill. Stir for 1 minute, then add the wine. Stir the sauce for 1 to 2 minutes and add the chicken broth and white pepper. Cook over medium heat until sauce is reduced to 3/4 cup. Gradually add the heavy cream, stirring until the sauce begins to thicken. Do not boil. Slowly add the Gorgonzola cheese and stir to get a smooth, creamy consistency. For a thicker consistency, the cornstarch paste may be whisked into the hot liquid and heated to boiling until mixture thickens (about 2 minutes). Turn heat to low to keep the sauce warm while cooking the fish. Arrange the red peppers around the edge of the grill. Cook the salmon around the outside of the flame, approximately 4 to 5 minutes per side, turning with a spatula only once, as the salmon will come apart. Remove peppers as they begin to blacken. In a medium saucepan, heat 2 cups cooking oil to a temperature suitable for frying. Fry thawed spinach until it darkens and gets crispy. Transfer it to paper towels with a slotted spoon. Serve the grilled salmon over the spinach with the sauce poured on top. Arrange the grilled peppers around the salmon.

(continued on next page)

Tips: The skin of the salmon should peel away easily once salmon is grilled. Peanut oil can be used if guests do not have peanut allergies, otherwise non-hydrogenated lard or coconut oil can be used.

Special Note: To test if oil is hot enough for frying, put the thin end of a wooden spoon to the bottom of the pan with oil. If bubbles rise briskly to the end of the wooden spoon, your oil is ready.

Joe and Jeanne Graber: Colleyville, Texas
Joe and Jeanne are dear friends and made this for me on my birthday several years ago. Joe is a great cook and Jeanne helps with the preparation. Jeanne recommends getting everything chopped and measured ahead of time. It definitely helps organize the process and leaves no room for error. The combination of ingredients in this dish is outstanding.

Orange Roughy with Parmesan and Green Onion Topping

Serves: 2

• cheese grater

1 1/2 pounds skinless orange roughy fillets
2 tablespoons freshly squeezed lemon juice (juice from 1 medium lemon)
1/2 cup freshly grated Parmigiano-Reggiano cheese
1/4 cup (1/2 stick) butter, softened
3 tablespoons Hellmann's or Best Foods Real Mayonnaise
3 tablespoons finely chopped green onion
Dash of Tabasco red pepper sauce

Arrange your broiler pan 4 inches from the broiler. Preheat the broiler. Place fillets in a greased glass baking dish; brush with the lemon juice and let sit 10 minutes. Broil the fish until it is predominantly white and flaky and no longer opaque. Combine the remaining ingredients in a bowl. Spread the mixture evenly over the fillets. Broil 2 to 3 minutes longer until topping is golden.

Variations: Fresh herbs (oregano, basil and thyme) may be added into the mixture for another variation of this recipe. Tilapia and other similar textured white fish may be substituted in place of roughy.

Salmon Sautéed with Shallots on a Bed of Spinach

Serves: 4

4 (8-ounce) skinless salmon fillets
Salt and pepper, to taste
4 tablespoons (1/2 stick) butter, divided use
6 medium shallots, thinly sliced, divided use
3 tablespoons chopped fresh tarragon, divided use
1 1/2 cups fresh spinach
2/3 cup dry white wine
1/2 cup heavy cream

Sprinkle salmon fillets with salt and pepper. Melt 2 tablespoons butter in a skillet. Sauté salmon until opaque in center, about 4 minutes per side. Place on a plate. Melt 1 tablespoon butter in the same skillet and add half of the shallots and half of the tarragon. Sauté 1 minute. Increase heat to high and add the spinach. Toss until wilted and divide between plates. Melt the remaining tablespoon of butter in the skillet over medium-high heat. Add the remaining shallots and tarragon. Sauté 1 minute. Add the wine and cream and bring to a boil until sauce is thick enough to coat a spoon, about 3 minutes. Season the sauce with salt and pepper, to taste. Return the cooked salmon to the skillet and simmer about 1 minute in the sauce. Place the salmon on top of the wilted spinach and top with sauce.

Becky Loboda: Mission Hills, Kansas
Becky and I have been friends since high school. We have always enjoyed stimulating conversation at dinner in a cozy restaurant that features unique and unusual items on their menu. Drew, her husband, told her this dish was "restaurant quality." The tarragon is not overpowering and the balance of the ingredients is very appealing.

Tuna Kabobs with Red Pepper Relish

Serves 8

• metal or wood skewers

2 pounds tuna steak, cut into
1-inch cubes
3/4 cup red pepper jelly
2/3 cup spicy brown mustard
1/4 cup red wine vinegar
1 teaspoon ground black pepper
1/2 teaspoon salt
2 red bell peppers, minced
2 green onions, minced (white
and pale green part only)
2 oranges, cut in 1-inch pieces
2 green bell peppers, cut into
1-inch pieces

If you are using wood skewers, soak the skewers in water for 30 minutes. Put the tuna in a large resealable plastic bag. Combine the jelly, mustard, vinegar, black pepper and salt in a glass bowl or measuring cup. Pour 1 cup of the marinade over the tuna. Seal the bag and refrigerate for 15 minutes. Combine the remaining marinade with the red pepper and onion in a serving bowl. (This will be the sauce you serve with the fish. Warm over low heat, if desired.) Once marinated, thread the tuna on the metal or wood skewers, alternating the tuna, orange pieces and green pepper. Grill kabobs over medium-low heat approximately 8 to 10 minutes. Tuna will be slightly opaque. Baste halfway through cooking with the marinade. Serve the tuna skewers with the sauce, rice and a vegetable or salad for a beautiful balance of color and flavor.

Bill and Jeanie Woody: Springfield, Missouri
Bill and Jeanie are the parents of our neighbor, Brian Compas. Bill is Brian's step-dad but the relationship is priceless. When Bill and Jeanne come to visit we eat dinner with Brian and Angie, Bill and Jeanne. Bill cooks, enjoys wine and we all partake in a wonderful meeting of the minds (and wines).

Red Snapper with Garlic Lime Butter

Serves: 2

2 fillets skinless red snapper
6 tablespoons clarified butter
Tony Chachere's Creole Seasoning,
  to taste
Flour
1 teaspoon olive oil
3 medium garlic cloves, minced
2 tablespoons freshly squeezed
  lime juice (juice from
  1 medium lime)

Have the butcher remove the skin from the fish when purchasing. Melt the butter in a saucepan. To clarify the butter, turn off heat and use a spoon to scrape the white foam off the top. Leaving the solids behind, pour the melted butter in a skillet large enough to sauté the fillets. Sprinkle fillets with *Tony Chachere's* seasoning. Dust fillets with flour. Add the olive oil to the butter and increase heat to sauté garlic until slightly brown. Add the fish to the pan and sauté until golden, approximately 10 minutes total, or until the fish is no longer opaque and is flaky. Remove the fillets from the pan and squeeze the lime juice into the butter. Pour the lime butter over the fish and serve hot.

Tip: This is great served with Steakhouse Creamed Spinach (page 251) and Naturally Sweet Carrots (page 252).

Salmon with Brown Butter Sauce

Serves: 4

1/3 cup unsalted butter
2 tablespoons balsamic vinegar
1 tablespoon honey
1 tablespoon Dijon mustard
1 tablespoon olive oil
4 (8-ounce) salmon fillets
1 tablespoon capers, drained
  and rinsed
1 medium tomato, seeded and
  diced (1/4-inch pieces)

Simmer the butter in a saucepan over medium heat, swirling the pan occasionally, until golden brown for about 4 minutes. Remove from the heat and add the vinegar, honey and mustard. (Have a lid ready to cover the pan because the vinegar will splatter when added to the hot butter.) In a separate large skillet, heat the olive oil. Sauté the fish until flaky and only a small bit of opaque center remains. (Fish needs to cook approximately 4 minutes per side.) Keep the fish warm in a low temperature oven (150°F) until ready to serve. Warm the sauce and pour over the fish. Sprinkle with capers and tomatoes.

Tip: If the skin is on the salmon, then cook skin side down. When you turn the salmon over on the other side, the skin should be easy to remove!

Tilapia with Tomatoes and Capers

Serves: 4

4 (8-ounce) tilapia fillets
Coarse sea salt
1/2 teaspoon ground white pepper, divided use
2 tablespoons olive oil
1/4 cup dry white wine
2 tablespoons freshly squeezed lemon juice (juice from 1 medium lemon)
4 tablespoons cold unsalted butter, cut into chunks
6 green onions, sliced diagonally into 1/4-inch pieces (white and pale green part only)
1 tablespoon capers, drained and rinsed
1 large tomato, seeded and chopped (1/4-inch pieces)

Preheat the oven to 150°F. Season both sides of the fish with salt and a sprinkle of white pepper. Heat the olive oil in a large pan over medium heat. Cook the seasoned fish on each side for 4 minutes or until lightly browned. Remove the fish from the pan and place in an ovenproof dish in the oven to keep warm while making the sauce. To make the sauce, heat the wine and lemon juice in the pan the fish was sautéed in. Bring to a boil and let the mixture reduce by half, adding the butter 2 tablespoons at a time until melted. The cold butter helps the sauce thicken. Add the onion, capers and tomatoes to the thickened sauce and cook for 1 more minute. Remove the warm fish from the oven and pour the sauce over the fillets before serving.

Variations: Vary the flavor of this dish by adding herbs, artichokes or sliced kalamata olives. This recipe is also delicious with halibut fillets. The original combination is also delicious as fish tacos. Cut the fish into bite-size pieces and serve with warmed flour or corn tortillas.

"When we have a friend who encourages us to be ourselves, who loves us as we are, we have an incomparable treasure."

~Alexandra Stoddard

Spicy Garlic Lemon Shrimp

Serves: 4

1/4 teaspoon black pepper

1/4 teaspoon cayenne pepper

1 teaspoon *Tony Chachere's Creole Seasoning*

1/4 teaspoon dried thyme

1/8 teaspoon dried oregano

1/4 teaspoon dried basil

1/2 cup (1 stick) unsalted butter

6 small or 3 large garlic cloves, minced or pressed

3 medium shallots, finely chopped (about 1/3 cup)

3/4 cup dry white wine

2 tablespoons freshly squeezed lemon juice (juice from 1 medium lemon)

1 tablespoon Worcestershire sauce

2 teaspoons cornstarch mixed with 2 teaspoons cold water

1 pound medium shrimp, peeled and deveined, tails removed

Cooked white rice, wild rice or brown rice

Chopped fresh parsley, for garnish (optional)

Measure out the spices and set aside. In a large saucepan, melt the butter and add the garlic and shallots. Sauté about 5 minutes until the shallots are translucent. Add the wine, lemon juice, Worcestershire and spices. Stir to blend. Stir the cornstarch mixture into the hot liquid and allow the sauce to come to a full boil for approximately 2 minutes until it thickens. Add the shrimp to the mixture and simmer until shrimp are pink and slightly coiled (approximately 2 minutes per side depending on the size). Serve hot over cooked rice and garnish with parsley.

Tip: Level off your spices with a knife otherwise heaping measurements can make a dish too spicy.

Variations: This dish is delicious prepared with a mild fish like tilapia or orange roughy instead of shrimp, or replace the seafood with 3 large, boneless, skinless chicken breasts cut into strips. For another twist, add 1 (14-ounce) can, drained and finely chopped artichokes.

Special Note: Two medium lemons yield about 4 tablespoons juice or 1/4 cup. Shrimp should never cook more than about 5 minutes or it becomes rubbery.

Renee Kent: Stilwell, Kansas

Renee was my boss at a previous job and is the mother of my sweet niece Audrey. Renee and I love wine and good food. She enjoys this dish and makes it with an added can of artichokes. Her daughter, Audrey, is a supertaster. Supertasters are highly sensitive to chili peppers, black pepper, fats and even carbonated water. If there is someone in your family similar to this, be sensitive to their taste buds (they have more of them) and eliminate the spicy seasonings for their portion. It is still delicious without all the spice or a reduced amount!

Shrimp with Blue Cheese Cream Sauce   Serves: 4

1 pound large shrimp, peeled
   and deveined, tails removed
2 tablespoons freshly squeezed
   lemon or lime juice (juice from
   1 medium lemon or lime)
1/2 cup (1 stick) unsalted
   butter, melted
3 ounces cream cheese
3/4 cup (3 ounces) blue cheese,
   or more to taste
Tony Chachere's Creole Seasoning,
   to taste

Preheat the oven to 350°F. Peel and butterfly shrimp. Place the shrimp in one layer in a baking dish. Pour the lemon or lime juice over the shrimp. Mix the melted butter, cream cheese and blue cheese together and spread over the shrimp. Cover (you can use foil) and bake for 15 minutes. (Time will vary depending on the size of the shrimp.) Serve with rice or pasta.

Tip: This dish makes a great appetizer served warm with a crusty baguette. To add some color, sauté some red pepper and zucchini and toss with the cooked shrimp mixture.

Special Note: To butterfly shrimp, split the shrimp down the center cutting almost but not completely through. The two halves open up to resemble a butterfly shape.

Rita Stanley: Austin, Texas
Rita is the sister of Gaylon Edwards, Donna's husband, and they have been in Dinner Club with us since 1989. Elizabeth (Rita's friend) and Rita's husband, Jerry, spend a lot of time with the Edwards doing "annual" activities like wine festivals, 10K runs and often spend weekends together. They love this recipe and passed it on to us!

Cornmeal Crusted Shrimp Tacos with Jicama Slaw

Serves: 4

• wire cooling rack

Chipotle Mayonnaise
1 can chipotle chile in adobo
sauce, minced
1 cup Hellmann's or Best Foods
Real Mayonnaise

Jicama Slaw
1 cup peeled and chopped
jicama
1/2 cup diced red bell pepper
(1/4-inch pieces)
1 (16-ounce) bag coleslaw
1/2 cup finely chopped red or
green onion
1/2 cup chopped cilantro

Lime Dressing
1 tablespoon minced or
pressed garlic
1/2 cup freshly squeezed lime
juice (juice from 4 medium
limes)
1/2 teaspoon salt
1 tablespoon sugar
1/8 teaspoon cayenne pepper
3/4 cup extra virgin olive oil

(ingredients continued on next page)

Mix together the minced adobo chile and mayonnaise. Set aside. To make the slaw, mix the jicama, red pepper, coleslaw, onion and cilantro in a bowl. To make the dressing, whisk the first 5 ingredients together in a separate bowl. Add the oil slowly while whisking. Toss the slaw with the desired amount of lime dressing and set aside. (Refrigerate remaining dressing.) Wrap the tortillas in foil and place in a slightly warm (150°F) oven. Combine the cornmeal with the next 5 ingredients and pile on a plate. Lightly brush the peeled shrimp with olive oil. Roll the shrimp in the cornmeal mixture. Put a small amount of peanut oil in a pan and heat to sizzling. Fry the coated shrimp approximately 2 minutes per side. Do not overcrowd the pan. Drain the shrimp on a wire rack so air circulates and shrimp do not get soggy. Place paper towels under the rack to catch any oil that might come off the shrimp. Spread a thin layer of chipotle mayonnaise on the warm tortilla, topping with the shrimp and slaw. Fold over and serve. Slaw may be made ahead but do not toss with dressing until just before serving.

Tips: Michelle Smith of Euless, Texas, suggests freezing leftover chipotle chiles individually in sealable plastic snack bags. They are delicious, adding a smoky, spicy flavor to any recipe, from hamburgers to soup. You will find canned chipotles in adobo in the Hispanic section of a grocery store. Refrigerate remaining mayonnaise and use to spice up sandwiches.

(continued on next page)

Cornmeal Crusted Shrimp Tacos

8 corn tortillas
2 tablespoons yellow cornmeal
1 teaspoon ground cumin
1 teaspoon garlic powder
2 tablespoons sweet paprika
2 tablespoons chili powder
1 teaspoon salt
1 pound medium shrimp,
  peeled and tails removed
Olive oil
Peanut oil for frying

Variations: *Salmon (skinned) may be substituted for the shrimp. Cut into 1-inch cubes. Beef tenderloin is another choice. Refrigerate a 3-pound beef tenderloin in a sealable plastic bag with 1 (12-ounce) can regular Dr. Pepper poured over it to tenderize and marinate (about 8 hours). Remove the beef from the Dr. Pepper and bring to room temperature for about 45 minutes before cooking. Thirty minutes before cooking rub the beef with a paste made of 1/2 cup brown sugar, 1 tablespoon* Tony Chachere's Creole Seasoning, *1 tablespoon lemon pepper, 1 tablespoon lemon or lime juice, 2 teaspoons minced garlic and just enough olive oil to make it a paste that adheres to meat. Grill or roast until the thickest part of the meat registers 140°F on a meat thermometer for medium.*

Special Note: Jicama (pronounced HEE-Kah-mah) is often referred to as a Mexican potato. It is a root vegetable with thin brown skin and white crunchy flesh. It has a sweet, nutty flavor and is good raw or cooked.

Ivan Vasquez: Fort Worth, Texas
Ivan taught for me at the cooking school and showed me many simple yet tasty recipes.
This is a favorite of ours!

Cajun Spiced Shrimp with Mushrooms   Serves: 4

1/2 cup lobster or shrimp stock (chicken stock may be substituted)

1 1/2 pounds shrimp

1 tablespoon freshly squeezed lemon juice (juice from 1/2 medium lemon)

Cooked white or brown rice

1/2 teaspoon salt

3/4 teaspoon ground cayenne pepper

1/4 teaspoon ground white pepper

1/4 teaspoon ground black pepper

1/4 teaspoon dried basil

1/2 teaspoon dried thyme

1/8 teaspoon dried oregano

1/2 cup (1 stick) cold unsalted butter, divided use

1/4 cup minced green onions (white and pale green part only)

1 teaspoon minced or pressed garlic

4 cups (8 ounces) thinly sliced fresh mushrooms (portobello, white or mixed)

3 tablespoons chopped fresh parsley

If you purchase lobster or shrimp base, dilute according to directions. Otherwise, peel and devein shrimp and reserve shells. Squeeze the lemon juice over the peeled shrimp. Boil the reserved shells in 2 cups water for 20 minutes. Remove shells and reserve 1/2 cup shrimp stock. For extra flavor, use the remainder of stock in place of the plain water to cook the rice. Cook rice according to package directions and keep warm. Measure out the salt and next 6 ingredients in a small bowl before starting. Measure out all remaining ingredients and put in individual bowls. In a large skillet melt 1/4 cup (1/2 stick) butter over high heat. When almost melted, add the chopped green onions, garlic and dried spices. Add the shrimp and sauté until they turn pink, shaking the pan rather than stirring. Flip the shrimp with spatula if necessary. Add the mushrooms and 1/4 cup stock. Add the remaining 1/4 cup (1/2 stick) butter cut into tablespoons and continue shaking the pan. Before the butter is completely melted, add the chopped parsley and remaining 1/4 cup stock. Continue cooking until butter thickens the sauce slightly. Serve over hot cooked rice.

Tip: Good stocks or broths are always needed. I use Better than Bouillon because they make a lobster stock. It is a paste that must have water added. When I don't have lobster stock, I use chicken stock. The spices are strong enough that no one would know. Vegetable stock is another replacement.

Scrumptious Shrimp Étouffée

Serves: 4

1/2 teaspoon cayenne pepper,
   or more to taste
3/4 teaspoon dried basil
1/2 teaspoon dried thyme
1 teaspoon *Tony Chachere's
   Creole Seasoning*
1/2 cup olive oil
1/2 cup flour
1/4 cup chopped green pepper
1/2 cup chopped green onion
1/3 cup chopped celery
3 cups lobster stock (chicken
   stock may be used)
2 medium garlic cloves,
   minced or pressed
1 teaspoon Tabasco red pepper
   sauce, or more to taste
1 pound shrimp, peeled,
   deveined and tails removed
8 ounces crawfish (or substitute
   more shrimp, if desired)
Cooked white or brown rice
   or grits

Measure all of the spices out in a small dish before starting. In a medium cast iron skillet, heat the oil over medium heat until hot (just reaching the smoking point) and add the flour. Start stirring immediately with a whisk and stir until you achieve a mixture the color of a pale brown paper bag (this is a roux). Never stop stirring or it will burn and you will have to start over. Add the green pepper, onion and celery to the roux and stir with a wooden spoon until the onions are translucent. Slowly add the broth, continuing to stir. Add the garlic, measured spices, and Tabasco and continue to stir. Turn the heat off under the skillet while you cook the rice or grits. Check the consistency of the sauce. It should be a thick sauce but not pasty. Add additional broth to achieve the desired consistency. Turn the heat back up and add the seafood to the sauce cooking until the shrimp are slightly coiled and pink, about 5 minutes. Serve over the hot cooked rice or grits.

Tip: For an elegant version, serve in a puff pastry shell with a salad on the side for a luncheon. We had a similar dish in Louisiana and it was divine! Be sure your pan is dry before starting. Water drops make oil pop.

Variation: *Add one (14-ounce) can diced tomatoes with juice, chopped for a more Creole versus Cajun twist. Vegetables must be tender and onion translucent before adding or they will not cook completely due to the acid in the tomatoes.*

Mary Hutchinson: Topeka, Kansas
Mary, originally from Tupelo, Mississippi, knows good food. She sent me a rendition of this recipe that I tweaked a little. She often serves Cajun dishes with grits, which is also delicious.

Shrimp with Cilantro Pesto Cream Sauce

Serves: 4

- cheese grater
- blender or food processor
- whisk

Pesto
1 bunch fresh cilantro
1/4 cup raw pumpkin seeds
1 1/2 teaspoons minced garlic
1/8 teaspoon ground black pepper
1/4 cup freshly grated
    Parmigiano-Reggiano cheese
1/4 cup olive oil

Shrimp
1 tablespoon olive oil
24 large shrimp, peeled and
    deveined

Pesto Cream Sauce
1/4 cup white wine
3 tablespoons prepared pesto
1 cup heavy cream
1 tablespoon cornstarch mixed
    with 1 tablespoon cold water
Salt and pepper, to taste
Cooked brown or white rice,
    or pasta

Wash the cilantro and remove the stems. In a blender or food processor, chop the pumpkin seeds. Add the cilantro, garlic, pepper and grated cheese to the blender. Blend until smooth and add the oil slowly to mixture. Set the pesto aside. In a large skillet, heat the tablespoon of oil and sauté the shrimp until pink. They should be slightly curled when done but not tightly coiled. Remove the shrimp from the pan. Deglaze the pan by adding the wine, heating it to boiling and reducing by half. Reduce the heat and add 3 tablespoons of pesto and the heavy cream. Once heated through, add half of the cornstarch mixture to the hot liquid. Bring to a boil so sauce thickens (allow approximately 2 minutes). Add additional cornstarch mixture if a thicker sauce is desired. Add the cooked shrimp back to the sauce to warm them. Season the pesto cream sauce with salt and pepper, to taste. Serve the shrimp and sauce over rice or pasta.

Pasta, Rice & Vegetables

Pasta, Rice & Vegetables

 **Kitchen tools needed**

 May be prepared ahead

Orange-Pineapple Spice Tea, page 105 • Hearts of Palm, Artichoke and Olive Salad, page 125
Jalapeño Cornbread, page 105 • Tomato Pie, page 246 • Coconut Cherry Bars, page 291

Pasta with Lemon Cream and Prosciutto

Serves: 8

• whisk

12 ounces angel hair pasta
4 tablespoons (1/2 stick) unsalted butter, softened, divided use
3 medium shallots, finely chopped (about 1/3 cup)
3/4 cup chicken stock or broth
1 cup heavy cream
1 teaspoon lemon zest
1/8 teaspoon cayenne pepper
1 tablespoon freshly squeezed lemon juice (juice from 1/2 medium lemon)
2 tablespoons flour
2 cups frozen peas, thawed
4 paper thin slices prosciutto, chopped

Prepare the pasta according to package directions in salted water and drain. Leave a lid on the pasta so it stays warm. Melt 2 tablespoons butter in a large skillet and add shallots. Sauté until translucent then add the broth. Simmer until the broth is reduced to 1/4 cup. Add the cream, zest, cayenne and lemon juice to the mixture. Mix the flour and the remaining 2 tablespoons butter into a paste. Add this mixture to the hot liquid, continuing to whisk until it starts to boil. Lower the heat and simmer until the sauce reaches the desired consistency about 5 minutes. Add the peas and cook 2 minutes longer. Finally add the prosciutto and warm through. Toss the lemon cream with the drained pasta and serve.

Variations: *This sauce alone can be used to jazz up a chicken breast or piece of fish. Feel free to experiment—add capers (drained and rinsed), fresh herbs or additional vegetables. This pasta dish can become a main dish if sautéed scallops, shrimp or chicken are added.*

Special Note: We have made the switch to whole-wheat pasta, brown rice pasta and brown rice. Whole-wheat pasta is higher in dietary fiber than regular pasta. Brown rice has only had the outer hull removed and retains an impressive number of vitamins and minerals. Brown rice contains four times more insoluble fiber than white rice.

Angel Hair with Pesto, Shrimp and Pancetta

Serves: 4

2 tablespoons unsalted butter
6 paper thin slices pancetta
(2 ounces), or prosciutto
1 cup (2 ounces) sliced fresh
mushrooms
1 red pepper, diced
(1/4-inch pieces)
1/3 cup prepared pesto
1 teaspoon lemon zest
8 ounces angel hair pasta
1 pound shrimp, peeled,
deveined, tails removed
1 large tomato, cored, seeded
and diced (1/4-inch pieces)

Melt butter over medium heat and add the pancetta, mushrooms and red pepper. Sauté until the mushrooms are tender, about 3 minutes. Add the pesto and lemon zest and remove from heat. Cook the pasta according to package directions in salted water. While preparing pasta or just before serving, reheat the pesto mixture. Add the shrimp and cook until they are pink and slightly coiled. Once pasta has been drained (do not rinse) toss with the pesto mixture, top with the chopped tomatoes and serve immediately. This recipe is easy and delicious. (The tomatoes may be heated by stir-frying in a separate pan if you do not like the idea of cold tomatoes added to a hot dish.)

Variations: Diced bacon that has been cooked can be used instead of pancetta or prosciutto or omit meat completely for a vegetarian version.

Try 1 tablespoon of the Creole Spice (page 224) in place of the pesto (add a bit of olive oil if needed to the pasta so the spice sticks) for a totally different version.

Add your favorite vegetables—red pepper, green onion or even chicken in place of the shrimp. You'll need to sauté the vegetables until they are al dente (cooked through but not mushy or overcooked, instead just tender to the bite). One red pepper, cored and cut into thin strips, 1 broccoli crown (1/2 pound) or 1 bunch asparagus and 3 peeled, sliced carrots is the perfect color assortment and is delicious!

For a nice Alfredo primavera (cream sauce with vegetables), add 1 cup heavy cream, bring to boil and stir in 1/2 cup (or more) freshly grated Parmigiano-Reggiano cheese to have a delicious Alfredo with a spicy twist!

Tomato Pancetta Sauce with Fresh Herbs

Serves: 4

12 ounces linguine, penne or
   other pasta
1 tablespoon olive oil
4 ounces pancetta, diced
   (1/4-inch pieces)
1 large garlic clove, minced or
   pressed
1 cup finely chopped onion
2 tablespoons balsamic vinegar
1 (28-ounce) can chopped
   tomatoes
1/2 cup red wine
1 teaspoon salt
1 (3-ounce) package fresh basil,
   thinly sliced (approximately
   1 cup loosely packed)
2 tablespoons fresh chopped
   oregano or 2 teaspoons
   dried oregano
3/4 cup freshly grated
   Parmigiano-Reggiano cheese

Cook the pasta according to package directions in salted water. While the pasta cooks, heat the olive oil in a large skillet over medium heat. Add the pancetta and fry until crisp. Add the garlic and onion to the pan and sauté until the onion is translucent. Add the vinegar and cook for about 2 minutes. Add the tomatoes, red wine and salt and simmer for about 8 minutes. Just before serving, remove from heat and add the basil, oregano and Parmigiano-Reggiano cheese. Stir to blend. Drain the pasta and toss with the sauce.

Tips: When cooking pasta, the water is salted so when the pasta is tasted it has some flavor. Drain pasta but do not rinse. Return the pasta back to the pan and keep warm. The Microplane grater is the best grater we have found for hard cheeses like Parmesan and to zest citrus fruits.

Variations: Cooked meat like Italian sausage may be added to this fresh tasting tomato sauce or spice (red pepper flakes) may be added to create a spicy red sauce. For our family this fresh tasting sauce is a vehicle for adding fresh vegetables like baby spinach. Add the spinach when you are adding the herbs so the leaves keep their color. If dried herbs are used, reduce the measurement to 1/3 of the fresh herb measurement. A (14-ounce) can of non-marinated chopped artichokes is another wonderful combination. Brown rice pasta is a healthier alternative to semolina pasta.

Special Notes: Pomi brand tomatoes are a preference, but other canned tomatoes can be used. Fine sea salt is our choice for cooking and baking. We keep coarse sea salt and kosher salt on hand for those recipes needing a coarser salt.

Pasta with Mascarpone, Parmesan and Fresh Sautéed Vegetables

Serves: 8

1 (16-ounce) package refrigerated or dried pasta of your choice
3 tablespoons olive oil
1 large yellow onion, finely chopped
6 ounces sliced prosciutto (paper thin), coarsely chopped
2 tablespoons minced garlic
1/4 teaspoon red pepper flakes
2 cups (4 ounces) sliced fresh mushrooms
1 large red bell pepper, diced (1/4-inch pieces)
1 cup frozen green peas
1 cup heavy cream
1 (8-ounce) container mascarpone cheese, softened
1 cup freshly grated Parmigiano-Reggiano cheese
Salt and pepper or **Tony Chachere's Creole Seasoning**, to taste
1/2 cup fresh basil, chiffonade (see below)

Special Note: To chiffonade basil, stack the leaves on top of one another and roll into a cylinder. Slice the cylinders of leaves crosswise into thin strips.

Cook pasta according to package directions in salted water and drain. Do not rinse so that the pasta remains hot. (You may place covered in a slightly warmed oven.) Heat the oil in a large sauté pan and add the onion, prosciutto, garlic, and red pepper flakes. Sauté over medium heat until garlic is fragrant and the onions are translucent. Add the mushrooms, bell pepper and green peas. Reduce heat and simmer 5 minutes or until liquid is evaporated. Add the cream and bring to a boil; boil for 5 minutes or until slightly thickened. Add the mascarpone and Parmigiano-Reggiano cheese, stirring until completely melted, about 5 minutes. Remove from the heat and gently toss with the cooked pasta. Return the pan back to the stove and simmer the pasta with the sauce for approximately 4 minutes, stirring to coat. Taste and add salt, pepper or *Tony Chachere's* if desired. Sprinkle each serving with fresh basil before serving or mix in just before serving. Fresh herbs will turn brown if mixed in too early.

Variation: This is another recipe that can be changed many ways to create a new recipe. Different vegetables (carrots cooked al dente (soft but not overcooked) or asparagus are great!), chicken, shrimp or various types of onion varieties (shallots, green or red) can be used to make it slightly different. Fresh herbs such as chives or chopped tomato are also wonderful as a garnish. As long as you have pasta, onion, garlic, cream and the cheeses— it is your recipe and the variations are endless! For this dish, we like a sturdy wheat pasta that has an opening (either a rigatoni or shell shape (chiocciole)), one that holds the sauce.

Spaghetti with Meat Sauce

Serves: 4

1 1/2 pounds ground beef
2 onions, finely chopped
1 (8-ounce) package sliced fresh mushrooms (optional)
1 (1.37-ounce) package McCormick Thick and Zesty Spaghetti Sauce
1 (6-ounce) can tomato paste
2 cups water
1 1/2 teaspoons *Tony Chachere's Creole Seasoning*
1 teaspoon coarse ground black pepper
1/2 teaspoon dried basil
1/2 teaspoon dried oregano
2 large garlic cloves, minced or pressed
2/3 cup red wine (Merlot or Cabernet)
1 teaspoon salt
1 (16-ounce) box spaghetti
Freshly grated Parmigiano-Reggiano cheese

Fry the ground beef until almost all the red is gone, breaking apart the large chunks with a spoon. Do not drain the cooked beef. Add the onion and sauté until almost translucent, then add the mushrooms. Continue to sauté until onion is translucent and stir in the dry spaghetti sauce mix. Add the can of tomato paste and slowly add 2 cups of water. Stir to blend. Bring to a boil and add remaining ingredients. Stir to blend and reduce heat to low. Simmer 1 hour or until ready to serve. While the sauce is simmering, cook the pasta in salted water according to package directions. Once cooked, drain and return to pot; cover to keep warm. Taste the simmering sauce, if you prefer more salt, add an additional 1/2 teaspoon; or for salt and spice, add additional *Tony Chachere's* if needed. Serve the pasta warm with sauce ladled over the top.

Tip: When cooking pasta, use a 6 to 8 quart capacity pot to prepare 1 pound of pasta. Fill with hot water 3/4 full. Add salt (approximately 1 tablespoon sea salt) to the hot water as it begins to boil and allow it to dissolve before adding the pasta. Never add oil to pasta water. Do not cover the pot, but stir the pasta gently several times while it is cooking, approximately every 3 minutes. Cook pastas according to the cooking time on the package and drain the pasta immediately into a large colander. Toss the cooked pasta gently to remove excess liquid, but do not rinse.

David Gore: Grapevine, Texas
David is the Texan who taught me the "spice of life." He got me hooked on Tony Chachere's and he puts it in everything he makes. My stepson, Ryan, shares his father's experienced palate which in recipe testing presents interesting challenges.

Variations: *One pound of Italian sausage links (sliced) may be substituted for ground beef. Serve with penne pasta and freshly grated Parmesan for a tasty Italian meal. Add 1 (2.25-ounce) can of sliced black olives, if desired.*

223

Pasta with Chicken, Cream and Creole Spice

Serves: 6

Creole Spice
1/4 cup sweet paprika
1 tablespoon onion powder
3/4 teaspoon dried thyme
1 1/2 teaspoons dried oregano
4 3/4 teaspoons salt
1 3/4 teaspoons black pepper
1 3/4 teaspoons ground white pepper
1 1/2 teaspoons cayenne pepper
1 1/2 teaspoons dried basil

Pasta
4 (8-ounce) boneless, skinless chicken breasts
2 (9-ounce) packages fresh angel hair pasta
4 tablespoons (1/2 stick) butter
4 teaspoons minced garlic
1/2 cup green onions, finely minced (white and pale green part only)
3/4 pound sausage (bulk pork sausage, not spicy)
2 cups chicken broth or stock
1 cup heavy cream (at room temperature)
1 tablespoon cornstarch mixed with 1 tablespoon cold water

Mix all of the dry spices together before starting and set aside 2 to 3 tablespoons depending on your preference. Store the remaining spice mixture in an airtight container for another use. Cut the chicken breasts into bite-size pieces. Prepare the pasta according to package directions in salted water (once boiled and drained, cover and keep warm until ready to serve.) Sprinkle the chicken pieces evenly with a tablespoon of the spice and rub into the chicken with your hands. In a large skillet, melt the butter and sauté the garlic and green onions for about 2 minutes. Turn the heat up to medium and add the chicken. Cook until the chicken pieces turn white, and no pink remains in the center. Remove the skillet from the heat. Cook the sausage in another skillet and drain. Add the sausage to the chicken and return the skillet to the heat. Add the chicken broth to the meats and simmer. Add the cream and bring to a boil. Add the cornstarch mixture to the skillet and cook until the liquid boils and thickens, about 2 minutes. Add 1 tablespoon of the remaining spice mix, stirring to blend. Taste test the sauce before adding any additional spice and adjust the spiciness accordingly to your tastes. Toss the meat sauce mixture with the warm pasta and serve immediately.

Tip: This Creole Spice mix can be used for fish, eggs or for grilling meat. Mix together ahead of time to quicken preparation time.

(continued on next page)

Variations: *For a different version, make the chicken breasts as directed and leave them whole. In a separate pan from the chicken breasts, sauté 2/3 cup each of julienned carrots, zucchini and yellow squash in 3 tablespoons butter and 1 tablespoon spice. Add 2/3 cup sliced mushrooms. When vegetables are tender, add 1 cup of heavy cream. Boil until slightly thick. Pour the sauce over the breasts that have been cooked with the spice, garlic and green onion. It is excellent!*

A tablespoon of the Creole Spice is a perfect rub for 4 chicken breasts or sprinkled over a pound of shrimp before sautéing in 1/4 cup butter (1/2 stick) and a bit of olive oil (1 tablespoon) and adding to pasta. You can find your own versatile combinations with any meat, seafood or vegetable. Zucchini, green onions and mushrooms are a super combination!

See the recipe for Creamy Lemon Chicken with Capers (page 188) using this spice.

Here's another great variation from my friends Cindy and Chip Kimbell, from North Richland Hills, Texas. Take 1 pound of shrimp (or crawfish) sprinkled with 1 tablespoon Creole Spice. In a skillet, heat a tablespoon of olive oil, sauté a minced clove of garlic with 1 cup sliced mushrooms and 1/2 cup green onions. Add 1 cup heavy cream and 1 cup freshly grated Parmigiano-Reggiano cheese. Heat the mixture and add the shrimp to the cream mixture. Cook just until shrimp coil. Toss the mixture with cooked pasta or serve over rice. Delicious!

Special Note: To julienne is to cut into thin, matchstick strips. When boiling pasta, cover pot after putting pasta in so it will quickly return to a boil and pasta won't stick together.

Joan Redhair:
Overland Park, Kansas
Joan gave me this recipe and I keep the spice mix on hand at all times and use it in a multitude of recipes. We have been friends since college and enjoy a few gatherings each year with our friend, Melissa. We appreciate good meals, good coffee and good conversation together!

225

Tarragon Meatballs with Fettuccine   Serves: 6

• whisk

4 tablespoons (1/2 stick)
  unsalted butter, divided use
1 cup finely chopped onion
1 tablespoon minced garlic
2 pounds ground beef
2 large eggs
1 teaspoon salt
1 teaspoon black pepper
1/4 cup flour
1 tablespoon dried tarragon
1 tablespoon dried marjoram
2 tablespoons olive oil
1 (6-ounce) can tomato paste
3/4 cup beef broth or stock
4 teaspoons Worcestershire sauce
2 teaspoons white or red wine
  vinegar
1 (8-ounce) package sliced
  fresh mushrooms
1 cup sour cream
1 (9-ounce) package fettuccine

In a large skillet, melt 2 tablespoons butter. Sauté the onion and garlic until the onion is translucent. With a slotted spoon, remove the onion and garlic and reserve. In a large bowl, mix together the ground beef, eggs, salt and pepper. Roll into walnut-size meatballs. In a shallow platter, mix the flour with the tarragon and marjoram. Roll the meatballs in the flour mixture to coat them. Heat the remaining butter with the olive oil and brown the meatballs. Do not overcrowd or they will be difficult to turn. Whisk the tomato paste, beef broth, Worcestershire and vinegar together. Stir the onions and garlic into the mixture. Pour the tomato mixture over the meatballs and simmer covered for one hour. Fifteen minutes before serving stir in the sliced mushrooms and sour cream. Prepare the pasta according to the package directions in salted water (once boiled and drained, cover and keep warm until ready to serve). Taste the sauce and add salt and pepper if needed. Enjoy over pasta with a green salad for a delicious dinner!

Tips: Noodles are named differently due to size or shape. Use what you have in the cupboard. We prefer whole wheat or rice noodles. We recommend fresh garlic versus the garlic minced in a jar. The 80/20 ground beef holds together well for making meatballs. If it is too lean, it falls apart.

Lee Martin-Terry: Colleyville, Texas
Lee passed this recipe to me via our friend and accountant, Julie Lancaster. This is child-friendly and delicious for adults as well. The flavor of tarragon and marjoram together make it spectacular.

Chicken with Pink Vodka Sauce

Serves: 4

Cream Sauce
1/4 cup (1/2 stick) unsalted
  butter, divided use
2 tablespoons flour
1 cup heavy cream

Seasoned Chicken Breasts
4 boneless, skinless chicken
  breasts, cut in strips
2 teaspoons dried oregano
1/8 teaspoon cayenne pepper
  (optional)
1/2 teaspoon coarse black pepper

Tomato Vodka Sauce
1 tablespoon olive oil
2 medium shallots, finely
  chopped (about 1/4 cup)
2 tablespoons minced garlic
1/4 teaspoon crushed red pepper
1 tablespoon fresh thyme or 1
  teaspoon dried thyme
1 tablespoon fresh chopped basil
  or 1 teaspoon dried basil
1/4 cup vodka
1/2 cup chicken broth
1 (26- to 28-ounce) container
  of prepared marinara sauce
1 (12-ounce) package penne
  pasta
Freshly grated Parmigiano-
  Reggiano cheese, served on
  the side

Make the cream sauce by melting 2 tablespoons of the butter slowly. Add the flour and whisk until it becomes a paste. Slowly add the heavy cream while whisking over low heat. Once thickened to the desired thickness, set aside. To season the chicken breasts, sprinkle the chicken strips with the oregano, cayenne pepper (if using) and black pepper and set aside. In a large skillet heat the olive oil and remaining 2 tablespoons butter. Sauté the shallots and garlic until the shallots are translucent. Add the chicken, crushed red pepper, thyme and basil to the skillet. Cook the chicken thoroughly, until no pink remains. Remove the chicken and set aside. With the heat still on medium, add the vodka to the pan to deglaze. Reduce the vodka by half and add the chicken broth. Boil the liquids, reducing them to 1/2 cup. Add the marinara, cooked chicken and whisk in just enough of the prepared cream sauce to reach the consistency you desire. Simmer on low until ready to serve. While sauce is simmering, prepare the pasta according to the package directions in salted water and drain. Serve the sauce over the cooked pasta. Pass freshly grated Parmigiano-Reggiano separately.

Tips: Marinara is a highly seasoned tomato sauce. When choosing a marinara, look for a marinara with limited sugar added.

Variations: This sauce is delicious with chicken but you can also replace it with ground sausage, salmon and asparagus or shrimp. Ouzo is an anise-flavored liquor that can replace the vodka for another delicious sauce.

Lemon Rice Pilaf

Serves: 6

- whisk
- cheese grater

2 1/2 teaspoons lemon zest
1 tablespoon plus 1 teaspoon
  freshly squeezed lemon juice
  (juice from 1/2 medium lemon)
2 large egg yolks
1/4 cup heavy cream
2 tablespoons butter
1 1/2 cups uncooked long grain
  white rice
3 cups low salt chicken broth
3 tablespoons freshly grated
  Parmigiano-Reggiano cheese
3 tablespoons minced fresh
  parsley
Salt and pepper, to taste

In a small bowl, combine the lemon zest, lemon juice, egg yolks and heavy cream. Whisk until blended and set aside. In a small saucepan, melt the butter and add the rice. Cook briefly, stirring until the rice turns opaque. Pour in chicken broth and sprinkle with salt. Heat to boiling and reduce heat to simmer. Cover and cook for 20 to 25 minutes. Just before serving, fold the lemon-cream sauce into the rice. Stir in the Parmigiano-Reggiano cheese and parsley. Season the pilaf with salt and pepper, to taste. Serve immediately.

Simple Garlic Potatoes

Serves: 6

3 baking potatoes, skins on,
  washed and cut into
  1/4-inch slices
1/3 cup melted butter
2 medium garlic cloves, finely
  chopped
Seasoned salt
1/3 cup freshly grated
  Parmigiano-Reggiano cheese

Preheat the oven to 350°F. Slightly overlap potato slices in a 9 x 13-inch baking dish. Pour the melted butter over the potatoes. Sprinkle the chopped garlic over the potatoes. Sprinkle with seasoned salt and grated Parmigiano-Reggiano cheese. Cover with foil and bake for 1 hour.

Jean Neill: Bella Vista, Arkansas
I got this recipe when I was around 10 years old, from Jean, a family friend. They lived two doors down from us when I was born. We then moved, and they moved into our new neighborhood a few years later. Jean's husband, Bill, was the principal at my high school, and a good friend of my father's.

Wild Mushroom Risotto

Serves: 4

4 tablespoons (1/2 stick) unsalted butter

2 medium garlic cloves, minced or pressed

2 medium shallots, finely chopped (about 1/4 cup)

1 cup (2 ounces) sliced fresh mushrooms (shiitake, portobella and oyster)

1 cup Arborio rice

2 1/3 cups chicken stock or broth mixed with 1 cup water

1/4 cup heavy cream

2 tablespoons freshly grated Parmigiano-Reggiano cheese

Salt and pepper, to taste

Melt the butter in a skillet and add the garlic, shallots and mushrooms. On medium-low heat sauté until the shallots turn translucent. Add the rice and sauté for another 2 minutes. Using either a measuring cup with a spout or a ladle, start to add the stock and water. Add the stock 1/3 cup at a time stirring constantly until all the stock is absorbed. Add more stock as all the liquid is absorbed. Continue to add the stock until you reach the desired consistency. Once the liquid is absorbed, about 20 minutes, add the cream and stir until it is also absorbed. The risotto should be tender, yet firm to the bite (al dente). Cover and lower heat or turn off heat until ready to serve. If the risotto appears too dry, add more broth, reheat and continue to stir until you reach the desired consistency. Just before serving, add the Parmigiano-Reggiano cheese, salt and pepper to taste. Stir and serve warm.

Variations: A few toasted pine nuts sprinkled over the top is a nice addition. Risotto is a nice accompaniment to many dishes as a substitute for potatoes or rice. A beef broth may be used or another cheese. Keep the risotto simple (no mushrooms) if pairing with Osso Buco (page 202).

Special Note: Arborio is an Italian-grown grain that is shorter and fatter than any other short grain rice. It is used in making risotto because it lends this dish its requisite creamy texture.

Ed Bamberger: Dallas, Texas
Ed owns the Single Gourmet in the Dallas Fort Worth area. Ed arranges dinner parties at fine restaurants, wine tastings, cooking classes and other exquisite culinary events for his members. Ed is also a freelance food writer and was one of the first to write an article about Good Friends Great Tastes when the first edition was published in the year 2000. Ed's original recipe inspired this dish.

Black Beans with Cilantro Pesto Rice   Serves: 12

 • blender or food processor

Beans and Rice
1 pound dried black beans
(do not use canned)
1 ham hock
4 cups water
2 cups long grain rice
2 1/2 teaspoons *Tony Chachere's
Creole Seasoning,* divided use
1/4 cup (1/2 stick) butter,
softened
1/8 teaspoon cayenne pepper

Cilantro Pesto
1/3 cup pine nuts
1/2 cup freshly grated
Parmigiano-Reggiano cheese
2 large garlic cloves
1 1/2 cups packed fresh basil
leaves
1 1/2 cups packed fresh
cilantro leaves
1 cup packed fresh parsley leaves
2 tablespoons freshly squeezed
lime juice (juice from
1 medium lime)
3/4 cup olive oil

Use a container large enough that beans can expand and soak them overnight in water 2 inches higher than the beans, or use the quick soak method on the package. On the preparation day, preheat oven to 350°F and toast pine nuts 3 to 4 minutes or until lightly golden and shiny. Cool completely. In a blender, mix cooled pine nuts with remaining pesto ingredients and set aside. Drain the soaked beans and place them in a large Dutch oven with the ham hock. Add enough fresh, cold water to cover beans with 2 inches remaining above beans. Simmer the beans, covered until tender, about 1 to 1 1/4 hours. While beans are simmering, bring the 4 cups of water to a boil in a large heavy skillet. Stir in the rice and 1/2 teaspoon *Tony Chachere's* seasoning. Cook rice covered over low heat, undisturbed for 18 to 20 minutes or until water is absorbed and rice is tender. Fluff rice with a fork. Drain the cooked beans, discard the ham hock and keep beans warm on the stove. Gently fold in the rice, butter, prepared pesto, remaining *Tony Chachere's* and the cayenne pepper. Taste and add a little more *Tony Chachere's* if more salt is needed; add more cayenne if you want a spicier dish. Serve warm.

Tips: This dish looks great when served in a hollowed out pineapple. This recipe can be cut in half to serve with the Tropical Fiesta Steak (page 159).

Special Note: To clean the blender after making pesto, squirt in a little dishwasher soap and fill half way with water. Blend and rinse out.

Potatoes Gruyère

Serves: 8

- potato peeler
- cheese grater

3 cups heavy cream
2 large garlic cloves, minced or pressed
10 medium russet potatoes, peeled and thinly sliced
Salt and pepper, to taste
1 1/3 cups Gruyère cheese, grated

Preheat oven to 400°F. Butter a 9 x 13-inch baking dish. In a large pot, bring the cream and garlic to a boil over medium heat. Gently mix in the sliced potatoes. Reduce heat to medium, cover and cook until the liquid returns to a boil, about 4 minutes. Transfer half of the potatoes to the prepared dish and season generously with salt and pepper. Sprinkle with half of the cheese. Top with the remaining potatoes and sprinkle with salt and pepper. Cover (you can use foil) and bake 45 minutes. Uncover the casserole and top with the remaining cheese and return to the oven until potatoes are tender, cheese melts and sauce bubbles, about 15 minutes. Let stand 10 minutes and serve.

Tips: Chopped shallot (a cross between onion and garlic), can be added. A variety of cheeses, such as white Cheddar or blue cheese may be used in place of the Gruyère for a totally different potato dish.

Lynn Holcomb: Raleigh, North Carolina
Lynn and I worked together years ago and we exchanged recipes often. We keep in touch at holiday time. She suggested adding a combination of shallots and red pepper to this dish.

Potato, Mushroom and Spinach Tart   Serves: 6

- pastry brush
- slotted spoon
- jelly roll pan

6 (18 x 12-inch) phyllo dough sheets

1 cup (2 sticks) unsalted butter

2 medium Yukon gold potatoes

1 (9-ounce) bag fresh spinach, tough stems removed

1 pound portobello mushrooms

Salt and pepper, to taste

5 medium shallots, finely chopped (about 2/3 cup)

1/4 cup chopped parsley leaves

2 tablespoons fresh chopped thyme

2 cups chicken broth

Thaw phyllo dough according to package directions. Preheat oven to 350°F. Clarify butter by slowly melting the butter. Once melted, skim the foam off the top and slowly pour into another pan, leaving the white solids in the bottom of pan. Leave the clarified butter (the butter free from foam and solids) on low heat. Brush the unpeeled whole potatoes with the clarified butter. Roast potatoes at 350°F for 1 hour, until they are soft when pierced with a fork. Cool before peeling. Coarsely chop the spinach leaves. Wipe the mushrooms with a damp paper towel to remove the dirt. Discard stems from the mushrooms and thinly slice the caps. Keep all of these vegetables separate. In a large skillet add 1 tablespoon of the clarified butter. Heat until foam subsides. Add the chopped spinach and cook for 1 minute or until just wilted. Drain the spinach on paper towels and sprinkle with salt and pepper. Add an additional tablespoon of butter to the skillet and cook 1/3 of the mushrooms over moderate heat; stir until browned. Remove the mushrooms from the pan with a slotted spoon and set aside on a plate. Cook the mushrooms in 3 batches, adding 1 tablespoon of butter each time. Add another tablespoon of the clarified butter to the skillet and cook the chopped shallots, stirring until translucent. Remove the shallots from the heat and add the parsley, 1 1/2 tablespoons thyme and the mushrooms. Add broth to the skillet and return to heat. As sauce boils, it will release the browned bits that add flavor to the sauce. Reduce the liquid to 1 cup. Whisk in 3 tablespoons of the clarified butter. Keep covered and warm.

(continued on next page)

232

Keep phyllo dough covered with a damp kitchen towel while you are working. On a jelly roll pan, lay 1 sheet of phyllo dough and brush with the clarified butter. Sprinkle this with about 1/4 of the remaining thyme, sprinkle lightly with salt and pepper. Repeat this process with 2 additional layers brushing with butter, sprinkling with thyme, salt and pepper. Cover this with plastic wrap and a damp cloth. Make another stack in the same manner; this will be the top layer. Be careful not to over salt. Arrange cooked and peeled potatoes down the middle of the first stack of phyllo that is on the jelly roll pan. Top the potatoes with the mushroom mixture and spinach. Brush edges with butter. Carefully drape remaining phyllo stack over the filling and roll edges to seal. Bake the tart at 350°F for 20 to 25 minutes until golden. Cut in slices, drizzle with any remaining sauce and serve.

Special Note: Deglazing is done by heating a small amount of liquid in a pan that has been used in cooking and stirring to loosen brown bits of food on the bottom. This flavored liquid then becomes the base for a sauce.

"The kitchen is the center of the home, luring family and visiting friends with enticing aromas and curious clatter."

~Nathalie Dupree

Portobello Mushrooms Topped with Whipped Sweet Potatoes

Serves: 8

- potato masher
- electric mixer
- pastry brush

- 1/2-inch star piping tip
- disposable piping bag

1 large sweet potato, peeled and diced (1-inch pieces)
4 medium russet potatoes, peeled and diced (1-inch pieces)
6 whole garlic cloves, peeled
1 bay leaf
1 teaspoon salt
4 tablespoons (1/2 stick) unsalted butter
2 large eggs, beaten
1/2 cup freshly grated Parmigiano-Reggiano cheese
Salt and pepper, to taste
8 medium portobello mushrooms
3 tablespoons olive oil, divided use
4 cups fresh baby spinach
1/2 cup finely chopped yellow onion

Preheat the oven to 400°F. In a large pot or Dutch oven, add the potatoes, garlic and bay leaf and cover with cold water. Add 1 teaspoon salt and bring to a boil. Boil the potatoes for 15 to 20 minutes or until potatoes are tender when pierced with a fork. Remove the bay leaf. Drain potatoes, add the butter and with a potato masher, mash the potatoes and garlic until smooth and colors of potatoes are completely blended. Cool slightly and with an electric mixer, quickly beat in the eggs and grated Parmigiano-Reggiano cheese. Add salt and pepper, to taste. Remove the stems from the mushrooms and chop. Set the caps aside. Heat 2 teaspoons of olive oil in a large skillet and add the mushroom stems, spinach and onions. Sauté the mixture 5 minutes and remove from heat. Season the spinach with salt and pepper. Drizzle the remaining 1 tablespoon olive oil over the rounded sides of the mushroom caps and use a pastry brush to distribute evenly. Place mushrooms on a baking sheet gill sides up (underside up) and bake 10 minutes. Remove the caps from the oven and reduce temperature to 350°F. Distribute the spinach mixture evenly over the gill side of the cap. Use a star piping tip and fill a disposable piping bag with the potato mixture. Pipe the potato mixture on top of the spinach. Bake 25 minutes. A beautiful side for any grilled or roasted meat!

Baked Mashed Potatoes Supreme

Serves 12

- potato masher
- cheese grater
- electric mixer

18 small to medium red skinned new potatoes, unpeeled
1 teaspoon salt
8 slices bacon
1/2 teaspoon black pepper
1 1/2 teaspoons *Tony Chachere's Creole Seasoning*
6 tablespoons unsalted butter
3/4 cup whole milk (enough to achieve a mashed potato consistency)
1 cup sour cream
5 green onions, finely chopped (white and pale green part only)
1 1/2 cups grated Cheddar cheese

Preheat oven to 300°F. In a large pot or Dutch oven, boil potatoes with 1 teaspoon salt until tender, about 30 minutes. If you are using the larger potatoes, cut into smaller pieces to boil. While potatoes are cooking, fry the bacon until crisp in a large skillet. Drain well and lay the cooked bacon on paper towels. Crumble when cool. When potatoes are tender, drain well and add pepper, *Tony Chachere's* and butter. With an electric mixer, mash potatoes, slowly adding enough milk to get mashed potato consistency. The amount of milk used will vary due to the potatoes holding some water. Add 1/2 cup sour cream and half of the chopped onions and crumbled bacon. Spoon the mixture into a 9 x 13-inch baking dish. Cover with the remaining sour cream, grated cheese and bacon. Bake 20 minutes or until cheese melts. Garnish with the remaining onions.

Tip: This is an excellent dish for a large group and can be made ahead. This recipe is similar in taste to twice baked potatoes and makes great leftovers.

"In water one sees one's own face, but in wine one beholds the heart of another."

~French proverb

Garlic Chive Mashed Potatoes

Serves: 8

- electric mixer
- vegetable peeler

12 medium russet potatoes, peeled and cut into quarters

1 teaspoon salt

1 (8-ounce) package cream cheese

1/4 cup (1/2 stick) butter, divided use

3 large garlic cloves, minced or pressed

1 cup sour cream

2 tablespoons chopped fresh chives

Whole milk or half-and-half, (at room temperature)

Salt and ground white pepper, to taste

Preheat the oven to 350°F. Place potatoes in a large pot or Dutch oven with enough cold water to cover and 1 teaspoon salt. Bring to a boil and cook until tender when pierced with a fork (approximately 20 minutes). Drain well. Soften the cream cheese in the microwave for about 10 to 20 seconds. Add the cream cheese, 2 tablespoons butter and garlic to the potatoes and whip with an electric mixer. Add the sour cream and chives. Gradually add half-and-half, adding only enough to get the desired mashed potato consistency. Do not over mix or the mixture will get shiny and pasty. (You may choose to use a potato masher.) Taste and season with salt and white pepper. Spread potatoes in a buttered 9 x 13-inch baking dish. This dish can be made ahead of time and refrigerated. Bring to room temperature before reheating. Dot the potatoes with the remaining butter and bake for 30 minutes until heated through.

Tip: Roasted garlic may be substituted for the chopped garlic. Cut 1/4-inch off a head of garlic and place in a baking dish. Drizzle with 2 tablespoons olive oil and stir around to coat. Cover dish with foil and bake at 350°F for 45 to 55 minutes until cloves are tender. Squeeze garlic from cloves and add to the potatoes. Use as many cloves as desired.

Nancy Wilson: Lee's Summit, Missouri

Nancy and I met years ago in Kansas. She and her husband Jeff, moved to Texas around the same time I did. Nancy cut my hair while she lived here and I got this from her on one of my visits. I changed it over the years, adding fresh garlic, herbs and half-and-half.

Mashed Potatoes with Caramelized Onions

Serves: 6

• potato masher

1/4 cup (1/2 stick) butter
2 tablespoons olive oil
2 red onions, thinly sliced
12 medium Yukon gold potatoes, unpeeled, diced (1-inch pieces)
1 teaspoon salt
1 1/2 cups half-and-half (at room temperature)
Salt and ground white pepper, to taste

In a sauté pan, over medium heat, melt the butter and stir in the olive oil. Add the onion and cook until translucent. Reduce heat to low and stirring occasionally, cook until caramelized, about 30 minutes. Remove from heat. Wash potatoes and put in a large pot or Dutch oven with enough cold water to cover. Add 1 teaspoon salt and bring to a boil. Continue to boil until tender when pierced with a fork (about 20 minutes). Drain well. Add half-and-half and mash potatoes until there are no lumps. Stir in the caramelized onions. Season the potatoes with salt and white pepper to taste. If you are making these ahead, put them in a buttered 9 x 13-inch baking dish and refrigerate. Bring to room temperature before baking. Preheat the oven to 350°F. Bake approximately 30 minutes or until warmed through.

> *"A true friends face lights up when they see you*
> *...celebrates your success*
> *...tells the truth*
> *...works to resolve conflict*
> *...nourishes and supports you."*
>
> ~SARK

Twice Baked Potatoes with White Cheddar and Rosemary

Serves: 8

4 large russet or baking potatoes, scrubbed
Olive oil
1 cup coarsely grated white Cheddar cheese
2 tablespoons unsalted butter
3/4 cup heavy cream
1 teaspoon *Tony Chachere's Creole Seasoning*
2 teaspoons finely chopped fresh rosemary or 3/4 teaspoon dried rosemary
Salt and pepper to taste
Sweet paprika

Preheat the oven to 400°F. Pierce potatoes in several places with a fork, then brush lightly with oil. Place potatoes directly on oven rack and bake until tender when pierced with a fork, about 55 minutes. Cool slightly. Turn oven down to 350°F. Cut off a thin slice from both ends of the potatoes and discard. Cut each potato crosswise in half; stand each on its flat end. Using a teaspoon, scoop out the cooked pulp from each half, leaving a 1/3-inch shell and forming a potato cup. Place potato cups in a 9 x 13-inch baking dish. Place potato pulp in a medium bowl; add the cheese, butter, heavy cream, *Tony Chachere's* and rosemary. Using a potato masher, mash the mixture until well blended and smooth. Season to taste with salt and pepper. Mound the mashed potato mixture in the potato cups. Bake potato cups until heated through, about 20 minutes. Sprinkle lightly with paprika and serve.

Tip: Piping potatoes with a pastry bag make a more impressive presentation.

Variation: *Substitute Gorgonzola for white Cheddar and top with fried, drained bacon crumbles if desired. Cheeses may be varied to balance your menu. For prime rib or steaks, we use horseradish Cheddar. Roasted garlic (page 236) is superb included in any of the combinations!*

Feta Potatoes

Serves: 6

• cheese grater
• vegetable peeler

3 large russet potatoes
(2 1/2 pounds)
1 teaspoon salt
1/4 cup finely chopped onion
1 teaspoon *Tony Chachere's
Creole Seasoning*
1/2 teaspoon coarse ground black
pepper
1 large garlic clove, minced or
pressed
1/4 cup (3 ounces) grated colby
cheese
1/4 cup (3 ounces) grated Swiss
cheese
1/4 cup (3 ounces) crumbled
feta cheese
3 tablespoons chopped fresh
parsley
1/2 cup (1 stick) butter, melted
1/2 cup bread crumbs

Peel potatoes and place in a large pot or Dutch oven with enough cold water to cover and 1 teaspoon salt. Bring to a boil and boil until tender when pierced with a fork (approximately 40 minutes.) Drain and refrigerate until cool. Preheat the oven to 350°F. Grate the potatoes once cool and mix with the chopped onion, *Tony Chachere's,* pepper, garlic, cheeses and parsley. Pour the melted butter on top and sprinkle with bread crumbs. Bake for 45 minutes in a buttered 9 x 13-inch baking dish or refrigerate until ready to bake. Let warm to room temperature before baking.

Special Note: Colby cheese is a mild, whole milk Cheddar cheese. It has a higher moisture content and it does not keep as long as other Cheddar cheeses.

Mariann Nichols: Grapevine, Texas
Mariann shops at Market Street where I am employed and we also see each other at some of my cooking demonstrations. She entertains family often and we discuss her culinary discoveries when we see one another. This is a favorite potato recipe.

239

Rosemary Potatoes

Serves: 6

• jelly roll pan

2 1/2 pounds small red skinned
potatoes
2 tablespoons olive oil
Salt and pepper, to taste
3 tablespoons coarsely chopped
fresh rosemary or 3 teaspoons
dried rosemary

Preheat the oven to 350°F. Wash and cut the
potatoes in quarters. Toss with olive oil and put
on a lightly oiled jelly roll pan. Sprinkle with
salt and pepper (I prefer sea salt). Sprinkle
rosemary over tops of potatoes. Do not stir.
Bake potatoes for 15 minutes and remove from
oven. Stir. Bake an additional 30 minutes or
until you can easily pierce the potatoes with a
fork. Serve hot from the oven.

*Variation: Add 1 pound cooked, drained
and crumbled Italian sausage (if sausage is
in links, remove casing). Experiment with
the flavor by replacing rosemary or mixing
rosemary with Greek oregano, garlic salt or
seasoned salt for a Mediterranean twist.
Create your own combination of herbs!*

Melinda Tomelleri: Los Angeles, California
*I met Markham in the Oklahoma airport en route to Kansas City during
Christmas in 1998. She has been very instrumental in guiding me toward my passion and
natural calling, which is the love of food, people and travel. She coaches and I took her
course "Trust What You Love" and this cookbook is the result of her coaching.*

Grandma's Potato Dressing

Serves: 8

- vegetable peeler
- potato masher

6 slices bacon
1 yellow onion, finely chopped
5 pounds russet potatoes
3 stalks celery, cut into 1-inch pieces (leaves included)
1/2 teaspoon salt
1 (14-ounce) package seasoned croutons
1/2 teaspoon dried rubbed sage
1/4 teaspoon dried ground thyme
Salt and ground black pepper, to taste
2 large eggs, beaten

Fry bacon until crisp. Remove the cooked bacon from the grease and drain on paper towels. Fry the chopped onion in the bacon grease until translucent, set aside. Peel and quarter the potatoes. Add the potatoes, celery and salt to enough cold water to cover the potatoes. Boil potatoes until tender when pierced with a fork (about 15 to 20 minutes, depending on the potato size). Do not overcook because they are not to be mashed completely, rather they will be left somewhat chunky. Drain water off potatoes leaving 1 cup water in pan. Slightly mash the potatoes and celery with a potato masher in the pan with the reserved potato water. Add the seasoned croutons. Stir in the crumbled bacon, onion and grease. Add the herbs and salt and pepper to taste. Mix and refrigerate overnight to let flavors blend. The next morning, thoroughly mix in the beaten eggs. Preheat the oven to 350°F. The dressing can be used to stuff a turkey cavity and the remainder can be baked in a glass 9 x 13-inch baking dish (or round casserole dish) for 30 to 45 minutes uncovered. Serve with roasted turkey and Turkey Gravy (page 201).

Louie Scherer: Kansas City, Kansas
This is my paternal grandmother's family recipe. My dad, Louie grew up in Atchison, Kansas, and this is the only dressing we have ever served during the holidays. Don't be afraid to pepper heavily. The bacon, onion and pepper combination is quite good.

Asparagus with Soy Sauce and Sesame Seeds

Serves: 4

2 pounds fresh asparagus
2 tablespoons less sodium soy sauce
2 teaspoons sugar
2 tablespoons sesame oil
2 large garlic cloves, minced or pressed
Salt and pepper, to taste
4 teaspoons sesame seeds

Wash and trim asparagus. Stir the soy sauce and sugar together until the sugar dissolves. Heat the oil in a large skillet and add the garlic. Sauté until fragrant, about 1 minute. Add the asparagus and stir-fry until crisp-tender, about 4 minutes. Add the soy mixture and toss until the asparagus is coated, about 1 minute longer. Season to taste with salt and pepper. Add the sesame seeds and toss. Transfer to a serving dish or to individual plates and serve hot.

> *Coleen Rossi: Paradise Valley, Arizona*
> *Coleen and I became friends when we were around 6 or 7 years old through our parents. Coleen entertains often and says friends have started enjoying lighter fare at her dinner parties so she often serves fish. This asparagus is especially good with grilled meats and seafood that has an Asian twist such as the Salmon with Honey-Soy Sauce on (page 205).*

Green Bean Bundles

Serves: 6

1/2 teaspoon *Tony Chachere's Creole Seasoning,* divided use
2 pounds fresh green beans, washed and ends snapped off
6 slices bacon, cut in half, partially cooked
Garlic salt
1/4 cup (1/2 stick) butter, melted
3 tablespoons packed brown sugar

In boiling water seasoned with 1/4 teaspoon *Tony Chachere's,* cook beans until al dente, about 8 to 12 minutes. Allow to cool. Preheat oven to 350°F. When beans are cool, wrap approximately 6 to 10 beans with the partially cooked bacon. Place bundles in a 9 x 13-inch baking dish. Sprinkle the bundles with garlic salt and the remaining *Tony Chachere's.* Pour melted butter over the bundles and sprinkle with brown sugar. Bake the bundles for 15 to 20 minutes or until bacon is done. To make ahead, complete all steps except the last (pouring the butter and brown sugar over beans). Put in a glass baking dish and refrigerate overnight until ready to bake. Before putting in oven, pour melted butter over bundles and sprinkle with brown sugar.

Asparagus and Mushroom Sauté

Serves: 4

• Microplane cheese grater

1 bunch asparagus (1/2 pound after ends are snapped)
1/4 cup minced green onions (white and pale green part only)
2 tablespoons olive oil
1 1/2 cups (3 ounces) sliced fresh mushrooms
1 tablespoon fresh thyme or 1 teaspoon dried thyme
1/2 teaspoon salt
1/4 teaspoon ground black pepper
3 tablespoons dry white wine
3/4 cup freshly grated Parmigiano-Reggiano cheese
1 teaspoon lemon zest

Wash and trim the asparagus. Cut asparagus (approximately 40 thin spears) into 1-inch pieces. Set aside. Sauté the green onions in olive oil in a large skillet over high heat, stirring constantly for about 1 minute. Reduce heat to medium and add the asparagus, mushrooms and seasonings. Cook, stirring constantly for 3 minutes. Add the wine and cover. Cook an additional 2 to 5 minutes until the asparagus is crisp-tender; drain. Sprinkle with Parmigiano-Reggiano cheese and lemon zest. Serve warm.

Tip: My mother-in-law, Linda Gore of Colleyville, Texas, gave me this tip. It is sometimes hard to know how much of the asparagus you should trim off. If you take the asparagus and bend it, it will break where the tender stalk meets the tough stalk.

Jane Langlais: Southlake, Texas
Jane from Dinner Club helped me proofread the cookbook and gave me this because it is such a great side vegetable as well as a light dinner. The combination of lemon and thyme is wonderful.

Oven Roasted Vegetables

Serves: 8

2 pounds assorted vegetables
(small potatoes, or peeled
cut up sweet potatoes; peeled,
quartered onions or shallots; red
peppers, sliced fennel, carrots
or parsnips; asparagus or
broccoli crowns)
2 tablespoons olive oil
1 teaspoon salt
1/4 teaspoon black pepper
1/4 teaspoon dried marjoram,
or more to taste
1 tablespoon minced garlic

Preheat the oven to 450°F. Wash and clean the vegetables. Toss all the vegetables with olive oil and sprinkle with salt, pepper, marjoram and garlic. Set tender vegetables such as asparagus and red peppers aside. In a shallow baking dish, arrange vegetables so they are in a single layer. Roast 20 minutes and stir. Add the tender vegetables and continue to roast 10 minutes. Serve hot.

Tips: Rosemary or your favorite herb may be included in this recipe. Potatoes should be almost finished roasting (tender when pierced with a fork), before adding the vegetables that roast more quickly, such as asparagus. Grilling adds a whole new flavor if you decide to try roasting the vegetables on the grill. They are delicious either way!

Paula Dyrhaug: Minneapolis, Minnesota
Paula and I went to grade school together and she threw a gathering for me when I visited her. She invited her closest girlfriends and they each made a recipe for me to try. They were all delicious and the evening was very memorable.

Julienne Vegetable Medley

Serves: 6

3/4 pound zucchini, cut in
1/4-inch julienne strips
3/4 pound carrots, peeled and
cut in 1/4-inch julienne strips
3/4 pound yellow squash, cut in
1/4-inch julienne strips
1/2 cup (1 stick) butter, softened
Salt and pepper, to taste (*Tony
Chachere's Creole Seasoning*
may be substituted for salt
and pepper)

Arrange vegetables in a vegetable steamer over 1 inch boiling water and steam until tender-crisp. Drain off water and toss with butter and salt and pepper, to taste. This is easy and colorful.

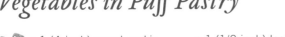

Vegetables in Puff Pastry

Serves: 8

- 1 (4-inch) round cookie cutter

- 1 (1/2-inch) leaf cookie cutter
- parchment paper
- pastry brush

2 (17.3-ounce) boxes frozen puff pastry sheets
2/3 cup finely chopped yellow onion
2 zucchini, diced (1/4-inch pieces)
4 carrots, peeled, sliced thin and finely chopped
2 yellow squash, diced (1/4-inch pieces)
1 tablespoon olive oil
1 tablespoon butter
1 large garlic clove, minced or pressed
2 teaspoons fresh thyme
1/4 teaspoon *Tony Chachere's Creole Seasoning*
1 large egg, beaten

Defrost the puff pastry sheets for 20 minutes and preheat oven to 400°F. Line the bottom of a jelly roll pan and a 9-inch round cake pan with parchment paper. Chop vegetables and measure. Vegetable mixture should equal approximately 7 cups before it is cooked. Heat oil and butter together and sauté all the vegetables with the garlic, thyme and *Tony Chachere's* for 15 minutes or until carrots are tender but not overcooked (al dente). Let mixture cool. On a floured surface cut out 16 circles, 4 inches in diameter from the puff pastry. Use any scraps to make decorative leaves with a leaf cookie cutter. Spoon the mixture of vegetables onto all pastry circles. Gather the pastry up to form a half moon, pinching to seal edges and then pull widest part together again to form a small round purse. Brush with egg and put a decorative dough leaf on top and brush it with egg. Place the pastries on the prepared baking dishes 2 inches apart and bake 18 to 22 minutes until they are puffed and slightly golden.

Variation: You may add crumbled goat cheese to the vegetable mixture.

"Bear in mind that you should conduct yourself in life as at a feast."

~*Epictetus*

Tomato Pie

Serves: 8

1 (9-inch) unbaked
  refrigerated pie crust
3 ripe tomatoes, sliced
  (1/4-inch slices)
1 bunch green onions, finely
  chopped (white and pale
  green part only)
Dried oregano leaves
Dried basil leaves or fresh basil,
  sliced in thin strips (chiffonade)
Italian seasoning
Salt and pepper
1 cup Hellmann's or Best Foods
  Real Mayonnaise
1 cup grated Cheddar cheese
3 Roma tomatoes, (1/8-inch
  slices), for garnish (optional)

Preheat the oven to 450°F. Using a glass pie dish, press the pie crust firmly against the sides of the dish so when pre-baked, the dough remains in place. Pre-bake the pie shell according to package directions. Remove from the oven and turn the oven down to 325°F. To protect the edges of the pie shell from getting too brown during the second baking, cover with foil. Drain the sliced tomatoes on paper towels for 15 minutes. Cover bottom of pie shell with the tomato slices. Cover tomatoes with the chopped green onions. Sprinkle liberally with the herbs, Italian seasonings and salt and pepper. In a small bowl, combine the mayonnaise and cheese and spread over the tomato layers. Thinly slice the Roma tomatoes and slightly overlap on the outside of the pie forming a decorative circle. Bake the filled shell approximately 30 minutes on the bottom rack of the oven until top is golden and bubbly. Allow to cool 10 minutes on a cooling rack before slicing. Garnish with Roma tomatoes, if desired. In the summer this can suffice as a light dinner with salad and bread. This is also a delicious vegetable accompaniment to beef, fish or poultry.

Variations: Add 6 slices cooked, drained crumbled bacon for variety. Experiment with different cheeses such as Gruyère. Sauté red onion in place of green onion and add sautéed red or green pepper. Add sliced zucchini, squash and garlic or any other vegetables to make your own combination vegetable pie.

Special Note: Tomatoes should not be refrigerated. They will retain their flavor and ripen correctly at room temperature.

Mary Hutchinson:
Topeka, Kansas
Mary and I met through work at my first job out of college in 1984. She was in the original Girl's Dinner Club and is a polished entertainer. Mary has traveled all over the world and has sampled a variety of cuisines, but claims nothing compares to sitting down in her home with good friends, food, wine and stimulating conversation. This is one of Mary's favorite dishes to make in the summertime with homegrown tomatoes.

Marinated Green Bean Bundles

Makes: 24

• slotted spoon

**12 slices bacon, cut in half,
partially cooked**
**2 (14.5-ounce) cans whole
green beans, drained**
1 (8-ounce) bottle French dressing
5 pimentos, cut in strips

In a large sauté pan, cook bacon over medium heat until golden, but still pliable. Drain on paper towels. Arrange beans in bundles of 8 to 10 and wrap with a half slice of bacon. Place in 9 x 13-inch glass baking dish. Pour dressing over the beans. Cover and chill at least 3 hours. Preheat the oven to 350°F. Bake uncovered for 40 minutes, turning once after 20 minutes. Remove with a slotted spoon. Garnish with pimento. You can make these beans the night before since they must marinate at least 3 hours.

Tip: When marinating foods, I prefer to use a glass dish or sealable plastic bag.

Marla Payne: Coppell, Texas
Marla enjoys cooking and passed on the idea of keeping a separate folder of recipes "to try." It is helpful when you are not feeling imaginative to comb through the items you've cut out from various publications. If you don't want to cut up your magazines, catalogue the issue, page number, add the title of the recipe and add it to your folder. This recipe that Marla makes for our Dinner Club is one of her most requested and you should add it to your list of recipes "to try."

Blue Cheese Green Beans

Serves: 4

2 pounds green beans, washed, ends snapped off
8 slices bacon, diced (1/4-inch pieces) and fried, reserve grease
1 (4-ounce) package blue cheese
1 cup walnuts, toasted
Salt and cracked black pepper, to taste

Cook the green beans in boiling water for 8 to 12 minutes or until tender-crisp. Add the beans to the pan with the bacon and bacon grease. Add the blue cheese and toss (these are to be served warm). Add the toasted walnuts and toss just before serving. Add salt and pepper, to taste.

Variation: Blue cheese is also delicious with asparagus, but for 1 1/2 pounds asparagus you only need about 3 tablespoons cheese. Top with toasted pecans instead of walnuts.

Pepper Hollingsworth: Fort Worth, Texas
Pepper works at one of my favorite interior design stores called Domain. These are a super complement to any grilled meat. Pepper eats these as his "complete meal" and likes them to be really gooey so he tends to use less beans, approximately 1 pound.

Red Cabbage

Serves: 8

• vegetable peeler

1 head red cabbage
1 cup Pinot Noir wine
1/3 cup brown sugar
1 tablespoon salt
1/2 teaspoon cayenne pepper
4 medium apples, peeled, cored and quartered
1/4 cup (1/2 stick) butter
1/4 cup cider vinegar
3 tablespoons cornstarch mixed with 3 tablespoons cold water

Core cabbage and cut into 4 quarters, then into strips. Place the cabbage in a Dutch oven or stockpot. Add the wine, brown sugar, salt, cayenne and apples. Cook on low for 60 to 90 minutes depending on the size of the head of cabbage. Apples will get so soft they will dissolve. Once apples dissolve, add the butter, cider vinegar and cornstarch mixture. Stir until thickened, about 2 minutes. Serve hot. This freezes nicely if you want to make for a later date. This is another specialty from my mother.

Curried Cauliflower

Serves: 8

1 large head cauliflower
1/2 teaspoon salt
1 (10.75-ounce) can cream of chicken soup
3/4 cup grated Cheddar cheese
1/3 cup Hellmann's or Best Foods Real Mayonnaise
1/2 teaspoon curry powder
3 tablespoons butter, melted
1/2 cup dried bread crumbs

Preheat the oven to 350°F. Break the cauliflower into florets. Cook in water with salt over medium heat for 10 minutes and drain. In a 2-quart casserole dish, stir in soup, cheese, mayonnaise, and curry powder. Add the cooked cauliflower. Melt the butter in a saucepan and stir in the bread crumbs. Sprinkle on top of the casserole. Bake 20 minutes or refrigerate until ready to bake. Let warm to room temperature before baking. This is great with turkey or ham.

"Jiffy's" Cornbread Casserole

Serves: 8

 • cheese grater

1 (15.25-ounce) can corn, undrained
1 (14.75-ounce) can cream style corn
1 (8.5-ounce) box "Jiffy" Corn Muffin Mix
1/2 cup (1 stick) butter, melted
1 (8-ounce) container sour cream
1 1/2 cups grated Cheddar cheese

Preheat the oven to 350°F. Mix together all ingredients except cheese. Put corn mixture in a 9 x 13-inch baking dish and bake uncovered, approximately 45 minutes or until top is golden. Sprinkle the grated cheese on top and return to the oven. Bake until the cheese melts, about 5 minutes. Serve hot.

Marla Payne: Coppell, Texas
Marla and her husband Steve are part of "Dinner Club." We alternate homes and the hostess picks a theme and the menu. She has her choice of assigning a dish and sending the recipe to you or assigning you a course (e.g. salad, vegetable or dessert). This cornbread casserole was served at one of our dinners and everyone requested the recipe.

Cauliflower Bake with Cream and Bacon

Serves: 4

- slotted spoon
- whisk

1 large head cauliflower, broken into florets
2 slices bacon, diced
2 tablespoons flour
1 cup heavy cream
3/4 teaspoon *Tony Chachere's, Creole Seasoning*
1/8 teaspoon nutmeg
1 cup grated Gruyère, Swiss or Parmigiano-Reggiano cheese

Preheat the oven to 325°F. Heat a pot of boiling water and add the cauliflower. Cook until cauliflower is soft when it is pierced with a fork. Drain off water and put cauliflower in a glass, baking dish. Fry the bacon pieces until crisp and remove from the grease with a slotted spoon, drain the bacon on paper towels. Heat the reserved grease and whisk in the flour to make a roux. Slowly add the cream and spices to make a sauce. Once the desired thickness is obtained, add in the cheese. Pour the cheese mixture over the cauliflower and sprinkle with bacon. Bake until cheese melts, approximately 20 minutes.

Tip: Bacon can be diced easiest if it has been put in the freezer about 10 minutes. Use kitchen shears to cut into small pieces before frying. If all of the components (cauliflower and sauce) are warm, you may mix together and serve immediately.

Variation: *Savoy cabbage is a nice replacement for cauliflower and was served by my friend, Darren McGrady (former chef to Princess Diana), in a cooking class.*

Steakhouse Creamed Spinach

Serves: 4

- whisk
- Microplane cheese grater

2 (10-ounce) boxes frozen spinach
4 slices bacon
1 tablespoon olive oil
1 bunch green onions, finely chopped (white and pale green part only)
4 large garlic cloves, minced or pressed
Pinch of nutmeg
1 (3-ounce) package cream cheese, cut into cubes
1 cup freshly grated Parmigiano-Reggiano cheese
Salt and pepper, to taste

White Sauce
3 tablespoons butter
3 tablespoons flour
2 cups whole milk
3/4 cup Cheddar cheese

Thaw spinach and squeeze to extract excess water. Cook the bacon in a medium skillet for about 8 minutes. Drain, crumble and set aside. In a separate medium skillet, heat the oil and add the onion, sautéing for 6 to 8 minutes until onions begin to soften. Add the garlic and continue to sauté 1 to 2 minutes longer or until fragrant. Add the spinach and sauté until minimal liquid remains. Set aside. For the white sauce, melt the butter in a saucepan on low heat. Once butter is melted, whisk in the flour. Turn heat up to medium and gradually whisk in the milk stirring constantly until the sauce begins to thicken. (Sauce will begin to have bubbles on outside edge but does not need to boil to thicken.) Add the Cheddar, continuing to whisk until the cheese melts. Fold the cheese sauce into the spinach and heat over medium heat, stirring to blend. Stir in a pinch of nutmeg and add cream cheese. Stir until melted. Gradually add the Parmigiano-Reggiano cheese. Stir until creamy. Add the bacon crumbles and stir. Reduce heat to low and simmer 5 to 10 minutes. Taste and season with salt and pepper, if desired.

Joe Graber: Colleyville, Texas
Joe and Jeanne do not live far from us and they often host dinner in their home.
Joe is a foodie and loves wine so when we get together it is quite a feast.

Naturally Sweet Carrots

Serves: 8

2 pounds carrots, peeled and sliced into uniform pieces
1 tablespoon unsalted butter

Place the carrots and butter in a saucepan over very low heat and cover with a tight-fitting lid. The carrots will slowly steam in their own moisture, turning a beautiful orange and will be sweet. Shake the pan from time to time. After 10 minutes on a low heat, check to see if the temperature is correct. Lift the lid and you should see steam and barely hear the carrots cooking. If there is no steam, raise the heat, but if you hear sizzling, reduce the heat. Cook until the carrots are tender. This process can take from 25 to 40 minutes. When the carrots are finished cooking they should be tender and only a small amount of butter that is clear should remain in the bottom of the pan. Toss the carrots with the butter in the pan and serve hot. These are delicious because the carrots are cooking in their own moisture that brings out their natural sweetness.

Variations: For orange glazed carrots melt together 1/2 cup (1 stick) unsalted butter, 1/4 cup brown sugar, 1/8 teaspoon nutmeg and 1/4 cup orange juice or Grand Marnier liqueur. Toss with warm steamed carrots.

One pound trimmed asparagus cut into thirds diagonally may be added the last 15 minutes for a beautiful and colorful vegetable combo. A tablespoon of pure maple syrup tossed with the carrot and asparagus combination is delicious.

One tablespoon of brown sugar, 2 tablespoons minced green onion and 1/4 cup fried, drained and crumbled bacon can be gently tossed with the carrots before serving for another palate pleaser.

1/4 cup peeled and finely chopped shallots (2 medium shallots peeled and finely chopped) can be added when you begin the carrots, and snow peas (1 cup) may be added in the last 15 minutes of cooking for a colorful and tasty addition.

1/4 cup (1/2 stick) butter, 1/4 cup bourbon and 1/4 cup brown sugar can be mixed together and boiled. (Mixture should be thick enough to coat the back of a spoon.) Gently mix with the cooked carrots.

Sliced fennel is a wonderful combination when cooked with the carrots. Season with salt and pepper if desired.

Corn Maque Choux

Serves: 6

3 cups fresh corn (7 to 10 ears)
1/2 cup olive oil
1 cup finely chopped yellow onion
1/2 cup diced green bell pepper
(1/4-inch pieces)
1 cup chopped fresh parsley
1 tablespoon minced garlic
1 cup dry white wine
Tony Chachere's Creole Seasoning,
to taste
Tabasco red pepper sauce, to taste
1 tomato, chopped (1/4-inch
pieces)

Remove the corn kernels by scraping close to the cob to get all of the juices. Heat the oil in a skillet and sauté the onions, pepper and parsley until the onion is translucent. Add the corn, garlic, wine and seasonings. Stir to blend ingredients. Reduce heat and simmer for 30 minutes. Add the chopped tomato. Taste and adjust seasonings before serving. The Choux is pronounced "Shoe" and is a fancy name for smothered corn.

Jalapeño Broccoli

Serves: 6

1/4 cup (1/2 stick) butter,
softened
2 tablespoons flour
2 tablespoons chopped white
onion
1/2 cup evaporated milk
3/4 teaspoon celery salt
1 teaspoon Worcestershire sauce
6 ounces processed cheese (such
as Cheez Whiz or Velveeta)
Chopped fresh or pickled
jalapeños, to taste
3 (10-ounce) packages frozen
broccoli, cooked, drained,
reserve liquid

Preheat the oven to 350°F. Make a paste with the butter and flour. Add all other ingredients, excluding broccoli and blend in a small saucepan, over low heat to make a cheese sauce. (This includes the reserved liquid.) Mix the cheese sauce with the broccoli and put in a buttered 9 x 13-inch baking dish. Bake 20 minutes. This may be made 1 to 2 days ahead.

Stuffed Zucchini

Serves: 4

1/4 cup grated Cheddar cheese
1/4 cup grated mozzarella cheese
2 medium zucchini
Olive oil
1 slice bacon, diced (1/4-inch pieces) (optional)
1 garlic clove, minced or pressed
1 green onion, finely chopped (white and pale green part only)
1 small tomato, cored and diced (1/4-inch pieces)
2 tablespoons thinly sliced fresh basil

Preheat the oven to 400°F. Mix the cheeses together and set aside. Halve the zucchini lengthwise. With a small spoon, scoop out the seeds and most of the flesh. Leave about a 1/4-inch thickness and be careful not to tear the skin. Reserve the flesh. Brush zucchini with oil and put cut side down on a baking sheet. Roast zucchini 10 to 12 minutes until skin is wrinkled and starting to brown. Using tongs, flip zucchini over and set aside. Heat a skillet slightly and add the bacon. Sauté until bacon is lightly crisp; add the reserved zucchini flesh, garlic, and onion. Continue to sauté until garlic is fragrant about 2 minutes. Add the tomato and cook an additional 2 minutes. (You may make up to this point and refrigerate for later.) Bring to room temperature and proceed by stirring in the basil. Divide the mixture evenly among the hollowed out zucchini shells and top with cheese. Bake 6 minutes or until cheese melts. Serve immediately.

Tip: This is a super side dish to those on a reduced carbohydrate diet. If you choose to leave bacon out, use a small amount of olive oil for sautéing.

Green Beans with Balsamic Brown Butter

Serves: 8

1 slice bacon
2 pounds fresh green beans, washed and ends snapped off
1/2 cup (1 stick) butter
1 tablespoon balsamic vinegar
1/4 teaspoon salt
1/4 teaspoon black pepper

Dice uncooked bacon into 1/4-inch pieces. Cook green beans and bacon in boiling water for 8 to 12 minutes or until crisp-tender (soft but not overcooked); drain. Melt the butter in a small saucepan over medium-high heat, stirring often until deep golden brown. Remove from heat; stir in vinegar, salt and pepper. Pour over the beans and serve. This is a nice alternative to plain steamed green beans.

Desserts

Desserts

 Kitchen tools needed

 May be prepared ahead

Pineapple Carrot Cake with White Chocolate Cream Cheese Frosting, page 269 • Puff Pastry Berry Napoleons with Mascarpone, page 275 • Raspberry Cheesecake (variation of Amaretto Cheesecake), page 255 • Fruit Torte, page 279

Amaretto Cheesecake

Serves: 12

- springform pan (9- or 10-inch)
- blender or food processor
- electric mixer

Crumb Crust
1 1/2 cups graham cracker crumbs
(1 pack from a 16-ounce box)
2 tablespoons sugar
1 teaspoon ground cinnamon
6 tablespoons butter, melted

Topping
1/4 cup chopped almonds
1 (8-ounce) container sour cream
1 tablespoon plus 1 teaspoon
sugar
1 tablespoon amaretto
1 (12-ounce) chocolate candy bar,
grated

Cheesecake
3 (8-ounce) packages cream
cheese, softened
1 cup sugar
4 large eggs
1/3 cup amaretto

Preheat the oven to 375°F. To make the crust, crush the graham crackers in a blender or food processor. Combine the graham cracker crumbs with the sugar, cinnamon and butter; mix well. Spray the bottom and sides of the springform pan with cooking spray. Press the crust mixture into the bottom and up the sides of a springform pan. For the topping, toast the almonds on a baking sheet in the oven until lightly golden, about 3 to 4 minutes. Remove the almonds and set aside. Increase the oven temperature to 500°F. To make the cheesecake, beat the cream cheese with an electric mixer in a large bowl until light and fluffy. Gradually add the sugar, mixing well. Add eggs, one at a time, beating well after each addition. Stir in 1/3 cup amaretto. Pour into the prepared pan. Bake the cheesecake for 45 to 60 minutes until set. Combine the sour cream, sugar and amaretto. Stir well and spoon over the cheesecake. Return to the oven and bake for another 5 minutes. Remove and let cool to room temperature. Once cooled refrigerate for 24 to 48 hours. Cheesecake is best when thoroughly chilled for at least 24 hours. Just before serving, garnish with the toasted almonds and grated chocolate.

Variations: This is a cheesecake recipe that can be a basic for many variations. Replace amaretto with a raspberry flavored liqueur, omit almonds and garnish the top with 2 pints fresh whole raspberries arranged neatly with pointed end up, covering the top. Use 1/3 cup grated white chocolate in the crust and reduce sugar in crust to 1 tablespoon. Frangelico will work nicely as a substitute for amaretto, using chopped hazelnuts instead of almonds, and white or dark chocolate as a garnish.

Chokahlúa Cheesecake

Serves: 12

- electric mixer
- springform pan (9- or 10-inch)
- blender or food processor

Chocolate Crumb Crust
1 1/3 cups chocolate cookies with white cream filling
1/4 cup (1/2 stick) butter, softened

Cheesecake
2 tablespoons butter
1 1/2 cups semisweet chocolate pieces
1/4 cup Kahlúa liqueur
2 (8-ounce) packages cream cheese, softened and cut into small pieces
2 large eggs
1/3 cup sugar
1/4 teaspoon salt
1 cup sour cream

Mocha Sauce
1 cup semisweet chocolate chips
1/3 cup Kahlúa liqueur
1/3 cup light corn syrup

Topping
1/2 cup sour cream

Preheat the oven to 325°F. To make the crust, crush the cookies in a blender. Mix the cookies with the butter in a small bowl. Spray the bottom and sides of the springform pan with cooking spray. Press the crust mixture into the bottom of a springform pan. To make the cheesecake, slowly heat the butter, chocolate pieces and Kahlúa in a small saucepan, stirring until the chocolate melts and the mixture is smooth. Cool and set aside. Beat the softened cream cheese with an electric mixer in a large bowl until smooth. Beat in the eggs one at a time then beat in the sugar, salt and sour cream. Gradually beat in the cooled chocolate mixture. Pour entire mixture over the chocolate crumb crust. Bake the cheesecake for 40 minutes or until the filling is barely set in the center. Remove from the oven and let stand at room temperature at least 1 hour. To make the mocha sauce, combine all the ingredients over low heat and stir until the chocolate melts. Spread a thin layer of sour cream over the cooled cheesecake and drizzle with the warm mocha sauce. If not serving until later, refrigerate the cheesecake and sauce until ready to serve. Before serving, bring to room temperature. Reheat the sauce over low heat in a small saucepan to serve warm with the cheesecake. The cheesecake may be made 1 to 2 days ahead and the sauce 1 week ahead. The mocha sauce is also delicious over ice cream.

Betty Krenger: Abilene, Kansas
Betty is the mother of a college boyfriend. We got along well back then and loved to discuss food and recipes. We've stayed in touch and still exchange recipes today. This is a recipe she gave me back in 1982. It is a chocolate lover's dream.

Pecan Pie

Serves: 8

- electric mixer
- pie pan

1 (10-inch) refrigerated pie crust
3 large eggs, beaten
1/2 cup sugar
1/2 cup dark corn syrup
1/2 cup light corn syrup
1/2 teaspoon vanilla
1/3 cup butter, melted
1 cup pecan halves
2 cups heavy cream, whipped

Preheat the oven to 350°F. Press the unbaked crust into a pie pan according to package directions. Combine the eggs, sugar, corn syrups, vanilla and butter together in a large bowl. Mix in the pecans and pour the entire mixture into the pie crust. Bake 45 to 50 minutes until the pie is set. Let cool and serve with whipped cream.

Tip: For extra flavor and sweetness, add confectioners' sugar (1 tablespoon or to taste) and vanilla (1 teaspoon) to your heavy cream as you whip.

Pumpkin Pie

Serves: 8

- electric mixer
- pie pan

1 (9-inch) refrigerated pie crust
1/2 cup sugar
1/2 cup brown sugar
1/4 cup flour
1/2 teaspoon ginger
1 teaspoon cinnamon
1/2 teaspoon allspice
1/4 teaspoon salt
1 (15-ounce) can 100% pure pumpkin
1/4 cup corn syrup
1 cup heavy cream plus extra to whip for garnish
2 large eggs

Preheat the oven to 375°F. Press the unbaked crust into a pie pan according to package directions. Combine all the dry ingredients in a large bowl. In another bowl, combine the pumpkin and corn syrup. Mix into the dry ingredients. Add 1 cup heavy cream and eggs; mix until well combined. Pour the mixture into the pie crust. Bake for 45 minutes. Cool and serve with whipped cream. This recipe can be made a day ahead. Once pie is served, refrigerate any leftovers.

Pumpkin Rum Cheesecake with Praline Sauce

Serves: 10

- blender or food processor
- springform pan (9- or 10-inch)
- electric mixer

Crust

1 1/4 cups honey graham cracker crumbs (1 pack from a 16-ounce box)
1/2 cup pecans
1/3 cup butter, melted
1/4 cup brown sugar
1/4 cup sugar

Filling

3/4 cup plus 6 tablespoons sugar, divided use
1 cup 100% pure pumpkin
3 large eggs
1 1/2 teaspoons cinnamon
1/2 teaspoon nutmeg
1/2 teaspoon ground ginger
1/2 teaspoon salt
3 (8-ounce) packages cream cheese, softened
1 tablespoon cornstarch
2 tablespoons heavy cream
1 teaspoon vanilla
1 tablespoon rum

Praline Sauce

1 cup light brown sugar
1 tablespoon cornstarch
1 1/2 cups water
2 tablespoons butter
1/2 cup coarsely chopped pecans

Preheat the oven to 325°F. To make the crust, crush the graham crackers and chop the nuts separately in a food processor or blender. Combine all the crust ingredients in a large bowl and mix well. Spray the bottom and sides of a springform pan with cooking spray. Press the crust mixture into the bottom and up the sides of a springform pan. Bake 15 minutes. Set aside until the filling is prepared. Lower the oven temperature to 300°F. To make the filling, mix the 3/4 cup sugar, pumpkin, eggs, cinnamon, nutmeg, ginger and salt in a large bowl. Set aside. Using an electric mixer, beat the cream cheese and 6 tablespoons sugar in a separate bowl until smooth. Add cornstarch, heavy cream, vanilla and rum, beating well after each addition. Add the pumpkin mixture to the cream cheese and mix thoroughly so the color is consistent. Pour the filling into the crust and bake 1 hour at 300°F. The center will be soft. Turn off the oven and let the cheesecake cool in the oven with the door closed for several hours or overnight. Refrigerate until ready to serve. To prepare the sauce, combine the sugar and cornstarch in a small saucepan. Add the water and bring the mixture to a boil, stirring constantly until sauce is thick, about 5 minutes. If you prefer a thicker sauce, make a thin paste of additional cornstarch (1 teaspoon) mixed with an equal amount of cold water. Whisk the cornstarch mixture into the hot liquid to avoid lumps. Allow the sauce to come to a boil and boil approximately 2 minutes or until thickened. Add the butter and pecans. Cool slightly before serving. Serve the praline sauce drizzled over the cheesecake.

(continued on next page)

Tip: If the cheesecake cracks on top, nothing is wrong. Just spread a mixture of 4 ounces (1/2 cup) sour cream and 1 teaspoon sugar over the cooled cheesecake. Refrigerate until ready to serve.

Susan Bee: Rockwall, Texas
I reported to Susan in two different jobs, and as a result, our friendship has blossomed. Dave and I enjoy restaurant outings with Susan and her husband, Russ. She and her friend Kathleen Wincorn created this tantalizing combination of pumpkin and praline. It is a unique alternative to traditional pumpkin pie.

Chocolate Sacks Filled with White Chocolate Mousse on Raspberry Sauce

Serves: 2

- pastry tube
- candy thermometer
- blender
- electric mixer
- double boiler
- mesh strainer

- pastry brush
- 2 (12-inch) wooden skewers and 4 toothpicks
- 1-inch wide ribbon for decorative bows
- 4 tall cans or glasses to balance the drying chocolate sacks

Raspberry Sauce
1 (10-ounce) bag frozen raspberries
2 tablespoons raspberry flavored liqueur (optional)
1/4 cup sugar or more, to taste

Chocolate Sack
2 small gift bags (approximately 7 3/4 x 4 x 2 1/2 inches)
1 (14-ounce) bag chocolate candy coating

White Chocolate Mousse
1 cup white chocolate morsels
1/4 cup heavy cream
1 tablespoon raspberry sauce
1 1/2 cups heavy cream, whipped
1 drop red liquid food coloring
Fresh raspberries, for garnish
Fresh mint, for garnish

To make the raspberry sauce, blend the frozen raspberries in a blender until smooth. Pour the raspberry liquid through a mesh strainer into a large bowl and discard the seeds. Add the liqueur and sugar to the raspberry mixture and stir until the sugar dissolves. For the chocolate sacks, cut 3 inches from the top of the sack so the sack is small enough to fit on a dinner plate. Insert wooden toothpicks on outside base of bag, parallel to the short edges of the bag, tucking ends of picks under the diagonal folds. Insert a long wooden skewer through the center base fold of bag under the wooden toothpicks. You will suspend it between cans to dry, so try not to have wooden skewer become part of the base of the bag that will be coated with chocolate. Melt the bag of chocolate candy coating in a double boiler and cool to 100°F using a candy thermometer to monitor the temperature. Pour the candy coating into the bag and tilt to coat the interior. You may need a pastry brush or a spoon to coat the inside. Shake the bag over the double boiler to remove excess chocolate. Heat the candy coating again and cool to 100°F. Hold the bag to the light to identify weak areas and reinforce them using a pastry brush. Heat the chocolate and coat the inside again, each time shaking off excess chocolate and suspending upside down between cans to dry. Repeat for the second bag. Once the chocolate sack has dried, about 1 hour, gently peel the bag off.

(continued on next page)

It comes off easily and any slight flaws can be disguised with the bow, mousse and garnishes. Do not refrigerate; the moisture will soften the coating. Handle the bag as little as possible to avoid melting. To make the mousse, combine the white chocolate morsels and 1/4 cup heavy cream in a saucepan. Melt over low heat, stirring constantly until chocolate melts. Let cool. Stir the raspberry sauce into the mousse and fold in the whipped cream. Add food coloring. The mousse can be made ahead and refrigerated until ready to serve. To serve, spoon 2 to 3 tablespoons raspberry sauce onto the center of a 10- to 12-inch dinner plate. Position the small chocolate sack diagonally across the pool of the raspberry sauce. Pipe about 3/4 cup of the mousse into the open end of the sack; allow the white chocolate mousse to spill out onto the sauce. Scatter fresh raspberries over the mousse and sauce. Garnish with mint leaves. Make a bow of gold ribbon, leaving the tails long. Place the bow on top of the chocolate sack.

Variation: Shannon Curry-Rackers from Pembroke, Massachusetts, gave me this time-saving variation. Melt the (14-ounce) bag of chocolate candy coating using microwave directions and paint the inside of paper cupcake wrappers. Place in metal cupcake holders and refrigerate. When firm, peel off the paper and use as you would the chocolate paper bag. It is quick and makes 6. The filling and raspberry sauce can be used to fill cups and garnish. The mini cupcake holders and muffin pans will also work as well and could be used for mousse or filled with liqueur to serve with coffee.

Fudge Truffle Cheesecake

Serves: 12

- blender or food processor
- electric mixer
- springform pan (9- or 10-inch)

Chocolate Crumb Crust
1 1/2 cups vanilla wafers
(about 45 wafers)
1/2 cup confectioners' sugar
1/3 cup unsweetened cocoa
1/3 cup unsalted butter, melted

Cheesecake
3 (8-ounce) packages cream
cheese, softened
1 (14-ounce) can sweetened
condensed milk
2 cups semisweet chocolate chips,
melted
4 large eggs
2 teaspoons vanilla

Preheat the oven to 300°F. Crush the vanilla wafers in a blender or food processor. Combine the vanilla wafer crumbs with the sugar, cocoa and butter in a small bowl. Spray the bottom and sides of the springform pan with cooking spray. Press the crust mixture into the bottom and up the sides of a springform pan. To make the cheesecake, beat the cream cheese with an electric mixer in a large mixing bowl until fluffy. Gradually beat in the condensed milk until smooth. Add the remaining ingredients and gently mix until combined. Pour the mixture into the prepared crust and bake for 1 hour and 5 minutes or until the center is set. Cool and chill.

Tip: Add the finishing touch to this dessert with a seasonal garnish such as red and white peppermints, mint leaves and cranberries or raspberries, or even edible flowers.

Variation: *Graham cracker crumbs may be substituted for vanilla wafers, if you are short on time. Graham cracker crumbs are sold already crushed on the baking aisle.*

Gail Davis: Colleyville, Texas
Gail helps match speakers with companies and she and I became acquainted when I began speaking on the art of entertaining. She brought this dessert to a dinner party that I hosted. The dessert and the party were a huge success and this dessert is touted as her "signature" dessert.

Chocolate Praline Squares with Coffee Whipped Cream

Serves: 12

- electric mixer
- wire cooling rack
- 9 x 13-inch baking dish

Crust
1 1/2 cups pecan pieces
1 1/2 cups flour
1/2 cup confectioners' sugar
3/4 cup (1 1/2 sticks) unsalted
   butter, softened

Filling
3/4 cup light corn syrup
1/2 cup dark corn syrup
1 cup packed brown sugar
1/4 cup (1/2 stick) unsalted
   butter, melted
4 large eggs
2 cups coarsely chopped pecans
1 teaspoon vanilla
1 1/2 cups mini semisweet
   chocolate chips

Topping
1 cup heavy cream
2 tablespoons confectioners' sugar
1 teaspoon vanilla
1 tablespoon coffee flavored
   liqueur or Irish cream flavored
   coffee syrup

Preheat the oven to 350°F. For the crust, toast the chopped pecans for approximately 3 to 4 minutes. Set aside. Stir together the flour and confectioners' sugar in a large bowl. Blend in the butter until the coarse dough resembles small peas. Stir in the toasted pecans. Spray a baking dish with cooking spray and press the dough into the dish. Bake the crust for 25 to 30 minutes or until it is slightly golden. In a medium bowl, mix the syrups, brown sugar and butter together. In a large bowl, beat the eggs until well combined. Beat the syrup mixture into the eggs then stir in the pecans and vanilla. Pour the filling into the crust and sprinkle with chocolate chips. Bake 30 to 45 minutes or until the center is set. Cool on a wire rack. To make the topping, whip the heavy cream until soft peaks begin to form. Add the sugar and continue to beat until stiff peaks form. Stir in the vanilla and the liqueur. To serve, cut into squares and top with whipped cream.

Jody Huerter: Leawood, Kansas
Jody is my mentor in cooking and entertaining and is a dear friend. We frequently call each other with cooking questions and I try to stop by for coffee when I am in Kansas City. Jody has been an inspiration to me throughout my life.

Chocolate Flowerpot Dessert

Serves: 8

- large flowerpot (8 x 8 inch) or small flowerpots for individual servings
- whisk
- blender
- electric mixer

1 (16-ounce) package chocolate sandwich cookies
11 ounces cream cheese, softened
1/2 cup (1 stick) butter, melted
1 cup confectioners' sugar
2 (3.5-ounce) packages instant chocolate fudge pudding mix
3 cups cold milk
1 teaspoon vanilla
1 (8-ounce) container whipped topping, thawed

Crush the sandwich cookies in a blender. They should resemble potting soil. If using a flowerpot, cover the hole in the bottom of the flowerpot with foil or wax paper. Put half of the crumbs in the bottom of the flowerpot (you may use a 9 x 13-inch baking dish as a substitute). With an electric mixer, beat together the cream cheese, butter and confectioners' sugar in a medium bowl. In a separate bowl, whisk together the pudding mix, cold milk, vanilla and whipped topping. Mix the pudding mixture with the cream cheese mixture and pour over the crumbs. Top with the remaining chocolate cookie crumbs. Chill for 10 hours. This may be served chilled or frozen.

Variations: Top the chocolate crumbs in the flowerpot with gummy worms for a boy's birthday party. For a more feminine touch, use small individual flowerpots and insert a flower into the center. For a more sophisticated look, layer in brioche dishes. Graham cracker crumbs can be substituted for chocolate cookies, and vanilla pudding and strawberries can be used instead of chocolate pudding for a completely different dessert.

Barb Homer: Houston, Texas
Barb is a teacher in Houston and has been a friend of mine since junior high school. I love her contribution because the ingredients are simple but make a creative dessert. The tips for serving may lead you to your own discovery—adding nuts, fruit or cookie variations.

Rum Bundt Cake

Serves: 10

- electric mixer
- nut chopper
- Bundt cake pan

Cake

1 cup chopped pecans
1 package yellow cake mix (without pudding added)
1 (3.5-ounce) package vanilla instant pudding and pie filling
4 large eggs
1/2 cup cold water
1/2 cup vegetable oil
1/2 cup 80 proof rum (can be white or amber)

Glaze

1/2 cup (1 stick) butter
1/4 cup water
1 cup sugar
1/2 cup rum (white or amber)
Whipped cream (optional)

Preheat the oven to 325°F. Generously spray the Bundt pan with cooking spray and dust with flour. Sprinkle the nuts in the bottom of the pan. Combine the rest of the cake ingredients in a large bowl. Blend well for about 2 minutes with an electric mixer at medium speed. Pour the batter over the nuts. Bake for 1 hour. Remove from the oven and let cool. Invert onto a serving plate. Prepare the glaze by melting butter over medium heat in a saucepan. Stir in water and sugar and boil 5 minutes. Remove from the heat and stir in the rum. Prick the top of the cake all over with a fork. Pour the glaze evenly over the cake, allowing it to absorb the glaze. Repeat until all of the glaze is used. Serve with a side of whipped cream.

Special Note: Add a festive touch to this Bundt cake by filling the center with fresh flowers. Crumble foil and place it in the center of the cake so you have a base for the stems and so fewer flowers are needed.

Louie Scherer: Kansas City, Kansas
I have some fun memories of eating popcorn with a side of tart apples with my dad. He liked food with nice presentation and made his breakfast look so appetizing you wanted a bite. This recipe was one of my dad's favorites. We have had this recipe in the family since I was ten years old. It is a very moist and flavorful cake.

Raspberry Bread Pudding with Cajeta Sauce

Serves: 12

- whisk
- 9 x 13-inch baking dish

6 large eggs, at room temperature
3 cups heavy cream
3/4 cup sugar
1 tablespoon vanilla extract
1 teaspoon ground cinnamon
1 (16-ounce) loaf Challah or French bread
1 (12-ounce) bag frozen raspberries

Cajeta Sauce
1 cup heavy cream
1 (13.4-ounce) can cajeta (Dulce de Leche, caramel)

Preheat the oven to 350°F. Lightly spray the baking dish with cooking spray. (Individual ramekins can be used as well.) In a large bowl, whisk the eggs. Add the heavy cream, sugar, vanilla and cinnamon and whisk until thoroughly blended. Remove the crust from the bread and cut the bread into 1-inch cubes. In a large bowl, toss the berries and bread together. Evenly place the bread mixture in the bottom of the baking dish. Pour the egg mixture evenly over the bread mixture and toss to coat so no dry areas remain. (Berries should be immersed or they will burn.) Bake for 30 to 40 minutes until the pudding is bubbling around the edges and golden on top. To make the cajeta sauce, heat the cream in a saucepan and gradually add the cajeta. Serve this warm drizzled over the warm bread pudding.

Special Note: Cajeta is a thick dark syrup or paste made from caramelized sugar and milk—traditionally goat's milk, although cow's milk is often used. It is most often found in Latin markets, but grocery stores that have a Hispanic section carry this product. In many instances the can states Dulce de Leche and then in small lettering says cajeta. Challah is an egg bread that is light yet rich in flavor.

Ivan Vasquez: Fort Worth, Texas
Ivan was one of the visiting chefs that taught for me at the culinary school. His recipe is one of my favorite desserts because you can make it in a more traditional manner with a bourbon sauce, but we liked his version as well as any bread pudding we have had!

Sour Cream Chocolate Cake with Cream Cheese Chocolate Frosting

Serves: 8

 • 8 x 8-inch or 11 x 7-inch baking dish

Cake
1/2 cup boiling water
1/3 cup unsweetened cocoa
1/2 cup (1 stick) butter
1 cup sugar
1 large egg
1 teaspoon vanilla
1 cup sifted flour
1 teaspoon sifted baking soda
1/2 cup sour cream

Frosting
9 ounces semisweet chocolate chips
1/4 cup (1/2 stick) unsalted butter
1 (8-ounce) package cream cheese
1 teaspoon vanilla extract
2 1/4 cups confectioners' sugar

Preheat the oven to 350°F. Pour the 1/2 cup boiling water over the cocoa in a bowl and stir until cocoa dissolves. Allow mixture to cool. In a separate bowl, cream the butter and sugar together until pale yellow. Add the egg and vanilla and beat. Add the cooled cocoa mixture to this mixture. Mix the flour and baking soda together in a small bowl. Alternating, add the sour cream and flour to the cocoa mixture. Spray the baking dish with cooking spray and lightly dust with flour or cocoa. Pour the batter into the baking dish and bake 30 to 40 minutes or until a toothpick inserted in the center comes out clean. Cool completely before frosting. To make the frosting, melt the chocolate chips and butter in a small saucepan over low heat then cool. Beat the cream cheese until fluffy in a large bowl, gradually adding the lukewarm chocolate mixture and the vanilla. Beat until smooth. Gradually add the confectioners' sugar, beating until well blended. You may have a bit more frosting than is needed but it is good spread between graham crackers for a child-friendly treat.

Tip: Cooking spray with flour is helpful for greasing pans for baking. It is found with the oils in the grocery store. It will not leave the sticky yellow residue on pans like other spays do.

"The discovery of a new dish does more for the happiness of mankind than the discovery of a new star."

~*Jean Anthelme Brillat-Savarin*

Chocolate Cake with Whipped Cream Filling

Serves: 8

- 3 (9-inch) round cake pans
- hand mixer
- sifter

Cake
1 cup cocoa
2 cups boiling water
1 cup (2 sticks) butter, softened
2 1/2 cups sugar
4 eggs
2 3/4 cups flour
2 teaspoons baking soda
1/2 teaspoon baking powder
1/2 teaspoon salt
1/2 teaspoon vanilla extract

Whipped Cream Filling
1 cup heavy cream
1 teaspoon vanilla extract
1/4 cup sifted confectioners' sugar

Chocolate Frosting
1 (6-ounce) package semisweet
  chocolate chips
1/2 cup half-and-half
3/4 cup (1 1/2 sticks) butter
2 1/2 cups sifted confectioners'
  sugar

Preheat the oven to 350°F. Spray the cake pans with cooking spray and lightly dust with flour or cocoa. Combine the cocoa and boiling water, stirring until smooth; set aside. In a large bowl, cream the butter and gradually add the sugar, beating well at medium speed with an electric mixer. Add eggs one at a time, beating well after each addition. Combine flour, soda, baking powder and salt in a medium bowl. Add to the creamed mixture, alternating with the cocoa mixture, beating at low speed, beginning and ending with the flour mixture. Stir in the vanilla but do not overbeat. Pour the batter evenly into the pans. Bake for 20 to 25 minutes or until a toothpick inserted in the center comes out clean. Cool in pans for 10 minutes; remove from the pans and cool completely. To make the whipped cream filling, beat heavy cream and vanilla in a medium bowl until foamy. Gradually add confectioners' sugar while beating. Beat until soft peaks form. To make the chocolate frosting, combine the first 3 ingredients in a saucepan and cook over medium heat, stirring until the chocolate melts. Remove from the heat and add confectioners' sugar. Set the saucepan on ice and beat at low speed until the frosting holds its shape and is no longer glossy. Add a few more drops of half-and-half to make a spreading consistency. Stack cake layers on top of each other spreading the whipped cream filling between layers and the chocolate frosting on the top and sides of the cake. Refrigerate until ready to serve.

Lisa Taylor-Richey: Wayne, Pennsylvania
Lisa gave me this delicious recipe. To add color to the presentation of this cake, Lisa decorates the cake platter with Gerber daisies.

Pineapple Carrot Cake with White Chocolate Cream Cheese Frosting

Serves: 8

- sifter
- cheese grater or food processor

- electric mixer
- 3 (9-inch) cake pans (optional) or 9 x 13-inch baking dish

Cake
1 1/2 cups vegetable oil
2 cups sugar
5 large eggs
2 1/2 cups sifted flour
2 teaspoons sifted baking powder
1 teaspoon sifted baking soda
2 teaspoons cinnamon
1 teaspoon salt
2 cups grated carrots
1 cup crushed pineapple (drained)
1 cup chopped pecans
2 teaspoons vanilla

Frosting
1 (8-ounce) package cream cheese
1/4 cup (1/2 stick) butter
2 ounces white chocolate, melted
2 teaspoons vanilla
1 (16-ounce) box confectioners' sugar

Preheat the oven to 350°F. Using an electric mixer, mix together the oil and sugar in a large bowl. Add the eggs one at a time, beating after each addition. Sift the flour, baking powder and baking soda separately, then measure them to the specified amounts. Mix the flour, baking powder, baking soda, cinnamon and salt together with the oil, sugar and egg mixture. Blend in the carrots, drained pineapple, pecans and vanilla. Spray the cake pans with cooking spray and lightly dust with flour. Pour the batter evenly into the pans. Bake 1 hour or until a toothpick inserted in the center comes out clean. Cake will be moist but should start to pull away from the sides of the pans. Let cool about 10 minutes before inverting onto wax paper, if making a layer cake. Loosen the cake from the edge of the pans with a knife. Let cakes cool completely. To make the frosting, mix the cream cheese and butter in a medium bowl until smooth. Mix in the white chocolate and vanilla. Gradually add the confectioners' sugar until the mixture is fluffy. Frost the cake.

Lenette Swaim: Arlington, Texas
Lenette is one of the original Knots Landing Girls' Night members. Back in the day of the television series, we used Thursday night as a girls' night to get together, eat, drink and watch Knots Landing. With our current schedules, we only see each other quarterly for dinner and for our special annual holiday slumber party and gift exchange.

Tip: If making this cake in three layers it may take less time to bake because it is not as dense. Check the cake after 25 minutes, inserting a toothpick in the center to check doneness. I used 1 1/2 times the frosting when making it a layer cake. For extra spice, add 1 teaspoon nutmeg and 1 teaspoon ground cloves along with the cinnamon. One cup of dark raisins may be added and walnuts substituted for pecans. In some grocery store produce departments, you may find carrots already grated.

Amaretto Cake

Serves: 10

- electric mixer
- Bundt cake pan

Cake
1 package yellow cake mix (without pudding added)
1 (3.4-ounce) package vanilla instant pudding and pie filling
4 large eggs
1 cup cold water
1 cup vegetable oil
1 cup chopped almonds
1 cup sweetened coconut flakes

Glaze
1/2 cup (1 stick) butter
1/2 cup amaretto
1/2 cup sugar

Preheat oven to 350°F. Generously spray the Bundt cake pan with cooking spray and lightly dust with flour. To make the cake, mix the first 5 ingredients together in a large bowl. Fold in the almonds and coconut. Pour the batter into the Bundt pan. Bake 50 to 60 minutes or until a toothpick inserted in the center comes out clean. Cool then invert onto a serving plate. Prepare the glaze by melting butter over medium heat. Stir in amaretto and sugar and boil 5 minutes or until sugar dissolves. Prick the top of the cake with a fork. Pour the glaze evenly over the cake, allowing it to absorb the glaze. Continue until all glaze is used.

Tip: Cooking spray with flour added is the best to use on your bakeware. Other cooking sprays leave a yellow sticky residue. The sprays with flour allow you to eliminate the two-step process of spraying and dusting pans with flour.

Variations: *This is an easy recipe to prepare and can be made with other liqueurs and nut combinations. Hazelnut liqueurs, such as Frangelico, and hazelnuts, or coffee flavored liqueurs and pecans make great combinations.*

Sharon Cordes: Sugar Land, Texas
Sharon and I lived together in college and she had many wonderful recipes, especially in her dessert collection. The basic cake can be changed up to suit your own tastes.

Peach Spice Cake with Cream Cheese Frosting

- electric mixer
- wire cooling rack
- 2 (9-inch) round cake pans

Cake
1 package (18.25-ounce) yellow cake mix
1 (8-ounce) can peaches, drained and chopped (liquid reserved)
3 ripe bananas, mashed
1/2 cup water
1/2 cup vegetable oil
3 large eggs
1 teaspoon vanilla
1 teaspoon cinnamon
1 cup chopped nuts, divided use

Cream Cheese Frosting
1 (8-ounce) package cream cheese, softened
1/2 cup (1 stick) unsalted butter, softened
1 (16-ounce) box confectioners' sugar
1 teaspoon vanilla

Preheat the oven to 350°F. Spray the cake pans with cooking spray and lightly dust with flour. Place the cake mix, chopped peaches with their juice, bananas, water, vegetable oil, and eggs in a large mixing bowl. With an electric mixer, mix on low for 1 minute. Add vanilla, cinnamon, and 1/2 cup chopped nuts and continue to mix for approximately 3 minutes or until well blended. Divide the batter evenly into pans and bake for 30 to 35 minutes or until a toothpick inserted in the center comes out clean. Let cool in pans for 10 minutes and then invert onto cooling rack until completely cool. To make the frosting, mix the cream cheese and butter together with an electric mixer in a large bowl. Gradually beat in the confectioners' sugar until well blended. Add vanilla and mix well. Place the bottom layer of the cake on a serving dish. Frost the cake and sprinkle with the remaining nuts. Top with the second layer and frost the top and sides.

Variation: For a slightly different frosting you may mix 12 ounces mascarpone cheese with 1 3/4 cups confectioners' sugar. The combination is decadent as well. When I am rushed I make this cake in a 9 x 13-inch baking dish, which takes slightly longer to bake.

Special Note: Consider making the Peach Spice Cake as a woman's hat or Easter bonnet centerpiece. Ice the cake as usual on the cake plate you would like to use. The cake plate must be flat enough and big enough to allow you to create the brim of the hat out of flowers at the base of the cake by placing the heads of the flowers up. Attach a ribbon close to the flowers around the iced cake just like a hat typically has. This is a beautiful centerpiece and conversation piece!

Sharon Sherley-Mylius:
Haltom City, Texas
Sharon is my banker that funded my first four printings of Good Friends Great Tastes *and has believed in my business venture since the beginning. This cake is called a "Hummingbird Cake" but the components make it an incredible spice cake.*

Coconut Cream Cake

- 3 (9-inch) round cake pans
- electric mixer

Cake
5 large eggs
2 cups sugar
1/2 cup (1 stick) unsalted butter
1/2 cup shortening
1 cup buttermilk
1 tablespoon baking soda
2 cups flour
1 teaspoon vanilla extract
1 teaspoon coconut extract
1 cup sweetened coconut flakes

Cream Cheese Frosting
1 (8-ounce) package cream cheese, softened
1/2 cup (1 stick) unsalted butter, softened
1 (16-ounce) box confectioners' sugar
1 teaspoon vanilla extract
1 teaspoon coconut extract
1 cup sweetened coconut flakes

Preheat the oven to 350°F. Spray the cake pans with cooking spray and lightly dust with flour. Separate the egg whites from the yolks in two separate bowls. With an electric mixer, beat the egg whites in a large bowl until they form stiff peaks. In a large mixing bowl, beat the egg yolks with the sugar until they are a pale butter-colored yellow. Combine the butter, shortening, and buttermilk together and blend with the mixer. Add the baking soda to the buttermilk to dissolve. Add the buttermilk mixture, flour and extracts to the egg yolk mixture and mix with the electric mixer until smooth. Gently fold the egg whites and coconut into the smooth mixture. Divide the batter evenly into the three prepared pans. Bake for 20 to 25 minutes until a toothpick inserted in the center comes out clean. Remove the cakes from the oven and let stand 10 minutes to cool before removing from the pans. While the cakes are cooling, make the frosting. Mix the cream cheese and butter together with the electric mixer in a large bowl. Gradually beat in the confectioners' sugar and extracts until well blended. Gently fold in the coconut. Stack the cake layers on top of each other, spreading the frosting between each layer and on the top and sides of the cake.

Elizabeth Fast: Kansas City, Missouri
Elizabeth loves to cook and bake. She and my brother, Tom, travel often and enjoy food and dining out. This cake is a favorite at her house and is the perfect end to any meal. If desired, you may toast additional coconut in the oven until golden and sprinkle over the top of the cake.

Crème Brûlée

Serves 6

- whisk
- double boiler
- kitchen torch

- 2 (9 x 13-inch) pans or a roasting pan
- 6 ramekins (3/4 inches deep x 2 1/2 inches wide) or custard cups (2 1/2 x 1 1/2 inches)

8 egg yolks (from large eggs)
1/3 cup sugar plus 1/4 cup, divided use
2 cups heavy cream
1 teaspoon pure vanilla extract

Preheat the oven to 300°F for the water bath (see below). In a large bowl whisk together the egg yolks and sugar until the sugar has dissolved and the mixture is thick and pale yellow. Set aside. Over a double boiler bring the cream to a gentle simmer but do not boil. Add the hot cream and vanilla to the egg mixture and whisk until well blended. If you feel there are a lot of bubbles or foam, you may strain this mixture. Divide the mixture into 6 ramekins. Place the ramekins in a 9 x 13-inch baking dish and place in the oven. With a pitcher, pour water in the bottom of the pans so the water comes up the sides of the ramekins halfway. Bake 40 to 50 minutes. Remove the pans from the oven, but let the crème brûlée cool in the water bath. Remove the ramekins from the water bath and chill for a minimum of 2 hours before serving. You may serve these up to 2 days later. When ready to serve, sprinkle 2 teaspoons of sugar over each custard and use a hand-held torch to melt the sugar. If you don't have a torch, place it under the broiler until the sugar melts and begins to brown. Chill again for a few minutes before serving.

Tip: The water bath is the way the crème brûlée sets into a thick custard. Use two 9 x 13-inch baking dishes or a roasting pan so you can have a dish with sides deep enough that the water can come halfway up the sides of the ramekins. A paper towel laid in the bottom of the pans keeps the glass dishes from slipping as you take them to and from the oven.

Vanilla Flan

Serves: 12

- whisk
- 12 ramekins or custard cups (2 1/2 x 1 1/2 inches)
- 2 (9 x 13-inch) baking dishes

3 large eggs
2 egg yolks (from large eggs)
1 1/2 cups sugar
1/3 cup water
2 cups half-and-half
1 cup heavy cream
1 (12-ounce) can sweetened condensed milk
1 tablespoon bourbon vanilla extract or 1 split vanilla bean
Coffee flavored liqueur

Special Note: Tempering is the technique used to blend uncooked eggs with a hot liquid without cooking the eggs in the process. Eggs are beaten as a little of the hot liquid is mixed into them. The warm liquid warms the eggs to temper them and this prevents the eggs from scrambling or cooking when blending two different temperature ingredients.

Preheat the oven to 300°F. Spray ramekins with cooking spray. In a medium bowl, whisk the eggs and yolks together and set aside. Stir the sugar and water together in a heavy medium saucepan over low heat until the sugar dissolves. Increase the heat and boil without stirring until the mixture turns a deep brown. Pour the mixture evenly into the ramekins and set aside. In another heavy bottomed saucepan, bring the half-and-half, cream and condensed milk to a simmer (185°F). Remove from the heat before it comes to a boil. With a ladle, add approximately 3/4 cup of the cream mixture to the eggs while whisking (see special note). Continue adding cream to the eggs while continuing to whisk. Add the vanilla extract. (If for any reason some of the egg cooked in the milk mixture, strain.) Place the ramekins in the 9 x 13-inch baking dishes. Ladle the custard evenly into the prepared ramekins and place in the oven. With a pitcher, pour enough water into the bottom of the 9 x 13-inch dishes to come halfway up the ramekins. Bake until the custards no longer move in the center when they are gently shaken, approximately 45 to 60 minutes. Remove the custard from water and let cool for 1 hour. Place in the refrigerator until ready to serve.

Tip: When I turn this onto the plate, I add a teaspoon of coffee flavored liqueur to the top of each adult's dessert. A good quality extract makes a big difference. You want pure vanilla, not imitation. If you use a vanilla bean as a replacement for the extract, split it open and be sure to remove it once it has had time to steep in the hot liquid at least 15 minutes before proceeding.

Variation: Orange-flavored, walnut or hazelnut liqueur would work equally well. The size of the ramekins just affects the number you make, but it is not crucial to the outcome.

Puff Pastry Berry Napoleons with Mascarpone

Serves: 16

- electric mixer
- sifter
- baking sheet

- serrated knife

1 (17.3-ounce) package puff pastry sheet, thawed
1 cup well-chilled heavy cream
1/2 cup sugar
16 ounces mascarpone cheese
1 quart fresh berries (if using strawberries, hull and slice)
Confectioners' sugar, for garnish
Mint leaves, for garnish
Orange slices, for garnish

Preheat the oven to 400°F. Unfold the puff pastry and cut each pastry sheet into 3 strips along the fold marks. Cut each strip into 4 rectangles. Keep the shapes uniform because you will be stacking them. Spray a baking sheet with cooking spray. Place the rectangles 2 inches apart on a baking sheet and bake approximately 15 minutes until the tops are lightly golden. Let cool. Once cooled, use a serrated knife and split the puff pastry into 2 layers, reserving the rounded portion for the top. (They will be most visible.) With an electric mixer, beat the heavy cream to soft peaks and mix in the sugar. Add the mascarpone to the whipped cream and gently and briefly blend the mascarpone cheese into the whipped cream. (You just want to blend together but not turn the mixture into butter.) Spread one side of the bottom layer with the cheese mixture and then put berries on top. Spread a small layer of the cheese mixture on the underside of the next layer so it adheres to the berries and top this layer with more cream and berries. Top with the rounded piece of pastry. Sprinkle the top with sifted confectioners' sugar and decorate plate or pastry with mint and orange slices.

Special Note: The color of your finished baked goods will be affected by the color of the bakeware you use. Light bakeware will result in lighter baked goods and darker bakeware will yield darker baked goods. Adjust cooking time accordingly.

Whipped Cream and Fresh Fruit Roll

Serves: 8

- 11 1/2 x 17-inch jelly roll pan (10 x 15-inch will work also)
- sifter

3/4 cup flour
1 teaspoon baking powder
1/2 teaspoon salt
4 large eggs, separated
1 1/4 cups sugar, divided use
2 teaspoons vanilla, divided use
Sifted confectioners' sugar
1 pint (2 cups) heavy cream
2 pints berries or 2 large peaches
or fruit of your choice

Preheat the oven to 375°F. Mix the flour with the baking powder and salt in a large bowl. Beat the egg whites in a separate bowl. Once peaks have formed, fold in a 1/2 cup sugar. Beat the egg yolks in a separate bowl with 1/2 cup sugar until pale yellow in color, then add 1 teaspoon vanilla. Use a spatula to fold the whites and yolks into the flour. Spray the bottom and sides of a jelly roll pan with cooking spray, press wax paper into it and generously spray the wax paper with cooking spray. Spread the batter evenly over the wax paper. Bake 10 to 15 minutes, or until lightly golden and firm to the touch. While cake is baking, spread out a dishtowel and sprinkle with sifted confectioners' sugar. In a large bowl, whip the cream until almost firmly peaking and slowly add the 1/4 cup of remaining sugar and remaining vanilla. Be careful not to whip the cream too long or it will turn to butter. Refrigerate until ready to use. When cake is removed from the oven, invert onto a towel and roll gently into a jelly roll. When the cake is cool, you are ready to fill. Unroll the cake and spread the whipped cream mixture over entire inside surface. Press the fresh fruit of your choice over the whipped cream. Roll up again like a jelly roll, cover and refrigerate. Cut into slices and serve with the remaining whipped cream. Make no more than 24 hours ahead.

Special Note: I mixed fruits I had available that included raspberries, peaches and strawberries and the combination was delicious! This cake lasts several days when wrapped and stored in the refrigerator unless the fruits are super juicy. The mascarpone cream in the recipe on (page 275) can be used instead of the whipped cream in this recipe for an even more decadent cake.

Fresh Fruit Tarts with Grand Marnier Cream

Serves: 6

- 6 glass custard cups
- electric mixer
- double boiler

Fruit Tarts
1 (15-ounce) package refrigerated pie crusts
1 cup fresh raspberries
1 cup fresh blackberries
1 cup fresh strawberries
2 kiwis, peeled and sliced
1 tablespoon sugar

Grand Marnier Cream
5 egg yolks, at room temperature
3/4 cup sugar
1/4 cup Grand Marnier
1 cup heavy cream
1 tablespoon sugar

Preheat the oven to 425°F. Unfold each pie crust and roll out on a lightly floured surface into a 9-inch circle. Place 6 custard cups upside down on a baking sheet and spray the bottoms with cooking spray. Cut out and drape a pastry circle over the bottom of each cup and pinch the dough to make pleats. Form the pastry around the outside of each cup. Prick the bottom and sides with a fork. Bake for 10 minutes until lightly brown. Carefully remove pastry cups, and turn right side up to cool. Two hours before serving, combine the fruit and sugar in a large bowl. To make the Grand Marnier cream, beat the egg yolks with an electric mixer in the top of a double boiler. Beat in the sugar and simmer, stirring until thickened, about 20 minutes. Remove from the heat and beat until smooth. Add the Grand Marnier and refrigerate until chilled. In a separate bowl, whip the cream until it starts to thicken and add the sugar. Continue to beat until cream is medium thick but will still pour. Fold into the prepared Grand Marnier cream and pour the entire mixture into a serving dish. Chill until serving time. The Grand Marnier cream can be made a day or two ahead and refrigerated. Spoon berries into the pastry cups and put a dollop of the Grand Marnier cream on top. Serve immediately.

Variations: *Lemon curd (approximately 3/4 cup) or any flavored curd can be mixed with whipped cream (approximately 2 cups) to replace the Grand Marnier cream or it can be used as a quick dessert topping for fresh fruit.*

Buttermilk Shortcake with Mascarpone Cream

Serves: 8

- whisk
- sifter
- electric mixer

- baking sheet

Shortcake
2/3 cup chilled buttermilk
1 large egg
1 teaspoon vanilla
2 cups cake flour
1/4 cup sugar
1 tablespoon baking powder
1/2 teaspoon salt
1/2 cup (1 stick) unsalted butter, cut into 1/2-inch pieces
Confectioners' sugar for dusting top of cake

Mascarpone Cream
1 cup chilled heavy cream
1/4 cup confectioners' sugar
1 teaspoon vanilla
1 (8-ounce) container mascarpone cheese

Fruit Filling
1 pint fresh raspberries
1 pint fresh blackberries
1 quart fresh strawberries, hulled and sliced
1/3 cup sugar

Preheat the oven to 425°F. To make the shortcake, whisk the buttermilk, egg and vanilla in a medium bowl. Set aside 1 tablespoon for the glaze. Sift the flour, sugar, baking powder and salt into a large bowl and add butter. Using an electric mixer, beat until the mixture resembles coarse meal, about 3 minutes. Add the buttermilk mixture and blend just until a soft dough forms. Turn the dough out onto a lightly floured surface. Coat your hands in flour and knead gently for 6 turns. Transfer the dough to an ungreased baking sheet. Shape into an 8-inch round. Brush the top of the dough with the reserved 1 tablespoon buttermilk mixture. Bake until the top is golden and a toothpick inserted in the center comes out clean, about 20 minutes. For mascarpone cream, beat the cream until firm peaks form; add the sugar and vanilla. Gently fold in the mascarpone cheese. Refrigerate until ready to use. To make the fruit filling, toss the berries with the sugar and let stand 30 minutes before serving. To serve, slice off the top 1/3 of the cake, then slice the cake in 8 wedges that will have a top and bottom. On each bottom piece of cake, put a dollop of cream then berries and slightly more cream and then place the top of the cake on the cream. Repeat for all 8 pieces. Dust with sifted confectioners' sugar.

Variation: Any summer fruits may be substituted to invent your own combination. Plums, peaches and raspberries are another colorful combination.

Fruit Torte

Serves: 8

- zester or cheese grater
- vegetable peeler
- 8 x 11-inch tart pan or 9- or 10-inch springform pan

Fruit Torte
1 (18-ounce) package refrigerated sugar cookie dough
1 (8-ounce) container mascarpone cheese, softened
1/4 cup sugar
1/3 cup chilled heavy cream
1 pint strawberries, sliced
1 pint raspberries
1 pint blueberries
2 kiwis, peeled and sliced

Fruit glaze
1/2 cup sugar
2 tablespoons cornstarch
Dash of salt
2 teaspoons freshly squeezed lemon juice
1/2 cup orange or cranberry juice

Preheat the oven to 350°F. Bring the cookie dough to room temperature. Spray a pan with cooking spray and press the dough into the pan. Bake 15 to 20 minutes until the top and edges are slightly golden. Cool the dough. Mix the mascarpone, sugar and cream together in a medium bowl. Spread this over the cookie dough. Arrange the fruit symmetrically starting at the outside working into the center. To make the fruit glaze; combine the sugar, cornstarch and salt. Whisk in the lemon juice and orange juice. Bring to a boil while continuing to whisk to avoid lumps. Boil 1 minute. Cool the sauce and spoon the sauce over the torte. Refrigerate the torte until ready to serve.

Tip: Due to the juices in the fruits, it is best to serve this the same day.

Variations: *You may use other fruits such as pineapple, mandarin oranges or blackberries. To make this more child friendly, you may use a pizza pan and replace the mascarpone mixture with 1 (8-ounce) package cream cheese mixed with 4 1/2 ounces whipped cream topping, thawed.*

Mary Pat Johnston: Overland Park, Kansas
Mary Pat has a busy schedule, but still manages to entertain family and friends. She is known for her creative and special table settings and makes it fun and entertaining for the children. Mary Pat likes this dessert because it has a colorful presentation and is easy to make.

Blackberry Cobbler

Serves: 8

• 9 x 13-inch baking dish

1 cup (2 sticks) unsalted butter, divided use
1 1/2 cups water
1 1/2 cups sugar plus 3 tablespoons sugar for extra sprinkling
3 cups self-rising flour
2/3 cup milk
Cinnamon for sprinkling
6 cups (about 2 pounds) fresh blackberries
Vanilla ice cream

Preheat the oven to 350°F. Place 1/2 cup (1 stick) of butter in a 9 x 13-inch baking dish. Place in the oven for 3 to 5 minutes to melt the butter. Remove the pan from the oven and set aside. In a small saucepan, combine the water and 1 1/2 cups of sugar. Heat over moderate heat, stirring to dissolve the sugar. Remove from heat and set aside. Cut the other 1/2 cup of butter into small chunks and mix with the flour in a large bowl. Add the milk and mix until dough forms. Turn the dough onto a lightly floured surface and roll into a large rectangle approximately 16 x 20 inches. Sprinkle dough with cinnamon and scatter blackberries over the top. Beginning with the long side, roll up dough like a jelly roll and cut into 1 1/2-inch slices. (Slices will be a bit messy but it is a "rustic" cobbler.) Arrange slices, cut side up, on the melted butter in the prepared baking dish. Pour the sugar syrup over the slices. Bake the cobbler on the middle rack for 45 minutes. Sprinkle the remaining sugar over the slices and bake an additional 15 minutes or until golden. Serve with ice cream.

Tip: You may use a food processor to mix the dough.

> *"Friends celebrate the things they have in common and delight in the things that make them different."*
>
> *~Author unknown*

Fall Harvest Apple Crisp

Serves: 6

- 8 1/2 x 11-inch baking dish
- vegetable peeler

4 large apples, peeled, cored and cut in large chunks
1/2 cup flour
1/2 cup sugar
3/4 teaspoon cinnamon
1/2 cup (1 stick) unsalted butter, melted
1 cup brown sugar
Rolled oats (not quick-cooking)
Vanilla ice cream

Preheat the oven to 350°F. Toss the apples with the flour, sugar and cinnamon in a large bowl. In a medium bowl, combine the melted butter and brown sugar. Add enough oats to the butter and brown sugar to make a granola-type topping. Spray a baking dish with cooking spray. Pour the apple mixture into the greased 8 1/2 x 11-inch baking dish. Top with the oatmeal mixture and bake for 1 hour. This is best served warm topped with ice cream.

Variation: Dried cranberries (1 cup) may be added to the apple mixture for a different twist!

Joan Redhair: Overland Park, Kansas
Joan and I have been friends since West Hall at Kansas State University, but our relationship blossomed more after college. We get together several times annually to nurture our friendship. Melissa Weikel, another friend from our college dorm, is part of this bonding experience. Those times are special and full of deep, soul-searching conversations.

Butterscotch Apple Crisp

Serves: 12

- vegetable peeler
- double boiler
- 9 x 13-inch baking dish

Filling
8 cups peeled Granny Smith apples

1 tablespoon freshly squeezed lemon juice (juice from 1/2 medium lemon)

1 cup sugar

1/2 cup flour

2 teaspoons cinnamon

1/8 teaspoon salt

Butter

Topping
1 (11-ounce) package butterscotch chips

1/2 cup (1 stick) unsalted butter

1 1/2 cups flour

1/4 teaspoon salt

1/4 teaspoon mace

Preheat the oven to 375°F. Measure out the dry ingredients for filling and topping before peeling and slicing the apples. Peel and slice the apples and toss with lemon juice in a large bowl. Add dry filling ingredients to the apples and toss. Spray a baking dish with cooking spray and spread the apple mixture over the bottom. Bake for 20 minutes. While the apple filling is baking, melt the butterscotch chips and butter in a double boiler until smooth. Add the dry topping ingredients with a fork so mixture becomes crumbly. Crumble topping over the hot apple mixture and bake an additional 25 minutes. Serve with vanilla ice cream.

Special Notes: For cooking and baking, it is best to use apples that remain flavorful and firm, such as Baldwin, Cortland, Northern Spy, Rome Beauty, Winesap, York Imperial or Granny Smith. Mace is a spice that is a pungent version of nutmeg.

"Friends...they cherish each other's hopes. They are kind to each other's dreams."

~Thoreau

Easy Fruit Pecan Crisp

Serves: 8

• 9 x 13-inch baking dish

2 (20-ounce) cans fruit pie filling
1/2 teaspoon almond extract
1/4 cup warm water
1 (1 pound 2.25-ounce) box white cake mix
1/2 cup (1 stick) unsalted butter, melted
1 (8-ounce) package pecan pieces
2 tablespoons warm water

Preheat the oven to 350°F. Mix together the pie filling, almond extract and warm water. Spread the mixture in a 9 x 13-inch baking dish. In a separate bowl mix together the cake mix, butter, pecan pieces and water. Drop this mixture by teaspoonfuls on top of the fruit mixture until it is completely covered. Bake 40 minutes until top is lightly golden. Serve with vanilla ice cream.

Tip: Any flavor canned pie filling can be used. This is a wonderful quick dessert.

Bananas Foster

Serves: 8

3/4 cup (1 1/2 sticks) unsalted butter
1 1/2 cups dark brown sugar
1 1/2 teaspoons cinnamon
6 very ripe bananas, halved lengthwise, then quartered
1/4 cup banana liqueur
1 cup dark rum, warmed
1 gallon vanilla ice cream

In a large skillet over medium heat melt the butter, sugar and cinnamon together until the sugar dissolves. Add the bananas and banana liqueur. Cook to coat, stirring gently. Add the rum and ignite liquor if desired (flambé). The flame should die down quickly. Spoon the mixture over vanilla ice cream. The ice cream will melt quickly due to the warm topping, so work quickly. It is best to give guests spoons to eat this dessert.

Variation: *Peaches may be substituted for the bananas. If using peaches, omit the banana liqueur.*

Special Note: Flambé safety: To extinguish the flame after you flambé, keep the skillet lid in close proximity to the stove. Immediately place lid over the skillet if necessary. Without oxygen, the flame cannot burn. Alcohol ignites easily, so keep your face and clothing at a distance.

Homemade Vanilla Ice Cream

Makes: 1 gallon

- electric mixer
- ice cream freezer

4 large eggs
2 cups sugar
3 cups heavy cream
1 pint half-and-half
1/4 cup vanilla extract
1/4 teaspoon salt
Whole milk to fill line on ice cream
   freezer
Ice and salt according to your
   freezer's directions

Beat the eggs in a large bowl with an electric mixer until pale yellow. Add sugar, heavy cream, half-and-half, vanilla and salt. Stir to dissolve the sugar. Pour into your ice cream freezer. Pour whole milk into freezer just to the fill line. Freeze according to your freezer directions.

Special Note: It is best to use a Madagascar vanilla extract rather than an inexpensive extract or an imitation vanilla. Also, liqueurs like crème de cacao (1 ounce) and brandy (2 ounces) per 2 cups of prepared ice cream are delicious additions. Mix together and serve as after-dinner drinks. Top with shaved chocolate.

Esther Rowley: Overland Park, Kansas
Esther is my friend Kathryn's mother and she made this rich ice cream in the summertime, so it brings back many memories. Kathryn and I roomed together at Kansas State and to relieve our stress, we would walk to the Dairy Science building to get scoops of homemade ice cream.

Pecan Crusted Ice Cream Pie with Caramel Sauce

Serves: 8

- nut chopper, blender or food processor
- pie pan

Crust
1 egg white, whipped
1/4 cup sugar
1 1/2 cups finely chopped pecans

Filling
1 pint coffee ice cream
1 pint French vanilla ice cream

Caramel Sauce
2/3 cup dark brown sugar
1/4 cup evaporated milk
1 egg yolk (from large egg), beaten
1/3 cup corn syrup
1/4 cup (1/2 stick) butter
1/2 teaspoon vanilla extract

Preheat the oven to 400°F. Generously spray a pie pan with cooking spray. Fold the crust ingredients together and press into the pan. Bake 12 minutes then cool for 1 hour. Spread 1 pint of coffee ice cream on the bottom of the crust and 1 pint of vanilla ice cream over the coffee ice cream. Freeze. To make the caramel sauce, stir the sauce ingredients together in a small saucepan (over no heat) until smooth and egg is thoroughly mixed into the sauce. Heat slowly until sauce resembles caramel sauce. This sauce may be refrigerated and reheated when you are ready to serve the pie. Cut pie into slices and put on individual serving plates. Drizzle a small amount of warm sauce over each piece of pie and serve.

Variations: This is a great basic recipe so use your imagination for other combinations of ice cream and sauce. The pairing of coffee, vanilla and caramel is still my favorite. You may add 1/2 cup coarsely chopped pecans to the sauce. The sauce makes a great gift as an ice cream topping.

Coleen Rossi: Paradise Valley, Arizona
Coleen and I have known each other since the days of our parents' elaborate dinner parties. This wonderful recipe came from her mother. This is the dessert I remember sampling before the adults even sat down to eat. It is still my favorite.

Baklava

Serves: 16

- pastry brush
- nut chopper, blender or food processor
- 9 x 13-inch baking dish

Baklava
1 1/2 cups (3 sticks) unsalted butter
1/2 cup vegetable oil
1 pound phyllo dough (18 x 12-inch sheets), thawed
4 cups shelled pistachio nuts or pecans, chopped in blender

Syrup
1 1/2 cups sugar
3/4 cup water
1 tablespoon freshly squeezed lemon juice (juice from 1/2 medium lemon)
1 tablespoon honey
1 tablespoon rosewater

Preheat the oven to 350°F. Cut the butter into small pieces. Clarify the butter by melting at a low heat and skimming foam off the top as it melts. Let rest 2 minutes. Drain the butter into another pan leaving solids behind. Add the oil to the butter. Using a pastry brush, grease the bottom and sides of a 9 x 13-inch baking dish with the butter and oil mixture. When working with phyllo you need to keep it moist. Take a clean dishtowel and wet it. Ring it out so it is just slightly damp. Completely cover the dough with the towel while working. The dough tends to get dry if not covered. Fold a sheet of dough in half crosswise. Lift it gently and put into the prepared pan and unfold. Press the pastry flat, pressing down the excess around the sides and flattening it against the bottom. Brush entire surface with the butter and oil mixture and repeat with another sheet of dough. Sprinkle the top of the second layer with 3 to 4 tablespoons of the chopped pistachios. Brush another sheet of dough with butter and sprinkle with 3 to 4 tablespoons of the pistachios. Butter 2 more sheets of dough, sprinkling 3 to 4 tablespoons pistachios on the top of the second layer. Repeat until you have only 2 sheets of phyllo left. Put the last 2 sheets on top and brush with the remaining butter and oil mixture. With a sharp knife score the top of the pastry with diagonal lines 1/2 inch deep and 2 inches apart both lengthwise and widthwise, then cross them diagonally to make diamond shapes. Bake on the middle oven rack for 30 minutes. Reduce oven to 300°F and bake 45 minutes longer until the top is crisp and golden.

(continued on next page)

Make the syrup while this is baking. Combine the sugar, water and lemon juice in a small saucepan over medium heat, stirring constantly. Cook until the sugar dissolves. Increase the heat to high and cook 5 minutes, uncovered. Mixture should be thick enough to coat the back of a spoon. Remove from heat and stir in the honey and rosewater. Let cool. Pour over Baklava once it is removed from the oven. Cool and follow the lines from the scoring done prior and continue cutting into diamond-shaped pieces with a sharp knife.

Variations: *You may substitute walnuts for pistachios or pecans. Orange blossom water may be substituted for rosewater in this recipe. For a party you may serve the triangle of Baklava with a small scoop of vanilla ice cream and fresh berries. If only 9 x 14-inch phyllo sheets are available, they fit nicely in a 9 x 13-inch baking dish, but you will need to use both packages (1 pound) of dough.*

Special Note: Rosewater has been a popular seasoning for centuries in the cuisines of the Middle East. You can find it in gourmet stores.

Sami El-Beheri: Colorado Springs, Colorado
This was a big hit at a Greek Dinner Club we had. I also won a bakeoff at work with this recipe. It looks more difficult than it is so don't be intimidated. Sami's daughter, Twila, is a member of our regular Dinner Clubs. Sami is a guest at Dinner Club when he comes into town.

287

Decadent Toffee Dessert Sauce

Serves: 8

3/4 cup plus 1 tablespoon sugar, divided use
1 (8-ounce) container sour cream
1/2 cup heavy cream
1/4 cup light corn syrup
3 (1.4-ounce) English Toffee Candy Bars (such as Heath or Skor), crumbled
2 tablespoons unsalted butter
2 quarts strawberries, cleaned, hulled and sliced

Stir the 1 tablespoon of sugar into the container of sour cream and set aside. Combine the 3/4 cup of sugar with the heavy cream and corn syrup in a saucepan and bring to a boil over medium-high heat. Boil 1 minute then remove from heat. Stir in the crumbled toffee bars (measurement should be approximately 1 cup) and butter. Stir until chocolate melts and butter is blended. Not all of the toffee will dissolve. (It makes the texture more interesting.) Put strawberries at the bottom of small serving dishes (I use martini glasses). Drizzle sauce over the berries and top with a dollop of the sour cream mixture. Serve immediately.

Variations: Peaches, pound cake or ice cream taste wonderful with this sauce as well. If you cannot find the Heath or Skor bars, buy the Heath Toffee Bits and milk chocolate chips in the baking section of the grocery store. Use approximately 3 ounces of toffee and 1 ounce chocolate.

Kathryn Jay: Rowlett, Texas
I met Kathryn at a Pi Beta Phi brunch where I did a cooking demonstration. The hostesses Mary Kay Griffin and her mother Patsy Hendrickson prepared recipes from the first edition of Good Friends Great Tastes. *Kathryn passed this recipe on to me and I have prepared this for numerous Red Hat Society members, a very special birthday group in Dallas and many guests. There is never a drop left!*

Pecan Lace Tacos with Margarita Mousse Filling

Serves: 4

- 2 wooden spoons
- pastry tube
- cheese grater or zester
- electric mixer
- baking sheet

Pecan Lace Shells

2 tablespoons firmly packed brown sugar

2 tablespoons butter, melted

2 tablespoons light corn syrup

1/4 cup flour

1/4 cup finely chopped pecans

3/4 teaspoon vanilla extract

Mousse

1 teaspoon unflavored gelatin

2 tablespoons tequila

2 tablespoons Grand Marnier

2 teaspoons lime zest plus additional for garnish

1/4 cup freshly squeezed lime juice (juice from 2 medium limes)

1 drop green food coloring (to make mousse pale green)

1 1/2 cups heavy cream

3/4 cup sugar

Preheat the oven to 350°F. Spray a baking sheet with cooking spray. To make the pecan lace shells, combine the first 3 ingredients in a saucepan over high heat, stirring constantly until mixture boils. Remove from heat. Add flour, chopped pecans and vanilla, stirring until well blended. Drop batter by level teaspoons onto the prepared baking sheet, spacing 3 inches apart. Do not bake more than 3 at one time. Bake for 8 minutes or until golden brown. Cool for 1 minute. When you remove the shells from the baking sheet, drape them over a greased handle of a wooden spoon so it takes the shape of a taco shell. Two should fit on the end of the wooden spoon handle. Repeat with remaining batter. The shells can be made 1 week ahead and stored in an airtight container. The mousse can be prepared 24 hours before serving. To make mousse, sprinkle gelatin over tequila and Grand Marnier in a small saucepan and let stand 1 minute. Cook over low heat, stirring until gelatin dissolves. Stir in the lime zest, lime juice and food coloring, if desired. Cool and set aside. Beat the heavy cream in a large bowl until foamy. Gradually add sugar and gelatin mixture, beating until soft peaks form. Cover and chill. Pipe into the pecan lace shells and sprinkle with lime zest for additional color. I kept this recipe in my file for years before trying it. This is a fun dessert especially if the meal is not overly complicated.

Tip: You will need to make 2 shells for each guest. You may need 4 cans of the same height for cooling the hardening shells. Suspend the wooden spoons between two cans while they are hardening. You can garnish dessert plates with mango and kiwi slices for additional presentation.

Tiramisu

Serves: 6

- electric mixer
- Microplane grater
- 2-quart glass dish

3 large eggs, separated
3/4 cup plus 1 tablespoon sugar, divided use
1 (8-ounce) container mascarpone cheese
Pinch salt
1/2 cup chilled heavy cream
3 cups strong brewed coffee, cooled
3 tablespoons Irish cream flavored coffee syrup or coffee liqueur
18 crisp Italian ladyfingers (savoiardi)
1/4 cup fine-quality bittersweet chocolate shavings
Raspberries and mint leaves, optional

Beat together egg yolks and 1/2 cup sugar in a large bowl with an electric mixer at medium speed until thick and pale yellow, about 2 minutes. Beat in the mascarpone until just combined (otherwise it turns to a butter consistency). In another bowl, with cleaned beaters, beat the egg whites with a pinch of salt until they just hold soft peaks. Add 1/4 cup sugar a little at a time, beating, then continue to beat whites until they just hold stiff peaks. In another bowl, with cleaned beaters, beat the cream. Add the remaining 1 tablespoon of sugar. This should be beaten until it also holds soft peaks. Fold the cream into the mascarpone mixture, gently but thoroughly, then fold in the egg whites. Stir together the coffee and flavored syrup in a shallow bowl. Dip 1 ladyfinger in the coffee mixture, soaking it for about 4 seconds on each side. It should not fall apart. (You may not need all of the coffee.) Transfer to a glass dish (2-quart capacity) and repeat with 8 more ladyfingers. Arrange in the bottom of the dish, trimming as needed so they fit snugly. Spread half of the mascarpone mixture evenly over the ladyfingers. Make another layer in the same manner with remaining ladyfingers and mascarpone mixture. Sprinkle the top with chocolate shavings. Chill the tiramisu, covered, for at least 6 hours. Spoon the tiramisu onto serving plates. Garnish with raspberries and fresh mint, if desired.

Tip: Tiramisu will hold up to 1 day in the refrigerator. Use the Microplane grater (also used for zesting) to get the chocolate finely shaved. It will resemble cocoa.

Coconut Cherry Bars

Makes: 24 bars

• 9 x 13-inch baking dish

Crust
2 cups flour
1 cup (2 sticks) butter, softened
6 tablespoons confectioners' sugar

Filling
4 large eggs
2 cups sugar
1/2 cup flour
2 teaspoons vanilla
1 teaspoon baking powder
1/2 teaspoon salt
1 1/2 cups chopped pecans
1 cup coconut flakes
1 cup chopped maraschino
  cherries, drained

Preheat the oven to 350°F. Spray a baking dish with cooking spray. Mix the crust ingredients together in a medium bowl and press the mixture into the bottom of the baking dish. Bake 10 minutes. To make the filling, beat the eggs in a large bowl and stir in the remaining 7 ingredients. Spread the mixture over the baked crust. Sprinkle the cherries on top. Bake an additional 30 to 40 minutes or until the center is set. Cool and cut into 2 x 1-inch bars.

Tip: If you cut the recipe in half, you may use an 8 x 8 x 2-inch pan.

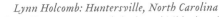

Lynn Holcomb: Huntersville, North Carolina
Lynn and I worked together years ago and she brought this decadent dessert to work.
They taste like a pecan pie cookie with chewy coconut and cherries. Superb!

Buttermilk Brownies with Buttermilk Icing

Serves: 12

 • jelly roll pan

Brownies
1/2 cup (1 stick) butter
1 cup water
1/4 cup cocoa
1/2 cup vegetable oil
2 cups flour
2 cups sugar
1/2 teaspoon salt
1/2 cup buttermilk
2 large eggs, beaten
1 teaspoon baking soda
1 teaspoon vanilla

Frosting
1/2 cup (1 stick) butter
1/4 cup cocoa
1/3 cup buttermilk
1 (16-ounce) box confectioners' sugar
1 cup chopped pecans
1 teaspoon vanilla
Dash of salt

Preheat the oven to 400°F. Spray a jelly roll pan with cooking spray and dust with flour. To make the brownies, combine the butter, water, cocoa and vegetable oil in a medium saucepan. Bring to a boil. Mix together the flour, sugar and salt in a large bowl. Pour the warmed cocoa mixture over the flour, sugar and salt. Add the buttermilk, beaten eggs, baking soda and vanilla and mix until combined. Pour the mixture into the jelly roll pan and bake for 20 minutes. To make the frosting, combine the butter, cocoa and buttermilk in a saucepan. Bring to a boil and add confectioners' sugar, pecans, vanilla and salt. Spread over the brownies while warm and serve.

> *"A meal cooked and eaten with good friends ranks among the supreme privileges of being human. Something almost alchemical seems to occur when we bring food substances and mind substances together; everything is enhanced in the process, and we make more of ourselves and one another."*
>
> ~ Gail Godwin

Peanut Butter Crispy Rice Cookies

Makes: 12

- double boiler
- 9 x 13-inch baking dish

1 cup sugar
1 cup corn syrup
1 cup peanut butter
6 cups crispy rice cereal
1 (6-ounce) package semisweet chocolate chips
1 (6-ounce) package butterscotch chips

In a saucepan over medium heat, combine the sugar, corn syrup and peanut butter until melted together. Bring to a boil for a short time so the peanut butter mixes with the corn syrup. (If you cook too long it will reach a candy state and cookies will be difficult to bite into.) Remove from the heat and pour over 6 cups crispy rice cereal in a large bowl. Mix well. Spray a baking dish with cooking spray and press the cereal mixture evenly into the baking dish. Melt chocolate chips and butterscotch chips together in a double boiler. Spread the chocolate and butterscotch mixture over the cereal and refrigerate until top hardens. Remove from the refrigerator 10 minutes before cutting. Cut into squares when ready to serve. I prefer to serve these at room temperature once the top is hardened.

Tip: If you spray your measuring cup with nonstick cooking spray, sticky ingredients like corn syrup will slide right out.

Marla Payne: Coppell, Texas
I have collected quite a few recipes from Marla over the years. This recipe is from one of the first invitations to her house. She made these and I ate more than a first-time guest should! They can be addicting to those of us with a sweet tooth!

293

Chewy Chocolate Caramel Bars

Serves: 16

- double boiler
- 9 x 13-inch baking dish

1 (14-ounce) bag of caramels or 60 unwrapped light caramels
1 (12-ounce) can evaporated milk, divided use
1 (18.25-ounce) box German chocolate cake mix
3/4 cup (1 1/2 sticks) butter, melted
1 cup chopped pecans
1 cup semisweet chocolate chips

Preheat oven to 350°F. Spray a baking dish with cooking spray and dust with flour. In a double boiler, melt the unwrapped caramels and 1/2 cup evaporated milk over low heat, stirring constantly. (Caramels should be completely melted and have a thin consistency.) In a large bowl mix the cake mix with the melted butter, 1/3 cup evaporated milk and pecans. Press half the dough into the prepared pan. Bake for 12 minutes. Sprinkle chocolate chips over the baked dough and drizzle the caramel over the chocolate chips. Crumble the remaining dough over the caramel and return to the oven for 18 to 25 minutes. The top dough should not resemble raw batter in the center. Test by pulling a small bit of the chocolate cake off the top; the center should not be too wet or gooey. These can be cut into uniform bars when cooled completely (you may chill to speed up cooling).

Tip: I prefer using my regular oven setting instead of convection. A shallow 9 x 13-inch baking dish (1 1/2-inch sides) works much better than a deep one. I use the good old-fashioned German chocolate cake and the easy to unwrap caramels called classic caramels. (Even the chocolate filled caramels work for this recipe.) Kids tend to prefer these bars without nuts, and for a great serving idea, try these warm with vanilla ice cream.

Jody Huerter: Leawood, Kansas
In 1978 Jody gave me my first recipe holder. It seemed so difficult to fill up at the time. Her oldest daughter Susie and I wrote out some of Susie's favorite recipes from Jody's collection. This recipe is still on the original card that matches the book and continues to be a favorite.

Favorite Oatmeal Cookies

Makes: 2 dozen

• baking sheet

1 cup brown sugar
1 cup sugar
1 cup vegetable oil
2 large eggs
2 teaspoons vanilla
3 1/2 cups rolled oats or quick-cooking oats
1 cup sweetened coconut flakes
1/2 teaspoon salt
1 teaspoon baking soda
1 cup flour

Preheat the oven to 350°F. Mix the brown sugar, sugar and oil together in a large bowl. Add eggs and vanilla. Mix in the oats and coconut. Add salt, baking soda and flour to the batter. Drop by teaspoonful onto an ungreased baking sheet. Bake approximately 10 minutes.

Amy Carro: Wichita, Kansas
I met Amy at Kansas State through her sorority sister Mary Pat Sasenick (now Johnston). We ran into one another at an alumni function in Dallas and decided to live together. Amy made these cookies regularly and I would eat the batter by the spoonful, therefore the yield is an approximation. This is one of my favorite cookie recipes because of the texture and rich flavor.

Mexican Wedding Cookies

Makes: 3 dozen

- blender
- sifter
- 1 1/2-inch cookie cutter

- electric mixer
- baking sheet

3 cups sifted flour
1 1/2 teaspoons baking powder
1/2 teaspoon salt
1/2 pound lard (do not substitute)
1 cup sugar, divided use
1/2 teaspoon chopped anise seeds (chop in blender or chopper)
1 egg, beaten
2 tablespoons Frangelico, amaretto or brandy (may not need entire amount)
1 tablespoon water (if needed)
2 teaspoons cinnamon (to mix with the 1/4 cup sugar for topping)

Preheat the oven to 350°F. Combine the sifted flour, baking powder and salt in a large bowl. Cream the lard with 3/4 cup sugar in a separate medium bowl. Add anise seeds to the lard and beat at medium speed with an electric mixer. Add the egg to the lard and continue beating. Add the dry ingredients and just enough liqueur to make the batter stiff. If the batter does not stick together, add 1 tablespoon water. Knead slightly and pat into 1/4 to 1/2 thickness. Cut into small shapes. I use a 1 1/2-inch heart cookie cutter. Mix 2 teaspoons cinnamon with the 1/4 cup sugar in a small bowl. Generously sprinkle the cookies with the cinnamon and sugar mixture. Bake approximately 9 minutes on an ungreased baking sheet.

Special Note: Baking powder goes flat fairly fast, so buy it in small tins.

Sylvia Muñoz: Addison, Texas
I used to buy 5 dozen for 5 dollars from my friend Sylvia when she brought these cookies back from her hometown of Edinburg, Texas. I had difficulty sharing these because I loved them so much and only got them a couple times a year. They are traditionally served at Hispanic weddings and are called by many different names, all meaning small pastry.

Mimi's Congo Cookies

Makes: 5 dozen

• baking sheet

2 large eggs
2/3 cup shortening
1 (16-ounce) box brown sugar
2 3/4 cups sifted flour
2 1/2 teaspoons baking powder
1/2 teaspoon salt
1 cup chopped pecans
1 (12-ounce) package semisweet chocolate chips
1/4 cup water

Preheat the oven to 350°F. Spray a baking sheet with cooking spray. Mix together the eggs, shortening and sugar with an electric mixer in a large bowl. Add the remaining ingredients and drop by the teaspoonful on the greased baking sheet. Bake until light brown, 10 to 12 minutes.

Variation: Spread the dough into a greased jelly roll pan or 9-inch square pan for bar cookies to save baking time. Bake 30 to 35 minutes until golden brown. If desired, add macadamia nuts in place of pecans and white chocolate instead of semisweet chocolate.

Special Note: Chocolate chip cookies taste better when they are made with shortening rather than butter. A few drops of butter flavoring can be added or butter flavored shortening can be used. Cookies hold up better over several days and stay moist without tasting stale.

Melissa Weikel: Topeka, Kansas
Melissa lived across from me in the dorm at Kansas State. She got this recipe from her grandmother, Mimi. She had never made these cookies because she thought they had a silly name. Now that Mimi has passed away, Melissa makes them in her memory.

Cappuccino Sundaes

Serves: 10

Coffee Sauce
1/2 cup strong brewed coffee
1/2 cup heavy cream
1/4 cup firmly packed brown sugar
1/4 teaspoon ground cinnamon
1 cup semisweet chocolate,
  chopped

Sundaes
3 pints coffee ice cream
3/4 cup coarsely chopped
  chocolate covered toffee bar
  (such as Heath or Skor)
Pirouline cookies

In a small saucepan, combine the coffee, cream, sugar and cinnamon. Bring to a simmer until sugar dissolves. Remove from heat and add the chocolate, stirring until melted. Simmer until smooth. (Make the sauce ahead if desired.) Scoop the ice cream into bowls, drizzle with sauce and sprinkle with crushed candy pieces. Serve with a cookie on the side.

Tip: The sauce can be made ahead and refrigerated. Reheat on low heat, stirring constantly. Pirouline cookies are round wafers typically sold in a can.

Marla Payne: Coppell, Texas
Marla served this simple dessert in elegant antique bowls after a dinner she hosted just for the Dinner Club girls. The combination of ingredients was a perfect finishing touch to the meal.

Praline Grahams

Makes: 24

• jelly roll pan

1 package graham crackers (from a 16-ounce box)
1 1/2 cups (3 sticks) butter
2 cups brown sugar
1/4 teaspoon cream of tartar
2 cups coarsely chopped pecans
1/4 teaspoon cinnamon (optional)

Preheat the oven to 350°F. Break the graham crackers into their natural rectangles and lay them out in a jelly roll pan. Melt butter in a medium saucepan and add the brown sugar and cream of tartar. Stir until mixture comes to a boil. Add the pecans and boil 3 minutes stirring frequently. Pour this mixture over the graham crackers and sprinkle with cinnamon. Bake for 10 to 12 minutes. Let cool and cut into bars following the outline of the graham crackers, keeping bars somewhat uniform in size. These are decadent! Serve with Homemade Vanilla Ice Cream (page 284) for an extra special treat.

Beth Martell: New York, New York
Beth and I have been friends since college and have been able to stay in touch since my career often took me to New York. Beth is a residential and commercial decorator and we have spent numerous hours over dinner discussing design details for the two homes she has helped me decorate. When I fly into the Big Apple, it is off to SoHo for shopping, but we always make plenty of stops for good food along the way!

Oma's Linzer Cookies

Makes: 12 Linzer Cookies

- blender or food processor
- sifter
- baking sheet

- approximately 1-inch round or heart cookie cutter
- approximately 2 1/2-inch round or heart cookie cutter

2 cups (4 sticks) unsalted butter
1 cup sugar
2 cups slivered, sliced or blanched almonds, ground
1 teaspoon vanilla
4 cups sifted flour
1 (8-ounce) jar red currant jelly
Sifted confectioners' sugar

Preheat the oven to 350°F. Cream the butter and sugar together in a medium bowl. Grind the almonds in a blender. Add the almonds, vanilla and flour to the butter and sugar. Mix well. Form into a ball and chill. Roll the dough out on a floured surface approximately 1/4 inch thick. With a round cookie cutter, cut out two circles. In the center of one of the circles, cut out a small heart. Repeat with the remaining dough, cutting out heart centers in half of the dough. Lightly spray baking sheets with cooking spray. Bake cookies approximately 10 to 13 minutes until edges are lightly golden. When cooled, spread the cookies without the cut-out center with a thin layer of jelly. Place the heart cut-out cookies on top. Sprinkle with sifted confectioners' sugar.

Special Note: If mom only made one cookie at Christmas, it would be this one! If the jam does not appeal to you, the cookies can be made as crescent moon shapes or snowballs. While warm, roll the shapes in confectioners' sugar. We prefer the tart and sweet combination with the jam!

> *"The good life, or living well often stems from simple pleasures, deeply felt."*
>
> ~Gail Zweigenthal

Crunchy Chocolate Peanut Cookies

Serves: 8

• double boiler

1 (12-ounce) package semisweet chocolate chips

1 (11-ounce) package butterscotch chips

1 (12-ounce) can shelled, salted peanuts

2 (3-ounce) cans or 1 (5-ounce) can chow mein noodles

Melt chocolate chips and butterscotch chips together in a double boiler. Once melted, pour the mixture over the peanuts and noodles in a large bowl. Stir to coat. Drop by tablespoons on wax paper to harden.

Heather Gray: Kansas City, Missouri

Heather and I have been friends since junior high and have always loved chocolate. We would buy candy by the piece from a specialty chocolate store when we went shopping together. She gave me this recipe years ago when I was making holiday cookies. These are easier than baking cookies when you want to take a treat to a friend.

Wine Basics

One of the highlights of my career was working as a buyer in a gourmet food store, Caviar to Cabernet. The customers were friendly and interested in food and wine. My day consisted of helping with menu selections, wine pairings and offering entertaining ideas. Wine sales represented a large portion of the business, so it was necessary to taste many of the wines to recommend to the customers. This section covers wine basics and some reasonably priced wine recommendations.

Cooking with Wine

I recommend cooking with wines you enjoy that are moderately priced. An inexpensive Merlot can be used for red wine sauces unless a certain grape variety or region (e.g. Burgundy) is specified. A Sauvignon Blanc is a nice dry white wine for cooking; Sauternes is a nice sweet white wine that can be used in recipes. It is best to cook with a wine that you would drink with dinner and that complements the food with which it's paired. I do not recommend using cooking wines sold in grocery stores, because they contain salt and affect the recipe's flavor.

When dining out in a restaurant, you can expect to spend anywhere from 1 1/2 to 3 times what you would pay at a wine merchant for a bottle of wine. Be sure the wine is the same year as the wine you ordered on the menu, otherwise you may find a difference in price when the bill arrives. Inhale the bouquet of the wine once poured in the glass. Swirl and taste the wine. Allow yourself two tastes before judging a wine. The cork is given to you not to smell, but so you may check it for moistness. The cork will tell you if the wine has been stored properly. If the cork is dried out, the wine may have been improperly stored. Air may have entered the wine bottle, causing oxidation, which may cause the wine to have an unpleasant flavor. This often happens when wines are served (by the glass) in a restaurant and they have been open several days. A "corked" wine smells strongly of mold, this is due to a bad cork, not poor winemaking. A wine that tastes more like a sherry or Madeira, may have been exposed to heat or poorly stored. In any of these cases, if the wine is unpleasant you should send it back.

White Wines

American Sauvignon Blanc

The Sauvignon Blanc grape produces crisp wines with fresh flavors. Certain styles taste slightly of herbs. Those aged in oak barrels resemble a Chardonnay. Robert Mondavi introduced Fumé Blanc, an oak-aged wine made with Sauvignon Blanc. The Fumé Blanc is no different than a Sauvignon Blanc. Sauvignon Blanc is the second best-selling white wine, just behind Chardonnay. Sauvignon Blanc goes well with appetizers, poultry, sautéed or grilled fish, oysters, veal, pasta and light cream or tomato based sauces. Acidic wines such as these are also recommended with salads that have vinegar or lemon in the dressing.

Recommendations:
- Benziger
- Murphy-Goode
- Hogue
- St. Supéry
- Markham
- Voss

American Chardonnay

The Chardonnay grape was for centuries the only grape used to make all French White Burgundy wines and is a primary source for champagne. Chardonnay was transplanted to American climates with great success. American Chardonnay ranges from light-bodied, delicate and crisp to full-bodied, rich and oaky. The light-bodied varieties are fruitier, sometimes tasting of melon or apple. Identify which type you prefer, and your wine merchant can then accommodate your taste. Chardonnay goes well with appetizers, spicy foods, salmon and shellfish when not served with a cream sauce. Smoked fish is excellent with an oak-aged Chardonnay. Buttery Chardonnay complements sauces made with butter.

Recommendations:
- Ferrari-Carano
- Clos Du Bois
- Morgan
- Geyser Peak
- Flora Springs
- Benziger
- Markham
- Joseph Phelps
- Morro Bay
- Château Ste. Michelle

American Viognier

Viognier is a rare varietal that was brought to the Rhône Valley of France over 2,000 years ago by either the Greeks or Romans. It was only planted in California in the late 1970s. In the 1990s, plantings in California increased from 10 acres to 1,000 acres with 90 percent planted in the late 1990s. It is medium-bodied and known for its spice, floral, citrus, apple and peach flavors. This wine is great before dinner or with fish or chicken.

Recommendations:
- Cline Cellars
- Arrowwood

American Gewürztraminer

Gewürztraminer wines are golden in color with distinctly floral scents that vary from dry to very sweet. The grape is slightly pink and is similar to that of the Alsace region. When it is allowed to ripen late, it can take on a slight clove flavor and is often described as spicy. Gewürztraminer complements appetizers, turkey, salmon, slightly spicy foods and Asian food.

Recommendations:
- Alderbrook
- Geyser Peak
- De Loach
- Fetzer

American Pinot Blanc

This wine is often made with tart orchard fruit and can vary from a crisp acidic taste to an oak-aged flavor, and is similar to a Chardonnay. Grown most often in California, its roots lie in Burgundy where this variety was used as a less expensive alternative to Chardonnay. Most consider Pinot Blanc an all-purpose wine that can be served with appetizers, brunch or fish in a white sauce.

Recommendations:
- Mirassou
- Murphy Goode
- Lockwood

Australian Chardonnay

Australia produces a huge volume of competitively priced, high quality Chardonnay. Many of their wines have more vibrant citrus flavors and less oak flavors. These wines proudly state "unwooded" on the label. Australian Chardonnay can easily be paired with poultry, ham, salmon and buttery pasta sauces.

Recommendations:
- Penfolds
- Yalumba
- Seppelt

New Zealand: Sauvignon Blanc

Marlborough on the South Island of New Zealand has a region that lies southeast of the north coast on a wide flat area called the Wairau Plains. It is now the largest grape growing region in New Zealand and consists of 5,110 acres. This has only been achieved since 1973 when Montana, the largest wine group in the country, planted the vines. This area is the sunniest and driest part of the whole country and the conditions are suitable for white varieties including Müller-Thurgau, Sauvignon Blanc, Chardonnay and Riesling. Watch for these wines to become more popular. Appetizers, sautéed or grilled fish, veal, pasta and light cream or tomato sauces go well with these wines.

Recommendations:
- Cloudy Bay
- Allan Scott
- Grove Mill

Bordeaux, France: White Bordeaux

These wines are a blend of Sauvignon Blanc and Sémillon in varying proportions. The wines are typically oak-aged and have a distinct toasted vanilla flavor. Serve with seafood and poultry dishes or enjoy them without a meal.

Recommendations:
- Maitre d' Estournel
- Verdillac
- Marquis de Chasse
- Château Bonnet (entre deux mers)
- Mission St. Vincent

Burgundy, France: Pouilly-Fuissé

Pouilly-Fuissé is a region located in southern Burgundy where they grow Chardonnay grapes exclusively. The soil is a key element to the creation of these wines that are rich, ripe and tinged with oak. These wines are moderately expensive, but those made by top wine producers are well worth the price. This wine goes well with scallops, whitefish (mild-flavored white fish, a member of the salmon family) and veal with a light cream sauce.

Recommendations:
- Louis Latour
- Antonin Rodet
- St. Veran

Northern Italy: Pinot Grigio

Pinot Grigio is Italy's favorite white wine. It is crisp, refreshing and acidic. In America we have a similar wine called Pinot Gris which is grown in Oregon. These wines complement smoked salmon, spicy food and pasta with seafood.

Recommendations:
- Alois Lageder
- Zenato
- Ecco Domani

Tuscany Italy: Vernaccia Di San Gimagnano

This white wine comes from vines surrounding the medieval city of San Gimagnano. It is a soft white wine with a crisp acidity. This is an affordable everyday table wine that can be purchased for less than $20. Most Italian whites are easy to drink and a good value. This wine is enjoyed with poultry, fish and pastas in a light cream or tomato sauce.

Recommendations:
- Teruzzi & Puthod
- Mormoraia

Red Wines

American Pinot Noir

Pinot Noir is grown in cooler climates. Oregon and cooler parts of California are known for this variety. There is a delicate balance between fruit and acidity and these wines are very food friendly. In a Pinot Noir that has not been aged long, there is often a plum or cherry flavor, but as they age the flavor leans toward spices, fig or chocolate. This wine is a nice complement to pork loin, salmon and veal.

Recommendations:
- Carneros Creek
- Bethel Heights
- David Bruce
- Saintsburg
- Sokol Blossor
- Testarossa

American Rhône Style Reds

American winemakers introduced the less popular Syrah and Mourvèdre grape varieties to the United States. These grapes make a full-bodied and flavorful wine while the Grenache is a lighter wine. California also has a Petite Syrah that continues to remain a good value with its rich and tannic characteristics. All of these varieties fall within the Rhône style red wines. They are good with poultry in a light sauce or with cheese.

Recommendations:
- Bonny Doon Blends
- David Bruce: Petite Sirah
- Guenoc: Petite Sirah
- Swanson: Syrah
- Carignane: Syrah
- Fess Parker: Syrah
- Zaca Mesa: Cuvée Z, Syrah
- Joseph Phelps: Blend; Syrah

American Merlot

Merlot and Cabernet Sauvignon are the two most popular grapes planted in Bordeaux. Merlot was often blended with Cabernet to add fruit and softness to the Cabernet. California winemakers began experimenting with the Merlot on its own and it quickly became America's red wine of choice. These are usually medium to dark red and have predominant flavors of currants and cherries. They are not as tannic as Cabernets and do not have the long range aging potential of Cabernets. Merlot is paired well with lamb and grilled duck.

Recommendations:
- Kunde
- Ferrari-Carano
- Merryvale
- Rombauer
- Columbia Crest
- Shafer
- Newton
- Markham
- Swanson

American Cabernet Sauvignon

The Cabernet Sauvignon grape is originally from Bordeaux and is a chief ingredient in California and Washington red wines. It is full-bodied, deeply colored and aged in oak.

The Cabernet Sauvignon improves with age because of the heavy tannins that give the wine its longevity and dryness. This flavor comes from the skin, pit, and stems of the grapes as well as the French oak barrels. For this reason, Cabernet Sauvignon complements lamb, duck, beef and game.

Recommendations:

- Arrowood
- Ridge
- Flora Springs
- Shafer
- Joseph Phelps: Bachus
- Markham

American Red Zinfandel

This red grape was brought to the United States from Italy. This grape produces a wine with a spicy, yet fruity flavor that can rival a Cabernet Sauvignon. It pairs great with steaks and kabobs.

Recommendations:

- Storybook
- Rabbit Ridge
- Kenwood
- Ridge
- Ravenswood

Australian Shiraz

Since the nineteenth century, Shiraz has been a widely planted red grape in Australia. Since the cuttings were brought from France's Rhône Valley Syrah vines, the grapes produce a slightly spicy wine similar to the Syrah wines in France. Americans have since discovered the quality of Australian reds, which has driven the price up. Larger producers will have more reasonable prices on Shiraz. The Shiraz grape is wonderful with barbecue and spiced chicken.

Recommendations:

- Penfolds: Grange
- Penfolds
- McGuigan Bros.
- Rosemount: Balmoral
- Lindemans
- Tyrell's
- St. Hallet
- Kingston
- Peter Lehmann

Australian Cabernet Sauvignon and Merlot

Cabernets in Australia gained popularity by blending with Shiraz, known as the Syrah grape in France. In more recent years it has gone back to the traditional pairing with Merlot. The finer quality Bordeaux styled wines come from a cooler climate and are rich and fruity in character. These wines have a higher alcohol content than their American counterparts. Serve with duck, lamb or beef.

Recommendations:

- Henschke
- Yalumba
- Rosemount
- Penfolds: All Bin Numbers

Spain: Rioja

Forty percent of all exported wine coming from Spain to the United States is from Rioja. Winemaking in this region dates back to the Romans. Tempranillo is Rioja's primary grape followed by Grenache (Garnacha Tinta), Garignan (Mazuelo) and Graciano. Because they are oak-aged they have a vanilla aroma. There are regulations as to the aging specifications; Crianza and Reserva must spend one year in the cask and Gran Reserva requires a minimum of two years. They can be consumed upon release or can be cellared for years. Rioja can be paired with paella, pizza and tapas.

Recommendations:
- Conde de Valdemar
- Bodegas Montecillo
- Faustino
- Sierra Cantabria

Spain: Ribera del Duero

The local grapes of this area (Tinto Fino, or Tinto del Pais [Tempranillo]) are grown following the course of the Duero River from Soria to Valladolid. Although wines have been made in this region since 1846, it was not until 1982 that this region was recognized for having world-class wines. Now wines from this area are becoming more popular. The high altitude and climate allows Ribera del Duero to produce a wine of balanced acidity and complexity without the addition of other grapes. Only red wines and rosé wines are produced in this region. Wines from this region are good with paella, pizza and manchego cheese.

Recommendations:
- Pesquera
- Arzvaga
- Vega Sicilia

Italy: Chianti

A Tuscan wine made in the area between Florence and Sienna. This region extends to six outlying regions that also produce wines identified as Chianti. These wines vary from light hues to dark and age worthy. This is due to the variety of grapes used including Sangiovese, Canaiolo Nero, Trebbiano, Malvasia and Cabernet Sauvignon. If it states reserve on the label it has been aged in oak at least three years. Chianti pairs well with grilled foods, pasta with a red sauce, some rich cream sauces (such as Carbonara) and pizza.

Recommendations:
- Badia a Colitbuono
- Terrabianca
- Monsanto: Il Poggio
- Fontodi
- Querceto

France: Côtes du Rhône

Most of the vineyards in the Rhône valley comprise the Côtes du Rhône region that is responsible for 80 percent of wines produced. This region makes some white and rosé wines but red wines made with the Grenache grape are most prevalent. Syrah, Carignan and Mourvèdre are sometimes used for blending. These wines vary from light and fruity to full and dark. They do not require aging. Cheese, mild meats and chicken in a light sauce go well with this wine.

Recommendations:
- Coudelet de Beaucastel
- Domaine de Mont Redon
- Guigal
- Perrin Reserve
- La Vielle Ferme

France: Pomerol and Saint-Emilion

Between the city of Bordeaux and the Medoc lie two of the finest wine producing areas in France. These regions are Pomerol and Saint-Emilion and they produce softer, less tannic wines than Cabernet Sauvignon. The grapes used are predominantly Merlot and Cabernet Franc. Pomerol uses Merlot that has a great concentration of fruit. Cabernet Franc is grown more often in Saint-Emilion and the characteristics of the wine from this region are the herbal and mineral flavors. Saint-Emilion is a larger region than Pomeral, so Saint-Emilion wines tend to be less expensive than wines from Pomerol. Try roast or grilled beef with wines from these regions.

Recommendations:
- Château Gazin
- Château La Fleur Petrus

Rhône, France: Châteauneuf-du-Pape

Châteauneuf-du-Pape means "new castle of the Pope." This region lies in the region near Avignon, France. Avignon was a summer residence used by the Avignon popes. This wine can be a blend of thirteen varieties of red or white grapes, but some of the finest contain high percentages of Syrah, Grenache and Mourvèdre. These wines are rich, ripe and heady and can be enjoyed with steak, venison and ripe cheeses.

Recommendations:
- Château Beaucastel
- Perrin
- Domaine du Vieux Telegraphe
- Guigal

South America: Chile and Argentina

The wines of Argentina and Chile definitely deserve mentioning. The climate found in the southern belt that encompasses Chile and Argentina is the same climate by latitude that allows southern Australia, South Africa and South America to produce wines at low or moderate prices. The Argentinean varietal, Malbec, is usually used in a blend and introduces interesting and spicy flavors to the wine. It has become quite popular. Grilled meats, spicy sauces and paprika are notable in South American cuisine and pair nicely with these wines.

Recommendations:
- Argentinean/Los Cardos/Crios/Norton
- Chilean/Casa Lapostolle/Los Vascos

South Africa: The Cape Area

Jan Van Riebeeck, a former ship's surgeon, sent for vines from Europe believing they prevented scurvy. He was able to plant these vines in 1655 in an area called the Cape. During the eighteenth century the wine industry flourished and today this area of South Africa produces most of the country's wines. The wines produced today span the spectrum from good dry whites to tannic reds and sparkling wines. Port and sherry is also produced. The vintner's recent focus has been on reassessing wine styles and making the reds softer and richer and some of their harsh whites fruitier. The white grape varieties include Chenin Blanc, Colombard, Chardonnay and Sauvignon Blanc. The red grape varieties include Pinotage, Merlot, Shiraz and Cabernet Sauvignon. Pinotage is unique to South Africa and produces some of the most exciting wines. The Pinotage grape only accounts for 5 percent of their production. A cross between Pinot Noir and Cinsaut, these two grapes combined produce complex fruity wines with age, but can also be enjoyed when young. Cinsaut is South Africa's most widely planted grape. The Steen also known as Chenin Blanc is the most widely planted grape for white wines.

Recommendations:
- Meerlust wines
- Goats do Roam

Germany: The Rhine and Mosel

The Riesling grape produces the best German wines of the Rhine (Rhein) and Mosel as well as the Alsace wines of France. This grape yields very dry wines to very sweet dessert wines. The finest have a fragrant nose that is fruity and flowery. The level of sweetness is determined by the length of time the grapes are left on the vine. The label will indicate the degree of sweetness.

Recommendations:
- Dr. Loosen Riesling
- Strub Riesling

Champagne

True champagne comes only from the Champagne region in northeast France. Sparkling wines may be labeled as "Spumante" in Italy and "Sekt" in Germany. French champagne is made from a blend of Chardonnay, Pinot Noir or Pinot Blanc grapes. Good champagnes are not expensive because of the grapes used, but because a second fermentation process in the bottle is required, which requires up to one hundred manual operations, some of which are mechanized today. The manual process does affect the price.

Champagnes vary from dry to sweet. A sugar and wine mixture called a dosage is added just before corking and determines how sweet the champagne will be. The label indicates the level of sweetness. Brut is dry, extra sec or extra dry (slightly sweeter), sec (medium sweet), demi sec (sweet) or doux (very sweet). It is recommended to use champagne glasses because the shape of the glass allows the champagne to hold bubbles longer. If you open a bottle of champagne and don't drink it all, stick a metal handle in the bottle, letting the bowl of the spoon rest on top. It will remain drinkable stored in the refrigerator for 1 to 2 days this way. Enjoy champagne with brunch entrées, fruit desserts or with caviar.

Recommendations:
- Roederer
- Carousel
- Taittinger
- Marwood Brut
- Rotari Brut

Port; Porto

Port is a sweet fortified wine often served after a meal. Grape alcohol is added to the wine partway through fermentation, stopping the process at a point where the wine has plenty of sweetness and alcohol. Vintage Ports are the most expensive, and are made from a single vintage bottled within two years. The best ports age fifty years or more. Late-Bottled Vintage Ports and Single Vintage Ports are not made from as high of quality of grapes as the Vintage Ports.

Tawny Ports are a blend of grapes from several different years that can be aged in wood as long as forty years. They are ready to drink when bottled. Ruby Ports are considered the lowest quality of port. They are blended from several vintages and wood-aged. Port is traditionally served after dinner with walnuts and Stilton cheese or enjoyed with cigars. It is also good with chocolate, a dessert or alone.

Recommendations:
- Dows
- Grahams
- Taylor
- Fonseca

Fortified Wines

Madeira, Marsala and sherry wines have a higher alcohol content and therefore cannot be sold where only beer and wine is sold. Marsala is from the western tip of Sicily and can range from sweet to dry. Madeira can be used for both sweet and savory recipes. Sherry is made in the Andalusia region of southern Spain. They range from dry to sweet. Sherry is often served with traditional Spanish appetizers (tapas), as an apéritif, after dinner drink, or used in recipes.

Vermouth is a white wine that originated in Italy that has been flavored with herbs and spices. It is used as an apéritif, in cocktails, and for cooking. Fortified wines such as vermouth, Madiera, Marsala and sherry have had brandy or another spirit added to them, increasing the alcohol content.

> *"Good wine is a necessity of life."*
>
> ~*Thomas Jefferson*

Common Wine Terms

Corked—wine tastes of a bad cork. Wine will taste slightly musty and will be unpalatable with an unpleasant smell.

Oxidized—exposed to air, flavor has changed. Open too long.

Tannin—identifies a dry sensation with flavors of leather and tea. Excess tannins can cause wine to be bitter.

Balance, Acid—alcohol, fruit and tannins should be balanced. The right amount of acidity and tannins means the fruit is refreshing and flavor lingers. Time will alter this balance.

Tasting Terms

Color-is largely due to grape variety but age and region of origin also play a part. The color of wine comes from the skin of the grapes. White wines can be made from red grapes when the skins are removed immediately after picking.

Smell-or nose of the wine will reveal the condition and character. Swirl it around in the glass and inhale deeply. What flavors do you smell? Swirling the wine aerates the wine and allows oxygen to mix with it, creating the bouquet. The "nose" is the term tasters use to describe the bouquet and aroma of the wine.

Length-the way in which flavor lingers in the mouth and is considered a positive description. The quality and sensation of the wine's aftertaste, combined with how it lingers, is described as finish.

Artichokes and asparagus are difficult to pair with wine because the acid called cynarin in artichokes makes wines taste sweet, and phosphorus and mercaptan in asparagus makes the wines taste bad. Avoid these foods if your guests are wine connoisseurs.

Flavors-have a lot to do with the scientific basis of the wine. You may not recognize the characteristics but these flavors may make the identification easier.

Banana or pear-will indicate wine was fermented at a low temperature, which is common for inexpensive whites and Beaujolais.

Black pepper-often a flavor from a Syrah grape.

Toast-can be a sign of new oak barrels or bottle aged Chardonnay or Sémillon.

Peach or apricot-suggests a Chardonnay, ripe Riesling or Muscat.

Honey-found in dessert wines or wines that were subject to noble rot. Noble rot is a mold that grows on the grapes and is necessary to make Sautérnes and sweeter German dessert wines such as Beerenauslese and Trockenbeerenauslese.

Nutty overtones-hazelnut or walnut is present in a mature white burgundy.

Green pepper-designates an inexpensive young red from Cabernet Sauvignon or Cabernet Franc.

Lemon or lime-is found in wines made from Sémillon and American Riesling.

Cherries, strawberries and red currants-are often associated with Pinot noir grapes.

Chocolate-may be sensed in a fine full-bodied red wine. These wines are ripe, mature and low in acidity.

Vanilla-is often associated with wine being aged in new oak barrels.

Raspberry flavors-are apparent in expensive red Rhône wines, often those from Syrah grapes.

Litchis-are found in wines made from Gewürztraminer grapes. This small fruit from China is deliciously sweet.

Rose petal-will be noticed in a Gewürztraminer.

Butter-is a distinct flavor of all styles of Chardonnay.

Gooseberries-are distinctive of Sauvignon Blanc.

Mint and eucalyptus-are indicative of Cabernet Sauvignon from Australia, South Africa and California.

Tasting Basics

Swirl wine and take a generous amount in your mouth, but do not swallow. Roll it around in your mouth and breathe over it to further release the flavors. Assess acidity, sweetness and alcohol content. There are four flavors you will taste on the different parts of the tongue. The back and top of the tongue recognize bitterness, possibly from the tannins. The sides of the tongue detect sharpness and acidity and the tip registers sweetness.

The oak from wood barrels imparts tannins to the wine and gives the wine a vanilla characteristic. The limited exposure to oxygen coming from the pores in the wood helps to mature the wine. You may hear the term oak-aged frequently. Corks are used to stop air from entering the bottle and have no affect on the wine. An older wine may have some air trapped between the wine and the cork. Mature wines are best if opened a half hour before serving; young wines will not benefit from opening early.

Wineglasses

Glasses should not obscure the color of the wine. A clear glass bowl is most appropriate for tasting wines, and a large enough glass is important for swirling. Ideally, a 10-ounce glass is the appropriate size. Large balloon-shaped glasses are more appropriate for red wines. A smaller glass, closed slightly at the top, is used for white wines and helps to concentrate on the bouquet and to keep the wine chilled.

Malolactic Fermentation

Malolactic fermentation is the fermentation of wine in a cask or tank that occurs naturally or is induced artificially by the vintner. This process will impart an oak flavor to the wine. Determine whether this process has caused too much oak flavor for your liking and ask your wine merchant to help you determine which wines would better serve your taste.

Storing Wine

Fluctuations in temperature can be harmful to wine. Store bottles horizontally, away from sunlight to ensure corks remain moist. The optimum temperature to store wine is 52°F, but wine is safe anywhere from 40°F to 65°F. Expensive wines age well. Cabernet Sauvignon, Zinfandel, Merlot and Syrah benefit from the aging process. Modestly priced reds should be enjoyed within two years and modestly priced whites within six months.

Chilling Wine

Immersing a bottle of wine in a bucket of ice and water for thirty minutes is the best way to chill a white wine or champagne and keep it cool while drinking. White wines and champagne should not be left in the refrigerator more than a few hours or they may oxidize.

Below are some guidelines for the correct temperature to serve wines:

Sparkling: 40°F to 45°F

White wine: 45°F to 50°F

Reds, rosé and light reds: 50°F to 55°F

Medium-bodied: 55°F to 60°F

Full-bodied: 60°F to 65°F

Light Reds-Rioja, Beaujolais, Chianti

Medium bodied reds—Beaujolais-Villages, wines from Burgundy, Pinot Noir, Merlot, Red Zinfandel, Cabernet Sauvignon, Chianti Classico, Rioja-Riserva.

Full bodied—Barbaresco, Barolo, Bordeaux wines, Rioja Gran Riserva, and some Cabernet Sauvignon, Merlot and Red Zinfandel from California.

In the summer it may be necessary to slightly chill a warm red wine. Chill in the refrigerator for thirty minutes. It is a recognized practice since temperatures for wine storage are based on properly cooled cellars, not our homes today.

Reading Labels

Wines from United States winemakers are required by law to state on the label the brand name and the year the wine was bottled. It is required that 100 percent of the grapes must come from the area stated on the bottle. The label may also indicate a broad growing area such as the northern coast in California. The county such as Napa or Sonoma may be stated and even a township such as Carneros. After branding and location are stated, the grape variety is named and by law the wine must contain 75 percent of that variety. If the grape of origin is identified, the wine may also reflect a higher cost. The vintage year is listed, which determines the year the grapes were harvested although the wine may have been stored several years. This is important because the conditions of a particular year determine the quality and readiness of the wine for drinking.

The same information appears on French labels, but order of emphasis varies. In France, the place the grapes were grown takes precedence over the vintner or grape variety since each region has ratings according to the excellence of the wines. The name of the proprietor is next followed by the location. Having the proprietor's name on the bottle places his or her reputation on the contents. Estate bottled means the proprietor has watched over the entire production.

Italian wine labels fall somewhere between the French and the California labels with the emphasis placed on the vintner and the region the grapes were grown. Italian wine has a government designation on the label that is either DOC or DOCG. The DOC is the name of the agency that controls the wine production in Italy. The DOCG on the label denotes that it is the finest of red wines. The G at the end is a guarantee that it is a premium wine and only five qualify for this label (Barbaresco from Piedmont, Barolo from Piedmont, Brunello di Montalcino-Tuscany, Chianti-Tuscany and Vino Nobile di Montepulcino from Tuscany.) Following the DOCG, the label will identify a prestigious site within a particular growing zone from which this wine originated. A regional DOC and the grape's variety will be listed on the label. When you find an Italian wine you like, try other wine varieties from that maker and use it to measure other wines.

The producer's name is the most important aspect on Australian labels. If the variety of grape is stated on the label, then the contents must contain 80 percent of that kind of grape. When the origin is listed, 80 percent of the grapes must come from that region. Australian wines are a very good value. If it was a good vintage year in California, it will also hold true for that year in Australia since they have similar climates.

On Spanish labels, the reputation of the Rioja wine producer and shipper is most important. After the shipper buys the grapes, they blend wines from several vintages to keep the style consistent. The label may give you the style of wine, but grape varieties are not found on the label. The label identifies appellation or region (e.g. Rioja or Penedes). DOCA is the top quality and then DO. VdM is considered table wine. Reserva on a Spanish label indicates that the shipper specially selected this wine and gave it further aging in cask or bottle.

The fancy artwork and crests on German wine labels are somewhat misleading. The important information is alongside or beneath the art. The greater degree of particularity the greater the quality of wine. The label may state all of the specifics (producer, vintage, township and the vineyard from which it comes, and the grape variety) and have a high price tag. The less detailed the information, the less expensive the wine. The sweetness of a German wine will depend on how long the grapes are left on the vine and will be denoted on the label. The driest German wine is a Kabinett followed by Spätlese, "spät" meaning late (as in late pick). The next level is even sweeter, which is Auslese, Beerenauslese and Trockenbeerenauslese or the picking of trocken (dry almost raisin-like grapes.) Eiswein is the sweetest because the grapes are harvested after the first freeze. Qualitätswein or Qualitätswein mit Prädikat with the addition of Prädikat is a climb up the ladder of sweetness. The wine grade will be listed at the bottom of the label.

The History of Wine

Winemaking encompasses a period of over seven thousand years. Tom Haas, one of my previous employers informed me that turning water into wine in Cana is the first recorded miracle in the Bible. There is little recorded about the early years, but it is generally accepted that wine was made for the first time in Asia Minor in the Caucasus and Mesopotamia, around 6000 to 4000 BC. From there, winemaking spread to Egypt where there are written references dating back to 5000 BC. At about the same time, they began making wine in Phoenicia. By 2000 BC the Greeks and Cretans began experimenting with winemaking. By 1000 BC the inhabitants of Sicily, Italy and most countries in North Africa had begun planting vineyards, and five hundred years later wine production began in Spain, the south of France and Arabia. By about 100 BC, wine was made in northern India and China. Shortly after the birth of Christ the practice spread to the Balkan States and Northern Europe. The history of wine halted during the next thousand years due to the decline of the Roman Empire and Europe's Dark Ages. Explorers in the sixteenth century accelerated the pace and by 1530 vine plantings had spread to Mexico and Japan. In 1560, Argentina imported plantings, and later Peru followed. South Africa planted vines in 1655 followed by Australia in 1697 and New Zealand in 1813. The birth of wine in America began in California when vines were planted in 1849 during the Gold Rush. Those that had no luck panning for gold turned to farming, and the most popular crop was grapes. Many Europeans that settled in California planted grapes and brought their winemaking tradition with them. In the 1970s California wines evolved into national and international prominence. Oregon, Washington, New York and Texas are a few other states that produce wines in the United States.

Here is a quick chart for your own wine pairings!

Salads: Sauvignon Blanc, Riesling, Pinot Blanc, Pinot Gris, Pinot Grigio, Unoaked Chardonnay, Sparkling Wine, Champagne, Gamay, Pinot Noir

Chicken (Cream Sauce): Sauvignon Blanc, Sparkling Wine, Champagne, Unoaked Chardonnay, Riesling, Pinot Blanc, Pinot Gris, Pinot Grigio

Chicken (Grilled): Riesling, Shiraz, Syrah, Zinfandel

Chicken (Lemon or Citrus): Riesling, Chablis, Unoaked Chardonnay

Game (Venison, Duck, Pheasant, Quail, Rabbit, Boar): Chardonnay, Pinot Noir, Shiraz, Syrah, Rioja

Turkey and Goose: Gewürtztraminer, Pinot Noir

Lamb: Bordeaux, Rioja, Syrah

Tomato based pasta and pizza dishes: Sangiovese, Chianti, Montepulciano d'Abruzzo, Barbaresco

Pork (Spicy): Gewürztraminer, Unoaked Chardonnay, Dry Riesling, Sauvignon Blanc, Chianti

Pork (Grilled or Plain): Chardonnay, Pinot Noir, Zinfandel

Red meats (Spicy): Pinot Noir

Red meats (Rich: Osso Bucco, Beef Bourguignonne): Cabernet Sauvignon, Shiraz, Syrah, Pinot Noir, Barolo

Red Meats (Grilled): Sangiovese, Chianti, Zinfandel, Cabernet Sauvignon, Shiraz

Seafood/Shellfish (Grilled/Smoked): Unoaked Chardonnay, Sauvignon Blanc, Pinot Noir

Seafood/Shellfish (Butter or Cream Sauce): Oaked Chardonnay, Chablis, Sparkling Wine, Champagne

Spicy/Asian dishes/Sushi/Cajun seafood dishes: Gewürztraminer, Chardonnay, Dry Riesling, Sauvignon Blanc

Chili or spicy tomato stews: Zinfandel, Shiraz

Cheese Basics

Cheese is always appropriate as an appetizer. It is great for quick and elegant gatherings even when dinner does not follow. Choosing cheese can be confusing if you don't purchase them for appetizers on a regular basis. In this section I explain flavors of the different varieties I purchase most often.

When arranging your cheese tray include red and green grapes cut in small bunches and piled on top of one another so the tray looks full in the empty spots. If fruit and cheese is your preference, sliced apples, pears and melon are a nice accompaniment. Sprinkle apples and pear slices with lemon juice so they do not turn brown. Grapes are also appropriate when you include olives and cornichons as garnish. Wine and cheese are a wonderful choice for an appetizer before a meal.

Premium olives cured in oil with herbs or brine (from a specialty grocer) complement cheese and cleanse the palate. The common black olive is called a Mission olive. This olive is a ripe green olive that obtains its color from lye curing and oxygenation. Olives that are tree ripened turn dark brown or black naturally. Two of the most popular imported olives are the niçoise and the kalamata. Spanish olives are picked young and are therefore green. They are lye fermented and are usually aged about six to twelve months. Dry-cured olives have been packed in salt, which removes moisture and makes them wrinkly in texture. Some of my favorite olives include amfissa, lucques, nyon, niçoise, kalamata and gaeta. Gourmet food stores usually have many choices. For the best flavor, it is recommended to buy olives with the pit.

Once cheese is unwrapped, it spoils quickly. When arranging a cheese platter, cheese should be removed from refrigeration one to two hours before consuming to experience the true flavor. In the summer, you may want to remove only one hour ahead since the soft cheeses may change in consistency. Serve with water crackers or a thinly sliced baguette to allow the palate to experience the flavor. Allow approximately 4 ounces of cheese per person for a cheese tray. Cut cheeses for your serving platter while they are cold. Do not cut cheese in cubes or slices; instead leave them in the shape they are sold in and serve with the appropriate utensil. (Use a spreader for soft cheeses and a knife or cheese cutter for harder cheeses.) If the group is large, some cheeses (such as manchego) can be sliced to make the buffet line move more quickly. When wrapping leftover cheese, wrap each individual piece of cheese with a new piece of plastic wrap or place in a sealable plastic bag.

Popular Cheese Varieties

Feta Cheese from Greece is made from sheep's milk and has a distinct strong, slightly acidic flavor. Feta is crumbly in texture and white in color. True feta should be stored in brine in the refrigerator and is usually found only in cheese stores and some supermarkets. This is wonderful with crackers. Today, feta cheese is also found packed without brine, and makes a great salad topping or can be used for making spreads.

Goat Cheese is made from goat's milk and comes in a variety of shapes (cones, cylinders and pyramids). A mild or more profound flavor depends on the aging process. Today many are made from a mixture of goat, cow and sheep's milk.

Stilton is a blue veined cheese with a rich and mellow flavor and a pungent taste similar to blue cheese. The wrinkled rind is not edible. Stilton is milder than Gorgonzola or Roquefort and is excellent on salads. It can also be served with port after dinner.

Roquefort is made from sheep's milk that has been aged three months or more in a limestone cavern near the village of Roquefort in southwest France, near the Spanish border. It is creamy in texture and has a pungent somewhat salty flavor. Blue veins throughout a creamy white interior characterize Roquefort. The name Roquefort is protected from imitators by law. True Roquefort has a red sheep emblem on the wrapper, but many retailers will repackage the original wheel so you may not see this label of authenticity.

Cambozola is a German cheese, creamy in texture with an edible, white, velvety rind. The flavor is a cross between a blue cheese and Brie.

Brie is compact, even textured, pale yellow in color, with an edible white rind. As it ages it takes on a nutty flavor. This creamy cheese is made from cow's milk and is noted as the French cheese "king of kings." The French exported Brie is stabilized and the maturing process stopped so it has a longer shelf life. Brie must be served at room temperature to enjoy its full flavor.

Camembert is made from raw cow's milk. True Camembert comes from only five parts of Normandy, France. Although often copied, a good Camembert mentions "affine," which means it is matured to the heart of the cheese. It is clean yellow with a subtly salty taste and has a white edible rind like Brie.

Saint André is a triple cream soft cheese that has been heavily enriched with cream during the manufacturing process. The double and triple cream cheeses have an exceptionally rich and creamy texture and are higher in fat content. This one is outstanding!

Explorateur is rich triple cream cheese that has a delicate piquant flavor. It is a wonderful appetizer substitute for Brie.

Boursin cheese is a triple cream cheese with a buttery texture. It is usually flavored with garlic, herbs or black pepper.

Gouda has a yellow rind covered by a red or black paraffin wax. This coating allows the cheese to breathe while losing some humidity. Gouda accounts for 50 percent of the cheese produced in Holland. The flavor is sweet and fruity and as it ages is more pronounced. Gouda is firm and supple and essentially mild tasting. This cheese goes well with fruit.

Port-Salut is a semi-soft cheese that was originally made by the Trappist monks in France. This cheese is made from cow's milk and has a pale yellow interior. It has a savory flavor and a satiny texture. Fruit complements the flavor of Port-Salut.

Manchego is Spain's most popular cheese that comes from the milk of the Manche sheep in the La Mancha region. The Manche sheep survives on shrubs and grass and produces an aromatic milk. It is a well-ripened hard cheese with ivory color. The taste is creamy, nutty and sharp to the palate. The exterior is decorative but not edible. This cheese can be thinly sliced for a cheese tray with the exterior intact or as a wedge with the proper utensils for slicing.

Gloucester is a natural hard English cheese with a creamy yellow almost orange color. It has a rich smooth flavor. Gloucester is often layered with Stilton, which is referred to as Huntsman. Gloucester is a form of Cheddar.

Gorwood Caerphilly is mild, yet tangy and is made from cow's milk. It is produced in England but gets its name from the village in Wales where it was first made. It may be one of the more difficult cheeses to find, but is truly worth the search if you can locate it at a specialty grocer or cheese shop.

Cheddar Cheese, originally made in the English village of Cheddar, is now produced all over the English speaking world. It is made from cow's milk and varies in color from white to deep yellow and has a mild to sharp taste. Colby is a mild Cheddar. Other types of Cheddar include Gloucester, Cheshire, Leicester, Lancashire, Derby, Wensleydale and Gorwood Caerphilly.

Cabot Cheddar Cheese is one of the best known American types of Cheddar and has won every major cheese-making prize in America. The Cabot Classic Private Stock and Vintage Choice are sold in specialty food stores.

Gruyère is famous for its use in Swiss fondue. Gruyère is a hard cheese that is similar to Emmentaler with smaller holes but with the characteristic tough outer rind. The holes in these Swiss cheeses are caused by an expansion of gas within the cheese curd during the ripening process. Its texture is chewy and it melts evenly. The flavor is mild and nutty.

Parmigiano-Reggiano is the finest of Parmesan cheese and is made in Italy. It comes in a 75-pound wheel. This cheese has a pungent smell. It is primarily a grating cheese with a granular texture. It is recommended to buy this in a small wedge and grate it yourself. The outside coating states Parmigiano-Reggiano and ensures you will not get an imitation.

Sage Derby has a greenish hue due to sage being introduced to the cheese during the production. It is a mild hard cheese with a slight sage flavor.

Buffalo Mozzarella is made in the south of Italy from a mixture of water buffalo and cow's milk. It is pure white and hand formed into balls. The consistency is soft and rubbery and it is stored in whey brine. To serve, slice and alternate with fresh sliced tomatoes and fresh basil, sprinkle with salt and pepper and drizzle with extra virgin olive oil and balsamic vinegar.

Fresh Mozzarella is made today predominantly from whole milk instead of from the milk of water buffaloes. It is usually packaged in whey or water and is labeled "Italian style." It can be found in Italian markets, cheese shops and some supermarkets. It differs from the regular mozzarella, which is factory produced. It has a much softer texture and a sweet delicate flavor and can be used in the same way as the buffalo mozzarella. You may order this cheese and a variety of other wonderful cheeses from The Mozzarella Company in Dallas. Visit their web site at www.mozzco.com or contact them at 1-800-798-2954.

Havarti is a pale yellow Danish cheese that is semi-soft with irregular holes. It is considered a mild cheese, but slightly tangy. It intensifies and sharpens with age.

Mascarpone is a cheese that is usually mixed with sugar and used in desserts. It is a solidified cream that has been whipped to a velvety consistency. Mix with whipped cream to make a delicious topping for fruit. It is also used in Tiramisu.

An odd assortment of cheeses on a tray is most appropriate. If choosing five cheeses for a platter, select a hard, a crumbly, a blue, a semi-soft and a goat cheese. This provides a variety to the milk types used and presents an array of flavors. Duplication will occur if Cambozola is paired with Stilton or Roquefort since they are all from the blue family. It would be acceptable to have a feta or goat cheese with a Stilton or Roquefort.

Crumbly Cheese	Hard Cheese	Soft Cheese	Semi-Soft
Feta	Manchego	Cambozola	Gouda
Goat Cheese	Gloucester	Brie	Mozzarella
Stilton	Cabot Cheddar	Camembert	Havarti
Roquefort	Cheddar	Saint André	Port-Salut
	Parmigiano-Reggiano	Explorateur	Gorwood Caerphilly
	Gruyère	Boursin	
	Sage Derby	Mascarpone	

There are several cheeses, which are used more often for cooking than on a cheese platter, e.g. Gruyère, mascarpone, mozzarella and Parmigiano-Reggiano.

Processed cheeses are not appropriate for a cheese tray. These cheeses have had the ripening process stopped at some point with a heat treatment and are usually a blend of varieties. A chemical process is used to smoke cheeses. Originally smoked cheeses were hung over a fire to develop the taste. I don't recommend placing smoked cheeses on a cheese tray unless you know the traditional process was used.

Grilling

Grilling is searing the outside of the meat while keeping the juices inside. Grilling time depends on the cut of meat, grid position, temperature of coals and desired doneness. You can grill both meats and vegetables. There are some simple instructions to follow for success. Trimming excess fat from meat keeps the flame from flaring up. Foods will cook faster if you cook with the grill covered.

Cooking times are helpful but the internal temperature is more important. A good meat thermometer is imperative.

Meat and Seafood

Meats and seafood typically do not have a lot of varied cooking techniques in order to prepare them perfectly each time. The crucial thing is to cook them to an internal temperature that suits everyones preferences. Page 324 has a temperature chart to use as a guide. Many cookbooks will indicate a higher temperature due to the food safety requirements used for restaurants or give you a certain time to cook meat that may not be accurate. It is best to follow temperature guidelines.

Invest in a good thermometer and use it when roasting or grilling meats. The best meat thermometer I have found has a timer attached to it and a wire that attaches the alarm to the probe thermometer that goes in the thickest part of the meat. You set the temperature you would like to reach and the alarm sounds when the meat reaches this temperature. This type of thermometer is best because you can check the temperature on the outside thermometer without opening the door of the oven or grill. If you overcook you cannot go back, but if you undercook, you may always put it back in the oven or back on the grill. Whether cooking in the oven or on the grill, set the temperature on the thermometer (and turn the alarm on) 8°F to 10°F less than the temperature desired. ALWAYS let meat rest a minimum of 10 minutes (not tented) before slicing. The meat will continue to cook, the temperature will rise and the juices from the meat will redistribute. If you cover the meat, it traps the heat and continues to cook.

To test your thermometer to be sure it reads correctly, fill a glass with ice and then with water. Insert the thermometer to see if it shows 32°F, the freezing temperature of water. If it does not, you will need to adjust the thermometer if possible or take into account the difference when cooking.

Silver skin is the thin pearlescent membrane found on certain cuts of meat such as beef and pork tenderloin. Trim off the silver skin on all meats, as it is not digestible and does not add any flavor or benefit to meat.

Rub meat with olive oil and spices about 10 minutes before searing (browning to seal in juices). Sear the meat on all sides for approximately 7 minutes per side. Lightly rubbing the meat with oil helps prevent sticking. It is also helpful if your grates on the grill are lightly oiled as well. You can roast in the oven on your broil setting on the middle rack or on the grill. Continue to cook the meat to the desired temperature in the oven (reducing heat to 350°F) or on the grill. When using a meat thermometer, be sure to insert in the thickest part of the meat and be sure it is not touching any part of the rack or coils. By inserting in the thickest part of the meat, the majority of the meat will be at the desired temperature. The thinner ends will be slightly more done. For beef tenderloin, a center cut tenderloin will be trimmed to be an even thickness. If it is not center cut, you may tuck the ends under to create a more even thickness.

Do not season very fatty meats with salt before cooking. Rib-eyes, short ribs and other fatty meats require salting just before serving. That way the salt does not draw the moisture out. (Kosher salt or sea salt sprinkled over these meats just before serving is recommended.)

Steaks require the same cooking temperatures as beef tenderloin for doneness. A dinner party tip is to sear them outdoors to get the grill marks and finish steaks off in the oven at 350°F with a meat thermometer. You can cook each steak to the desired temperature this way without guessing.

For food safety purposes, do not put cooked meat on a platter that was previously used for raw meat. Do not re-use marinade.

For marinating any food, I prefer to use glass or a large sealable plastic bag versus aluminum.

Tongs and spatulas are better for turning meat, as forks pierce and allow juices to escape.

Pork

The old tale of trichinosis in pork is no longer relevant. Trichinosis is a parasite caused by eating undercooked meat, but with the new processing of today it is no longer a threat. Freezing pork and cooking pork eliminates trichinosis and almost all pork in supermarkets is previously frozen.

Pork tends to be overcooked in America. It is fine to be slightly pink inside. Use the chart on page 324 as a guide for the proper temperatures for the most common cuts. We prefer to cook pork to around 150°F for a tenderloin and 155°F for a pork roast.

Prime Rib or Standing Rib Roast

For a perfect prime rib it will take approximately 18 to 22 minutes per pound. For seasoning you may dust the outside fat of the roast with 2 tablespoons kosher salt and black pepper. Cut some small slits in the fat of the rib roast and insert slivers of fresh garlic or just smear pressed garlic all over the standing rib. The Juniper-Rosemary Marinade on page 163 is wonderful for prime rib and tenderloin, whether cooked as filets or whole, we prefer a sauce. The Perfect Red Wine Sauce (page 148) or the Perfect Cream Sauce variation (page 150) made with black pepper and bourbon are two of our favorites.

Internal Temperatures for Cooked Meat

Doneness	Beef	Pork	Lamb	Chicken
Rare	120°F-125°F	n/a	135°F	n/a
Medium-rare	130°F-135°F	n/a	140°F-150°F	n/a
Medium	135°F-140°F	145°F	n/a	n/a
Medium-well	145°F	n/a	150°F	150°F
Well Done	155°F	160°F	160°F	165°F-175°F

Chicken Breast done 160°F

Chicken Thighs done 165°F

Turkey 165°F-175°F

Safety Tips

Clean all cutting surfaces well.

Do not use the knife or cutting board used for raw meats for other dinner items without washing first.

Lettuce & Salads

Salad adds such a wonderful balance to a meal whether served before the main course or with dinner. You can be creative with salads and develop your own combinations. Mixing lettuce helps to incorporate color and texture. Nuts take on a more interesting flavor when toasted. Here is an abbreviated list of possibilities and tips for combinations. Allow approximately 1 1/4 to 1 1/2 cups of slightly packed lettuce per person, as a side dish. When you have a fruit and lettuce combination you may want a dressing with a touch of sugar.

Lettuce	Nuts	Fruits	Vegetables	Cheese
Butterhead or Boston	Pine Nuts	Kiwis	Artichokes	Asiago
Crisphead	Pecans	Strawberries	Olives	Parmesan
Romaine	Walnuts	Apples	Hearts of Palm	Mozzarella
Red leaf or green leaf	Macadamia Nuts	Grapes	Red Onions	Gorgonzola
Frisèe	Cashews	Avocados	Green Onions	Stilton
Mesclun	Sunflower Seeds	Oranges	Tomatoes	Blue
Spinach	Pistachios	Pears		Monterey Jack
Arugula	Almonds	Dried Cherries		Brie
Radicchio				Goat
				Feta

Lettuce should be washed in lukewarm water and drained completely or blotted with a paper towel to remove excess moisture before refrigerating. Do not soak. I like to wash lettuce ahead of time and roll it in paper towels to remove excess water. Store this way in the refrigerator for several hours before serving. Lettuce can be stored three to five days in an airtight bag once washed and dried.

Butterhead (Bibb or Boston lettuce) is a delicate lettuce. This lettuce is a small round head that is usually pale yellow green on the inside to pale green on the outside.

Crisphead Lettuce is a tightly packed head otherwise known as iceberg lettuce. It is not very flavorful but is good for Mexican dishes because it is so crisp. This lettuce is not recommended for formal gatherings.

Leaf Lettuce ranges in color from medium to dark green with some tipped in red (oakleaf or red leaf) lettuce. Look for any wilting or yellowing of leaves when selecting.

Romaine lettuce is the common choice for Caesar salad. The elongated head is crisp with green leaves that go to pale green at the center. There is little waste with romaine lettuce. Tear off any brown that may be on the edges and cut off the root end in a v shape. Wash in lukewarm water and dry off. This lettuce gets crisper if it is wrapped in paper towels and stored in the refrigerator for 30 minutes to an hour after washing.

Mesclun lettuce is sold in most grocery stores. It is a mixture of young small salad greens and is also referred to as gourmet salad mix. Even if the whole salad is not made from this, it is nice to mix a few handfuls with other lettuce for variety in color and texture. Baby spinach, frisée, arugula and radicchio are usually included in this mix.

Frisée is a member of the chicory family and has a slightly bitter flavor. Leaf color ranges from yellow white to yellow green and the ends are feathery. Curly endive can be used as a substitute for frisée.

Endive is closely related to, and often confused with chicory. Belgian endive, curly endive and escarole are the three main varieties. Belgian endive is a small (6 inches long) cigar-shaped head of cream colored, tightly packed, slightly bitter leaves. Curly endive, often mistakenly called chicory, grows in loose heads of lacy, green-rimmed outer leaves that curl at the tips. The off-white leaves in the center form a compact heart. Escarole has broad, slightly curved, pale green leaves and has a milder flavor than either Belgian or curly endive.

Radicchio is a red-leafed Italian chicory often used for its pink to dark red color. It is slightly bitter and comes in a small loose head.

Arugula is an aromatic salad green with a bitter flavor that comes in small bunches. It must be thoroughly washed before using.

> *"There is no love sincerer than the love of food."*
>
> *~George Bernard Shaw*

Keeping Things Interesting

It is always good to expand your social circles and mix people up to make events more entertaining and exciting. Sometimes a lull in the conversation, whether before or after dinner, requires a little encouragement from the host! Included in this section are some favorite games to help energize the party. Most games you can only use once with the same guests, but they are sure to stimulate lively conversations with each new group! One game per event is usually enough. There are also books on games that offer additional options. (I have found many of these games through the internet, the original author is unknown.)

Activity 1

The Secret Language of Birthdays is a great book that gives the characteristics of people born on a certain day. As the host, you will know enough about the guests to look for characteristics they may recognize in themselves. Type a few sentences about each guest, then cut and paste to the inside flap of a place card. Once guests arrive and have time to drink a cocktail, randomly pass out the place cards. This alone will have people mingling and searching for the one card that best suits them. Another option is to have one person take all of the cards and start by picking out one with characteristics they think best suits him or her. Pass the remaining cards on to the next person. When everyone has a card, let each person read it aloud. After everyone has finished you can then reveal to each person whose card they picked. Few people see themselves as they really are, so the conversation can be very engaging! Afterwards, you can write the correct name on each card and set them on the dinner table.

Activity 2

This game needs the host to organize answers for all of the players, so he or she will not participate. Have each guest start by drawing a cross on an index card to separate the four quadrants. In the upper left box ask the guests to list four descriptive words that identify their favorite color. They are to keep their answers and adjectives to themselves until they are revealed later. Next in the upper right box have guests list four adjectives to describe their favorite animal. In the left lower box have them describe their favorite body of water (which can be an ocean, pond or even the bathtub). They can be imaginative! Finally in the fourth box they should describe how they would feel in a dark room with no windows or doors.

Starting with the upper left box, have each guest reveal what their favorite color is and the four words used to describe it. Go around to each person. You then can tell them that these words describe how they see themselves. Once the first box is done repeat the process, revealing the meaning after they have revealed the animal and four words to describe the animal. Their favorite animal describes how others see them. Their favorite body of water describes their intimate life, and the dark room with no windows describes their view of death. Tell them what it means after everyone has disclosed their word and four words to describe the word. Other than the room with no doors or windows they all have an object and adjectives. This activity works well in groups that are not too large.

Activity 3

For this game you will need paper and pen for each guest. First ask each guest to write down the following five animals, starting with their most favorite to least favorite: Cow, Sheep, Horse, Tiger, and Monkey. Second, ask them to write down one word to describe each of these words: Dog, Rat, Cat, Coffee, and Ocean. Third, have them write down the name of a person with whom they relate to each of the following five colors: Yellow, Orange, Red, White, and Green. Finally, you can reveal the special meanings found in what they wrote.

1.) The animals from part one relates to the following and the order is how they prioritize things in their life.

Cow is career
Tiger is pride
Sheep means love
Horse means family
Monkey means money

2.) The description of each object in part two reveals how you view certain personalities:

Dog implies your personality
Rat implies your enemy's personality
Cat implies your partner's personality
Coffee implies how you interpret your intimate life
Ocean implies how you interpret your own life

3.) The colors in part three describe where people stand in your life according to which color you associated them with:

Yellow is someone who will never forget you
Orange is someone you can consider a real friend
Red is someone you really love
White is your soul mate
Green is a person whom you will remember for the rest of your life

Whether these descriptions are accurate or not, they certainly will liven up the group as each guest shares their answers!

> *"A friend reaches for your hand and touches your heart."*
>
> ~Unknown

Activity 4

You can either type out the next game or copy and give to each person or just read it aloud to the group. If you decide to read aloud, give each guest paper and pen to write down the numbers 1 through 10. With each question they will write down their answer a, b, c or d. Each answer corresponds to a certain amount of points, which when added up will reveal something about each guest's habits and personality.

1.) When do you feel your best?

    a.) in the morning
    b.) during the afternoon and early evening
    c.) late at night

2.) You usually walk:

    a.) fairly fast with long steps
    b.) fairly fast but with short, quick steps
    c.) slower, head up, looking the world in the face
    d.) slower, head down

3.) When talking to people, you:

    a.) stand with arms folded
    b.) have hands clasped
    c.) have one or both hands on your hips
    d.) touch or push the person to whom you are talking
    e.) play with your ear, touch your chin or smooth your hair

4.) When relaxing, you sit with:

    a.) your knees bent and your legs neatly side by side
    b.) your legs crossed
    c.) your legs stretched out or straight
    d.) one leg curled under you

5.) When something really amuses you, you react with:

    a.) a big appreciative laugh
    b.) a laugh, but not a loud one
    c.) a quiet chuckle
    d.) a sheepish smile

6.) When you go to a social gathering, you:

    a.) make a loud entrance
    b.) make a quiet entrance, looking around for someone you know
    c.) make the quietest entrance, trying to stay unnoticed

7.) You are working hard, concentrating hard, and then you are interrupted. How do you react?

a.) welcome the break
b.) feel extremely irritated
c.) vary between the two extremes

8.) Which of the following colors do you like most?

a.) red or orange
b.) black
c.) yellow or light blue
d.) green
e.) dark blue or purple
f.) white
g.) brown or gray

9.) When you are in bed at night those last few moments before going to sleep, you lie:

a.) stretched out on your back
b.) stretched out face down on your stomach
c.) on your side, slightly curled
d.) with your head on one arm
e.) with your head under the covers

10.) You often dream that:

a.) you are falling
b.) fighting or struggling
c.) searching for something or somebody
d.) flying or floating
e.) you usually have dreamless sleep
f.) your dreams are always pleasant

Here is the point system for what each answer means. Read aloud and have each guest keep track of their own points.

1.) a-2, b-4, c-6
2.) a-6, b-4, c-7, d-2, e-1
3.) a-4, b-2, c-5, d-7, e-6
4.) a-4, b-6, c-2, d-1
5.) a-6, b-4, c-3, d-5, e-2
6.) a-6, b-4, c-2
7.) a-6, b-2, c-4
8.) a-6, b-7, c-5, d-4, e-3, f-2, g-1
9.) a-7, b-6, c-4, d-2, e-1
10.) a-4, b-2, c-3, d-5, e-6, f-1

Have guests add up their score and then read what the points reveal about their personality. They can choose what to share about themselves, since they do not have to read their answers out loud.

Over 60 points:

Others see you as someone that they should "handle with care." You are seen as self-centered and extremely dominant. Others may admire you and wish they could be more like you, but they do not always trust you and hesitate to become too deeply involved with you.

51 to 60 points:

Your friends see you as exciting, highly volatile, with a rather impulsive personality. You are a natural leader, quick to make decisions (although not always the right ones). They see you as bold and venturesome, someone who will try anything once. They enjoy being in your company because of the excitement you radiate.

41 to 50 points:

Others see you as fresh, lively, charming, amusing and always interesting. You are seen as someone who is constantly the center of attention, but sufficiently well balanced not to let it go to your head. You are seen as kind, considerate and understanding, someone who will cheer them up and help them out.

31 to 40 points:

Others see you as sensible, cautious, careful and practical. They see you as clever, gifted, and talented but modest. Not a person who makes friends too quickly or easily, but someone who is extremely loyal to the friends they have and expects the same loyalty in return. Those who really get to know you realize it takes a lot to shake your trust in your friends, but it takes equally as long to reestablish the trust if broken.

21 to 30 points:

Your friends see you as painstaking and fussy. You are extremely cautious and careful, a slow and steady plodder. It would really surprise them if you ever did anything impulsively or on the spur of the moment. They expect you to examine everything carefully from every side and then usually decide against it. They think this reaction on your part is caused partly because of your careful nature and partly due to laziness.

Under 21 points:

People think you are shy, nervous and indecisive. You are someone who needs to be looked after, who always wants someone else to make the decisions and who does not want to become involved with anyone or anything. They see you as a worrier who sees problems that do not always exist. Only those that know you well know that you are not boring. The problem is that you let very few people get close to you.

Activity 5
(Especially recommended for couples.)

For evenings with married or unmarried couples, or even wedding showers, it is fun to do a takeoff of the old Newlywed Game. Think of funny questions for the group before they arrive and be as imaginative as possible. Have one mate of each couple leave the room and put them somewhere where they cannot hear the host asking the questions. Have pen and paper ready for the mates remaining in the room, so they can write a single answer on a piece of paper. Ask questions such as:

- What does the other one usually order in a restaurant: beef, chicken, pork or fish?
- What is their favorite show on TV?
- Where did you go on your first date?
- What size shoe does the other one wear?
- What does your mate do when lost...immediately ask for directions, look up directions before even leaving, try to convince you that they know what they are doing?

The group answering the questions can write down either an abbreviated or complete version of the answer they think their mate is most likely to use. Once done, have them turn the answers upside down on their lap in the same order the questions were asked. Four questions are usually enough, but you can ask more depending on the crowd's interest. The point is to see how well the guests know their mate, so be creative!

Bring the mates back into the room and start asking questions. Points accumulate when the one who left the room answers the same as their mate. Conversations can get exciting and lively, especially when couples differ in their answers! Continue the game by having the other mate leave the room, asking the new contestants four new questions.

"There are people whom one loves immediately and forever. Even to know that they are alive in the world with one is quite enough."

~Nancy Spain

332

Activity 6

The last game is a quick one. Have the guests imagine there are five things going on at the same time that they need to take care of. They must decide what to take care of first. Once they have listed each of the five in the order they would prioritize them, reveal what each incident means in terms of their own priorities.

The events are:

• The telephone is ringing.

• The baby is crying.

• Someone knocks on the front door or rings the doorbell.

• There is laundry hanging outside and it begins to rain.

• The water faucet in the kitchen is running.

Each answer represents a different aspect of life and your priorities:

• Phone represents job or career.

• Baby represents family.

• Visitor represents friends.

• Laundry represents your intimate life.

• Running water represents money or wealth.

All of these fun, quick games inspire women and men to interact, laugh and discuss topics that we can all relate to. Sharing anecdotes with each other about children, politics, sports and other personal interests encourages guests to relax in each others' company and ultimately to enjoy the party!

Organized Shopping List

Meats, Deli & Seafood	Produce	Dairy & Specialty Cheeses

Baking, Crackers, Chips, Nuts & Bakery	Frozen Foods	Jars, Cans, Bottles & Tubes

Rice, Bean, Pasta, Spices, Tea & Coffee	What do I need to check if I already own?	Errands & Supplies

Measurements to Remember

3 teaspoons	=	1 tablespoon
4 tablespoons	=	1/4 cup
8 tablespoons	=	1/2 cup
16 tablespoons	=	1 cup
4 ounces	=	1/2 cup
8 ounces	=	1 cup
16 ounces	=	1 pound
2 cups	=	1 pint
1 pound butter	=	2 cups or 4 sticks
2 pints	=	1 quart
4 cups	=	1 quart
1 quart	=	32 ounces
2 quarts	=	1/2 gallon
4 quarts	=	1 gallon

Sifting passes ingredients through fine mesh to remove large pieces. It incorporates air and will change measurements. When a recipe calls for sifting, measure ingredients after they are sifted.

Instead of relying on package labels, use a measuring cup instead. It is best to measure liquids in glass measuring cups and solids in metal or plastic measuring cups. Solid and dry ingredients can then be leveled off with a knife to ensure proper measurements.

Trademark Credits

Microplane® is a Registered Trademark of Grace Manufacturing, Inc.

TABASCO® marks, bottle and label designs are registered trademarks and servicemarks exclusively of McIlhenny Co., Avery Island, LA 70513.

Hellmann's® is a registered trademark of BestFoods, Englewood Cliffs, NJ 07632.

KNORR® is a registered trademark of BestFoods, Englewood Cliffs, NJ 07632.

Kitchen Bouquet® Browning and Seasoning Sauce and Hidden Valley® Original Ranch® Dressing are both registered trademarks of Hidden Valley Products Company.

Ro*Tel® is a registered trademark of International Home Foods, Inc.

Tony Chachere's® Creole Seasoning is a registered trademark of Creole Foods of Opelouses, Inc.

BRIANNAS® is a registered trademark of Del Sol Food Co., Inc., Brenham, TX.

"JIFFY®" Corn Muffin Mix is a registered trademark of Chelsea Milling Company, Chelsea, Michigan.

GRAND MARNIER® is a registered trademark of Société des Produits Marnier-Lapostolle.

MAGGI® is a registered trademark of Société des Produits Nestlé S. A.

A.1.® Steak Sauce is a registered trademark of Nabisco, East Hanover, N.J. 07936 ©Nabisco, Inc.

Better than Bouillon™ is a registered trademark of Superior Quality Foods, Ontario, California 91761

Bibliography

Anderson, Jean. *1001 Secrets of Great Cooks.* The Berkeley Publishing Group, 1995.

Food Epicurious.com

Herbst, Sharon Tyler. *Food Lover's Companion.* Barron's Educational Series, 1995.

Maresca, Tom. *Mastering Wine.* Grove Press, 1992.

Stevenson, Tom. *101 Essential Wine Tips.* DK Publishing, 1997.

Zraly, Kevin. *Windows On The World Complete Wine Course.* Sterling Publishing Co. Inc., 1994 Updated Edition.

Index

Index

343

Index

Index